The Evolving Role of China in the Global Economy

CESifo Seminar Series

Edited by Hans-Werner Sinn

The Evolving Role of China in the Global Economy

edited by Yin-Wong Cheung and Jakob de Haan

CESifo Seminar Series
The MIT Press
Cambridge, Massachusetts
London, England

MIT Press books may be purchased at special quantity discounts for business or sales promotional use. For information, please email special_sales@mitpress.mit.edu or write to Special Sales Department, The MIT Press, 55 Hayward Street, Cambridge, MA 02142.

This book was set in Palatino by Toppan Best-set Premedia Limited. Printed and bound in the United States of America.

Library of Congress Cataloging-in-Publication Data
The evolving role of China in the global economy / edited by Yin-Wong Cheung and Jakob de Haan.
    p.   cm. — (CESifo seminar series)
Includes bibliographical references and index.
ISBN 978-0-262-01823-4 (hbk. : alk. paper)
1. China—Economic policy. 2. China—Foreign economic relations. 3. Finance—China.
I. Cheung, Yin-Wong. II. Haan, Jakob de.
HC427.95.E954   2013
337.51—dc23
2012012951

10 9 8 7 6 5 4 3 2 1

Contents

Contributors

Jinzhao Chen, Paris School of Economics

Yin-Wong Cheung, City University of Hong Kong, MIFN, and CESifo, Munich

Menzie David Chinn, University of Wisconsin and National Bureau of Economic Research

Jakob de Haan, De Nederlandsche Bank, University of Groningen and CESifo, Munich

Galina Hale, Federal Reserve Bank of San Francisco

Dong He, Hong Kong Monetary Authority

Juann H. Hung, Congressional Budget Office

Yueqing Jia, George Washington University and The World Bank

Cheryl Long, Colgate University

Guonan Ma, Bank for International Settlements

Robert N. McCauley, Bank for International Settlements

Rong Qian, The World Bank

Xingwang Qian, SUNY, Buffalo State College

J. James Reade, University of Birmingham

Gunther Schnabl, University of Leipzig

Tara M. Sinclair, George Washington University

Lukas Vogel, European Commission

Ulrich Volz, German Development Institute

Wang Yi, The People's Bank of China

Shu Yu, University of Groningen

Series Foreword

This book is part of the CESifo Seminar Series. The series aims to cover topical policy issues in economics from a largely European perspective. The books in this series are the products of the papers and intensive debates that took place during the seminars hosted by CESifo, an international research network of renowned economists organized jointly by the Center for Economic Studies at Ludwig-Maximilians-Universität, Munich, and the Ifo Institute for Economic Research. All publications in this series have been carefully selected and refereed by members of the CESifo research network.

Preface

The chapters in this book were presented at a CESifo Summer Institute conference on "The Evolving Role of China in the World Economy" held in Venice in July 2010. As organizers we brought together a group of researchers who shared interest in China, all addressing topics that are highly relevant in analyzing China's role in the world economy.

Of course, there are plenty of books about China. Here we outline how our book differs from some recent publications. Probably the best-known textbook on China is Barry Naughton's *The Chinese Economy: Transitions and Growth* (MIT Press, 2007). The book offers a broadly focused introduction to China's economy since 1949, analyzing patterns of growth and development. It places China's economy in a comparative context. According to Naughton, China has achieved the establishment of a market-based economy though the formation of market institutions is still incomplete. He argues that China's economic growth is caused by three factors. First, labor and savings have been channeled into investment in human and physical capital on a large scale. Second, the transition from planning to markets has improved efficiency of resource allocation while utilizing the industrial experience gained from the socialist period. And finally, the long history of entrepreneurship has brought access to savings and capital, a chance to catch up technologically, and a revival of domestic and international trading relationships. In Naughton's view, there have been two distinct phases so far in the process of transition. In the first phase, 1978 to 1992, economic change was characterized by unique experiments and forms of economic organization, such as township and village enterprises promoted by local governments. The post-1992 phase has seen China's economic institutions converging to those of other economies in transition.

Gregory Chow's book *Interpreting China's Economy* (World Scientific, 2010) covers many important topics. The book consists of articles that Chow wrote for leading Chinese newspapers, as well as some lectures he gave. Chow's book is not a textbook; it is a collection of essays (many only a few pages long) designed to give readers insight into how China made the transition from central planning to a market system, and how economic theory can be applied to help interpret the Chinese economy and inform policy-making. The book covers a variety of issues ranging from the roles of entrepreneurs and the non-state sector in transforming the Chinese economy to the problems plaguing farmers in their quest to obtain more secure property rights.

Three recent books contain a collection of papers, like the present volume. The first one, *China, Asia and the New World Economy*, edited by Barry Eichengreen, Yung Chul Park, and Charles Wyplosz (Oxford University Press, 2008). The book deals with three issues: the implications of China's growth for global energy and the environment, the impact of Asia's emergence on the global trading system, and the macroeconomic problems of China. Unlike the present volume, *China, Asia and the New World Economy* does not only focus on China. Still, in the last part of the book some of the same topics that are also addressed in this volume are covered, like China's savings rate and the effectiveness of capital controls.

The second collection of papers is *China and India in the World Economy*, edited by Barry Eichengreen, Poonam Gupta, and Rajiv Kumar (Oxford University Press, 2010) has a very different focus than the current volume. It takes the growth experiences of China and India and places these issues in a comparative perspective.

The book that probably comes closest to our volume, is *Rising China Global Challenges and Opportunities*, edited by Jane Golley and Ligang Song (ANU E Press, 2011). The chapters contained in the Golley–Song volume reflect upon a wide range of opportunities and challenges that has emerged in the context of a rising China. While some chapters focus on key bilateral relationships (including with the United States and Australia), others offer either comparative perspectives (e.g., with Indonesia on migration and with India on sources of economic growth) or Chinese perspectives on global goals (e.g., constraining climate change and reforming the international economic system). Some chapters focus on particular markets (e.g., petroleum), others on key internal problems (e.g., urbanization and aging) or on certain aspects of China's global integration (e.g., China's outward direct investment and China's official finance to Africa). These last topics are also covered in our book but from a different perspective.

Overview of the Book

The present volume provides a systematic analysis of four broad aspects that have led to China's rapid economic growth. These four broad aspects are China's exchange rate policy (four chapters), China's savings and investments (three chapters), China's monetary policy and its capital controls (3 chapters), and China's foreign direct investments (FDIs) (two chapters). We believe that these issues are crucial both for academic studies and for policy-making. One of the reviewers of the manuscript wrote that to the best of his knowledge the present volume is the first one that analyzes China's economic growth from the perspective of a developed economy rather than a developing one.

Let us briefly dwell on the issues covered. According to many observers, the renminbi remains substantially below the level consistent with medium-term fundamentals. The contributions in this volume offer a novel perspective on this issue. China's large net foreign assets and current account surplus reflect a persistent excess of domestic savings over domestic investment. The contributions in this volume come up with new and refreshing information concerning this issue. Prices in China are currently on an upward trajectory and an important question is whether the Chinese monetary authorities are able to control inflation with its fixed exchange rate policies. Surprisingly, there has been relatively little empirical research on the impact of the Chinese dollar peg on the conduct of and constraints on Chinese monetary policy. The contributions in the present volume offer some new insights. Last, an important concern that has been raised in relation to China's economic growth is its growing demand for energy and raw materials. Access to energy and other resources is imperative for maintaining China's economic growth. Two chapters in the present volume address this issue focusing on Chinese Foreign Direct Investment (FDI), examining the factors that determine China's FDI in the conventional oil-producing countries and the factors that drive China's FDI in Africa.

Acknowledgments

We would like to thank Michael Stimmelmayr, Karin Fournier, and Deirdre Weber from CESifo for their support in organizing the conference, three referees from MIT Press for their useful feedback on the manuscript, and John Covell and Emily Taber from MIT Press for their support in publishing the book.

Yin-Wong Cheung
Jakob de Haan

1 Introduction

Yin-Wong Cheung and Jakob de Haan

1.1 China's Position in the World Economy

China has recently overtaken Japan as the world's second largest economy. According to the Conference Board, China doubled its share of global output during the past ten years (from 8 percent in 2000 to 16 percent in 2010) and may soon top the United States as the world's largest economy.[1] Between 1979 (when economic reforms began) and 2008, China's real gross domestic product (GDP) grew at an average annual rate of nearly 10 percent. China's economy grew 14-fold in real terms, while real per capita GDP increased over 11-fold (Morrison, 2009).[2] Despite these extraordinarily rapid growth rates, China still has a relatively low per capita income that is only 20 percent of that in the United States today (Conference Board 2011).

Not so long ago the developments as outlined above would have been considered science fiction. For a long time China maintained a centrally planned economy, under the leadership of Chairman Mao Zedong. Most of the country's output was directed and controlled by the state, which set production goals, controlled prices, and allocated resources. Chinese living standards were substantially lower than those of many other developing countries. However, shortly after the death of Chairman Mao in 1976, the Chinese government decided to gradually reform the economy according to free-market principles, opening up trade and investment with the West in the hope that this would significantly increase economic growth and raise living standards.[3]

Despite these reforms, China considers itself as a "socialist-market economy," in that the government allows free-market forces in a number of areas but still plays a major role in the country's economic development. For example, the banking sector in China is largely state-controlled. In addition, although the number of state-owned enterprises has declined sharply, several sectors (e.g., petroleum) are still dominated by the state. Furthermore the government continues to issue five-year and ten-year development plans and also promotes the development of industries deemed vital for future economic growth.

Economic reforms and trade and investment liberalization have indeed transformed China into a major trading country. Chinese exports rose from $14 billion in 1979 to $1,429 billion in 2008, while imports over this period grew from $16 billion to $1,132 billion. Between 2002 and 2008, China's exports grew by 339 percent, while its imports grew by 283 percent. The United States has been China's largest single country trade partner since the 1990s, but Japan, South Korea, and Germany also have strong trade relations with China. According to the IMF direction of trade database, 20 percent of China's exports between 2000 and 2009 went to the United States, while the remaining six countries of the G7 made up another 22 percent of China's export market.

As shown in figure 1.1, large trade surpluses have enabled China to accumulate the world's largest foreign exchange reserves, with $2.3 trillion at the end of September 2009 making it the world's largest holder of such reserves. During the recent crisis the Chinese current account surplus shrank from 11 percent of GDP in 2007 to an estimated 5 percent in 2010, but many analysts view this as a temporary respite related to the contraction in trade, so they expect China's surplus to rise again. However, according to the Chinese government, the surplus is driven by structural factors and the exchange rate has little role to play in influencing the saving–investment balance.

Although it is often believed that China has an export-led economy, investment rather than net exports has been the major driver of Chinese growth. In 2008, investment (plus inventory changes) accounted for about 42 percent of GDP, thereby constituting the most important GDP expenditure component. Still, much of the debate about China focuses on China's trade surpluses, which are often seen as caused by an under-valued currency.

1.2 China's Exchange Rate Policy

According to Paul Krugman (2009), "China has become a major financial and trade power. But it doesn't act like other big economies. Instead, it follows a mercantilist policy, keeping its trade surplus artificially high. And in today's depressed world, that policy is, to put it bluntly,

(a)

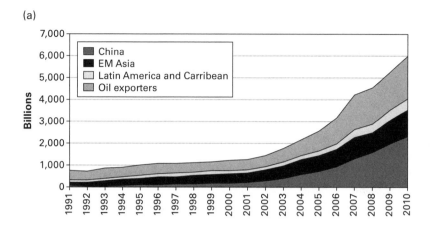

(b)

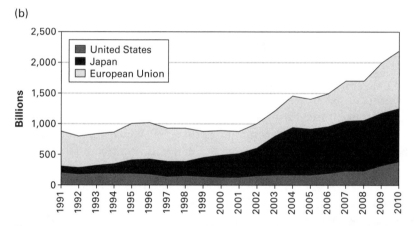

Figure 1.1
Foreign exchange reserves of industrial and emerging countries (billions of constant 2000 US$). Source: Korinek and Servén (2010).

predatory. Here's how it works: Unlike the dollar, the euro or the yen, whose values fluctuate freely, China's currency is pegged by official policy at about 6.8 yuan to the dollar. At this exchange rate, Chinese manufacturing has a large cost advantage over its rivals, leading to huge trade surpluses."

In 1994, the Chinese authorities decided to peg the renminbi to the US dollar. This has forced the People's Bank of China (PBOC) into large Forex operations. The PBOC has sterilized the impact of Forex interventions on domestic money supply by offsetting sales/purchases of domestic bonds. However, in July 2005, the central bank allowed the renminbi to appreciate. At its peak, the appreciation against the US dollar was around 1 percent per month (IMF 2010). But during the financial crisis, the central bank returned to pegging the renminbi to the US dollar in July 2008. According to the IMF (2010), Chinese authorities motivated their decision to return to a managed floating regime as part of an effort to overcome the temporary interruption to the reform process that was caused by the global financial crisis. On June 19, 2010, the PBOC announced the return to a managed floating exchange rate regime under which the spot exchange rate can move intraday +/- 0.5 percent from a central parity (as determined at the opening of trading by a truncated weighted average of primary dealers' offer rates and announced by the China Foreign Exchange Trading System). The central parity itself has not moved by more than +/- 0.5 percent each day. Since then the renminbi has appreciated slightly (see figure 1.2). However, with the increasing inflation (as discussed in section 1.4) China's real exchange rate appreciated at an annual rate of 10 percent in the second half of 2010, rising almost 5 percent in December (Bottelier 2011).

According to the IMF staff, the renminbi remains substantially below the level consistent with medium-term fundamentals. This assessment is based upon three broad arguments. First, the pace of accumulation of international reserves continues to be rapid. However, according to Chinese authorities, the recent accumulation of international reserves was more a product of the unprecedented expansion of global liquidity, a result of monetary policy decisions in the large industrial economies. Second, the current level of the real exchange rate is close to the level of the late 1990s even though productivity in China has increased more

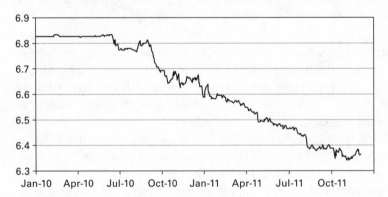

Figure 1.2
US dollar versus China renminbi, 2010 to 2011. © www.advfn.com.

than productivity of its trading partners. However, according to Chinese authorities it is arbitrary to judge the current level of the exchange rate by referencing a particular point in time when the currency may or may not have been in equilibrium. Third, China's current account is expected to turn into a sizable surplus in the coming years. However, according to Chinese authorities, reforms put in place over the past several years are already resulting in a structural change in saving and investment behavior in China. They view the level of the renminbi right now as much closer to equilibrium than at any time before and expect that the current account surplus will level off at around 4 percent of GDP, a level they regard as appropriate for China (IMF 2010).

Various studies have addressed the issue of undervaluation of the renminbi. In chapter 2, Menzie Chinn reviews academic research on the equilibrium level of the Chinese currency. His main conclusion is that each estimate of misalignment is subject to considerable imprecision. Apart from the issue of misalignment, Chinn addresses the positive question of how much of an impact an exchange rate change will have on trade flows. Again, estimates differ widely across studies. For instance, estimates of the impact on Chinese exports of a 20 percent renminbi appreciation after four years range from 50 billion to 400 billion US dollars. So, in contrast to popular belief, it is quite uncertain whether an appreciation of the Chinese currency will lead to substantially lower global imbalances.[4] Indeed, as figure 1.3 shows, China's

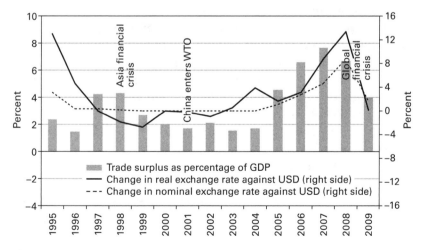

Figure 1.3
China's trade surplus and the exchange rate, 1995 to 2009. Source: Adams (2010).

trade surplus as a share of GDP shrank in periods when the exchange rate was pegged to the dollar and grew in periods when the exchange rate appreciated against the dollar.

In chapter 3, Gunther Schnabl offers a rather unconventional analysis of the costs and benefits of pegging the renminbi to the dollar. He sees many benefits. For instance, pegging the exchange rate stabilized the economy, which laid the foundation for increasing investment and boosting trade. Furthermore the dollar peg stabilizes financial markets. Without the peg, sustained appreciation expectations would depress interest rates below the interest rate of the anchor country thereby pushing China into a near-zero interest liquidity trap. According to Schnabl, China's exchange rate peg as well as decisive countercyclical macroeconomic policies played also a crucial role in stabilizing the East Asian region. The Chinese peg is the core of an informal dollar standard with the dollar as first (external) anchor and the Chinese yuan as a second (internal) anchor, which Schnabl argues is currently the (second) best solution to maintain the intraregional exchange rate stability and growth. The most important drawback of the current policies consists of the distortions caused by the fact that the Forex interventions are sterilized by the Chinese central bank so that the real exchange rate does not increase.

Schnabl also argues that China has moved from a regional to a global stabilizer. Indeed China's recession following the global financial crisis of 2008 was the shortest and lightest among major economies. According to the Conference Board (2011), in 2009 and 2010 China accounted for about half of global economic growth. However, in chapter 4, Yueqing Jia and Tara Sinclair find that China is little affected by the developed world's aggregate GDP. They apply a correlated unobserved components model to explore the relationships between the real output fluctuations of China with those of developed countries over the period 1978Q1 to 2009Q4, focusing on China's relationship with the G7 and the OECD. The model allows distinguishing correlations driven by permanent movements from those due to transitory movements. The authors find that the correlations between the real output fluctuations of China and the developed world are insignificant both in terms of permanent and transitory shocks, which indicates that domestic factors would have been the major drivers of China's macroeconomic fluctuations during the sample period.

In chapter 5, Lukas Vogel focuses on China's external position using a multiple-country version of the QUEST III macroeconomic model that is extended using (1) a portfolio approach that distinguishes gross/net and private/government sector foreign asset positions and accounts for limited cross-border capital mobility, and (2) exchange rate management in the form of sterilized foreign exchange intervention. The simulations show that the selected shocks (TFP catch-up, labor supply growth, labor reallocation, precautionary savings, and export growth) are able to replicate China's external position quite well in the benchmark setting with limited capital mobility and Forex intervention, though the fit is less satisfactory for domestic demand shares. The results also highlight that effective capital controls, namely binding restrictions on cross-border capital flows, are crucial for the viability of China's exchange rate management. Finally, the simulations suggest that enhanced exchange rate flexibility would lead to renmimbi appreciation under the selected set of shocks, reduce China's NFA position, and contribute to changing the composition of China's growth from exports toward domestic demand.

1.3   Chinese Savings and Investment

China's large net foreign assets and current account surplus reflects a persistent excess of domestic savings over domestic investment. The external surplus is difficult to reconcile using the neoclassical textbook model, in view of China's productivity catch-up and growing labor supply. According to the standard textbook model, these factors should lead to net capital inflows. China has historically maintained a high rate of savings. When reforms were initiated in 1979, gross domestic savings as a percentage of GDP stood at 32 percent. Since then, Chinese savings have increased substantially. As a result China's gross domestic savings as a percentage of GDP stood at 52 percent in 2008 (compared to a US rate of 8 percent), among the world's highest savings rates. Although household sector savings in China is high, it is not inordinately so. For instance, the household savings rate for India is quite similar to China's. Corporate and government sector savings are what really differentiate China from other developing countries (Adams 2010). Corporate saving—including that of state-owned enterprises—has risen sharply in recent years. But also government saving has increased, while the share of household saving in national saving has not changed much; this is mainly due to a fall in the share of household income in national income rather than a decline in the household saving rate (Prasad 2011).

In chapter 6, Guonan Ma and Wang Yi review the debate over factors shaping the Chinese saving dynamics and explore its medium-term outlook and policy implications. They come up with some very interesting conclusions. For instance, they question the more recent wisdom on the principal drivers of high Chinese saving. In particular, the evidence does not support the proposition that distortions and subsidies are the principal causes of China's rising corporate profits or high saving rate. Instead, the three major microeconomic factors driving Chinese savings are (1) major institutional reforms that include tough corporate restructuring, pension reform, and spread of private home ownership; (2) a marked Lewis-model transformation process as labor left the subsistence sector where its marginal product was less than its average wage; and (3) a rapid aging process. Finally, structural factors point to a peak in the Chinese saving rate in the medium term. Policy measures promoting job creation and a stronger social safety net would contribute to the transition to more balanced domestic demand.

In chapter 7, Juann Hung and Rong Qian adopt a different approach to examine Chinese savings. They estimate a national savings model using a large cross-country panel data and find that their benchmark model can explain over 70 percent of Chinese savings. In that sense, the Chinese saving behavior is not different from that of the rest of the world. Based on their panel regression results, the authors attribute the observed high Chinese savings to the following conditions in China: (1) a low old dependency ratio, (2) a low level of urbanization, (3) strong economic growth, and (4) a weak social safety net. Exchange rate valuation, however, has limited impact on the saving rate.

In chapter 8, Galina Hale and Cheryl Long analyze the financing of Chinese investment. They thus address the puzzle that the Chinese economy has experienced one of the fastest growth rates in the world, while the formal financial sector in China performs poorly in providing finances to the private sector. How did the private sector in China manage to grow so rapidly with limited access to external finance? The authors use balance sheet data from Chinese Industrial Surveys of Medium-Sized and Large Firms for 2000 to 2006 and survey data from the Large-Scale Survey of Private Enterprises in China to address this puzzle. They show that private firms are more financially constrained compared to state-owned firms. In addition they find that the ratios of inventory to sales and accounts receivable to sales are substantially lower in private firms than in other firms, even after controlling for various firm characteristics, industry, and location. Their results suggest that not only firms with less access to credit have lower ratios of inventories and accounts receivable to sales but also that firms make greater adjustments in their inventories and accounts receivable when credit gets tighter. The lower levels of inventory and accounts receivable increase firms' profitability through both higher productivity and lower financial costs.

1.4 China's Monetary Policy and Capital Controls

Inflation in China has been moderate over the past decade or so. Despite rapid economic growth and high credit growth in many years, China's headline CPI inflation has remained below 5 percent since the late-1990s, with non–food inflation rising even more modestly—never above 2 percent (Porter 2010). The People's Bank of China (PBOC) loosened monetary policy in response to the global financial crisis, which served to support growth. However, monetary aggregates have been growing at a very fast pace while the growth rebound has been rapid. This has raised concerns about inflationary pressures (Bottelier 2011). Indeed, after a period of deflation in 2009, prices are currently on an upward trajectory (see figure 1.4). The consumer price index (CPI) in China increased to 4.9 percent in January 2011, according to the National Bureau of Statistics (NBS).

In response to the increasing inflationary pressures, the PBOC increased reserve rates for banks seven times and hiked interest rates thrice between October 2010 and February 2011. An important question

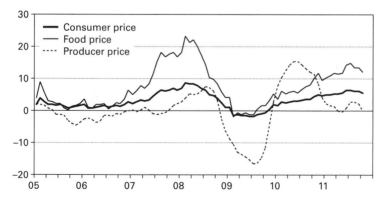

Figure 1.4
Inflation in China, 2005 to 2010. Source: Bloomberg.

is whether the Chinese monetary authorities are able to steer inflation in view of its fixed exchange rate policies. Surprisingly, there has been relatively little empirical research on the impact of the Chinese dollar peg on the conduct of and constraints on Chinese monetary policy.

In chapter 9, James Reade and Ulrich Voltz address two questions. First, they examine how much monetary policy independence the PBOC enjoys, where monetary independence is understood as the central bank's ability to conduct its own interest rate policy without having to follow any outside influences like US monetary policy. Second, they analyze how effective the PBOC's monetary policy tools (interest rate changes, changes in the reserve requirement ratios and open market operations) have been in managing monetary growth and containing inflation. For this purpose they estimate a monetary model for China that includes the PBOC's policy rate, the required reserve ratio, a measure of the PBOC's open market operations as well as mac-roeconomic indicators that policy might be expected to respond to, namely inflation, economic activity, growth in broad money and growth in foreign currency reserves. The authors conclude that China has been able to largely insulate its monetary policy from international monetary movements. However, in terms of monetary instruments, the interest rate tool does not seem to exert much influence on the economy. Rather, the PBOC has made more extensive use of less market-based policy tools like reserve ratio requirements.

In chapter 10, Dong He and Robert McCauley analyze the challenges posed to monetary and financial stability by offshore markets in domes-tic currencies with a special reference to developments in the extrater-ritorial use of the renminbi (notably in Hong Kong), owing to the several measures taken to allow its use outside the mainland. An off-shore market in a given currency can increase the difficulty of defining and controlling the money supply and bank credit in that currency. The questions addressed are: Can authorities promote offshore use of their currencies while maintaining a significant degree of capital account control, and do they have policy options to manage potential risks to monetary and financial stability posed by the offshore markets of their currencies? The authors' answers to both questions are positive.

In chapter 11, Jinzhao Chen investigates the intensity and the effec-tiveness of the capital controls in China from 2003 to 2010, with special attention to the period of financial turbulence that erupted in the summer of 2007. The author employs a two-regime threshold autore-gressive model to study the renminbi yield differential between the onshore interest rate and its non-deliverable forward (NDF)-implied offshore interest rate. Chen concludes that the de facto intensity of capital controls measured by the threshold increases over time, even during the period of financial turbulence. Furthermore the slightly lower speed of adjustment to the threshold implies that the capital controls are effective.

1.5   China's FDI and Quest for Resources

An important concern that has been raised in relation to China's economic growth is its growing demand for energy and raw materials. In its quest for resources China increased economic ties with numerous countries around the world, including traditional US allies, as well as countries in which the United States has major foreign policy concerns (e.g., North Korea, Sudan, and Iran). Once a top oil producer in Asia, China became a net oil importer in 1993. High rates of economic growth caused soaring demands for oil, resulting in China's inability to produce enough domestic oil to meet the desired consumption. China's consumption of oil increased fivefold from 1.7 in 1982 to 8.2 million barrels per day in 2009, making China the second-largest oil consumer in the world. Access to energy and other resources is imperative for maintaining China's economic growth (Morrison 2009).

Two chapters address this issue focusing on Chinese Foreign Direct Investment (FDI). In 2000, China's leaders initiated a new "going global" strategy, which sought to encourage firms to invest overseas. The Chinese government generally refers to these activities as overseas direct investment (ODI). According to Chinese data, its annual ODI increased from $2.9 billion in 2003 to $55.9 billion in 2008. China's state-owned enterprises accounted for 64 percent of ODI in 2008.

According to Morrison (2009), several factors drive ODI. First, the increase in foreign exchange reserves has led China to seek more profitable ways of investing these reserves (which traditionally have mainly been put into relatively safe, low yield assets, e.g., US Treasury securities). Second, China purchases existing companies and their brand names. For example, in April 2005 Lenovo Group Limited—a Chinese computer company—purchased IBM Corporation's personal computer division for $1.75 billion. Third, acquisition of energy and raw materials has been an important priority of China's ODI strategy. For example, in June 2005, the China National Offshore Oil Corporation (CNOOC) tried to buy UNOCAL (a US energy company) for $18.5 billion. Eventually, the bid was withdrawn in view of opposition by several members of Congress. The China National Petroleum Corporation (CNPC), China's largest oil company, has signed energy deals with Sudan worth $10 billion, with $4 billion in actual investment.

In chapter 12, Xingwang Qian investigates the factors that determine China's ODI in the conventional oil-producing countries, including oil producers in Middle East, Africa, Russia, and Central-Asia and in Latin America. While China's ODI has put more weight on Africa and other oil nations, it has reduced its degree of reliance on the Middle East area. Nevertheless, the Middle East remains China's main source of imported oil. He employs both a Tobit model and a Heckman two-stage model that allows separating the investment decision into two stages (i.e., whether to invest and how much to invest). Qian finds that China does not make the "invest or not-to-invest" decision based on a country's energy output. Once a positive investment decision is made, however, China tends to invest more in oil countries with a higher energy output. Qian also finds that China's ODI is generally averse to political risks. China's "going global" policy induces a higher volume of ODI to oil countries and a higher concentration in countries with higher oil production. Finally, some common economic factors are found to be significant determinants of China's ODI in oil-producing countries. For instance, China invests in oil-producing countries with a large market size and a high level of exports to China.

In chapter 13, Yin-Wong Cheung, Jakob de Haan, Xingwang Qian, and Shu Yu examine which factors drive China's ODI in Africa. While ODI from China is still small relative to total flows into Africa, its growth is rapid. Importantly, this recent growth in Chinese presence in Africa coexists with relatively stagnant OECD FDI inflows. The authors find that the likelihood that a country receives ODI from China increases if the country concerned is a political ally of China, has diplomatic relations with China, is corrupt, democratic, and politically stable. This result is based on a dataset that refers to 1991 to 2005. In contrast, for a second dataset that refers to the period 2003 to 2007 most political variables turn out to be insignificant. Instead, China's ODI in Africa is mainly driven by economic ties (trade and projects) and the drive for natural resources. The Heckman models suggest that the decision to invest in a country is driven by different factors than the decision how much to invest in a country.

Interestingly, both studies on Chinese FDI report that corruption attracts investments from China. This finding is in line with the view of Cuervo-Cazurra (2006). This author argues that investors who have been exposed to bribery at home will not be deterred by corruption abroad, but instead seek countries where corruption is prevalent. The similarities in the conditions of the institutional environment induce these investors to focus their FDI there.

Notes

1. See van Ark (2010) and sources cited therein for a further discussion. If China's official GDP growth rates are used with the most recent PPP estimates from the World Bank, China will reach a higher GDP level than that of the United States by 2016.

2. There is some debate about whether China will be able to maintain these high growth rates. For instance, Maddison (2007) argues that its growth would decelerate to 4.98 percent for several reasons related to demographic trends, environmental damage, the rural–urban divide, and a natural slowdown as Chinese wages rise and the technological frontier gets closer to that of the advanced countries. However, Fogel (2010) suggests that the Chinese economy will account for 40 percent of global GDP in 2040, implying a 9 percent growth rate sustained over the next three decades due to investments in education, decentralized control over economic decision-making, burgeoning consumer demand, and to the spread of growth from the coastal areas toward the rural hinterlands. Mold (2010) revises Madison's growth forecast to 5.80 percent.

3. van Ark et al. (2009) report that between 1995 and 2004 labor productivity and labor compensation both increased in China. However, labor productivity in 2004 is four to ten times that in 1995 and the labor compensation in 2004 is two to four times relative to its level in 1995. As a result the unit labor cost declined by 20 to 80 percent.

4. If the US trade deficit is reduced via a nominal appreciation of the renminbi, the disinflationary effect of cheap Chinese imports will be reversed. As nearly a sixth of all US consumption of manufactured goods is made in China, an appreciation would have a substantial direct impact on US inflation. According to Auer (2011), in the covered sectors, a 1 percent appreciation of the renminbi causes American producer prices to increase by a little over half a percentage point.

References

Auer, Raphael. 2011. What the renminbi means for American inflation. Available at: http://www.voxeu.org/index.php?q=node/6128.

Adams, William. 2010. *China View*. New York: Conference Board.

Bottelier, Pieter. 2011. *China's Potential Stimulus Hangover*. Carnegie Foundation, February 2011. Available at: http://carnegieendowment.org/ieb/?fa=show&id=42653.

Conference Board. 2011. *Global Economic Outlook 2011*. New York: Conference Board.

Cuervo-Cazurra, Alvaro. 2006. Who cares about corruption? *Journal of International Business Studies* 37 (6): 807–22.

Fogel, Robert. 2010. $123,000,000,000,000*. *Foreign Policy*, January.

IMF. 2010. IMF Country Report 10/238. Washington, DC.

Korinek, Anton, and Luis Servén. 2010. Undervaluation through foreign reserve accumulation: Static losses, dynamic gains. Available at: http://www.voxeu.org/index.php?q=node/5022.

Krugman, Paul. 2009. Chinese New Year. *New York Times*, December 31.

Maddison, Angus. 2007. *Contours of the World Economy 1–2030: Essays in Macro-economic History*. Oxford University Press.

Mold, Andrew. 2010. Maddison's forecasts revisited: What will the world look like in 2030? Available at: http://www.voxeu.org/index.php?q=node/5708.

Morrison, Wayne M. 2009. *China's Economic Conditions*. Congressional Research Service 7–5700.

Porter, Nathan. 2010. Inflation dynamics in China. Working Paper 10/221. IMF, Washington, DC.

Prasad, Eswar. 2011. Rebalancing growth in Asia. *International Finance*, forthcoming. Working Paper 15169. NBER, Cambridge, MA.

van Ark, Bart. 2010. *The Conference Board Global Economic Outlook 2011*. New York: The Conference Board.

van Ark, Bart, Abdul Azeez Erumban, Vivian Chen, and Utsav Kumar. 2009. The cost competitiveness of the manufacturing sector in China and India: An industry and regional perspective. Conference Board and Growth and Development Center, University of Groningen.

I China's Exchange Rate Policy

2 United States, China, and the Rebalancing Debate: Misalignment, Elasticities, and the Saving-Investment Balance

Menzie David Chinn

2.1 Introduction

China's global trade has loomed large in policy debates along a number of dimensions. This has been more pronounced ever since China's external balances have shifted from balance to surplus (including the current account and trade account), and foreign exchange reserves have increased. China's trade balance and reserve accumulation are depicted in figure 2.1. The increasing integration into world trade is illustrated in figure 2.2; both exports and imports have nearly returned to pre-recession levels. Figure 2.3 illustrates the fact that the Chinese trade surplus has been increasing even as the yuan (measured both against the USD and against a broad basket of currencies) has appreciated in real terms.

China has been cast in several roles in the ongoing drama. At first, it was tapped as a villain, as the source of the global imbalances that in turn have been interpreted as the cause of the global financial crisis. See, for instance, the last Bush Administration *Economic Report of the President* (Council of Economic Advisers 2009):

• The roots of the current global financial crisis began in the late 1990s. A rapid increase in saving by developing countries (sometimes called the "global saving glut") resulted in a large influx of capital to the United States and other industrialized countries, driving down the return on safe assets. The relatively low yield on safe assets likely encouraged investors to look for higher yields from riskier assets, whose yields also went down. What turned out to be an underpricing of risk across a number of markets (housing, commercial real estate, and leveraged buyouts, etc.) in the United States and abroad, and an uncertainty about how this risk was distributed throughout the global financial system, set the stage for subsequent financial distress.
• The influx of inexpensive capital helped finance a housing boom. House prices appreciated rapidly earlier in this decade, and building increased to well

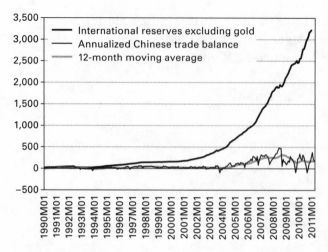

Figure 2.1
Chinese trade balance, annualized, and Chinese reserves excluding gold (bn USD).
Sources: IMF, *International Financial Statistics*, and author's calculations.

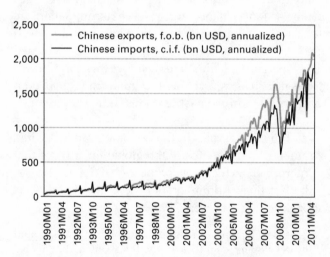

Figure 2.2
Chinese exports (gray line) and imports, c.i.f., annualized (bn USD). Sources: IMF,
International Financial Statistics, and author's calculations.

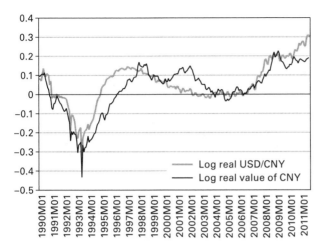

Figure 2.3
Log USD/CNY real exchange rate (gray line), and log real trade weighted value of CNY, both normalized to 2005 = 0. The series are adjusted to use swap rates instead of official rates pre-1994 (see Fernald, Edison, and Loungani 1999). Sources: IMF, *International Financial Statistics*, and author's calculations.

above historic levels. Eventually house prices began to decline with this glut in housing supply.

The importance of China's current account in global imbalances in the run-up to the global financial crisis is illustrated in figure 2.4.[1] Now China has been either implicated as the obstacle to global rebalancing or held up as the source of growth in the wake of the world-wide Great Recession. The latest IMF projections maintain a continued presence of a Chinese (plus emerging Asia) current account surplus out to 2015.

In this chapter, I review the current state of research on these issues. In addition I discuss how the academic research has informed the policy debates. My definition of "academic" research is fairly expansive, in that I do not restrict my attention to research conducted by economists in academe. I also include studies conducted in think tanks, investment banks, and policy organizations.[2] The criterion for inclusion is that the study incorporate either an econometric or theoretical component.

I first address the currency misalignment debate, the closely related exchange over the size of trade elasticities, and finally the research regarding the "normal" current account balance for a country such as China should be.

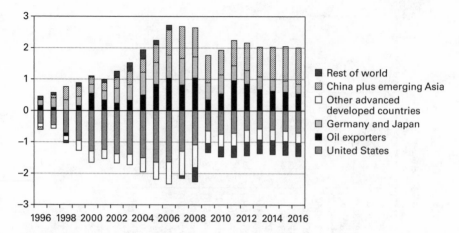

Figure 2.4
Current account balances as a share of world GDP; 2011 to 2016 data are IMF projections.
Source: IMF, *World Economic Outlook*, September 2011.

2.2 Defining Currency Misalignment[3]

The literature on the exchange rate misalignment, even when restricted to the Chinese yuan, is voluminous and diverse. Hence it is helpful to lay out a typology of approaches. Most of these theoretical approaches fall into familiar categories:

• Relative purchasing power parity (PPP)
• Absolute purchasing power parity and the "Penn effect"
• The productivity approach and the behavioral equilibrium exchange rate (BEER) approach
• The macroeconomic balance effect
• The underlying or basic balance approach

Table 2.1 lays out where some key studies fall in these categories. Once one adds in the divergences in statistical methodologies, one clearly sees why there is such a diversity of estimates.

2.2.1 Relative PPP
Relative PPP asserts that the nominal exchange rate moves with relative price levels in the long run, up to a constant:

$$s = p - p^* + \Psi, \tag{2.1}$$

Table 2.1
Studies of the equilibrium exchange rate of the renminbi

	Relative PPP, competitiveness	Penn effect	Balassa–Samuelson	BEER	Macroeconomic balance/external balance
Time series	CCF (2009a); Wang (2004)		CCF (2009a)	Wang (2004); Funke and Rahn (2005)	Bosworth (2004); Goldstein (2004); Wang (2004); Cline and Williamson (2010)
Cross section		Bosworth (2004); Frankel (2006);Coudert and Couharde (2005);			
Panel		Cairns (2005b); Wang and Yao (2008); CCF (2007, 2010); Reisen (2009) Subramanian (2010)			Coudert and Couharde (2005)

Notes: Relative PPP indicates the real exchange rate is calculated using price or cost indexes and no determinants are accounted for. Absolute PPP indicates the use of comparable price deflators to calculate the real exchange rate. "Balassa–Samuelson" (with productivity) indicates that the real exchange rate (calculated using price indexes) is modeled as a function of sectoral productivity levels. "BEER" indicates composite models using net foreign assets, relative tradable to nontradable price ratios, trade openness, or other variables. "Macroeconomic balance" indicates cases where the equilibrium real exchange rate is implicit in a "normal" current account (or combination of current account and persistent capital inflows, for the "external balance" approach). CCF denotes Cheung, Chinn, and Fujii.

where s is the log exchange rate expressed as Chinese yuan per unit of foreign currency, p is the Chinese price index, p^* is the foreign price index, and the constant ψ accounts for the fact that the indexes are just that—indexes, with given base years. Nobody expects that relative PPP holds in the short run, but it is plausible to argue that it would hold in the long run. Equation (2.1), as a long-run relationship, implies that the real exchange rate would revert to the average value ψ:

$$q \equiv (s + p^* - p) = \Psi ,\tag{2.2}$$

where q is the log real exchange rate.

Application of this method requires the assumption that at least at some time over the sample period, the exchange rate has been at its equilibrium level—and for the Chinese currency, this is a difficult proposition to maintain. To illustrate this contention, consider the log trade weighted real *value* of the Chinese yuan, in figure 2.5 (the series is $-q$).[4] Using the average value over the 1980 to 2009 period as a measure of the equilibrium rate leads to the conclusion that the yuan is only slightly undervalued in December 2009 at 7.5 percent (all misalignment is in log terms unless otherwise stated).

Even if one allows for some sort of time trend in ψ, whether the currency is deemed to be overvalued or undervalued depends critically

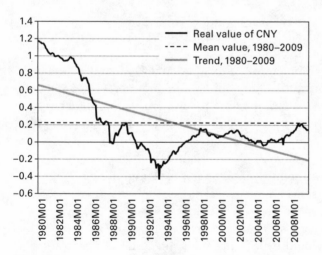

Figure 2.5
Log trade weighted real value of the Chinese yuan, deflated using CPIs, normalized to 2005 = 0. The upward direction indicates appreciation. The dashed line is the mean value over the 1980 to 2009 period; the gray line is the linear trend estimated over the 1980 to 2009 period. Source: Cheung et al. (2010b).

on the sample period used to estimate the trend; using the 1980 to 2009 sample, one finds a 36 percent *over*valuation.

Clearly, one can get pretty much any answer one wants by judicious choice of sample period. For instance, using a shorter, 1990 to 2009, sample, the yuan is overvalued by 13.5 and 1.6 percent in terms of the mean and trend, respectively. Further note that the standard calculation of the real exchange rate uses consumer price indexes (CPIs). One could use alternative deflators, such as producer price indexes, or unit labor costs (Chinn 2006). Doing so would provide alternative conclusions regarding differing estimates of misalignment.[5]

One of the most encouraging developments in the renminbi mis-alignment debate of the 2000s is that most of the policy discussion eschewed reference to simple trends in real exchange rates.

2.2.2   Absolute PPP and the "Penn Effect"

It seems like one could get around the problem of estimating ψ by using actual prices of identical bundles of goods across countries, rather than price indexes. Now p and p^* represent prices of identical bundles of goods

$$s = p - p^* \text{ or } p = s + p^*. \tag{2.3}$$

In principle, one can see then whether the "price level" differs between countries. In practice, one problem is that prices of identical bundles of goods are not usually available on a consistent basis. The "price levels" constructed by Summers and Heston (1991) and reported in the Penn World Tables, or in the related World Bank *World Development Indicators*, circumvent this problem by constructing the price levels in a way that they pertain to similar bundles across countries. One can then examine whether

$$r \equiv -q = (p - s - p^*) \tag{2.4}$$

is equal to 0 across countries.

Figure 2.6 presents a scatter plot of the observations on r for over 170 countries over the period 1980 to 2008, using the 2009 vintage of data the World Bank's *World Development Indicators*. If absolute PPP held, then one would expect that the scatter plot of observations to align horizontally. In fact the scatter of observations slopes upward—in words, higher income countries evidence higher prices.

A similar pattern obtains if one uses a bundle called a Big Mac (Parsley and Wei 2003), popularized by the *Economist*. Express the

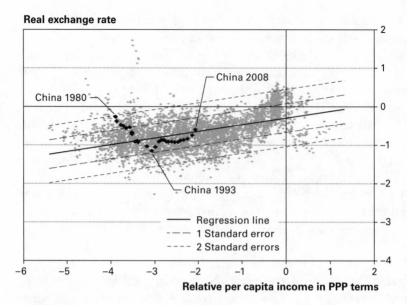

Figure 2.6
Log real exchange rate R and log per capita income relative to that of the United States, expressed in PPP terms. The upward direction indicates appreciation. The solid line denotes the regression line; the long (short) dashed lines represent ±1 (±2) standard error bands. The black boxes denote the path of the RMB over time. Sources: World Bank, *World Development Indicators* (accessed March 2010) and author's calculations.

prices of Big Macs across the globe in dollar terms, and one finds a positive correlation between per capita income and the US dollar price of a Big Mac. *Absolute* PPP using Big Macs indicates a January 2010 undervaluation of 67 percent.[6] This is not too dissimilar to the approximately 50 percent undervaluation (the distance from the 0 line to the China's observation for 2008) shown in figure 2.6.

The positive exchange rate–income relationship illustrated in figure 2.6 is so robust that it has a name—the Penn effect, after the Penn World Tables. Instead of viewing the Penn effect as a problem, one can *exploit* this stylized fact. One can estimate the relationship between (log) R and log relative per capita income, and interpret the deviation from this line as the degree of misalignment. Using a basic pooled cross-sectional regression, the elasticity of the price level with respect to relative per capita income is 0.2, whether using dollar-based price levels or PPP-based price levels (in general, PPP-based price levels are used). This correlation is shown in table 2.2.

Table 2.2
Panel estimation results of the real exchange rate–income relationship

	USD-based GDP				PPP-based GDP			
	Pooled OLS	Between	Fixed effects	Random effects	Pooled OLS	Between	Fixed effects	Random effects
GDP per capita	0.211**	0.196**	0.552**	0.482**	0.194**	0.188**	0.415**	0.302**
	(0.002)	(0.012)	(0.008)	(0.006)	(0.004)	(0.019)	(0.023)	(0.013)
Constant	−0.099**	−0.157**	—	0.623**	−0.276**	−0.310**	—	−0.078*
	(0.008)	(0.040)		(0.026)	(0.010)	(0.045)		(0.035)
Adjusted R^2	0.541	0.585	0.894	0.541	0.300	0.365	0.740	0.300
F-test Statistic			82.484**				42.765**	
Hausman test statistic				112.50**				35.122**
Number of observations	3,946				4,031			

Source: Cheung et al. (2010a).
Notes: The data cover 168 countries over the maximum of a twenty-seven-years' period from 1980 to 2006. The panel is unbalanced due to some missing observations. ** and * indicate 1 and 5 percent levels of significance, respectively. Heteroskedasticity robust standard errors are given in parentheses underneath coefficient estimates. For the fixed effects models, the F-test statistics are reported for the null hypothesis of the equality of the constants across all countries in the sample. For the random effects models, the Hausman test statistics test for the independence between the time-invariant country-specific effects and the regressor.

The regression line is plotted in the graph as the solid blue line.[7] The path of the yuan, and particularly the 2008 end point, in figure 2.6 is clearly counterintuitive. The yuan was estimated to be *over*valued by 5 percent by 2008. Note that while one cannot reject the no-misalignment null, one also cannot reject the 20 percent undervaluation null hypothesis at conventional significance levels.

2.2.3 The Productivity Approach and the Behavioral Equilibrium Exchange Rate Approach

Usually a Balassa–Samuelson model that focuses on the differential between traded and nontraded sectors is used to incorporate productivity in exchange rate determination. To my knowledge, few researchers have attempted to *estimate* the connection between sectoral productivity trends and the real exchange rate for China, with the exception of Cheung, Chinn, and Fujii (2009a).

The impact of productivity differentials can be illustrated in a highly simplified version of the Balassa–Samuelson model. Suppose that the economy price level is the average of the prices of tradable and nontradable goods. If the relative price of nontradables moves inversely with the relative productivity levels in the two sectors, then the faster tradable productivity grows relative to nontradables (relative to the same ratio in the foreign country), the stronger is the exchange rate.[8]

A highly simplified version of this approach can be expressed as

$$q = \alpha\left(a^{T^*} - a^{N^*}\right) - \alpha\left(a^T - a^N\right),\tag{2.5}$$

where α is the share of nontradables in the total basket of goods, and a is log total factor productivity in sector i ($i = N, T$).

In Cheung, Chinn, and Fujii (2009b), implementation of this approach is hampered by data limitations. Indeed reliable estimates of productivity levels in the tradable and nontradable sectors are hard to come by.[9] Estimates of equation (2.5) over the 1988 to 2004 period suggest that the Chinese yuan was undervalued in 2004 by as much as 6.1 percent, and as little as 1.4 percent, depending on the productivity series used.

The preceding approach restricted the exchange rate determinants to solely productivity differentials. Allowances for other effects can be made by augmenting the productivity variable with other variables, such as real interest differentials, government spending, or the terms of trade. Additionally more easily obtained proxy measures are often substituted for the intercountry productivity differential. The resulting composite models, called behavioral equilibrium exchange rate (BEER) specifications, are often used to evaluate equilibrium exchange rates for developed country currencies (Cheung, Chinn, and Garcia Pascual 2005).

Wang (2004), Funke and Rahn (2005), and Wang et al. (2007) use particularly simple BEERs to evaluate the Chinese currency. They relate the real exchange rate to the relative price of nontradables (to proxy for productivity ratios), and other variables such as net foreign assets, foreign exchange reserves, the terms of trade, money growth, and trade openness. These models are also used in the private sector. The Goldman Sachs version (GSDEER) relates the real exchange rate to productivity differentials and the terms of trade.

2.2.4 The Macroeconomic Balance Approach

The macroeconomic balance approach views the current account as being driven by saving and investment rates. Recall the national saving identity

$$CA \equiv (S - I) + (T - G).$$

In words, the current account is, by an accounting identity, equal to the budget balance and the private saving–investment gap. This is a tautology, unless one imposes some structure and causality. One can do this by treating the budget balance as an exogenous variable (or by using a cyclically adjusted budget balance) among the determinants of investment and saving to obtain "norms" for the current account (Chinn and Prasad 2003). Then, using trade elasticities, one can back out the real exchange rate, which would yield that "normal" current account.

The IMF regularly conducts analyses where it calculates equilibrium exchange rates via the Consultative Group on Exchange Rate Issues (CGER) (Lee et al. 2008; Isard and Faruqee 1998). However, the IMF has not publicly reported recent numerical estimates for China's equilibrium exchange rate.

The closely related fundamental equilibrium exchange rate (FEER) determines the current account norm on a more judgmental basis (i.e., the current account norm is not estimated econometrically, just imposed per the analysts' priors).

Cline and Williamson (2010) recently updated their estimates of the FEER-based exchange rate. They found that as of March 2009, the degree of undervaluation was about 32.8 percent, and only slightly larger as of December 2009.

2.2.5 The Underlying or Basic Balance approach

One could take a more ad hoc approach and ask what is the "normal" level of stable inflows—for instance, look at the sum of the current account and foreign direct investment (the "basic balance") to see whether that value "makes sense." Or one could look at the sum of the current account and private capital inflows after accounting for cyclical factors (the "underlying approach"). If one of the flows is "too large," then the currency would be considered undervalued (since a stronger currency would imply a smaller current account balance).

Interestingly two observations can be made in this regard. First, note the need for many non–model-based judgments. Recall the balance of payments accounting definition:

$$CA + KA + ORT \equiv 0 ,$$

where CA is current account, KA is private capital inflows, and ORT is official reserves transactions (+ is a reduction in Forex reserves). Saying that $CA + KA$ is too big is the same as saying that ORT is too small, namely that the reserves are rising "too fast."

Alternatively, running surpluses that are "too large" for "too long" will lead to foreign exchange reserves that are "too large." Obviously a lot of judgment calls are necessary for this approach.

Once one makes a judgment about what would be an appropriate trade surplus, for instance, the mechanics of making a judgment about exchange rate misalignment are fairly straightforward—what amount of exchange rate appreciation achieves a given reduction in the trade surplus. In this vein Goldstein and Lardy estimated the end-2008 undervaluation at 20 to 25 percent (in level terms), if the goal is a balance for China's current account (Goldstein and Lardy 2009: 67).[10]

The external balances approach also depends on a determination of which components of the balance of payments are "persistent." For instance, Prasad and Wei (2005), examining the composition of capital inflows into and out of China, argue that much of the reserve accumulation that has occurred in the preceding years was due to speculative inflow; hence the degree of misalignment was small.

One final observation: the implied exchange rate adjustment (and hence degree of currency misalignment) is *conditional* on the constellation of all other macro policies, including monetary, fiscal and regulatory being in place. If the $CA + KA$ is judged to be "too large," one could conclude the exchange rate is "too weak," but one could conclude with equal validity that the fiscal policy is "insufficiently expansionary." This is one point that is often forgotten when interpreting misalignment estimates in the basic balance approach.

2.2.6   Assessing the Assessments

The onset of US–China friction over the valuation of the renminbi began in earnest in 2003, with the confluence of stagnant employment growth in the United States and a widening Chinese trade surplus.[11]

One way to organize the discussion is to note the general characteristics of the estimates. In general (at least up until 2008), estimates based on PPP or the Penn effect yield the biggest estimates of yuan misalignment, while single country currency approaches, such as the BEER approaches, provide the smallest (Cairns 2005a, b).[12]

Frankel's 2006 paper was one of the earliest to use the Penn effect in a large cross-sectional analysis to measure the extent of misalignment.[13] He found that the Chinese yuan was about 44.8 percent in logarithmic terms (36.1 percent undervalued in absolute terms). Extrapolating to 2003, he concluded the gap had widened. Cheung, Chinn, and Fujii (2007, 2009b) exploited this relationship using panel data up to 2004 and found a yuan misalignment in excess of 50 percent.

In 2008, the International Comparison Program reported the results of a new benchmark survey of prices, conducted in 2005. These new estimates were incorporated into their comprehensive revision of the *World Development Indicators* database. While the estimates for many countries were affected, China's price and income data were substantially modified in light of the new benchmark data (Elekdag and Lall 2008). The Chinese price level was revised approximately 40 percent upward, and hence Chinese per capita income downward by roughly the same amount. Using updated data, Cheung et al. found something closer to 10 percent undervaluation in 2007 (with the 2004 estimated misalignment reduced to 18 percent). The 2008 yuan *over*valuation of 5 percent was obtained from the most recent *WDI*. While Chinese per capita income rose about 15 percent by the end of 2009, and the equilibrium rate should have risen by about 2.8 percent, the trade weighted real exchange rate was about the same now as it was in 2008; thus according to Cheung, Chinn, and Fujii's calculations, the yuan is currently slightly *over*valued.[14]

Using a smaller sample, Reisen (2009) finds a 12 percent 2008 undervaluation, and extrapolated a 15 percent undervaluation in 2009. Wang and Yao (2008) estimate a specification similar to that of Cheung, Chinn, and Fujii (2007), augmented by government spending, terms of trade, openness, and other variables (similar to Chinn 1999). Their model is estimated over the 1974 to 2004 period, for 184 economies. Extrapolating to 2007, they find a 16 percent undervaluation.

Since the 2008 data revisions, the prominence of the Penn approach in debates of the renminbi's valuation has diminished somewhat. This could be due to the decline in novelty of the approach, or because the message is not as "headline catching." Subramanian (2010) recently published estimates that contrast with those of Cheung et al. (2010b). He argues that it is best to estimate the slope coefficient off benchmark data years, with the last one being 2005. With this approach he finds the 2005 undervaluation to be 14.5 and 47.5 percent (in level terms), using the *World Development Indicators* and Penn World Tables, respectively. Extrapolating the path of the equilibrium exchange rate using income growth over the intervening period, he concludes that the current degree of undervaluation is roughly the same as it was in 2005.

Moving to the BEER approach, an interesting aspect of these studies is that the estimated extent of CNY misalignment was never typically large, at least relative to the estimates obtained using the Penn effect. This observation reflects a key difficulty with this approach. If the entire sample period were one in which the Chinese economy were *adjusting*, without ever achieving, an equilibrium in which the Balassa–Samuelson (and other effects) held, then a single-equation approach would tend to find smaller misalignments than alternative approaches that did not impose this condition.

One way to address this particular concern is to adjust the constant in the BEER equation by some factor. Goldman Sachs has recently incorporated such an adjustment, based on the Penn effect. Their assessment is that "the CNY no longer seems strongly undervalued against the dollar" (O'Neill 2010), with the degree of undervaluation equal to 2.7 percent against the US dollar and 23.1 percent against the euro (Stupnytska, Stolper, and Meechan 2009).

The macroeconomic balance approach and the basic balance approach are, in my view, the most relevant to the ongoing debates over the appropriateness of the value of the yuan. The Peterson Institute for International Economics has been at the forefront of applying the basic balance approach and—along with the IMF—the macroeconomic balance approach. I think that there has been a certain wariness of the basic balance approach because of the judgment calls that have to be made on what exactly is the sustainable level of external balances. The macroeconomic balance approach has a big policy impact, by definition, to the extent that it is a key input into the IMF's Consultative Group on Exchange Rate (CGER) assessments. Unfortunately, for obvious reasons, outside observers do not have a clear picture on what specific estimates are generated by this approach.

2.2.7   Impact

What was the impact of the academic research on the policy debate? This is a difficult question to answer, particularly with respect to the Chinese side, since much of the debate takes place internally.[15] However, we can see how the academic research was assimilated into the policy debates to get a feeling for how the academic research was mustered to take specific actions (or not take actions, as the case may be). The Bush Treasury's view is summarized in a 2007 Treasury *Occasional paper* (McCown, Pollard, and Weeks 2007). After reviewing the PPP, BEER, and FEER approaches (in a manner strikingly similar to the schema laid out above), the authors remark:

. . . different models can produce different estimates of equilibrium. Different models may specify different sets of fundamental variables and produce different levels. One model might find a substantial under-valuation of a currency, while other models might find little or no under-valuation or might even find over-valuation. For example, cyclical or transitory factors may affect the level of an exchange rate so that models that account for these factors will yield different results from those of models that do not. Some would argue that it is reasonable that different models should be used for different economies, reflecting the idiosyncratic factors that influence each economy's behavior. Since there is no broadly accepted "right model," a range of models should be employed when attempting to discern misalignment. If many models and indicators provide similar information, then the basis for rendering a judgment is strengthened." (p. 18)

This paper essentially expands on appendix II to the December 2006 Treasury Department *Semiannual Report on International Economic and Exchange Rate Policies*.[16] I like to think that the fundamental message of Cheung, et al. (2007) —that each estimate of misalignment is subject to considerable imprecision—is part of the reason why policy makers have been a little more circumspect in their use of point estimates. It is a message echoed by Dunaway et al. (2006). However, I may be over-optimistic in this regard.[17]

2.3   Trade Elasticities[18]

Separate from the issue of the degree of exchange rate misalignment is the positive question of how much of an impact will an exchange rate change have on trade flows (although, as in the macroeconomic balance and basic flows approaches, trade elasticities are an important input into the exchange rate misalignment methodologies).

2.3.1 The Framework

The basic approach is quite straightforward. It involves estimation of separate export and import flow equations for China, relative to the rest of the world:[19]

$$ex_t = \beta_0 + \beta_1 y_t^* + \beta_2 q_t + \beta_3 z_t + u_{1,t} \tag{2.6}$$

and

$$im_t = \gamma_0 + \gamma_1 y_t + \gamma_2 q_t + \gamma_3 w_t + u_{2,t}, \tag{2.7}$$

where ex is real exports, im is real imports, y is an activity variable, q is a real exchange rate (defined conventionally, so that a rise is a depreciation). In the studies cited below, a trade-weighted or "effective" exchange rate is used. The variable z is a supply side variable. An asterisk (*) superscript denotes the foreign variable. The variable w is a shift variable accounting for other factors that might increase import demand. The u's denote random error terms.

2.3.2 Discussion

Before the jump in the Chinese trade surplus, few academic studies aimed at estimating Chinese trade elasticities, at least over the relevant period. Many of the studies used data spanning the 1980s, which arguably pertained to an economy substantially different from that of the 1990s and 2000s (e.g., Cerra and Dayal-Gulati 1999; Cerra and Saxena 2000). With respect to the recent debate, one widely cited estimate from Goldman Sachs was for a Chinese export price elasticity of 0.2 and an import price elasticity of 0.5[20]—which is relatively low.

Garcia-Herrero and Koivu (2007) estimate equations (2.6) and (2.7). They examine data over the 1995 to 2005 period, breaking the data into ordinary and processing/parts imports and exports, and relate Chinese exports to the world, imports, and the real effective exchange rate, augmented by a proxy measure for the value-added tax rebate on exports, and a capacity utilization variable. In both import and export equations, the stock of FDI is included. One notable result they obtain is that for Chinese imports, the real exchange rate coefficient has a sign opposite of anticipated in the full sample. Additionally they find that post-WTO entry, Chinese income and price elasticities for exports rise considerably. On the import side, no such change is obvious with respect to the pre- and post-WTO period.

Marquez and Schindler (2007) argue that the absence of useful price indices for Chinese imports and exports requires the adoption of an alternative model specification. They treat the variable of interest as world (import or export) trade shares, broken down into "ordinary" and "parts and components." Using monthly Chinese imports data from 1997 to July 2006, they find ordinary trade-share income "elasticities" ranging from –0.021 to –0.001 (i.e., the coefficients are *in the wrong direction*), and price "elasticities" from 0.013 to 0.021.[21] The parts and components price elasticities are in the wrong direction, and statistically significantly so. Interestingly, the stock of FDI matters in almost all cases. Since the FDI stock is a smooth trend, it is not clear whether to attribute the effect explicitly to the effect of FDI, or to other variables that may be trending upward over time, including productive capacity.

For export shares (ordinary goods), they find income elasticities ranging from 0.08 to 0.09, and price elasticities ranging from 0.08 to 0.068. For parts and components export share, the income coefficient ranges from a 0.042 to 0.049. Their preferred specification implies that a 10 percent real appreciation of the Chinese RMB reduces the Chinese trade balance between $75 billion and $92 billion.

Thorbecke and Smith (2010) do not directly examine the implications for both imports and exports, but they do consider the impact of RMB appreciation on exports, taking into account the integration of the production chain in the region. Using a sample of 33 countries over the 1994 to 2005 period, and a trade-weighted exchange rate that measures the impact of how bilateral exchange rates affect imported input prices, they find that a 10 percent RMB appreciation in the absence of changes in other East Asian currencies would result in a 3 percent decline in processed exports and an 11 percent decline in ordinary exports. If other East Asian currencies appreciated in line with the RMB, then the resulting change in the processed exports would be 9 percent.

Cheung et al. (2010a) estimate equations (2.6) and (2.7) over the 1993 to 2006 period, using the Stock and Watson (1993) dynamic OLS regression method. The import and export data are examined as aggregates, and as series disaggregated into ordinary and processing and parts trade. The data are converted into real terms using a variety of deflators, including US CPI, PPI for finished goods, and country-specific Chinese price indexes due to Gaulier et al. (2006),[22] as well as (for Chinese exports) Hong Kong re-export indexes. The real exchange rate,

q, is the IMF's CPI deflated trade-weighted index, and foreign activity is rest-of-the-world GDP evaluated in current US dollars, deflated into real terms using the US GDP deflator, while y is measured using real GDP (production based) expressed in real 1990 RMB. For z, they assume that supply shifts out with the capital stock in manufacturing. This capital stock measure was calculated by Bai et al. (2006).

The results are reported in table 2.3. For the aggregate exports (panel A), the estimated income and price coefficients are not typically signifi-cantly significant, although they point in the right direction; only the supply variable coefficient is statistically significant.

As suggested by Marquez and Schindler (2007), the differing behav-ior of ordinary and processing exports suggests that aggregation is inappropriate. Panel B reports the results for ordinary exports. Here one finds that the rest-of-the-world activity is not a good predictor of exports, while the price variable is an important determinant. Using either a specific estimate of export prices from Gaulier et al. (2006) (hereafter GUL-K) or price indexes for Hong Kong exports,[23] one finds that the export elasticity of approximately 0.6. At the same time, a 1 percent increase in the Chinese manufacturing capital stock induces between a 2.2 and 2.5 percent increase in real exports.

Strangely, the rest-of-the-world GDP does positively affect the pro-cessing output. Thorbecke and Smith (2010) argue that the Chinese processing output is fairly sophisticated in nature; if so, that might explain the greater income sensitivity of such exports.

Table 2.4 (from Cheung et al. 2010a) shows that in the case of Chinese imports, aggregate imports respond strongly to income, and in the expected direction. But where Marquez and Schindler's results are replicated with regard to the price elasticity, a weaker RMB induces more imports, rather than less. This is true also for ordinary imports. Only when moving to parts and processing imports does one obtain some mixed evidence, and there the results are still toward finding a wrong-signed coefficient.[24]

Previously Ahmed (2009) used data that spans the recent recession and sharp drop-off and rebound in Chinese imports and exports (1996Q1–2009Q2). Using first differences specifications corresponding to equations (2.6) and (2.7), he found that (in the long run) a one per-centage point increase in the annual rate of appreciation of the real exchange rate would have a cumulative negative effect on real export growth of 1.8 percentage points, which is statistically significant. A one percentage point increase in foreign consumption growth would

Table 2.3
Chinese export elasticities

Panel A: Aggregate exports

	(1) PPI	(2) GLUK	(3) HK UV
y^*	0.57	−0.56	0.31
	(0.40)	(0.53)	(0.40)
q	−0.06	0.26	0.27
	(0.23)	(0.22)	(0.22)
z	1.68***	2.35***	2.06***
	(0.16)	(0.16)	(0.15)
Adjusted R^2	0.98	0.98	0.99
SER	0.077	0.080	0.076
sample	93Q3–06Q2	93Q3–04Q2	93Q3–06Q2

Panel B: Ordinary exports

	PPI	GLUK	HK UV
y^*	0.04	−1.26	−0.22
	(0.55)	(0.75)	(0.55)
q	0.31	0.61*	0.64*
	(0.32)	(0.31)	(0.32)
z	1.83***	2.51***	2.22***
	(0.22)	(0.22)	(0.22)
Adjusted R^2	0.96	0.96	0.97
SER	0.106	0.108	0.105
sample	93Q3–06Q2	93Q3–04Q2	93Q3–06Q2

Panel C: Processing and parts exports

	PPI	GLUK	HK UV
y^*	0.98***	0.26	0.72**
	(0.30)	(0.32)	(0.31)
q	−0.47**	−0.62***	−0.14
	(0.19)	(0.16)	(0.18)
z	1.52***	1.99***	1.91***
	(0.11)	(0.10)	(0.11)
Adjusted R^2	0.92	0.99	0.99
SER	0.065	0.060	0.062
sample	93Q3–06Q2	93Q3–04Q2	93Q3–06Q2

Source: Cheung et al. (2010a).
Notes: Point estimates are obtained from DOLS(2, 2). Robust standard errors are given in parentheses. *, **, and *** indicate significance at the 10, 5, and 1 percent levels. The price elasticity estimate should be positive for Chinese exports. PPI indicates US PPI-finished goods is used as the deflator; GLUK indicates the Gaulier et al. (2006) consumer good index is used as the deflator; HK UV indicates the Hong Kong unit value index for re-exports to the world is used as the deflator. Supply is the Bai et al. (2006) measure of the Chinese capital stock in manufacturing.

Table 2.4
Chinese import elasticities

Panel A: Aggregate imports

	(1)	(2)	(3)
	PPI	GLUK	HK UV
y	1.78***	1.41***	2.16***
	(0.06)	(0.04)	(0.06)
q	1.48***	0.39**	1.54***
	(0.38)	(0.19)	(0.32)
Adjusted R^2	0.99	0.98	0.99
SER	0.056	0.050	0.055
sample	94Q4–06Q2	94Q4–04Q2	94Q4–06Q2

Panel B: Ordinary imports

	PPI	GLUK	HK UV
y	2.16***	2.40***	2.54***
	(0.26)	(0.32)	(0.27)
q	2.75**	2.25**	2.80**
	(1.18)	(1.06)	(1.19)
Adjusted R^2	0.85	0.94	0.94
SER	0.209	0.152	0.196
sample	94Q4–06Q2	94Q4–04Q2	94Q4–06Q2

Panel C: Processing and parts imports

	PPI	GLUK	HK UV
y	1.68***	0.85***	2.06***
	(0.08)	(0.13)	(0.06)
q	1.15***	−0.25	1.20***
	(0.35)	(0.34)	(0.28)
R^2	0.98	0.88	0.99
SER	0.072	0.080	0.060
sample	94Q4–06Q2	94Q4–04Q2	94Q4–06Q2

Table 2.4
(continued)

Panel D: Processing and parts imports

	PPI	GLUK	HK UV
y	−0.40*	−1.86*	−0.04
	(0.20)	(0.93)	(0.25)
q	−0.13	−1.64***	−0.16
	(0.23)	(0.58)	(0.22)
w	1.10***	1.20***	0.96***
	(0.13)	(0.40)	(0.12)
Adjusted R^2	0.99	0.89	0.99
SER	0.037	0.074	0.035
sample	94Q4–06Q2	94Q4–04Q2	94Q4–06Q2

Source: Cheung et al. (2010a).
Notes: Point estimates are obtained from DOLS(2, 2). Robust standard errors are given in parentheses. *, **, and *** indicates significance at the 10, 5, and 1 percent levels. The price elasticity estimate should be negative for Chinese imports. PPI indicates US PPI-finished goods is used as the deflator; GLUK indicates the Gaulier et al. (2006) capital goods and parts index is used as the deflator for aggregate, capital goods for ordinary and parts for processing and parts; HK UV indicates the Hong Kong unit value index for re-exports is used as the deflator. The demand shift variable w is total real exports.

increase export growth by 5.9 percentage points, which is also statistically significant, and appears to be an implausibly large effect. Also a one percentage point increase in the growth rate of the FDI capital stock, comparable to the supply shift term in Cheung, Chinn, and Fujii, raises export growth by a cumulative and statistically significant 0.3 percentage points.

In practical terms, the difference in impacts is substantial. Consider estimates of China's export elasticities. Ahmed (2009) found that after four years, 20 percent yuan appreciation induces a $400 billion decrease in Chinese exports. In contrast, in Cheung et al. (2010b), we found a $50 billion impact. Chinn (2010), using a data sample extending up to 2010Q2, obtained a long-run impact of $144 billion impact, still lower than Ahmed's estimate.

It is unclear how much these results have affected the debate over the efficacy of exchange rate appreciation on the Chinese trade surplus, in that the estimates are only intermittently in line with priors. Nevertheless, it is apparent that the humility imparted by the lack of empirical success had a positive impact. There is further the fact that most of the earlier debate (circa 2005) relied on rule-of-thumb estimates, as noted in policy documents such the Congressional Research Service reports.[25]

A shortcoming of all of the estimates is that they are not the product of theoretically grounded, econometrically estimated economic models. Rather, they are "back of the envelope" estimates based on a few simple "rule of thumb" assumptions. "Rules of thumb" such as the Preeg [2003] 10%–$1 billion estimate or the Goldman Sachs [2003] import and export elasticities may not be accurate over time or over large changes in the exchange rate.

Perhaps the most important contribution of this literature is that rule-of-thumb estimates are no longer the norm in policy discussions, and the wide dispersion in actual estimates is now acknowledged.

2.4   Global Imbalances: Saving–Investment Norms

China and other Asian emerging market countries have often been identified as the main causes of the widening US current account deficits. In particular, these economies' underdeveloped and closed financial markets are alleged to be insufficiently attractive to absorb the excess saving in the region, resulting in a "saving glut." Clarida (2005a, b) argues that East Asian, particularly Chinese, financial markets are so less sophisticated, deep, and open that Asian excess saving inevitably flows into the highly developed US financial market. Bernanke (2005) contends that "some of the key reasons for the large U.S. current account deficit are external to the United States" and remediable only in the long run. The saving glut of the Asian emerging market countries, driven by rising savings and collapsing investment in the aftermath of the financial crisis, is the direct cause of the US current account deficit. Therefore the long-term solution is to encourage developing countries, especially those in the East Asian region, to develop financial markets so that the saving rate would fall. Once policies improving institutions and legal systems amenable to financial development and liberalizing the markets are implemented, "a greater share of global saving can be redirected away from the United States and toward the developing nations." He reiterated these views as recently as 2007 (Bernanke 2007).

Standing in stark contrast to the saving glut thesis is the more prosaic view that a fall in the US national saving, notably in the form of its government budget deficit, is the main cause of the ongoing current account deficits—the "twin deficit" argument. While the twin deficit effect has been empirically investigated in the literature (e.g., Gale and

Orszag 2004), as far as we are aware, very little investigation has been made to shed light on the effect of financial development on current account balances, with the exception of Chinn and Ito (2007, 2008) and Gruber and Kamin (2009).[26] In this investigation encompassing a sample of 89 countries over the 1971 to 2004 period, they find that more financial development—measured as private credit as a share of GDP—leads to *higher* saving for countries with underdevelopment institutions and closed financial markets that includes most of East Asian emerging market countries.[27]

Other factors are suggested by the current debate. Bernanke argues that the *openness* of financial markets can also affect the direction of cross-border capital flows. Alfaro et al. (2004), on the other hand, show that institutional development may explain the Lucas paradox, that is, why capital flows from developing countries with presumably high marginal products of capital to developed countries with low ones. In short, financial development might be mediated by financial openness and institutional development. Gruber and Kamin (2007) find an important role for financial crises, implicitly supporting the view that reserve accumulation (and accompanying current account surpluses) are driven by self-protection.

2.4.1 Empirics

Chinn and Ito (2007) examine the hypothesis that financial development is an important determinant of current account imbalances, building upon the saving-investment framework in Chinn and Prasad (2003). They use data for 19 industrial and 69 developing countries for the period of 1971 to 2004, focusing on three variables—the current account balance, and its constituents, national saving, and investment, all expressed as a ratio to GDP.[28] The determinants include the budget balance, demographic variables, relative per capita income, average growth rates, initial net foreign assets, terms of trade volatility, and trade openness, in addition to key variables of interest, namely financial development (proxied by private credit creation as a share of GDP), institutional development (proxied by LEGAL, the first principal component of three ICRG indexes), and capital account openness (a de jure measure due to Chinn and Ito 2006).

Because the economic environment may affect the way in which financial development might affect saving and investment, they include interaction terms between the financial development and legal variables (*PCGDP* times *LEGAL*), interaction terms between the financial development and financial openness variables (*PCGDP* times *KAOPEN*), and interaction terms between legal development and financial openness (*LEGAL* times *KAOPEN*). The financial and legal interaction effect is motivated by the conjecture that deepening financial markets might lead to higher saving rates, but the effect might be magnified under conditions of better developed legal institutions. Alternatively, if greater financial deepening leads to a lower saving rate or a lower investment rate, that effect could be mitigated when financial markets are equipped with highly developed legal systems. A similar argument can be applied to the effect of financial openness on current account balances.

Table 2.5 displays results from panel OLS regressions with institutional variables. First, as is typically the case, a positive relationship between current account and government budget balances is detected in almost all sample groups. The point estimate on budget balances is a statistically significant at the 0.15 level for the industrialized countries group (note that a ±2 standard error confidence interval encompasses values as high as 0.34).

Using this model, one finds that China's current account during the 2001 to 2004 period is within the 95 percent confidence band for the predicted values from this model. However, the point estimate for the 2001 to 2004 period is at the upper end, and slight modifications to the specification (or changing the sample periods) would place the actual current account balance closer to the top of the 95 percent confidence band (Chinn et al. 2010).

Second, financial development has different, and nonlinear, effects, depending on the group and also on the development of the institutional environment and openness to capital flows. For instance, higher financial development results in a smaller current account surplus, but the estimated effect is only statistically significant for the emerging market economies. Further, since the financial development variable (*PCGDP*) interacts with other institutional variables (*LEGAL* and *KAOPEN*), one must be careful about interpretation of the effect of financial development. Using these estimated nonlinear effects, Chinn and Ito find that Hong Kong and Singapore are the only East Asian countries for which financial development will cause a negative impact on national savings. Other countries will experience an *increase* in the ratio of national savings to GDP if financial markets develop further.

How does China fit into the estimated impacts on saving and investment? China experienced a remarkable 32.4 percentage point increase

Table 2.5
Determinants of the current account

Dependent variable: Five-year average of current account (% of GDP), 1971–2004

	(1) Full	(2) IDC	(3) LDC	(4) LDC without Africa	(5) EMG
Government budget balance	0.159 [0.065]**	0.154 [0.095]*	0.168 [0.079]**	0.251 [0.091]***	0.23 [0.075]***
Lane's NFA (initial)	0.049 [0.005]***	0.069 [0.011]***	0.047 [0.005]***	0.051 [0.006]***	0.041 [0.009]***
Relative income	0.062 [0.028]**	0.058 [0.028]**	0.115 [0.096]	0.16 [0.106]	0.216 [0.103]**
Relative income squared	0.032 [0.038]	−0.097 [0.120]	0.057 [0.102]	0.157 [0.121]	0.166 [0.111]
Relative dependency ratio (young)	−0.061 [0.018]***	−0.027 [0.082]	−0.076 [0.022]***	−0.099 [0.030]***	−0.044 [0.023]*
Relative dependency ratio (old)	−0.2 [0.058]***	0.099 [0.098]	−0.368 [0.096]***	−0.331 [0.114]***	−0.529 [0.127]***
Financial development (PCGDP)	−0.008 [0.009]	0.01 [0.012]	−0.043 [0.032]	−0.038 [0.040]	−0.082 [0.038]**
Legal development (LEGAL)	−0.003 [0.004]	0.002 [0.007]	−0.017 [0.008]**	−0.02 [0.009]**	−0.018 [0.010]*
PCGDP × LEGAL	−0.003 [0.004]	−0.035 [0.015]**	−0.021 [0.011]*	−0.025 [0.012]**	−0.037 [0.016]**

Table 2.5
(continued)

Dependent variable: Five-year average of current account (% of GDP), 1971–2004

	(1) Full	(2) IDC	(3) LDC	(4) LDC without Africa	(5) EMG
Financial openness (KAOPEN)	-0.001 [0.003]	-0.002 [0.003]	0.002 [0.007]	0.005 [0.008]	0.008 [0.010]
KAOPEN × LEGAL	0.002 [0.001]*	0.012 [0.003]***	0.002 [0.002]	0.002 [0.002]	0.005 [0.003]
KAOPEN × PCGDP	-0.003 [0.005]	0.002 [0.009]	0 [0.007]	0.002 [0.008]	-0.002 [0.009]
TOT volatility	-0.013 [0.017]	0.1 [0.054]*	-0.015 [0.018]	-0.002 [0.019]	-0.003 [0.022]
Average GDP growth	-0.123 [0.087]	-0.036 [0.243]	-0.09 [0.096]	-0.107 [0.124]	-0.132 [0.118]
Trade openness	0.006 [0.009]	0.046 [0.014]***	0.005 [0.013]	0 [0.014]	0.004 [0.014]
Oil-exporting countries	0.041 [0.013]***	—	0.04 [0.013]***	0.035 [0.012]***	0.025 [0.013]*
Observations	471	126	345	234	203
Adjusted R^2	0.47	0.55	0.46	0.54	0.51

Source: Chinn and Ito (2008).

Notes: Robust standard errors in brackets, * significant at 10 percent; ** significant at 5 percent; *** significant at 1 percent. The estimated coefficients for the time-fixed dummies and constant are not shown.

in private credit creation (net of change in the world weighted average) in 2001 to 2004. This financial development *alone* implies a national savings increase of 1.7 percentage points, but the investment increase of 2.4 percentage points suggests a negative effect of financial development on net saving; the directly estimated zero net effect on the current account reflects the uncertainty surrounding these point estimates.

In sum, these results present evidence against part of the argument that emerging market countries, especially those in East Asia, will experience lower rates of saving once these countries achieve higher levels of financial development and better developed legal infrastructure. More open financial markets do not appear to have an impact on current account balances for this group of countries, either. If anything, arguments to this effect have inappropriately extended a characterization applicable to industrialized countries to less developed countries.

Gruber and Kamin (2009) obtain results that are similar to these, in the sense that financial development measured by private credit to GDP fails to show up as an important determinant of current account balances. One similarity across these analyses is the reliance upon private credit to GDP as the proxy measure.

Ito and Chinn (2009) investigate whether alternative measures of financial development change these conclusions. Generally, they find that for emerging market countries, financial development may lead to deterioration of current account balances *if* the economy exhibits greater than the average openness and a legal system below the top decile. In other cases this linkage is not apparent. Moreover greater financial opening tends to make an emerging market economy run a smaller current account surplus, especially if the economy is financially underdeveloped.

2.4.2 Impact on the Policy Dialogue

It would be overstating the case to say that these analyses have proved definitively what current account norms should prevail, and how well America's—and China's—behavior can be explained by observable macro variables. However, I think this approach is a step beyond the ad hoc approach that had prevailed until then in some policy circles. From a 2005 Congressional Research Service report:[29]

The main source of contention in all of the estimates of the yuan's undervaluation is the definition of an "equilibrium" current account balance. All three estimates are defined as the appreciation that would be required for China to attain "equilibrium" in the current account balance. But there is no consensus based on theory or evidence to determine what equilibrium would be; rather, the authors base equilibrium on their own personal opinion.

Another aspect of these analyses does support the view that there is something special about China. Specifically, China's current account balance is underpredicted by these panel regressions. Depending on the specification, the misprediction is sometimes just barely statistically significant at the 95 percent level. At the same time the US current account is overpredicted. Hence no strong conclusions can be derived from these regression analyses.[30]

These types of analyses have focused attention on the fact that the current account is related to public sector savings and the gap between investment and private saving. This in turn has meant a greater degree of attention to the determinants of the private saving–investment balance as a critical factor, rather than on elasticities and income, arising from a simple Keynesian/Mundell–Fleming approach.

In this regard private sector analysts and policy makers cite research that emphasizes the importance of corporate saving on aggregate private saving, de-emphasizing household saving. One analyst mentioned Kuljis's 2005 World Bank paper as being very influential. In my view, this assessment is correct. Economists who stand at the nexus of policy and academe now typically cite the importance of the corporate sector in saving behavior, while recognizing the trends in the household sector (particularly the decline in the labor share of national income) (e.g., Prasad 2009).

This point has become increasingly central as the debate has moved to whether wage rates are rising. Those familiar with the Lewis–Fei–Ranis model of development will recall that as the supply of excess labor declines and wages rise, the share of national income going to capital decreases. If the propensity to save of labor is less than that of capitalists, then the overall saving rate should decline (Kroeber 2010).

2.5 Concluding Thoughts

The debate over the role of China in the development of global imbalances has been waged in both the policy and academic arenas. While it would be naïve to assert that academic research has driven the thrust of policy in the policy leadership in the United States or China, I believe the academic research has been important in moderating the impulse for superficially appealing measures.

In the currency misalignment debate, the proliferation of estimates, derived from a variety of methodologies, has forced a closer examination of what exactly misalignment means. To the extent that the debate over the appropriate model highlights the fact that any given misalignment estimate is conditional on other macro aggregates emphasizes the point that re-balancing the global economy will require more than merely a readjustment of exchange rates.

It is also of interest that in the latest round of legislation aimed at labeling China a currency manipulator,[31] the designation of an undervalued currency heavily depended on a series of criteria drawn from the fundamental equilibrium exchange rate literature.

In the end, policy positions will be driven primarily by national interests and pressure groups. But at the margin, research can and will inform the debate over what macroeconomic policy measures will be effective.

Notes

1. A critique of this hypothesis of global imbalances as primary cause is in Chinn and Frieden (2011).

2. IMF, World Bank, ADB, and OECD, and Federal Reserve.

3. This section draws on Cheung et al. (2010b).

4. The series was merged in 1994 with an older IMF series, which accounts for the fact that some transactions were conducted at "swap market" rates rather than official rates. See the discussion in Fernald, Edison, and Loungani (1999).

5. For the real exchange rate to be stationary, the exchange rate and price indexes must be cointegrated with the unit coefficients (Chinn 2000a).

6. The US price is $3.58, while the Chinese price (in US dollars) is $1.83; in level terms, this is a 50 percent undervaluation. See Anonymous (2010).

7. Ferguson and Schularick (2009) apply a variant of this approach to ten emerging market economies relative to the United States. In their case R is the dollar wage rate. By this criterion the yuan is undervalued by 34 to 48 percent (in level terms).

8. PPP must hold for traded goods, capital must be perfectly mobile internationally, and the factors of production must be free to move between sectors.

9. Following Chinn (2000b), average labor productivity is obtained by dividing real output in sector i by labor employment in the same sector. The tradables sector is proxied by the manufacturing sector, while the nontradables sector is proxied by the "other" sector.

10. They use the rule of thumb that a 10 percent appreciation induces a 2 to 3.5 percent reduction in the current account.

11. John Snow, "Testimony of Treasury Secretary John Snow before the Senate Committee on Banking, Housing and Urban Affairs," October 30, 2003. Senators Schumer and

Graham first submitted a bill to levy tariffs on Chinese imports in the fall of 2003, and they submitted further versions in 2005 to 2007.

12. I skip the absolute PPP approach because it is well accepted in the academic literature and policy discourse that there are very good reasons for the price level to be higher in high-income countries versus low-income countries.

13. Bosworth (2004) uses a smaller sample to evaluate misalignment according to the Penn effect.

14. In the IMF *World Economic Outlook* (April 2010) database, year on year growth in per capita GDP is around 10 percent in both 2009 and 2010. Using this growth rate and the 0.2 coefficient estimate yields the implied 2.8 percent appreciation.

15. Some research published in English does make it into Chinese analyses; see, for instance, Huang (2010). In addition the use of the Penn approach has appeared in Chinese analyses (Wang and Yao 2008). An insight into Chinese thinking can be obtained by reading what is published in *People's Daily*. See "Yuan Is Undervalued" (2010).

16. All the reports from November 2005 onward are available at http://www.treasury.gov/resource-center/international/exchange-rate-policies/Pages/index.aspx.

17. Frankel and Wei (2007) show that domestic variables influence whether a country is declared a currency manipulator, which is at odds with the view that only international macro factors determine the Treasury determination.

18. This section is drawn from Cheung et al. (2010a).

19. I don't address bilateral trade elasticities despite the prominence of the US–China trade balance in political debates because bilateral balances are of limited importance in the open economy macroeconomic context. The literature and estimates are discussed in Cheung et al. (2009b).

20. O'Neill and Wilson (2003) as cited in Morrison and Labonte (2007).

21. Marquez and Schindler (2007) conjecture that this counterintuitive result arises from the role of state-owned enterprises. They also observe that this result can occur under certain configurations of substitutability between imported and domestic goods.

22. The GLU-K indexes have the drawback of being available only at the annual frequency, and then only up to 2004. Cheung et al. (2010b) used quadratic interpolation to translate the annual data into quarterly.

23. The Gaulier et al. (2006) consumer good index, and the HK unit value index for re-exports to the world, are used as the deflator, respectively.

24. The Marquez and Schindler results suggest including a role for foreign direct investment as a w variable. However, inclusion of a cumulative *FDI* variable is insufficient to overturn this result on a consistent basis.

25. See, for instance, Morrison and Labonte (2005: 9).

26. Theoretical explanations for this phenomenon now abound. See Caballero, Farhi and Gourinchas (2008a, b) and Mendoza et al. (2009).

27. Among East Asian countries, most of countries (except for Hong Kong and Singapore) could experience worsening current account balances if financial markets develop further, but that effect is achieved, not through a reduction in savings rates, but through higher increases in the levels of investment than those of national savings.

28. One potential problem with developing country data is the possibility of significant measurement error in annual data. To mitigate these concerns, and to focus our interest in medium-term rather than short-term variations in current accounts, we construct a panel that contains non-overlapping five-year averages of the data for each country. Furthermore all the variables, except for net foreign assets to GDP, are converted into the deviations from their GDP-weighted world mean prior to the calculation of five year averages. The use of demeaned series controls for rest-of-world effects. In other words, a country's current account balance is determined by developments at home as well as abroad.

29. Morrison and Labonte (2005: 9–10).

30. That being said, it's hard to avoid this sort of framework for making judgments about the course of current account balances. See Chinn, Eichengreen, and Ito (2010).

31. HR 2378: Currency Reform for Fair Trade Act, in the second session of the 111th Congress.

References

Ahmed, S. 2009. Are Chinese exports sensitive to changes in the exchange rate? International Finance Discussion Paper 987. Federal Reserve Board, Washington, DC.

Alfaro, L., A. Chanda, S. Kalemli-Ozcan, and S. Sayek. 2004. FDI and economic growth: The role of local financial markets. *Journal of International Economics* 64 (1): 89–112.

Anonymous. 2010. The Big Mac index: Exchanging blows: Our Big Mac index shows the Chinese yuan is still undervalued. *Economist*, March 17.

Bai, C.-E., C.-T. Hsieh, and Q. Qian. 2006. Returns to capital in China. *Brookings Papers on Economic Activity* 2006 (2): 61–101.

Bernanke, B. 2005. The global saving glut and the U.S. current account. Remarks at the Sandridge Lecture, Virginia Association of Economics, Richmond, VA, March 10.

Bernanke, B. 2007. Global imbalances: Recent developments and prospects. Remarks at the Bundesbank Lecture, Berlin, Germany, September 11.

Bosworth, B. 2004. Valuing the renminbi. Paper presented at the Tokyo Club Research Meeting, February 9–10.

Caballero, R., E. Farhi, and P.-O. Gourinchas. 2008a. An equilibrium model of "global imbalances" and low interest rates. *American Economic Review* 98 (1): 358–93.

Caballero, R., Farhi, E., and Gourinchas, P.-O. 2008b. Financial crash, commodity prices, and global imbalances. *Brookings Papers on Economic Activity* 2: 1–68.

Cairns, J. 2005a. China: How undervalued is the CNY? IDEAglobal Economic Research, London.

Cairns, J. 2005b. Fair value on global currencies: An assessment of valuation based on GDP and absolute price levels. IDEAglobal Economic Research, London.

Cerra, V., and A. Dayal-Gulati. 1999. China's trade flows—Changing price sensitivies and the reform process. Working Paper 99/01. IMF, Washington, DC.

Cerra, V., and S. Saxena. 2000. An empirical analysis of China's export behavior. Working Paper 02/200. IMF, Washington, DC.

Cheung, Y.-W., M. Chinn, and E. Fujii. 2010a. China's current account and exchange rate. In R. Feenstra and S.-J. Wei, eds., *China's Growing Role in World Trade*. Chicago: Chicago University Press, 231–71.

Cheung, Y.-W., M. Chinn, and E. Fujii. 2010b. Measuring misalignment: Latest estimates for the Chinese yuan. In S. Evenett, ed., *The US–Sino Currency Dispute: New Insights from Economics, Politics and Law*, London: Center for Economic Policy Research.

Cheung, Y.-W., M. Chinn, and E. Fujii. 2009a. The illusion of precision and the role of the renminbi in regional integration. In K. Hamada, B. Reszat, and U. Volz, eds., *Towards Monetary and Financial Integration in East Asia*. London: Elgar.

Cheung, Y.-W., M. Chinn, and E. Fujii. 2009b. Pitfalls in measuring exchange rate misalignment: The yuan and other currencies. *Open Economies Review* 20: 183–206.

Cheung, Y.-W., M. Chinn, and E. Fujii. 2007. The overvaluation of renminbi undervaluation. *Journal of International Money and Finance* 26 (5): 762–85.

Cheung, Y.-W., M. Chinn, and A. Garcia Pascual. 2005. Empirical exchange rate models of the nineties: Are any fit to survive? *Journal of International Money and Finance* 24: 1150–75.

Chinn, M. 1999. Productivity, government spending and the real exchange rate: Evidence for OECD countries. In R. MacDonald and J. Stein, eds., *Equilibrium Exchange Rates*. Boston: Kluwer Academic, 163–90.

Chinn, M. 2000a. Before the fall: Were East Asian currencies overvalued? *Emerging Markets Review* 1 (2): 101–26.

Chinn, M. 2000b. The usual suspects? Productivity and demand shocks and Asia–Pacific real exchange rates. *Review of International Economics* 8 (1):20–43.

Chinn, M. 2006. A primer on real effective exchange rates: Determinants, overvaluation, trade flows and competitive devaluations. *Open Economies Review* 17 (1): 115–43.

Chinn, M. 2010. Back of the envelope estimates of Chinese trade elasticities. *Econbrowser*, September 25. Retrieved from: http://www.econbrowser.com/archives/2010/09/back_of_the_env.html.

Chinn, M., Eichengreen, B., and Ito, H. 2010. Rebalancing global growth. Paper prepared for the World Bank's Re-Growing Growth Project. World Bank, Washington, DC.

Chinn, M., and J. Frieden. 2011. *Lost Decades: The Making of America's Debt Crisis and the Long Recovery*. New York: Norton.

Chinn, M., and H. Ito. 2006. What matters for financial development? Capital controls, institutions, and interactions. *Journal of Development Economics* 81 (1): 163–92.

Chinn, M., and H. Ito. 2007. Current account balances, financial development and institutions: Assaying the world "saving glut." *Journal of International Money and Finance* 26 (4): 546–69.

Chinn, M., and H. Ito. 2008. Global current account imbalances: American fiscal policy versus East Asian savings. *Review of International Economics* 16 (3): 479–98.

Chinn, M., and E. Prasad. 2003. Medium-term determinants of current accounts in industrial and developing countries: An empirical exploration. *Journal of International Economics* 59 (1): 47–76.

Clarida, R. 2005a. Japan, China, and the U.S. current account deficit. *Cato Journal* 25 (1): 111–14.

Clarida, R. 2005b. Some thoughts on "The Sustainability and Adjustment of Global Current Account Imbalances." Speech given at the Council on Foreign Relations, March 28.

Cline, W. R., and J. Williamson. 2010. Notes on equilibrium exchange rates: January 2010. *Policy Brief PB10–2*. Washington, DC: Peterson Institute for International Economics.

Coudert, V., and C. Couharde. 2005. Real equilibrium exchange rate in China. Working Paper 2005–01. CEPII, Paris.

Council of Economic Advisers. 2009. Economic Report of the President. Washington, DC: US Government Printing Office.

Dunaway, S. V., L. Leigh, and X. Li. 2006. How robust are estimates of equilibrium real exchange rates: The case of China. Working Paper 06/220. IMF, Washington, DC.

Elekdag, S., and S. Lall. 2008. International statistical comparison: Global growth estimates trimmed after PPP revisions. *IMF Survey Magazine, January 8*. Available at: http://www.imf.org/external/pubs/ft/survey/so/2008/res018a.htm.

Ferguson, N., and M. Schularick. 2009. The end of Chimerica. Working Paper 10–037. Harvard Business School, Boston.

Fernald, J., H. Edison, and P. Loungani. 1999. Was China the first domino? Assessing links between China and other Asian economies. *Journal of International Money and Finance* 18 (4): 515–35.

Frankel, J. 2006. On the yuan: The choice between adjustment under a fixed exchange rate and adjustment under a flexible rate. In G. Illing, ed., *Understanding the Chinese Economy*. CESifo Economic Studies, vol. 52 Oxford: Oxford University Press, 246–75.

Frankel, J., and S.-J. Wei. 2007. Assessing China's exchange rate regime. *Economic Policy* 22: 575–627.

Funke, M., and J. Rahn. 2005. Just how undervalued is the Chinese renminbi? *World Economy* 28: 465–89.

Gale, W., and P. Orszag. 2004. Budget deficits, national saving, and interest rates. *Brookings Papers on Economic Activity* 2004 (2): 101–210.

Garcia-Herrero, A., and T. Koivu. 2007. Can the Chinese trade surplus be reduced through exchange rate policy? BOFIT Discussion Paper 2007-6. Bank of Finland, Helsinki.

Gaulier, G., F. Lemoine, and D. Ünal. 2006. China's emergence and the reorganization of trade flows in Asia. Working Paper 2006–05. CEPII, Paris.

Goldstein, M. 2004. China and the renminbi exchange rate. In ed. C. F. Bergsten and J. Williamson, *Dollar Adjustment: How Far? Against What? Special Report 17*. Washington, DC: Institute for International Economics, 197–230.

Goldstein, M., and N. Lardy. 2009. *The Future of China's Exchange Rate Policy, Policy Analyses in International Economics 87*. Washington, DC: Peterson Institute for International Economics.

Gruber, J., and S. Kamin. 2007. Explaining the global pattern of current account imbalances. *Journal of International Money and Finance* 26: 500–22.

Gruber, J., and S. Kamin. 2009. Do differences in financial development explain the global pattern of current account imbalances? *Review of International Economics* 17 (4): 667–88.

Huang, Y. 2010. Krugman's Chinese renminbi fallacy. *VoxEU* (March 26). Available at: http://www.voxeu.org/index.php?q=node/4801.

Isard, P., and H. Faruqee. 1998. Exchange rate assessment: Extension of the macroeconomic balance approach. Occasional Paper 167. IMF, Washington, DC.

Ito, H., and M. Chinn. 2010. East Asia and global imbalances: Saving, investment, and financial development. In T. Ito and A. Rose, eds., *Financial Sector Development in the Pacific Rim*. Chicago: University of Chicago Press for NBER, 117–50.

Kroeber, A. 2010. Economic rebalancing: The end of surplus labor. *China Economic Quarterly* 14 (1): 35–46.

Lee, J., G. M. Milesi-Ferretti, J. Ostry, A. Prati, and L. A. Ricci. 2008. Exchange rate assessments: CGER methodologies. Occasional Paper 261. IMF, Washington, DC.

Marquez, J., and J. W. Schindler. 2007. Exchange-rate effects on China's trade. *Review of International Economics* 15 (5): 837–53.

Mendoza, E. G., V. Quadrini, and J.-V. Ríos-Rull. 2009. Financial integration, financial deepness and global imbalances. *Journal of Political Economy* 117 (3): 317–416.

McCown, T. A., P. Pollard, and J. Weeks. 2007. Equilibrium exchange rate models and misalignments. Office of International Affairs Occasional Paper 7. US Treasury, Washington, DC.

Morrison, W., and M. Labonte. 2007. China's currency: Economic issues and options for US trade policy. Report for Congress RL32165. Congressional Research Service, Washington, DC.

O'Neill, J. 2010. The issue of the CNY. *Global Economics Weekly 10/09*. New York: Goldman Sachs Global Economics.

O'Neill, J., and D. Wilson. 2003. How China can help the world. Goldman Sachs Global Economics Paper 97. Goldman Sachs, New York.

Parsley, D., and S.-J. Wei. 2003. A prism into the PPP puzzles: The micro-foundations of Big Mac real exchange rates. Working Paper 10074. NBER, Cambridge, MA.

Prasad, E. 2009. Rebalancing growth in Asia. Working Paper 15169. NBER, Cambridge, MA.

Prasad, E., and S.-J. Wei. 2005. The Chinese approach to capital inflows: Patterns and possible explanations. Working Paper 11306. NBER, Cambridge, MA.

Reisen, H. 2009. On the renminbi and economic convergence. *VoxEU*, December 17.

Schindler, J. W., and D. H. Beckett. 2005. Adjusting Chinese bilateral trade data: How big is China's trade surplus? International Finance Discussion Paper 2005–831. Federal Reserve Board, Washington, DC.

Stock, J., and M. Watson. 1993. A simple estimator of cointegrated vectors in higher order integrated systems. *Econometrica: Journal of the Econometric Society* 61: 783–820.

Stupnytska, A., T. Stolper, and M. Meechan. 2009. GSDEER on track: Our improved FX fair value model. *Global Economics Weekly 09/38*. New York: Goldman Sachs Global Economics.

Subramanian, A. 2010. New PPP-based estimates of renminbi undervaluation and policy implications. *Policy Brief PB10–18*. Washington, DC: Peterson Institute for International Economics.

Summers, R., and A. Heston. 1991. The Penn World Table (Mark 5): An expanded set of international comparisons. *Quarterly Journal of Economics* 106: 327–68.

Thorbecke, W., and G. Smith. 2010. How would an appreciation of the RMB and other East Asian currencies affect China's exports? *Review of International Economics* 18 (1): 95–108.

Wang, T. 2004. Exchange rate dynamics. In E. Prasad, ed., *China's Growth and Integration into the World Economy*. Washington, DC: IMF, 21–28.

Wang, Y., X. Hui, and A. S. Soofi. 2007. Estimating renminbi (RMB) equilibrium exchange rate. *Journal of Policy Modeling* 29: 417–29.

Wang, Z., and Y. Yao. 2008. Estimation of renminbi equilibrium exchange rate. China Center for Economic Research Working Paper C2008006. Peking University, Beijing.

3 The Role of the Chinese Dollar Peg for Macroeconomic Stability in China and the World Economy

Gunther Schnabl

3.1 Introduction

The financial and economic crisis from 2007 to 2009 has brought a new dimension to the US–Chinese exchange rate dispute. Whereas the crisis caused China to return to the pre-2005 tight dollar peg to stabilize industrial production and employment, the Federal Reserve aggressively cut interest rates to prevent a meltdown in financial markets. As the recovery in the United States continues to lag behind China, the re-emergence of carry trades and the re-acceleration of Chinese reserve accumulation have added new fuel to the highly controversial exchange rate dispute. For instance, Krugman (2010) welcomed the Chinese New Year by calling China mercantilistic and predatory. In the US Congress, pressure is rising to label China as a "currency manipulator" and to introduce trade sanctions (*Economist* 2010).

The political pressure for a nominal yuan appreciation is based on scientific investigations which find the Chinese yuan to be strongly undervalued, for instance 25 percent on a trade-weighted basis and 40 percent against the dollar (Goldstein and Lardy 2009; Cline and Williamson 2009). In contrast, Cheung, Chinn, and Fujii (2009) argue that the assessment concerning the misalignment of the Chinese yuan strongly depends on the underlying methodology. Reisen (2010) argues that the undervaluation of the yuan originates in the Balassa–Samuelson effect rather than mercantilistic trade policies. McKinnon and Schnabl (2009) stress—with reference to the Japanese experience with yen appreciation—that the US–Chinese trade-imbalance cannot be cured by the nominal appreciation of the Chinese currency. Freitag and Schnabl (2010) scrutinize the direction of causality between US monetary and Chinese exchange rate policies and conclude that the Chinese current account balance cannot be delinked from the US low interest rate policies.

Given the heterogeneous policy recommendations concerning the future path of the yuan/dollar rate combined with the fact that China has become an engine of global growth, this chapter aims to analyze the benefits and costs of pegging the yuan to the dollar. It stresses the stabilizing role of the nominal dollar peg for China, East Asia, and the world and identifies the risks of (inevitable) real exchange rate stabilization. A coordinated exit from US low interest rate and Chinese real exchange rate stabilization policies is recommended to rebalance China and the United States.

3.2   The Dollar Peg as a Domestic Stabilizer

In both crisis and noncrisis periods China's dollar peg has fulfilled the role of a macroeconomic stabilizer. Since the tight dollar peg was introduced in 1994, it provided a robust framework for the economic catch-up process. Defying the international pressure to allow the yuan to float, to appreciate in a one-time step, or in a controlled gradual fashion, the fixed exchange rate has brought stability to fragile goods and underdeveloped financial markets.

3.2.1   The Peg as a Stabilizer of Chinese Goods Markets
Before 1994 China's currency was inconvertible in the strong sense. There were multiple exchange rates,[1] exchange controls on both current and capital account transactions. Exports and imports had to be funneled through state trading companies. Tight capital controls insulated domestic relative prices from world markets. Without free arbitrage between domestic and foreign prices the official exchange rate was set arbitrarily and was devalued in steps from 1.5 yuan per dollar in 1979 to 5.8 yuan per dollar by the end of 1993 (figure 3.1). Tight capital controls prevented "hot" money flows.

Starting from 1994, Chinese authorities abolished exchange controls on current account transactions (exporting, importing, transfers, interest, and dividends) and unified the exchange rate at 8.7 yuan per dollar in 1994. The substantial devaluation of the official rate from 5.8 yuan per dollar was followed by rising inflation, which rendered real depreciation minimal. By 1995, the nominal exchange rate had settled down to about 8.28 yuan per dollar and became for about ten years a stabilizing moment for the Chinese economy.

During the phase of currency inconvertibility China had suffered from a bumpy ride in real growth and inflation—peaking out with the

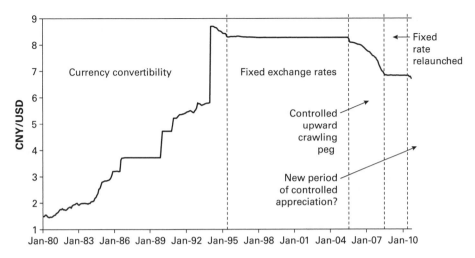

Figure 3.1
Yuan–dollar exchange rate, 1980 to 2010. Source: IMF.

high inflation of 1993 to 1995 (figure 3.2). With a very small domestic capital market the Peoples Bank of China had faced problems in anchoring the overall price level. With the unification of the exchange rate regime in 1994, the move to full current account convertibility by 1996 presented an opportunity to stabilize expectations. Pegging the exchange was equivalent to stabilizing the domestic price level. Inflation and growth stabilized (figure 3.2).

The stabilization of the macroeconomic performance laid the foundation for increasing investment and buoyant trade, which became the backbone of the Chinese growth miracle. After the steady expansion during the 1990s, the speed of trade growth accelerated in the new millennium. Overall dollar exports mushroomed from 200 billion dollars in 2000 to 1.4 trillion dollars in 2008 (figure 3.3). From 1994 to 2008 Chinese investment grew by an average 16 percent per year. Given the resulting fast growth of industrial production, employment in the manufacturing sector soared together with productivity and wages. The wealth of the Chinese working and new middle class was boosted.

Because the success of the Chinese export industry was accompanied by a rising current account surplus, in particular versus the United States (figure 3.4), conflicts about global imbalances and the dollar peg emerged. Dooley, Folkerts-Landau, and Garber (2004) created the notion of economic success, which was based on a mercantilist trade strategy. Cline (2005) argued that the Chinese yuan was substantially

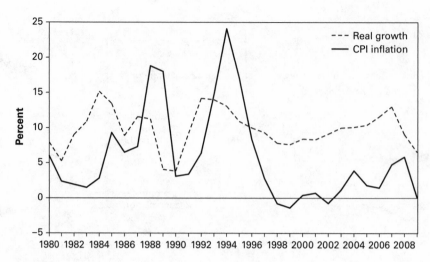

Figure 3.2
Real GDP growth and consumer price inflation, China, 1980 to 2009. Source: IMF.

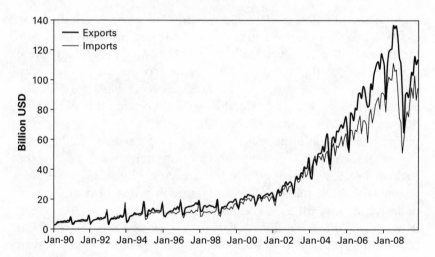

Figure 3.3
Chinese exports and imports. Source: IMF.

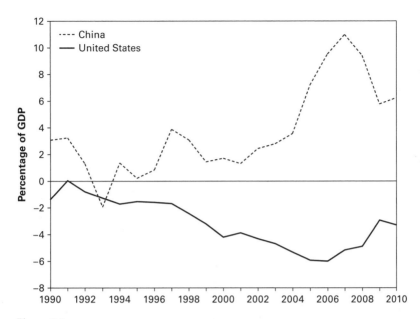

Figure 3.4
Chinese and US current account balance. Source: IMF; data for 2010 based on IMF staff estimates.

undervalued and called for a new Plaza Agreement to correct the imbalances. Bergsten (2010) stresses the leading role of the Chinese exchange rate policy for other East Asian countries, which he accuses of mimicking the Chinese undervaluation strategy.

3.2.2 The Peg as a Stabilizer of Chinese Financial Markets

China resisted international pressure to appreciate the yuan as the dollar peg not only promotes exports, but also stabilizes financial markets. Financial markets have assumed a crucial motivation for pegging the yuan to the dollar, as—based on persistent current account surpluses (figure 3.4)—China has accumulated a rising stock of foreign assets, which transformed China into an immature creditor country. While the stock of international assets gradually increased, Chinese creditors remained unable to internationally lend in yuan to finance the persistent current account surpluses.

There are two possible reasons for the inability to lend in its own currency. First, because (as in the case of China) domestic financial markets are shallow and fragmented and the currency is not convertible, the yuan is not accepted for international lending. Second, due to network externalities (as in the case of the Japanese yen) international capital markets have been preempted by major currencies from areas with highly developed financial markets. Aside from relatively illiquid foreign direct investment outflows, an immature creditor economy continually accumulates liquid claims on foreigners denominated in international currencies such as the dollar or the euro.

The resulting currency mismatch makes monetary management and securing portfolio equilibrium in domestic financial markets more difficult. If the exchange rate (potentially) fluctuates, private financial intermediaries face currency risk. With China's large saving surplus being invested in dollar claims on foreigners, in the balance sheets of private financial institutions sharp exchange rate appreciations can cause substantial losses and can wipe out the net worth of well-capitalized banks or enterprises. The currency mismatch and the problems of risk management are further aggravated if foreigners exert pressure to have the creditor country's currency appreciate—as most recently with Krugman's (2010) and Bergsten's (2010) "China bashing."

Such complaints lead to what McKinnon and Schnabl (2004) call the syndrome of *conflicted virtue*. Countries that are "virtuous" by having a high saving rate (like China, Japan and Germany, but unlike the United States) cumulate a stock of liquid dollar claims. Whereas domestic holders of dollar assets worry about an appreciation of the domestic currency, foreigners start complaining that the country's ongoing flow of trade surpluses is unfair and threaten trade sanctions unless the currency is appreciated. Because of the destabilizing properties of open-ended currency appreciation, the virtuous country becomes "conflicted."[2]

Thus in immature creditor economies, stabilizing the exchange rate is equivalent to stabilizing the financial sector, which holds dollar assets. This is even more the case because world and Chinese interest rates have reached historical lows. As long as the exchange rate is stabilized, Chinese interest rates are prevented from falling toward zero. Otherwise, from the principle of open interest rate parity sustained appreciation expectations would depress interest rates below the interest rate of the anchor country (Goyal and McKinnon 2003) thereby pushing China (like before Japan) into a near-zero interest liquidity trap.

3.2.3 The Destabilizing Effect of the Upward Crawling Peg

Given the stabilizing role of the dollar peg for an immature creditor economy any move away from the peg is likely to cause turmoil. This was experienced during China's upward crawling peg from July 2005 to August 2008, when one-way bets on the Chinese yuan led to an acceleration of speculative capital inflows and to extensive sterilization operations by the Chinese central bank. Today, as unprecedented and unconventionally low interest rate policies in the large industrial countries have created a quasi-unlimited amount of global liquidity, the potential to bet on the appreciation of the yuan has become even larger.

China bowed to international pressure and released its fixed rate anchor on July 21, 2005 (figure 3.1), allowing for one time revaluation of 2.1 percent and a controlled nominal appreciation of about 6 percent per year. During this period, despite monetary tightening in the United States between 2004 and 2007, Chinese foreign reserves soared from 415 billion dollars in 2004 to 1,884 billion dollars in 2008 (figure 3.5). At a first glance the tremendous increase in Chinese foreign reserves is closely linked to the drastic rise of the current account surplus from 3.5 percent of GDP in 2004 to 9.9 percent in 2008. Speculative capital inflows seem absent, as in the balance of payments statistics, errors and omissions (as a proxy for unrecorded capital flows) and short-term capital inflows remain small and negative suggesting net capital outflows rather than inflows during the gradual appreciation period (figure 3.6).

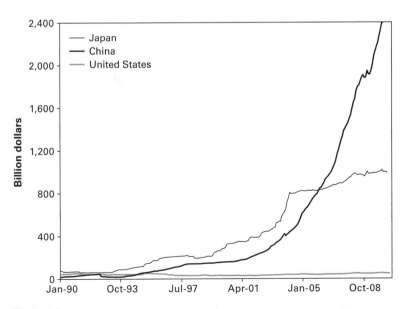

Figure 3.5
Foreign reserves, China, Japan, United States, 1990 to 2010. Sources: IMF and Peoples Bank of China.

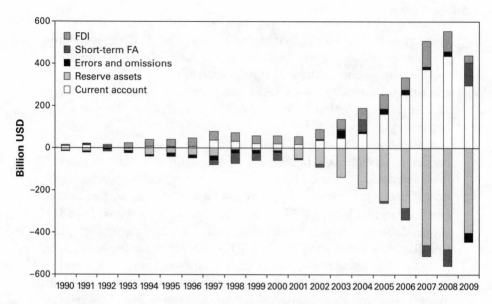

Figure 3.6
Chinese balance of payment. Source: IMF.

The official balance of payments statistics may, however, provide an incomplete picture of hot money inflows, as China's international capital transactions remain subject to tight controls (Ma and McCauley 2007).[3] Bouvatier (2006), who indentifies US interest rates and exchange rate expectations as main determinants of Chinese hot money flows, argues that they may be hidden in "other investments" of the financial account or in errors and omissions. But both items do not show respective changes after 2005. Martin and Morrison (2008) trace hot money inflows on the asset side of the Chinese balance of payments statistics, as speculators are argued to circumvent Chinese legislation by overreported or false foreign direct investment, underreported import and overreported export values. Also transfers (labeled as remittances) are identified as channels of speculative capital inflows.

Indeed, from 2004 to 2008 both net FDI inflows and the current account surplus increased substantially (figure 3.6). Net foreign direct investment rose from 53 billion dollars in 2004 to 94 billion dollars in 2008 by about 80 percent. The trade surplus increased from 58 billion in 2004 dollars to 360 billion dollars in 2008. Net transfers doubled from 23 billion dollars in 2004 to 46 billion dollars in 2008. Net income surged from –3 billion in 2004 to 31 billion in 2008. Martin and Morrison

(2008) quantify the total sum of hot money inflows from 2004 to the first half of 2008 to be within a range of 500 billion dollars to 1.75 trillion dollars.

The surge of speculative capital inflows in form of FDI, transfers and overreported trade surpluses had to be financed by the buildup of official exchange reserves as shown in figure 3.6. Because the accelerating speed of reserve accumulation would have led to excessive monetary expansion, the Peoples Bank of China (PBC) was forced to sterilize the immediate impact on the monetary base. The liability side of the Peoples Bank of China's balance sheet (figure 3.7) shows—with negative signs—sterilization instruments, namely central bank bonds, required reserves, and government deposits at the central bank.

As long as the sales of central bank bonds occurred at market rates, the monetary tightening threatened to drive interest rates upward, in particular as the underdeveloped Chinese capital markets could only absorb a limited amount of central bank bonds. When Chinese interest rates started to rise after 2005, to contain sterilization costs an increasing proportion of the rapidly accumulating foreign reserves was sterilized by reserve requirements both in domestic and foreign currency at

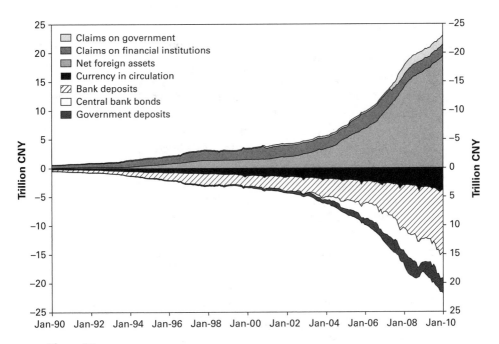

Figure 3.7
Peoples Bank of China balance sheet. Source: IMF.

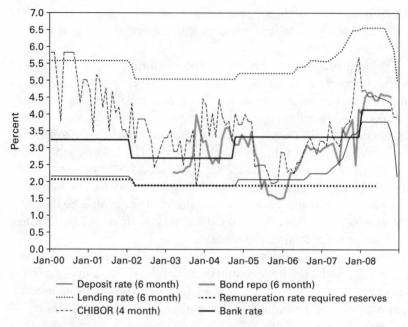

Figure 3.8
Fragmented structure of Chinese interest rates, 2000 to 2009. Source: Datastream.

a substantially lower rate than the remuneration of central bank bills (figure 3.8).

Figure 3.9 shows as proxy for the international portfolio balance the deviation from UIP, namely the deviation of the US–Chinese interest rate differential from yuan–dollar exchange rate changes. Before mid-2004, when the yuan–dollar rate was expected to remain stable, there was no substantial deviation of the interest differential from exchange rate changes. By mid-2004, Chinese interest rates started falling relative to US interest rates as if the market was anticipating the revaluations, which started in July 2005. The interest differential became negative in early 2005 when the Federal Funds Rate started to climb. By the end of 2006, Chinese interest rates were as much as 4 percentage points less than in the United States but were matched by an respective yuan appreciation to equilibrate the international portfolio balance.

However, when the US federal funds rate fell sharply from 5.25 percent in August 2007 to 2 percent by August 2008, the interest rate differential became positive in favor of China and the PBC began to increase some interest rates on yuan assets to steer against inflation in

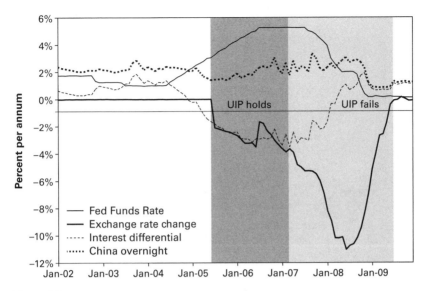

Figure 3.9
China's deviations from uncovered interest rate parity, 2002 to 2010. Source: Datastream.

2007 (figure 3.8), the continuing yuan appreciation opened the door for one-way bets on yuan appreciation. Hot money inflows into China accelerated. The result was a "corner" solution: no private holdings of dollar assets unless subsidized by the government (McKinnon and Schnabl 2009). The international portfolio balance—defined as UIP—was lost (figure 3.9) and inflation started to rise (figure 3.2). UIP was restored when the global crisis led to a reversal of international capital flows.

3.3 The Chinese Dollar Peg as an International Stabilizer

The large size of the Chinese economy combined with its dynamic growth performance, which remained robust during both regional and global crisis periods have transformed China into a stabilizer for East Asia and the world economy.

3.3.1 China and East Asia

The economic weight of China in East Asia has grown steadily, taking over Japan's role as dominating economic power in the region (upper panel of figure 3.10).[4] In 1990, when the Japanese bubble burst, Japan made up roughly 70 percent of East Asian GDP, whereas China

(a)

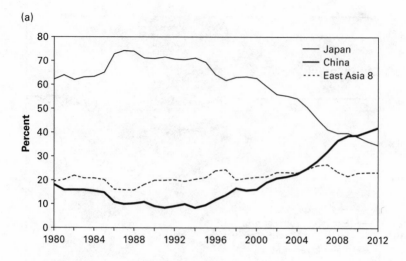

(b)

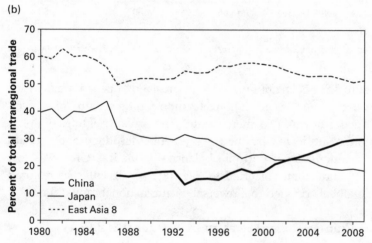

Figure 3.10
Economic weights in East Asia: (a) as percentage of East Asian GDP; (b) as percentage
of intra–East Asian exports. Source: IMF.

accounted only for roughly 10 percent. Due to the lasting stagnation of Japan and the dynamic expansion of China, by 2009 both countries accounted for roughly 38 percent of East Asian GDP, with trends pointing in two different directions. During the same time period the weight of the smaller East Asian (East Asia 8) economies—namely Indonesia, Hong Kong, South Korea, Malaysia, Philippines, Singapore, Taiwan, and Thailand—remained widely constant at around 24 percent.

Also intra–East Asian trade volumes soared, with China becoming the hub of a dense intraregional production network. China's buoyant industrial sector assumed the role of an export platform to the industrial countries (in particular to the United States) that links Japanese production technologies (imported in form of FDI) with inputs from the smaller East Asian economies. The lower panel of figure 3.10 shows that between 1990 and 2009 the share of Chinese exports as percent of total East Asian intraregional exports increased from 17 to 30 percent. During the same period the share of Japan's intra-regional exports declined from 30 to 18 percent. The share of the smaller East Asian countries on intra–East Asian trade remained widely constant at slightly above 50 percent.

Given its high and robust trade and growth performance China assumed the role of the East Asian growth engine. As shown in upper panel of figure 3.11, China excels with the highest growth performance in the region. In crisis periods China proved to be more resilient to global and regional shocks than its smaller neighboring countries. China's exchange rate peg as well as decisive countercyclical macroeconomic policies played a crucial role in stabilizing the region. During the 1997–98 Asian crisis sharp devaluations by the crisis countries (Indonesia, Malaysia, Philippines, South Korea, and Thailand) as well as by Japan, Taiwan, and Singapore imposed strong deflationary pressure on China, which ignored advice to let the yuan become more "flexible" and depreciate in turn. By keeping the yuan tightly pegged to the dollar China did not add further momentum to the competitive depreciations in the region. China's one trillion dollar fiscal expansion program allowed its neighbors to recover even faster.

In contrast, the depreciating Japanese yen caused and aggravated the Asian crisis. Because the East Asian countries except Japan pegged their currencies to the dollar, the fluctuations of the yen against the dollar have been a major source of regional business cycle fluctuations (McKinnon and Schnabl 2003). When the yen depreciated against the dollar since the mid-1990s—while the other East Asian currencies remained pegged to the dollar—growth in Japan's small neighboring

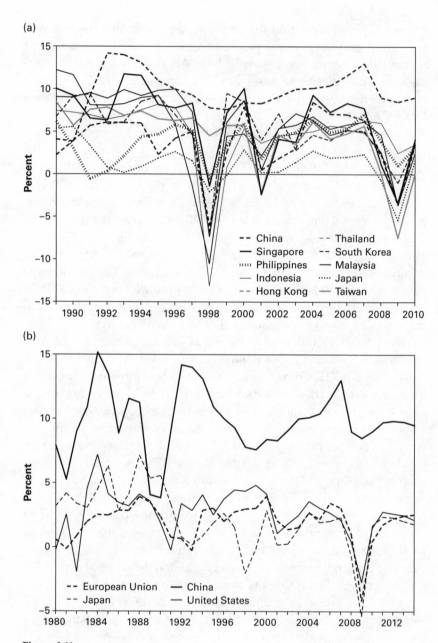

Figure 3.11
Regional and global growth performance: (a) East Asia; (b) world. Source: IMF.

countries declined. As South Korea, Taiwan, Hong Kong, and Singapore lost market shares in Japan and third markets—with the United States being the most important one—current account deficits increased. The resulting loss of confidence in the East Asian tiger miracle culminated into the Asian crisis. The depreciation of the Japanese yen during the crisis further aggravated the slump.

After the Asian crisis the Chinese yuan assumed a prominent role within the informal East Asian dollar standard. Before the Asian crisis intraregional exchange rates including the yuan, won, ringgit, baht, and so on, were all stabilized against the dollar without a particular role being attributed to one of them. By commonly pegging to the dollar, the East Asian countries stabilized intraregional exchange rates to reduce transactions costs for intraregional trade, which makes up about half of international trade in the region (McKinnon and Schnabl 2004. The floating yen was an important outlier, which caused substantial fluctuations in intraregional trade.

After the Asian crisis, while some smaller East Asian countries allowed for more—but by far not full—exchange rate flexibility against the dollar, the Chinese yuan assumed the role of an informal internal anchor next to the dollar as an informal external one. In figure 3.12 the

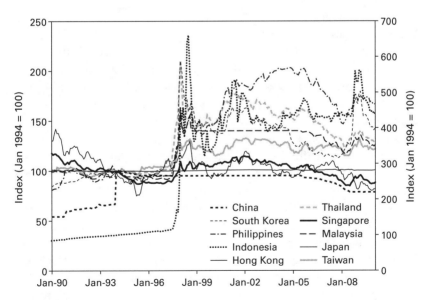

Figure 3.12
East Asian exchange rates against the dollar. Source: IMF.

East Asian exchange rates are indexed at 100 in January 1994 when China unified its multiple exchange rate and pegged it tightly to the dollar. The Chinese yuan exhibits—beside the Hong Kong dollar—the highest degree of exchange rate stability. Whereas the yuan remains stable in both crisis and noncrisis periods, the East Asian currencies (including the Japanese yen) seem to pursue a "dual exchange rate target" against the dollar and the yuan.

In contrast to a currency basket—as a monetary framework, which allows targeting directly more than one currency with specific (predefined) weights—the dual target is more a sequential one. First, the smaller East Asian countries observe the move of the yuan against the dollar. Then, they decide about the degree of exchange rate stabilization against the dollar to maintain exchange rate stability against the dollar and the yuan. With all smaller members of the East Asian dollar standard stabilizing their exchange rates against dollar and yuan also intraregional cross rates—for instance, between ringgit and won or Singapore dollar and baht—are fixed.

The dollar remains the intervention and reserve currency because the dollar markets are liquid and dollar reserves can be easily invested in the US financial markets. In contrast, outright exchange rate stabilization against the yuan is impossible or costly because the Chinese yuan is inconvertible. Foreign reserves are difficult to invest in yuan because Chinese financial markets are shallow and fragmented. Therefore mimicking the exchange rate path of the yuan against the dollar is the best way to create the public good of intraregional exchange rate stability. Figure 3.12 shows that when the yuan embarked on its appreciation path from July 2005, the East Asian countries followed—to a lesser or greater extent—the appreciation of the yuan against the dollar to keep intraregional exchange rates stable.

By choosing flexibly the parities against the dollar, while the yuan remains tightly pegged, the smaller East Asian economies including Japan[5] can stimulate growth in two ways. First, growth is stimulated because of China's higher and stable growth performance. Second, with the decided degree of depreciation against the Chinese yuan, growth can be shifted from China into the smaller East Asian countries, in particular during recessions. Figure 3.12 shows that during the Asian crisis (1997–98), the crisis in the semiconductor sector (2001), and the US subprime crisis (2007–08), the smaller East Asian countries, including Japan, allowed for significant depreciations against the yuan to beggar the large and healthy neighbor. Since 1994 all East Asian coun-

tries, including Japan, have kept their exchange rates on the depreciation side of the yuan against the dollar.

If, as desired by the United States, the Chinese yuan were to be
floated against dollar, the informal dollar standard would fall apart and
the intra–East Asian production network would suffer from fluctuations in intraregional competitiveness. In contrast to the European
countries, which floated their currencies against the dollar in the early
1970s and used the German mark as an internal anchor, it is difficult
to find an internal East Asian anchor. There are two good reasons. First,
the Chinese yuan does not fulfill the structural prerequisites of an
anchor currency in form of currency convertibility and developed
financial markets. Second, the Japanese yen fulfills the structural criteria of convertibility and developed financial markets but does not
qualify as long as the zero interest rate policy persists. To this end, the
informal East Asian dollar standard with the dollar as first (external)
anchor and the Chinese yuan as a second (internal) anchor is currently
the (second) best solution to maintain the intraregional exchange rate
stability and growth.

3.3.2 From a Regional to a Global Stabilizer

Whereas during the Asian crisis China fulfilled the role of a regional
stabilizer, the 2007 to 2009 subprime-rooted global financial and economic slump transformed China into a global stability hub. Rising
shares of Chinese exports and GDP as percentage of world exports and
world GDP combined with a highly dynamic growth have transformed
China into a global player. China's share of world GDP has risen from
2 percent in 1980 to more than 13 percent in 2010. Average yearly real
growth between 1994 and 2010 was close to 10 percent compared to 0.8
percent in Japan, 2 percent in European Union, and 2.6 percent in the
United States. Whereas during the crisis year 2009 growth slumped to
−4.2 percent in the European Union, −5.4 percent in Japan and −2.8
percent in the United States, China proudly reported a robust growth
of 8.5 percent (lower panel of figure 3.11). Whereas zero interest policies
and fiscal stimuli failed to jumpstart the advanced economies, China's
macroeconomic policies proved effective.

When by mid-2008 the global crisis had reached China via the export
channel[6] and unemployment among migrant workers had soared, the
Chinese government took decisive action with the exchange rate peg
being in the center of the stabilization measures. The Peoples Bank of
China could terminate the gradual appreciation and re-peg the yuan

to the dollar at a rate of 6.83, since during the crisis hot money flows were redirected toward the US and Chinese dollar assets were not any more threatened by revaluation losses. Chinese reserve accumulation was interrupted between August 2008 and February 2009 (figure 3.5) and the uncovered interest rate parity was restored (figure 3.9).

In November 2008 the Chinese government announced a four trillion yuan stimulus package for the years 2008–09 combined with an industrial policy program for promoting key sectors such as automobile, steel, machinery, and textile. The return to the tight dollar peg served as a backbone of the macroeconomic stimulus program (McKinnon and Schnabl 2009). As suggested by the seminal Mundell–Fleming open macroeconomics model, an isolated credit financed fiscal expansion would have been ineffective. Rising domestic interest rates would have triggered an appreciation of yuan, with both effects crowding out the expansionary effects of fiscal expansion.

This effect was prevented by the monetary expansion with the exchange rate peg acting a coordinating mechanism for the fiscal and monetary stimulus. As reserve accumulation stopped, the Peoples Bank of China was able to engineer a credit expansion by moving from sterilization to desterilization. Shadowing the monetary expansion in the United States, reserve requirements on commercial banks were reduced and other credit constraints were loosened (figure 3.7). Bank lending rates, deposits rates, and the remuneration rate of required reserves were cut (figure 3.8). From November 2008 bank lending increased significantly with a focus on loans to nonfinancial corporations (lower panel of figure 3.13). Soon the Chinese growth locomotive started over.

3.4 Distortions and Fragility

As unemployment in the United States remains high, the Federal Reserve is expected to keep interest rates close to zero until 2013 or even longer. In contrast, the success of the Chinese fiscal, monetary, and exchange rate stabilization measures have strengthened expectations that China will continue its dynamic catch-up path. With an (expected) real growth rate of about 10 percent for the years 2010 and 2011 China has become an attractive target of a new wave of carry trades (Roubini 2010; McKinnon et al. 2010). Hot money inflows resumed as indicated by newly accelerating reserve accumulation (figure 3.5). At the latest the June 2010 announcement that the yuan will become more flexible has put the scenario back to the period before 2008. Reserve accumulation

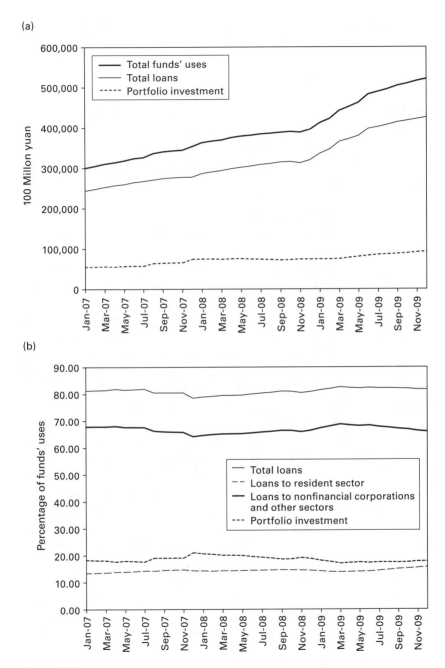

Figure 3.13
Uses of funds of the Chinese banking sector: (a) uses of funds of financial institutions (yuan and foreign currency); (b) percentage of overall uses of funds. Source: Peoples Bank of China.

combined with sterilization is likely to gain speed and thereby aggra-
vate distortions in the Chinese and world economy.

3.4.1 Global Surplus Liquidity and Overinvestment

From a global perspective the current Chinese boom with growth rates
well above 8 percent may be unsustainable, since an unprecedented
low level of global interest rates has driven China's investment beyond
what could be sustainable in the long run. The business cycle theories
of Knut Wicksell (1898) and Friedrich August von Hayek (1929) help
explain the long-term risks linked to interest rates at nearly zero in the
United States (and other large industrial countries) combined with
buoyant inflows of FDI and hot money into China.

In modeling business cycle fluctuations both Wicksell (1898) and
von Hayek (1929) distinguished between "good" investment—which
yields returns above a "natural" equilibrium interest rate[7] – and low
return (speculative) investment—which is induced by an interest rate
below the equilibrium ($I > S$). Overinvestment is triggered when the
central bank (Wicksell 1898) or the banking sector (von Hayek 1929)
keep interest rates below the natural interest rate during the economic
upswing. Whereas the monetary overinvestment theories were modeled
for closed economies, in today's liberalized international capital
markets interest rates in emerging markets can decline below the
"natural interest rate" due to buoyant capital inflows from highly
liquid, low yield developed capital markets.

Because growth in the United States, Japan, and the eurozone
remains sluggish, the Federal Reserve, the Bank of Japan, and the
European Central Bank continue to keep interest rates exceptionally
low. Because the recovery is faster in East Asia, the low interest rates
in the large countries feed carry trades into East Asia rather than
domestic investment. If, as since June 2010, the Chinese yuan can
be expected to appreciate, there is a double incentive to borrow in
dollars and to invest in higher yield foreign currency assets. For
instance, a carry trader can borrow for close to zero in the United
States and earn a return of 2 percent in buoyant China. Assuming that
the yuan will appreciate—say by 3 percent per year—the overall
return would be 5 percent (if a way is found to circumvent Chinese
capital controls).

Enterprises compare the expected return on investment with the
financing conditions on capital markets. A falling interest rate allows
for additional investment with lower returns, namely a lower marginal efficiency. Overinvestment in China is likely to be triggered

because (in the sense of Wicksell 1898) the large central banks have cut policy rates to unprecedented low levels and (in the sense of von Hayek 1929) private capital inflows have brought the Chinese interest rate to a level, which is uncommonly low for fast growing emerging markets. In China, money market rates have been floating between 1 and 3 percent, while the economy has been growing at real rates around 10 percent.

In the models of Wicksell (1898) and von Hayek (1929) the upswing continues as—how currently observed in China—the demand for investment goods rises. Capacity reserves are activated. Wages and consumption increase. The positive economic expectations can be transmitted to asset markets where speculation may set in (Schumpeter 1912).[8] With credit growth becoming speculative, productivity increases slow down. Consumer price inflation accelerates which conveys a signal supportive of building up additional capacities and increasing wages further. Finally, the central bank has to tighten money supply to contain inflation. Alternatively, financial institutions tighten credit when they regard the upswing as unsustainable.

Figure 3.14 shows a wave of wandering bubbles as described by Schnabl and Hoffmann (2008), augmented with Chinese exports. The

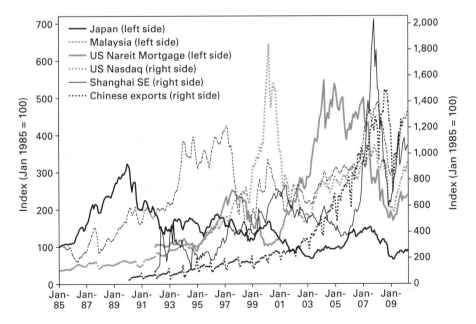

Figure 3.14
Wandering bubbles. Sources: IMF and Shanghai stock exchange, 1991: 01=100.

wave of wandering bubbles, which are argued to be triggered and per-petuated by a gradual decline of nominal and real interest rates in the large industrial countries, sets in the mid-1980s when Japan cut interest rates to contain the post-Plaza yen appreciation. The substantial accelera-tion of credit growth in Japan led to a boom in real estate and stock markets, the well-known Japanese bubble economy. The burst of the Japanese bubble in December 1989 marked the starting point of two lost decades of economic stagnation. Attempts to revive the Japanese economy by further interest rate cuts triggered the first wave of carry trades to the East Asian tiger countries, where a boom in the export-oriented industrial sectors emerged. The burst of the bubbles in the stock and real estate markets culminated into the 1997–98 Asian crisis.

The Asian crisis led to a flight to the safe havens of the large financial markets, where the dotcom bubbles emerged. The Federal Reserve's decision to counteract the sharp decline in US stocks market at the end of the dot-com boom is widely seen as the starting point for the US subprime boom and the second wave of carry trades from US, Japan and eurozone to East Asia, central and eastern Europe, and the raw materials exporting countries (Hoffmann and Schnabl 2011).

The period of lost international portfolio balance between China and the United States was accompanied by a bubble in Chinese stock markets, as represented by the Shanghai stock exchange in figure 3.14, and ended when hot money inflows were reversed. The subprime crisis triggered the advent of the current (close to) zero interest rate policies on a global level and therefore the third—and up to now largest—wave of carry trades (Roubini 2009). Currently Chinese monetary authorities aim to prevent new bubbles in stock and real estate markets by steril-ization measures and credit constraints. Figure 3.14 shows that prices in Chinese stock markets have more recently remained moderate. Nev-ertheless, the Chinese export sector could currently experience an overinvestment boom because of preferential treatment with respect to capital allocation and real exchange rate stabilization.

3.4.2   Administrative Capital Allocation, Real Exchange Rate Stabilization, and Structural Distortions

Despite the general notion of an export-led economy, investment rather than net exports has been the major driver of Chinese growth and employment. Figure 3.15 shows that by 2008 investment (plus inven-tory changes) accounted for about 42 percent of GDP, thereby constitut-ing the most important GDP expenditure component. In addition net

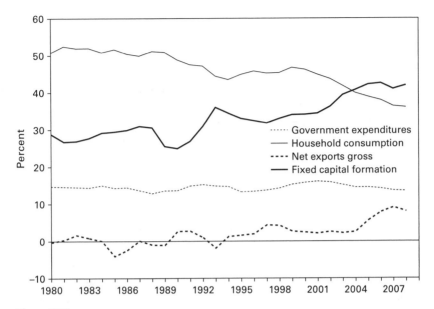

Figure 3.15
Chinese GDP by expenditure. Source: IMF.

exports accounted for 8 percent of GDP by expenditures in 2008. Because investment and exports make up about half of the Chinese GDP, Chinese economic policies have been keen to sustain investment of Chinese enterprises, with focus on the export sector.

The system of Chinese investment-based export promotion hinges on two programs connected to the Peoples Bank of China's sterilization policies: subsidized capital allocation via the state-owned banking sector to promote investment in the export sector and real exchange rate stabilization to promote sales of exports. The outcome is structural distortions in the Chinese goods and financial markets that endanger the long-term growth performance.

In capital markets sterilization policies lead to distortions, because non–market-based sterilization allows for "centrally planned" capital allocation via a dependent central bank and a state controlled private banking sector. As sterilization is widely non–market based—with required reserves being remunerated at around 2 percent—the general interest rate level in China is kept extremely low (figure 3.8). This keeps in a high-growth economy the demand for capital high, whereas sterilization and direct credit constraints keep the supply of capital tight.

The resulting surplus demand for capital puts the monetary authorities into the position of directing capital into sectors with preferential treatment, via so-called window guidance:[9] "The PBC will strengthen window guidance and credit guidance to intensify efforts to adjust the credit structure. Efforts will be made to optimize the credit structure, to encourage growth in some sectors while discouraging growth in others."[10] Two strategies of credit allocation are likely. First, the enterprise sector (which has a preference for investment) is likely to receive preferential treatment instead of the household sector (which has a preference for consumption). Second, within the enterprise sector export enterprises are likely to be (among others) the prime beneficiary of state-directed capital allocation.

The lower panel of figure 3.13 shows the uses of funds of the Chinese banking sector since 2007 when data became available. The shares of nonfinancial corporations and the residential sector are stable over a wide spread, and can be seen as characteristic of "centrally planned" capital allocation. The share of loans to nonfinancial corporations dominates with roughly 65 percent, while the share of loans to the residential sector remains small at around 15 percent. The state-controlled flows of funds in favor of the enterprise sector can explain why the share of GDP of household consumption has gradually declined, whereas gross fixed capital formation and net exports have gradually increased (figure 3.15).

Within the enterprise sector, the likelihood is large that export enterprises have been subsidized by the provision of low cost capital. For instance, Hale and Long (2011) provide evidence that Chinese large and state-owned firms have better access to lost-cost capital than small private firms. Tighter capital constraints (preferential capital allocation) in smaller (larger) firms are linked to higher (lower) efficiency. Prasad (2009: 227) argues that Chinese export enterprises are subsidized via the provision of low cost capital, including interest rate subsidies to agricultural and energy sectors to hold down the cost of inputs for industrial production.

On goods markets the structural distortions originate in real exchange rate stabilization. Nominal exchange rate stabilization—for instance, as criticized by Cline (2005), Bergsten (2010), and the US public (*Economist* 2010)—cannot be distorting, as fixed exchange rates do not alone cause balance of payments misalignments.[11] But exports are subsidized, if the Peoples Bank of China is forced to stabilize the price level in addition to the nominal exchange rate. This helps clear export production on international markets, but the economic structure is tilted toward the production of export goods at the expense of the domestic oriented economy (e.g., services).

The real exchange rate targeting discourages domestic consumption as expenditure switching from traded to nontraded goods via real appreciation is disturbed. If the Peoples Bank of China would leave the foreign currency purchases unsterilized, the monetary base would grow and prices would increase. The resulting real appreciation would raise nontraded (domestic) goods prices relative to traded (foreign) goods prices thereby shifting the demand (and consumption) to foreign (i.e., imported) goods. Chinese net exports and US net imports would decline, but this process is disrupted by the sterilization policies.

The impact of sterilization policies on the real exchange rate (and the current account position) in the face of buoyant capital inflows is shown in figure 3.16, which compares the real exchange rate of the Chinese yuan (with the dollar as reference currency) with the real exchange rate of the Estonian kroon (with the euro as reference currency) since 1994. Both countries have maintained tight pegs to their anchor currencies since 1994 and experienced fast capital market driven economic convergence toward their anchor countries. In contrast to China, the currency board arrangement of Estonia and its membership in the European Union strongly restricts non–market-based sterilization of foreign reserve accumulation.

Notice that the outcome for the real exchange rate is a gradual real appreciation of the Estonian kroon against the euro. In China, however, despite the considerable fluctuations, the real exchange rate of the yuan against the dollar has remained widely unchanged since 1994, although substantial productivity gains should have led to a significant real appreciation of the yuan. Not surprisingly, until the 2007 to 2009 crisis Estonia had substantial current account deficits, whereas in China the current account surplus increased.

In the view of Wicksell (1898) and von Hayek (1929) overinvestment occurs if interest rates are held below the (natural) market rate as in the case of subsidized preferential credit allocation. In addition the marginal efficiency of investment in the export sector is artificially biased upward by real exchange rate stabilization. Both factors suggest that investment in the export sector has grown beyond what is sustainable in the long term. In figure 3.14 the wave of wandering bubbles is augmented by Chinese nominal exports, which have experienced tremendous growth since the turn of the millennium. The

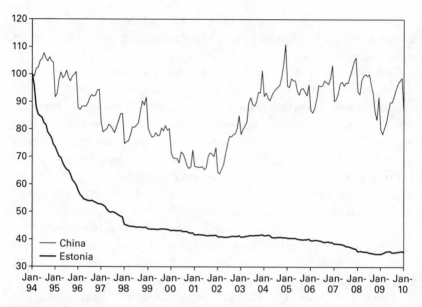

Figure 3.16
Real exchange rates of China and Estonia against anchor currencies (index January 1994 = 100). Source: IMF.

growth of Chinese exports has been invigorated by the most recent close-to-zero interest rate policies after the great crisis, while Chinese stock and real estate prices have grown at more moderate levels due to sector specific credit constraints and regulations. The investment in the export sector with a low marginal productivity is only sustainable as long as low interest rate subsidies and real exchange rate stabilization persist.

3.4.3   International Distortions

From an international perspective, the distortion of the Chinese economy toward industrial production and exports matches the decline of the industrial sector in the United States, which is China's most important trading partner. This corresponds to US claims that Chinese exports have contributed to its deindustrialization (Cline 2005; Bergsten 2010). Yet international trade is a mutual enterprise. Rising comparative advantage in one sector in one country is linked to rising comparative advantage in another sector in the other country.

The US–Chinese distortions in the goods markets are matched by distortions in the financial markets, which are inflated in the United States because of low interest rate policies and giant US government bond purchases by the Chinese central bank. In contrast, Chinese financial markets remain underdeveloped because the potential size of capital markets is reduced when foreign exchange intervention redirects capital flows toward the United States. Non–market-based sterilization and state-controlled capital allocation contribute to further fragmentation.

Thus, in the view of the overinvestment theories, the Ricardian international partition of labor between China and the United States with respect to goods and financial markets has gone beyond the market-based equilibrium. The expansionary US monetary policy keeps prices in the international financial markets artificially low, whereas sterilization policies in China nudge prices in international goods markets down. A correction of both types of price distortions would end the mutual (i.e., global) imbalances.

3.5 International Policy Coordination to End Global Imbalances

Because of artificially low prices in US and Chinese goods and financial markets, structural distortions have occurred in the both countries, so the current pattern of international partition of labor between China and United States is not sustainable. If interest rates in the United States increase or the rising inflation in China forces the PBC to further tighten its credit supply, new economic turmoil is likely to emerge. Therefore an exit from the current policy patterns—exceptionally low interest rates in the United States and real exchange rate stabilization in China—is in the interest of both countries.

However, one-sided exits of the United States or China from the current policies would further becloud their growth perspectives. If China would end its nominal exchange rate stabilization and the United States keep its interest rates low, one-way bets on yuan appreciation would further grow and the Peoples Bank of China would be forced to even larger foreign reserve accumulation and sterilization measures. Chinese capital markets would experience additional fragmentation and much larger future adjustment costs.

If the Peoples Bank of China should stop sterilization—while US interest rates remain low and Chinese nominal exchange rate stabilization persists—a tremendous inflationary pressure would be created, which would erode the competitiveness of the Chinese export industry and stir up more asset price bubbles. If the United States should unilaterally end its low interest rate policies, US unemployment is likely to further rise because of painful adjustments in the financial sector. The industrial sector would not be able to provide compensating growth because of persistent fierce low-cost competition from China.

For this reason an international policy agreement between the United States and China is necessary to rebalance both economies. The United States has to commit to gradually increase interest rates. China has to commit to end real (but not nominal) exchange rate stabilization. If interest rates in the United States increase, speculative capital inflows into China and thereby nominal appreciation pressure will slow down.

The resulting real appreciation of the Chinese yuan would give the US industrial sector room to regain domestic and international competitiveness. The revival of the industrial sector in the United States would provide a substitute for adjustment in the financial sector. The persistence of the nominal peg of the yuan to the dollar is necessary to stabilize Chinese, East Asian, and US growth. In both the United States and China, industrial and financial sectors would be allowed to rebalance with a positive impact on global growth.

Notes

I thank Stephan Freitag, Andreas Hoffmann, Axel Löffler, Tim Reichardt, Ronald McKinnon, Jakob De Haan, Yin-Wong Cheung, Tara Sinclair, Guonan Ma, Robert McCauley, Ulrich Volz, and the participants of the CESifo Venice Summer Institute on "The Evolving Role of China in the Global Economy" for useful comments and support.

1. An official rate and floating swap rates for exports of manufactures in different parts of the country.

2. In contrast to Germany, Japan is also an immature international creditor. Japan runs large current account surpluses but does not lend much abroad in yen. In contrast to China its overseas direct investment finances a substantial part of its current account surplus.

3. Ma and McCauley (2007) see substantial gaps between onshore and offshore yuan yields as indication for capital account restraints.

4. East Asia is defined as Japan and China plus eight smaller East Asian economies (Hong Kong, Indonesia, Malaysia, Philippines, Singapore, South Korea, Taiwan, and Thailand). The weights are calculated based on US dollar GDPs (at market exchange rates).

5. Note that although Japan stopped active foreign exchange intervention in 2004 the level of the yen against the dollar via monetary expansion is influenced by (unconventional) monetary policy measures.

6. From August 2008 to February 2009 nominal Chinese exports dramatically declined from 134 billion dollars to 64 billion dollars (figure 3.3).

7. At the equilibrium interest rate, saving is equal to investment: $S = I$.

8. A speculative mania may emerge, in which speculative price projections and "the symptoms of prosperity themselves finally become, in the well known manner, a factor of prosperity" (Schumpeter 1912: 226).

9. Preferential treatment of specific sectors and enterprises via window guidance (*madoguchi shidô*) was a common way of credit allocation during the catch-up process of the Japan (Hamada and Horiuchi 1987: 244–46).

10. Peoples Bank of China (2008: 13).

11. Whereas with a floating exchange rate the monetary policy is determined by the central bank and the exchange rate is left to float, under a peg the exchange rate is targeted and money supply is left to market forces. Economies with underdeveloped goods and capital markets have been using pegs ever since to import macroeconomic and financial stability (McKinnon and Schnabl 2004).

References

Bergsten, F. 2010. Correcting the Chinese exchange rate: An action plan. *Testimony before the Committee on Ways and Means, US House of Representatives*, March 24.

Bouvatier, V. 2006. *Hot Money Inflows in China: How the People's Bank of China Took up the Challenge.* Paris: Centre d'Economie de la Sorbonne, Cahiers Economique.

Cheung, Y.-W., M. Chinn, and E. Fujii. 2009. China's current account and exchange rate. CESifo Working Paper 2587. Munich.

Cline, W. 2005. *The United States as a Debtor Nation.* Washington, DC: Institute for International Economics.

Cline, W., and J. Williamson. 2009. 2009 Estimates of fundamental equilibrium exchange rates. Policy Brief 09–10. Peterson Institute for International Economics, Washington, DC.

Dooley, M., D. Folkerts-Landau, and P. Garber. 2004. An essay on the revived Bretton-Woods system. *International Journal of Finance and Economics* 4: 307–13.

The Economist. 2010. China policy: Yuanimpressed (June 3–9): 41.

Freitag, S., and G. Schnabl. 2010. Reverse causality in global current accounts. Working Paper 1208. ECB, Frankfurt.

Goldstein, M., and N. Lardy. 2009. *The Future of China's Exchange Rate Policy.* Washington, DC: Peterson Institute for International Economics.

Goyal, R., and R. McKinnon. 2003. Japan's negative risk premium in interest rates: The liquidity trap and fall in bank lending. *World Economy* 26 (3): 339–63.

Hale, G., and C. Long. 2011. If you try, you'll get by: Chinese private firms' efficiency gains from overcoming financial constraints. Working Paper 2010-21. Federal Reserve Bank of San Francisco.

Hamada, K., and A. Horiuchi. 1987. The political economy of the financial market. In *The Political Economy of Japan*, vol. 1. The Domestic Transformation. Stanford: Stanford University Press, 223–60.

von Hayek, F. 1929. *Geldtheorie und Konjunkturtheorie.* Salzburg: Philosophia Verlag.

Hoffmann, A., and G. Schnabl. 2008. Monetary policy, vagabonding liquidity and bursting bubbles in new and emerging markets—An overinvestment view. *World Economy* 31 (9): 1226–52.

Krugman, P. 2010. Chinese New Year. *New York Times*, January 1.

Ma, G., and R. McCauley. 2007. Do China's capital controls still bind? Implications for monetary autonomy and capital liberalisation. Working Paper 233. BIS, Basel.

Martin, M., and W. Morrison. 2008. China's "hot money" problem. Report for Congress. CRS, Washington D.C.

McKinnon, R., and G. Schnabl. 2003. Synchronized business cycles in East Asia and fluctuations in the yen/dollar exchange rate. *World Economy* 26 (8): 1067–88.

McKinnon, R., and G. Schnabl. 2004. A return to soft dollar pegging in East Asia? Mitigating conflicted virtue. *International Finance* 7 (2): 169–201.

McKinnon, R., and G. Schnabl. 2009. The case for stabilizing China's exchange rate: Setting the stage for fiscal expansion. *China and the World Economy* 17: 1–32.

McKinnon, R., B. Lee, and D. Y. Wang. 2010. The global credit crisis and China's exchange rate. *Singapore Economic Review* 55 (2): 253–72.

Peoples Bank of China. 2008. China Monetary Policy Report Quarter Two. Beijing.

Prasad, E. 2009. Effects of the financial crisis on The U.S. –China economic relationship. *Cato Journal* 29 (2): 223–35.

Reisen, H. 2010. Is China's currency undervalued? In S. Evenett, ed., *The US–Sino Currency Dispute: New Insights from Economics, Politics and Law*. London: VoxEU, 61–68.

Roubini, N. 2009. Mother of all carry trades faces an inevitable bust. *Financial Times*, November 1.

Schnabl, G., and A. Hoffmann. 2011. A vicious cycle of financial market exuberance, panics and asymmetric policy response—An overinvestment view. *World Economy* 34 (3): 382-403.

Schumpeter, J. 1912. *Theorie der wirtschaftlichen Entwicklung*. Berlin: Duncker and Humblodt.

Wicksell, K. 1898. *Geldzins und Güterpreise*. Jena: Gustav Fischer.

4   Permanent and Transitory Macroeconomic Relationships between China and the Developed World

Yueqing Jia and Tara M. Sinclair

4.1   Introduction

Although research on business cycles and economic growth has traditionally focused on developed countries, there is increasing interest in the economic fluctuations of developing countries. In particular, policy makers and researchers have focused on the growing importance of China, the largest developing country, within the global macroeconomic environment. Recent research by Jia and Sinclair (2009) explored the connection between the macroeconomic fluctuations of China and the United States. This chapter extends that analysis to examine the relationships between the real GDP of China and that of developed countries more generally.

In terms of the discussion about China's modern role in the global economy, much of the focus has been placed on China's connection with the United States, given that they are the largest developing and developed economy respectively, and on China's connection with neighboring Asian and Pacific economies. Most research in terms of business cycle synchronization has focused on the relationships of China with Asian and Pacific economies. These studies are based on regional economic integration and the discussion of the possibility of an Optimal Currency Area (OCA) for the region (Genberg, Liu, and Jin 2006). Trade has been recognized as the major determinant of the output fluctuation correlation of China with other East Asian and Pacific economies (Sato and Zhang 2006; Shin and Sohn 2006). Beyond the region Calderón (2009) finds increasing output co-movement of China's output fluctuation with Latin America countries along with the growing trade integration among the countries.

Much has also been made of the "special relationship" between China and the United States, with terms such as "G2" and "Chimerica"

(Ferguson and Schularick 2007). China is, however, also tightly connected with developed countries other than the United States. For example, although the United States has been China's largest single country trade partner since the 1990s, Japan, South Korea, and Germany are also large trade partners with China. In total, developed countries comprise the majority of both China's export and import sources, but the United States comprises less than 25 percent. According to the IMF direction of trade database, the United States averaged only 20 percent of China's export market between 2000 and 2009, but the remaining six countries of the G7 were another 22 percent of China's export market and the remaining members of the developed OECD countries[1] were another 10 percent (OECD other countries account for 7 percent).

In terms of imports, the United States on average supplies only 8 percent of China's imports, whereas the remaining countries of the G7 supply an additional 24 percent and the remaining developed OECD members another 7 percent. There is limited literature that addresses the output fluctuation correlations between China and developed countries. Fidrmuc and Batorova (2008), using quarterly CPI deflated GDP data from 1992 to 2006, analyze the dynamic correlations of China's business cycles with selected OECD countries under different cyclical frequencies. They find that despite the increasing trade and financial links between China and other economies, China's business cycle behaves differently from most other economies. Non-European OECD countries such as the United States, Korea, Australia, and Japan; which have more intensive economic linkage with China; show relatively high positive correlation of long-run cycles (over 8 years). In general, the dynamic correlations tend to increase in more recent years. The United States has a positive correlation with China in both long run cycles (over 8 years) and short run cycles (less than 1.5 years). Chen et al. (2004), using classical correlation techniques, document the business cycle correlations of China with the United States, Japan, and select European developed countries and find positive weak correlation between the output fluctuations of the United States and China, while the correlations between China and Japan and the European countries are negative. Zong (2007), using a VAR model on annual data of China's GDP, G7 countries aggregate GDP and China's FDI, reports that G7 GDP Granger-caused the fluctuation of China's FDI and China's GDP, while there is no evidence for an effect in the opposite direction. Lowe (2010) shows that the rolling correlation of real quarterly growth of China and Australia outpaces the correlation between growth of the

United States and Australia since 2000. Fidrmuc and Korhonen (2010) show that business cycle correlations between China and developed countries are zero on average.

Given the increased emphasis on China's role in the global economy, it is important to investigate further the nature of the relationships between China and the developed countries. In particular, we focus on China's relationship with two different aggregate measures for developed economies, the G7 and the OECD. The model employed in this chapter is based on the two-series correlated unobserved components (UC) model employed in Jia and Sinclair (2009), which was applied to examine the relationships between China and the United States. The model was developed in Sinclair (2009) as a two-series extension of the correlated unobserved component model proposed by Morley, Nelson, and Zivot (2003). Similar multivariate UC models have been applied to macroeconomic variables within single economies such as the United States (Morley 2007; Sinclair 2009) and Canada (Basistha 2007) and for an aggregate of the eurozone countries (Berger 2011). The model has also been applied for a cross-country study of the real output fluctuations of the G7 countries (Mitra and Sinclair, forthcoming). The model specifically allows us to distinguish cross-country correlations driven by the relationships between permanent shocks, caused by real shocks such as changes in technology and economic and social institutions, from those between transitory or cyclical movements, caused by changes in aggregate demand or monetary shocks. The model also allows us to explore the role of information from the dynamics of each series in identifying fluctuations in the other series. The correlated unobserved components model applied in this chapter does not require any prior transformation or detrending of the data and places fewer restrictions among the series than other models. In particular, our method combines the detrending and correlation estimation into a single stage which improves both the estimates of the trend and cycle as well as the estimates of the correlations. Furthermore this model nests many of the common detrending methods (Trimbur and Harvey 2003) and is thus more general than most other methods.

We present two different estimates: one with quarterly real GDP data for China with aggregate real GDP for the G7 countries and the other with quarterly real GDP data for China with aggregate real GDP for the 25 OECD member countries. Both models are estimated with quarterly data from 1978 through 2009.[2] We also compare these estimates with those based on a univariate unobserved components model of

Chinese real GDP as well as a trivariate model of the real output of
China, the United States, and Japan. To preview the results, we find
that China has little connection with the developed world aggregate.
We cannot reject that there is no cross-series correlation, and the estimates of the components for both China and the developed world
aggregates are not substantially different from the findings based on
univariate models. The results are similar whether we use the G7 or
the OECD aggregate.

The structure of the rest of the chapter is as follows: Section 4.2
presents the econometric model and estimation method. Section 4.3
discusses the data used in this chapter. Section 4.4 presents the results
of the model estimation. Section 4.5 concludes.

4.2   Model

This chapter applies a two-series correlated unobserved components
model similar to Sinclair (2009) and Jia and Sinclair (2009) to distinguish the correlation of the permanent shocks to output of China from
permanent shocks to aggregate developed country output (in one
model measured as an aggregate of OECD countries and in the other
measured as an aggregate of the G7 countries), separately from the
correlation of the transitory shocks. The model simultaneously decom-
poses each output series into a stochastic trend, or permanent component, and a stationary transitory component. The trend, or permanent
component, is assumed to be a random walk with drift (Stock and
Watson 1988) in order to capture the steady-state level or long-term
potential output of the economy. The transitory component, defined as
real GDP deviations from the permanent trend, is assumed to be stationary following a second order autoregressive process, or AR (2). The
two-series approach enables us to (1) identify the correlation of the
shocks to permanent and transitory components of real output for each
series with information from the dynamics of the other, in order to
examine the linkages of permanent shocks and transitory shocks
between the two economies, and (2) obtain new estimates of the permanent and transitory components for each series using the information of the other series.

This model is general enough to be applied to cointegrated series,
but it does not require cointegration or common trends. The model
allows any amount of correlation between permanent shocks to the
series, from zero correlation to a common trend. If the series do share

a common trend, then cointegration can be imposed in this framework to improve the efficiency of the estimates (Morley 2007). Johansen cointegration tests were applied to our series for both models, and we cannot reject the null of no cointegration allowing for either a constant or a linear deterministic trend in our data. We thus do not impose cointegration.

It is important to note that the transitory component captures transitory deviations from the permanent or steady-state level, which may be fundamentally different from the traditionally defined business cycle (Morley and Piger, forthcoming). The traditional business cycle is often isolated from the series with a filter such as the Hodrick–Prescott (HP) or bandpass (BP) filter. In this chapter we follow a more general definition of permanent and transitory components, which is associated with the Beveridge and Nelson (1981) decomposition and the Harvey (1985) and Clark (1987) unobserved components models. The permanent component, or the trend, follows a stochastic process (a random walk with drift in the model) rather than a fixed or predetermined path. The transitory component is stationary and is defined as the deviation from the stochastic trend, rather than the alternative definition of a cycle that captures alternating phases. The notion is more general than the alternating-phases definition in that it avoids any prior determination of appropriate business cycle frequencies. This is particularly important for macroeconomic fluctuations of developing countries such as China, which may not experience typical traditional business cycle fluctuations. Under the "deviation from trend" definition, the permanent and transitory components of the economic fluctuations can be directly formulated in structural time-series models (Harvey and Shephard 1993), cast in state space form, and estimated using the Kalman filter for maximum likelihood estimation (MLE) of the parameters using prediction error decomposition.

The measurement equation of our model is:

$$y_{it} = \tau_{it} + c_{it}, \tag{4.1}$$

where τ_{it} is the unobserved trend component and c_{it} is the unobserved cycle component for series i (where $i = DW$ represents the aggregate for the developed world and $i = C$ represents China).

The transition equations are

$$\tau_{it} = u_i + \tau_{it-1} + \eta_{it}, \tag{4.2}$$

$$c_{it} = \varphi_{1i} c_{it-1} + \varphi_{2i} c_{it-2} + \varepsilon_{it}. \tag{4.3}$$

where η_{it} and ε_{it} are assumed to be normally distributed with mean zero. There are no restrictions on the correlations between any of the contemporaneous shocks; that is, no restrictions are imposed on the variance-covariance matrix, which allows us to estimate all potential contemporaneous correlations within and across series.

The variance-covariance matrix is

$$
\Sigma = \begin{bmatrix}
\sigma^2_{\eta_{DW}} & \sigma_{\eta_{DW}\eta_c} & \sigma_{\eta_{DW}\varepsilon_{DW}} & \sigma_{\eta_{DW}\varepsilon_c} \\
\sigma_{\eta_{DW}\eta_c} & \sigma^2_{\eta_c} & \sigma_{\eta_c\varepsilon_{DW}} & \sigma_{\eta_c\varepsilon_c} \\
\sigma_{\eta_{DW}\varepsilon_{DW}} & \sigma_{\eta_c\varepsilon_{DW}} & \sigma^2_{\varepsilon_{DW}} & \sigma_{\varepsilon_{DW}\varepsilon_c} \\
\sigma_{\eta_{DW}\varepsilon_c} & \sigma_{\eta_c\varepsilon_c} & \sigma_{\varepsilon_{DW}\varepsilon_c} & \sigma^2_{\varepsilon_c}
\end{bmatrix}.
\tag{4.4}
$$

We cast equations (4.1) through (4.3) into state space form and estimate the unobserved components and the parameters of the model using the Kalman filter and maximum likelihood in GAUSS. The unobserved components are estimated with the Kalman smoothing algorithm, which uses information from the whole sample period, namely the future data as well as the past data.[3]

4.3   Data

4.3.1   Data Sources
The model is estimated with quarterly real GDP data for China and a developed country aggregate from 1978 through 2009. The Chinese data are from the National Bureau of Statistics of China (NBS), the nation's statistical authority.[4] Our study focuses on the real output fluctuations since 1978, when China embarked on the market-oriented and openness economic reform. Our data include the most recent official revisions for 2005 through 2009 based on the information collected through the second economic census completed at the end of 2009. For quarterly real GDP before 1992, when quarterly real GDP data were not published officially, the data are disaggregated from annual data using the Chow and Lin (1971) related series method based on Abeysinghe and Rajaguru (2004).[5] Their disaggregation uses money supply and international trade data, both available at the quarterly frequency, as related series. Abeysinghe and Rajaguru estimate the quarterly growth rates of real GDP for 1978 through 1994 based on the estimated relationship of annual real GDP growth rates and the related series from 1978 through 1996.[6] The results of the disaggregation are tested by the authors through model fitting and out-of-sample forecast

evaluation. The Abeysinghe and Rajaguru estimates are the only published estimates of quarterly real GDP data for China for this period. The data allow us to investigate the relationship of the Chinese economy with the developed world since it started to integrate with the world economy. This longer time series provides more information on China's macroeconomic fluctuations and improves the efficiency of the estimation. To investigate the possible irregularity caused by the difference of data sources and the robustness of the result, the model was also estimated with official Chinese real output data from 1992 through 2009. We find that the results are remarkably similar to the full sample results.

The Chinese real output data are seasonally adjusted using the X-12 ARIMA method. The X-12 ARIMA (2, 1, 2) and Tramo/seat (time-series regression with ARIMA noise, missing values, and outliers/signal extraction in ARIMA time series) methods give similar results. The finding is consistent with Blades (2007), who performed similar tests on current price quarterly GDP of China. The seasonal pattern of China's quarterly real GDP is regular and predictable. The method is consistent with the one applied by the OECD for the developed world data.

For the developed countries data, we focus on two measures: real GDP for the G7 countries and real GDP for 25 OECD countries (although a model of 30 OECD countries yielded equivalent results). The data come from the OECD and are measured as millions of US dollars, volume estimates, fixed PPPs, OECD reference year, annual levels, seasonally adjusted.[7] The 25 OECD countries included in the OECD aggregate are: Australia, Austria, Belgium, Canada, Denmark, Finland, France, Germany, Greece, Iceland, Ireland, Italy, Japan, Luxembourg, Mexico, Netherlands, New Zealand, Norway, Portugal, Spain, Sweden, Switzerland, Turkey, United Kingdom, and United States (the 30-country aggregate adds the Czech Republic, Hungary, Korea, Poland, and the Slovak Republic).[8] The G7 countries are Canada, France, Germany, Italy, Japan, United Kingdom, and United States. It is important to note that all of the G7 countries are also included in the OECD aggregate.

4.3.2   Chinese Data Quality

Along with the increasing interest in China's economic performance, the quality of Chinese official macroeconomic statistics, including the GDP data,[9] has been repeatedly questioned by a number of researchers and media reports. Despite the efforts made by NBS to explain and improve the GDP estimates over years, confidence in the accuracy of official data is still low. The data quality still remains a problem that must be addressed for empirical research on Chinese macroeconomic issues.

In the early 2000s heated discussions on the quality of Chinese macro data generated a large number of publications on this issue. The criticisms of China's official data are based on evidence from alternative GDP calculations (Maddison 1998; Wu 2000; Young 2003), comparison with energy and transportation consumption data (Rawski 2001), and suspects of data falsifications, especially on the local level, under the nondemocratic political system.[10] In the media, people are also concerned about the quick publication, only two weeks after the end of reporting periods, of the preliminary national account data for such a big economy.[11] This criticism persists even though before 1988 the Bureau of Economic Analysis released real GDP estimates for the United States just 15 days after the end of the quarter (Young 1993).

Refutations to the criticisms show the alternative data series constructed or corrected by researchers have not been proved to be more precise or reliable (Holz 2006). Many researchers find that GDP data problems are unlikely to be unique to China, and the evidence is not robust for a conclusion of data manipulation or systematic data falsification (Holz 2005, 2006; Chow 2006; Klein and Ozmucur 2003). Chinese statistical authorities explain most of the questions as lack of understanding of China's transitional statistical system and the nature of a transitional economy. Some problems have gained acknowledgment from the authorities (Xu, 2002, 2004) and efforts have been made to improve the data quality. The data are compiled and revised based on the information gained from recently established regular surveys and economic censuses, revised financial statement reports for enterprises and the more sophisticated data sources system. Manipulating statistics to meet political objectives, as the most usual concerns, are much harder at the national level. Xu Gao of the World Bank provides evidence of the consistency of data from different government institutes for recent years in his official blog.[12]

After carefully reviewing the literature on Chinese data quality and their national accounting system, and comparing different data resources and data construction methods, we agree with many researchers and most international organizations (OECD, IMF[13]) that although there are weaknesses or short-comings in the statistical system that provides Chinese national accounts estimation, the Chinese official macroeconomic data after 1978 are not proved to be politically manipulated or systematically biased. The official data can serve as "a reliable guide" to the level and growth pattern of GDP, even though the margins of error are "certainly larger than that of the most developed countries" (Lequiller and Blades 2006).

4.4   Results

Table 4.1 presents the classical correlations of the Hodrick and Prescott (1997) and Baxter and King (1999) cycles and the growth rates of real GDP of China with the G7 and the OECD aggregates over the entire sample period.[14] Note that the correlations of Hodrick–Prescott and the Baxter–King cycles may be due to spurious cycles generated by the detrending methods (Cogley and Nason 1995; and Murray 2003). Compared with the correlations between the United States and China as reported in Jia and Sinclair (2009), the pattern is similar but in all cases the correlations are lower between the G7 and the OECD with China than between the United States and China. Depending on the choice of method to address the nonstationarity that is present in the real GDP series the conclusion about the tightness of the relationship between China and the developed world differs substantially. In general, it appears that China and the developed world share somewhere between less than 10 and 25 percent of their fluctuations. This lack of clear conclusion suggests that further investigation is warranted.

4.4.1   Correlated Unobserved Components Model Parameter Estimates

Tables 4.2 through 4.5 report the parameters of the maximum likelihood estimation of our two correlated unobserved components models for the entire sample period. The results are strikingly similar for China when we use either aggregate, although the standard errors suggest

Table 4.1
Correlations of cycles for China and the developed country aggregates

Developed country aggregate	Quarterly growth rates	Year-on-year growth rates	Hodrick–Prescott cycles (lamda = 1,600)	Baxter–King cycles (cycle periods 6–32)
G7	0.09	0.18	0.28	0.21
OECD	0.11	0.16	0.24	0.14

92   Yueqing Jia and Tara M. Sinclair

Table 4.2
Estimation results

	China and G7		China and OECD	
	−251.16		−247.13	
Log likelihood	China (SE)	G7 (SE)	China (SE)	OECD (SE)
Drift	2.40 (0.18)	0.56 (0.09)	2.39 (0.18)	0.58 (0.09)
phi1	1.31 (0.04)	0.56 (0.25)	1.31 (0.05)	0.56 (0.15)
phi2	−0.48 (0.04)	−0.07 (0.20)	−0.48 (0.05)	−0.10 (0.17)

that the results based on the larger OECD aggregate are more precisely estimated than for the model using the G7 aggregate. The estimates for both aggregates are similar as well, and are consistent with estimates for developed countries individually, such as those reported in Morley, Nelson, and Zivot (2003)for the United States and in Mitra and Sinclair (forthcoming) for the G7 countries.

Drift Terms Since each series is in logs and multiplied by 100, the estimated drift term multiplied by 4 can be interpreted as the average annual growth of the permanent component. According to our estimates, China's average permanent real growth rate is 9.6 percent annually whereas for the G7 it is 2.2 percent and for the OECD it is 2.3 percent. These estimates are similar to other estimates reported in the literature.

Autoregressive Parameters The estimated autoregressive coefficients, which reflect the dynamics of the transitory components, are similar across the different models. The sum of the autoregressive coefficients, which provides a measure of persistence of the transitory components, suggests that China has a more persistent transitory component than either the G7 or the OECD aggregate. Both the G7 and the OECD have persistence measures less than 0.5, whereas for China it is 0.83.

Permanent and Transitory Standard Deviations Presented in table 4.3, the estimated standard deviations of the permanent and transitory shocks are similar across models. The standard deviation of the perma-

Table 4.3
Standard deviations of shocks

	China and G7	China and OECD
Developed	1.04	0.99
Permanent	(0.68)	(0.05)
China	1.97	1.97
Permanent	(0.96)	(0.08)
Developed	0.59	0.62
Transitory	(0.61)	(0.08)
China	1.43	1.43
Transitory	(0.09)	(0.03)
Developed ratio Permanent/transitory	1.76	1.60
China ratio Permanent/transitory	1.38	1.38

nent shocks is larger than the standard deviation of the transitory shocks for both China and the developed country aggregate for both models. The result implies that the trend or permanent component for each series is much more variable than the traditional HP and BP smoothed trends. Furthermore permanent shocks are relatively more important than the transitory shocks for each series. Permanent shocks to Chinese real GDP are substantially more variable than permanent shocks to the developed aggregates. Chinese permanent shocks have almost twice the standard deviation of the developed world permanent shocks. For the transitory components the difference is even more dramatic, with transitory shocks for China having almost three times the standard deviation as transitory shocks to the developed world. Thus, although the absolute magnitudes of both the transitory and the permanent standard deviations are higher for China than for the developed world aggregates, as might be expected given China's higher average growth rate, the ratio of permanent to transitory variability is less for China than the developed world aggregates. In both cases they are greater than one, however, suggesting an important role for permanent shocks for all series. It is possible in our case to have both more variable permanent components and more variable transitory components, since allowing for correlation opens up the possibility that there may be offsetting movements between the two components.

Within-series Correlations   Based on our two-series correlated UC model, the correlations between the permanent and transitory shocks

Table 4.4
Within-series correlations of shocks

	China and G7	China and OECD
Permanent developed	−0.99	−0.97
with transitory developed	(0.03)	(0.02)
Permanent China with	−0.99	−0.99
transitory China	(<0.01)	(0.01)

within the economies of China and the developed world are all significantly negative (table 4.4). In fact the correlation of permanent and transitory shocks for all series is nearly perfectly negative based on both models. Negatively correlated permanent and transitory shocks are a common finding for real GDP. These results are consistent with prior research that has examined the correlation between permanent and transitory shocks for the real GDP of the United States (Morley, Nelson, and Zivot 2003; Sinclair 2009), Canada (Basistha 2007), the United States and the United Kingdom (Nagakura 2008), and the G7 countries (Nagakura 2007; Mitra and Sinclair, forthcoming). The negative correlation has been interpreted as due to slow adjustment of the actual output of the economy to the permanent shocks to output. As Stock and Watson (1988) and Morley, Nelson, and Zivot (2003)explained, strong negative correlation of the permanent shocks with the transitory shocks may be interpreted as implying that the economic fluctuations are driven mainly by permanent shocks, while the permanent shocks immediately shift the long term path of the output, the short-run movements may include adjustments toward the shifted trend.

Cross-series Correlations   Table 4.5 shows the estimates of the correlations of the permanent-permanent shocks, the transitory—transitory shocks cross country—and the permanent-transitory cross correlations. The correlations are estimated simultaneously with the components. We find that for the G7 aggregate we cannot reject the null that there is no cross-series correlation. A likelihood ratio test with four restrictions results in a chi-squared statistic of 3.45, which has a p-value of 0.49. Similarly, for the OECD aggregate, the likelihood ratio test statistic is 4.51 with a p-value of 0.34. This finding is consistent with the finding of Fidrmuc and Korhonen (2010) that business cycle correlations between China and developed countries are zero on average.

Table 4.5
Cross-series correlations of shocks

	G7	OECD
Permanent China with permanent developed	0.07	0.07
	(0.17)	(0.04)
Transitory China with transitory developed	0.03	−0.02
	(<0.01)	(0.01)
Permanent developed with transitory China	0.07	0.07
	(0.19)	(<0.01)
Permanent China with transitory developed	−0.16	−0.11
	(0.02)	(0.06)

4.4.2 Estimated Permanent and Transitory Components

Figure 4.1 shows the estimated permanent and transitory components of the real GDP of China based on our two different bivariate models as well as the estimated components for the G7 and the OECD aggregates. These estimates suggest that the transitory components for the developed-world aggregates are small and noisy, similar to previous findings for estimates of the developed countries individually (e.g., see Mitra and Sinclair, forthcoming, for the G7 countries). The permanent components appear very similar to the series themselves. For China, however, there appears to be more substantial transitory movement. Some of this more substantial transitory movement is simply due to the larger size of fluctuations more generally as compared to the developed countries. Recall from section 4.4.1 that the transitory fluctuations for China are almost three times as variable as those of the developed world. The permanent component for Chinese real GDP still appears quite similar to the series itself.

The role of the information of the other countries is presented in the estimated transitory components in figures 4.2 and 4.3. In figure 4.2 we compare the estimated transitory component from two different models—the bivariate model with China and a developed country aggregate (the G7 and the OECD aggregate provide cycle estimates for China that are indistinguishable from each other) and the univariate correlated UC model applied to China alone. We see that the estimated components are broadly similar. Figure 4.3 shows that separating out two of the key members of the G7, namely the United States and Japan, to create a trivariate model does not substantially change the estimated transitory component for China either. We also estimated a model with a larger OECD aggregate, which included the real GDP of 30 OECD

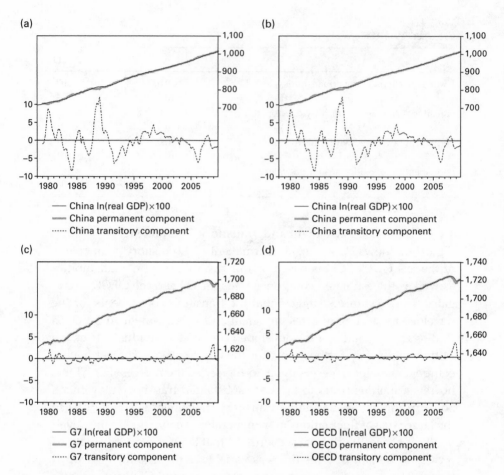

Figure 4.1
Estimated permanent and transitory components: (a) China based on bivariate model
with G7; (b) China based on bivariate model with OECD; (c) G7 based on bivariate model
with China; (d) OECD based on bivariate model with China.

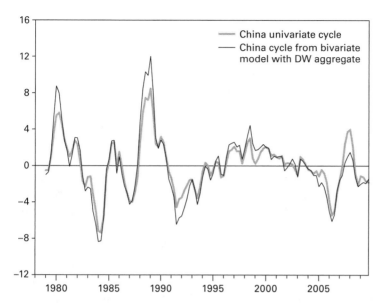

Figure 4.2
Comparing the different filtered cycle estimates: Univariate and bivariate models.

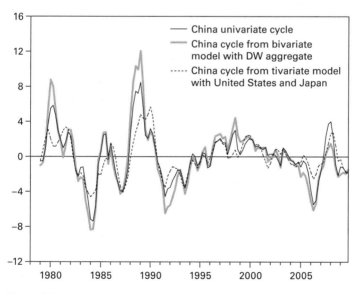

Figure 4.3
Comparing the different cycle estimates: Univariate, bivariate, and trivariate models.

member countries: Australia, Austria, Belgium, Canada, Czech Repub-
lic, Denmark, Finland, France, Germany, Greece, Hungary, Iceland,
Ireland, Italy, Japan, Korea, Luxembourg, Mexico, Netherlands, New
Zealand, Norway, Poland, Portugal, Slovak Republic, Spain, Sweden,
Switzerland, Turkey, United Kingdom, and United States. The results
were unchanged.

Jia and Sinclair (2009) showed that adding information from US
economic fluctuations does not visibly change the amplitudes and
movement pattern of the transitory component of China as compared
to the univariate results. They further show that adding other alternative external information sets such as the real GDP of Hong Kong or
the oil price does not change this result. A further investigation of the
China's real GDP fluctuation with China's international trade variables, using the bivariate model shows similar result (figure 4.4). Here
we show that even a large aggregate of developed world GDP provides
little new information for China's real output fluctuations. Possible
interpretations for the stability of China's transitory components across
different bivariate models could be: first, most of the external shocks
are permanent shocks to China, and thus do not change the transitory
components; second, domestic factors such as domestic demand or
monetary policy may be the major sources of China's real GDP fluctua-

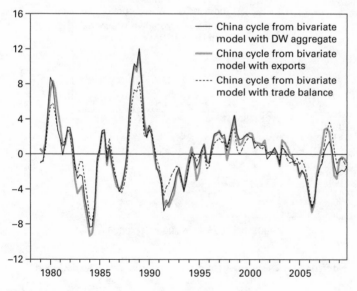

Figure 4.4
Comparing the cycle estimates: DW aggregate, exports, and trade balance.

tions,[15] thus external information sets do not provide much forecasting information; third, China's macroeconomic controls or adjustment policies could have largely isolated the external shocks from greatly influencing the macroeconomic performance of the country.

The result is in agreement with the finding of Jia (2011). Using a global vector autoregression model (GVAR), Jia (2011) shows that supply side shocks and domestic factors play an important role in China's real output movements, while none of the foreign variables, such as the trade-weighted aggregate real output, interest rates, and equity price of the rest of the world and the world oil price, appears to be significant for China's real output fluctuations.

4.4.3 The "Great Recession"

From 2007 through 2009 most of the world experienced the "Great Recession." Although China did not experience an absolute decline in real GDP, according to most sources, including the Economic Cycle Research Institute (ECRI),[16] China experienced a growth cycle peak in May 2007 and a trough in December 2009. Similarly the G7 and OECD countries all experienced business cycle peaks and troughs during this period. Therefore we next investigate what the model suggests about this important episode in our sample. Figure 4.5 presents a "zoom-in"

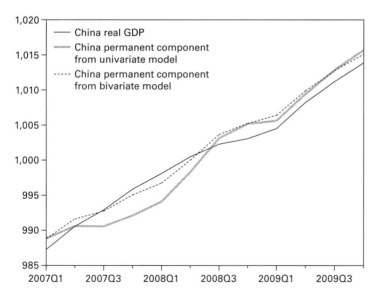

Figure 4.5
2007 to 2009 Chinese real GDP and permanent component estimates.

on Chinese real GDP and our estimates for the permanent component based on three different models for the period 2007 to 2009. The estimates show that although the estimates are broadly similar, if we relied on a univariate model to estimate the permanent component for China, then we would assume that the permanent component moved substantially below the series between the second quarter of 2007 and the third quarter of 2008. According to the bivariate model, however, the permanent component remained much closer to the series. By contrast, the estimates for both the G7 and the OECD aggregates suggest that there was substantial downward movement in their permanent components during this recession (figure 4.6).[17]

4.5 Conclusion

In this chapter we presented the estimates of two different bivariate correlated UC models for the real GDP of China with aggregate measures of developed country real GDP with quarterly data from 1978 through 2009: one with a G7 country aggregate and one with an OECD country aggregate. Our model permits us to examine both the within-country long-term and short-term properties of the output fluctuations of the two-series and the cross-series relationships of the two series

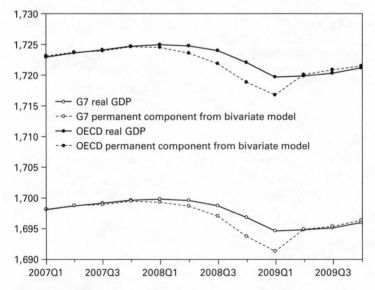

Figure 4.6
2007 to 2009 G7 and OECD real GDP and permanent component estimates.

simultaneously. The estimation results also reveal the relative importance of permanent versus transitory movements in the relationship. We find that although China and the developed world share substantial trade connections, we cannot reject that there are no cross-series correlations between Chinese real GDP and an aggregate of developed world GDP measured by either the G7 countries or the OECD countries.

Although there seems to be little correlation between the real output fluctuations of China and the developed world in terms of the permanent and transitory shocks and also little evidence of additional information for each other's fluctuations, there remain interesting similarities between China and the developed world. Like the findings for both individual developed countries reported in the literature as well as for the developed country aggregates reported here, we find that China has significant negative correlation between permanent and transitory shocks to its real GDP. We also find that China has an important role for permanent shocks in its real GDP fluctuations, which is similar to the finding for the developed countries. China does, however, have a much larger drift term, such that permanent shocks are substantially larger on average. These larger permanent shocks drive China's faster growth rate. Consistent with this faster growth rate, both the permanent and transitory shocks are substantially more variable for Chinese real GDP than those of developed countries. The similarities suggest that similar macroeconomic policies may be appropriate for China as for developed countries, although the lack of correlation and the greater size and variability of shocks may mean that different timing and size of policy may be necessary. The small correlation of China's output fluctuations with the developed world indicates that domestic factors such as economic reforms, domestic demand, and economic policies may be the major drivers of China's macro economic fluctuations.

Acknowledgments

The authors gratefully acknowledge support from GW-CIBER and the Institute for International Economic Policy (IIEP) of the Elliott School at GWU. We thank our discussant James Reade for his insightful comments and suggestions. We thank Deanna Jensen, Kavita Patel, and Rajeer Patel for excellent research assistance. We also thank Jinzhao Chen, Yin-Wong Cheung, Menzie Chinn, Jakob de Haan, James Morley, Tom Rawski, Alessandro Rebucci, Bruce Reynolds, and Stephen Smith for helpful comments and discussions. The views in this chapter are those of the authors and do not necessarily represent those of the institutes.

Notes

1. The developed OECD countries include the 25 OECD members in the aggregate data: Australia, Austria, Belgium, Canada, Denmark, Finland, France, Germany, Greece, Iceland, Ireland, Italy, Japan, Luxembourg, Mexico, Netherlands, New Zealand, Norway, Portugal, Spain, Sweden, Switzerland, Turkey, United Kingdom, and United States. The developing OECD members include: the Czech Republic, Hungary, Korea, Poland, the Slovak Republic, and Mexico. The data do not include Chile, Slovenia, and Israel, new members that joined the OECD after May 2010.

2. We also estimated two additional models for robustness. One was a model for a 30-country OECD aggregate. The other was for a subsample from 1992 to 2009 to consider only the officially reported quarterly real GDP for China. The estimates were both quantitatively and qualitatively similar to those reported in this chapter. These estimates are available from the authors upon request.

3. The smoother does produce different estimates of the components as compared to the filter, particularly for Chinese real GDP. The cycle based on the smoothed estimates is substantially larger. Results for the filtered estimates are available from the authors upon request.

4. The official data are published as cumulated year on year growth rate at comparable price. Data from 1992 to 2005 are from the publication of National Bureau of Statistics of China: Historical Data on China Quarterly GDP Estimator 1992–2005, 2/2008 China Statistics Press ISBN/ISSN 9787503753565.

5. The year 2000 is chosen as the base year because the inflation rate (CPI inflation) was close to zero during that year, which will minimize the distortion from inflation on the quarterly data within the base year.

6. We only use Abeysinghe and Rajaguru's data through 1991 and then use the NBS data.

7. The data were extracted on September 29, 2010, from OECD.Stat.

8. The 30-country aggregate was the largest available OECD aggregate at the time of the writing of this chapter. According to OECD.stat, "Chile became a member of the OECD on 7 May 2010, Slovenia on 21 July 2010 and Israel on 7 September 2010 and data for them now appears in the list of OECD member countries. Nevertheless, Chile, Israel and Slovenia have not yet been included in OECD area aggregation in the quarterly national accounts database for technical and timing reasons." The estimates using the 30-country aggregate are available from the authors upon request.

9. An article in The Economist (2008) cited Goldman Sachs' ranking of the reliability of Chinese statistics from high to low as: foreign trade, money supply, industrial production, consumer prices, GDP, retail sales, fixed investment, employment, average earnings, unemployment, where GDP is in the middle.

10. See Holz (2006) for a detailed survey of the literature.

11. The most recent official announcement on the timing of revisions of the quarterly data has become more cautious and leaves more time for the first and final revisions of the number.

12. http://blogs.worldbank.org/eastasiapacific/are-chinese-statistics-manipulated.

13. The World Bank criticized the Chinese national account statistics and revised their GDP estimation for China upward for 34 percent from the officially reported number in 1993. In 1996 the World Bank accepted China's reformed statistical system and the official GDP number again. But the World Bank revision and method of estimation are also questioned by many researchers.

14. The quarterly growth rate is defined as the first difference of the log of real GDP. The year-on-year growth rate is defined as log changes from the same quarter of the previous year, which is often used by articles published in Chinese, that is, $y_t = \log(realGDP) \times 100$ Year-on-year growth rates $g_t = y_t - yt_{-4}$.

15. We do not consider domestic information sets because, first, availability of quarterly data of domestic economic indicators for our sample period are very limited and, second, the data construction of the data before 2000 has used the total international trade and money supply—the only quarterly series available.

16. www.businesscycle.com.

17. Comparing the smoothed estimates reported here with the filtered estimates (available from the authors upon request) does suggest that hindsight improves our understanding of the role of permanent versus transitory shocks particularly for China in this episode. The filtered estimates suggest a much larger drop in the permanent component for China (more similar to the estimates reported for the developed country aggregates) as compared to the smoothed estimates.

References

Abeysinghe, T., and G. Rajaguru. 2004. Quarterly real GDP estimates for China and ASEAN4 with a forecast evaluation. *Journal of Forecasting* 23 (6): 431–47.

Basistha, A. 2007. Trend-cycle correlation, drift break and the estimation of trend and cycle in Canadian GDP. *Canadian Journal of Economics, Revue Canadienne d'Economique* 40 (2): 584–606.

Baxter, M., and R. G. King. 1999. Measuring business cycles: Approximate bandpass filters. *Review of Economics and Statistics* 81 (4): 575–93.

Berger, T. 2011. Estimating Europe's natural rates. *Empirical Economics, Springer* 40 (2): 521–36.

Beveridge, S., and C. R. Nelson. 1981. A new approach to decomposition of economic time series into permanent and transitory components with particular attention to measurement of the business cycle. *Journal of Monetary Economics* 7: 151–74.

Blades, D. 2007. *Decumulating China's Quarterly National Accounts*. Paris: OECD.

Calderón, C. 2009. Trade, specialization and cycle synchronization: Explaining output comovement between Latin America, China and India. In D. Ledeman, M. Olarreaga, and G. E. Perry, eds., *China's and India's Challenge to Latin America: Opportunity or Threat?* Washington, DC: World Bank, 39–100.

Chen, K., Y. Zhou, and L. Gong. 2004. The fluctuations of China's business cycles: Based on different filters. [In Chinese] *World Economy* 10: 47–57.

Chow, G., and A. Lin. 1971. Best linear unbiased interpolation, distribution, and extrapolation of time series by related series. *Review of Economics and Statistics* 53: 372–75.

Chow, G. 2006. Are Chinese official statistics reliable? *CESifo Economic Studies* 52: 396–414.

Clark, P. K. 1987. The cyclical component of U.S. economic activity. *Quarterly Journal of Economics* 102: 797–814.

Cogley, T., and J. M. Nason. 1995. Effects of the Hodrick–Prescott filter on trend and difference stationary time series Implications for business cycle research. *Journal of Economic Dynamics & Control* 19 (1/2): 253–78.

Anonymous. 2008. Finance and economics: An aberrant abacus. Economics Focus. *The Economist*, 387 (8578): 85. Available at: http://www.economist.com/node/11290833.

Ferguson, N., and M. Schularick. 2007. "Chimerica" and the global asset market boom. *International Finance* 10 (3): 215–39.

Fidrmuc, J., and I. Batorova. 2008. China in the world economy: Dynamic correlation analysis of business cycles. Working Paper RP2008/02. World Institute for Development Economic Research, United Nations University, Helsinki.

Fidrmuc, J., and I. Korhonen. 2010. The impact of the global financial crisis on business cycles in Asian emerging economies. *Journal of Asian Economics* 21: 293–303.

Genberg, H., and L. Liu, and X. Jin. 2006. Hong Kong's economic integration and business cycle synchronisation with mainland China and the US. Working Paper 0611. Hong Kong Monetary Authority.

Harvey, A. C. 1985. Trends and cycles in macroeconomic time series. *Journal of Business and Economic Statistics* 3: 216–27.

Harvey, A. C. and N. Shephard. 1993. Structural time series models. In *Handbook of Statistics*, vol. 2. Amsterdam: Elsevier Science, 261–302.

Hodrick, R., and E. C. Prescott. 1997. Postwar U.S. business cycles: An empirical investigation. *Journal of Money, Credit and Banking* 29 (1): 1–16.

Holz, C. 2005. The institutional arrangement for the production of statistics, OECD—China governance project. Statistics working paper STD. OECD, Paris.

Holz, C. 2006. China's reform period economic growth: How reliable are Angus Maddison's estimates? Response to Angus Maddison's reply. *Review of Income and Wealth* 52 (3): 471–75.

Jia, Y., and T. M. Sinclair. 2009. Permanent and transitory macroeconomic relationships between the US and China. Working Paper. GW-CIBER, Washington, DC. Available at: http://business.gwu.edu/CIBER/research/deliverables/2008-2009/Sinclain%20-%20US_China%20Sept%202009%20WP%20version.pdf.

Jia, Y. 2011. A new look at China's output fluctuations: Quarterly GDP estimation with an unobserved components approach. Working Paper. Department of Economics, George Washington University.

Klein, L. R., and S. Ozmucur. 2003. The estimation of China's economic growth rate. *Journal of Economic and Social Measurement* 28 (4): 187–202.

Lequiller, F., and D. Blades. 2006. *Understanding National Accounts*. Paris: OECD.

Lowe, P. 2010. The development of Asia: Risk and returns for Australia. Speech on Natstats 2010 Conference, Sydney. Available at: http://www.rba.gov.au/speeches/2010/sp-ag-160910.html.

Maddison, A. 1998. *Chinese Economic Performance in the Long Run*. Paris: OECD.

Mitra, S. and. T. M. Sinclair (forthcoming). Output fluctuations in the G-7: An unobserved components approach. *Macroeconomic Dynamics*.

Morley, J. C. 2007. The slow adjustment of aggregate consumption to permanent income. *Journal of Money, Credit and Banking* 39: 615–38.

Morley, J., and J. Piger (forthcoming). The asymmetric business cycle. *Review of Economics and Statistics*.

Morley, J. C., C. R. Nelson, and E. Zivot. 2003. Why are the Beveridge–Nelson and unobserved-components decompositions of GDP so different? *Review of Economics and Statistics* 85 (2): 235–43.

Murray, C. J. 2003. Cyclical properties of Baxter–King filtered time series. *Review of Economics and Statistics* 85: 472–76.

Nagakura, D. 2007. Inference on the correlation between permanent and transitory shocks for unidentified unobserved components models. SSRN Working paper, SSRN. Available at: http://ssrn.com/abstract=981646.

Nagakura, D. 2008. How are shocks to trend and cycle correlated? A simple methodology for unidentified unobserved components models. Discussion paper 2008-E-24. IMES, Bank of Japan, Tokyo. Available at: http://www.imes.boj.or.jp/research/papers/english/08-E-24.pdf.

Rawski, T. G. 2001. What is happening to China's GDP statistics? *China Economic Review* 12 (4): 347–54.

Sato, K., and Z. Zhang. 2006. Real output co-movements in East Asia: Any evidence for a monetary union? *World Economy* 29 (12): 1671–89.

Shin, K., and C. H. Sohn. 2006. Trade and financial integration in East Asia: Effects on co-movements. *World Economy* 29 (12): 1649–69.

Sinclair, T. M. 2009. The relationships between permanent and transitory movements in U.S. output and the unemployment rate. *Journal of Money, Credit and Banking* 41 (2/3): 529–42.

Stock, J. H., and M. W. Watson. 1988. Variable trends in economic time series. *Journal of Economic Perspectives* 2 (3): 147–74.

Trimbur, T., and A. C. Harvey. 2003. General model-based filters for extracting cycles and trends in economic time series. *Review of Economics and Statistics* 85: 244–55.

Wu, H. X. 2000. China's GDP level and growth performance: Alternative estimates and the implications. *Review of Income and Wealth* 46 (4): 475–99.

Xu, X. 2002. Study on some problems in estimating China's gross domestic product. *Review of Income and Wealth* 48 (2): 205–15.

Xu, X. 2004. China's gross domestic product estimation. *China Economic Review* 15: 302–22.

Young, A. 2003. Gold into base metals: Productivity growth in the People's Republic of China during the reform period. *Journal of Political Economy* 111 (6): 1220–61.

Young, A. H. 1993. Reliability and accuracy of the quarterly estimates of GDP. *Survey of Current Business* 73 (10): 29–43.

Zong, J. 2007. The economic fluctuations of developed countries on China: Empirical analysis on G7 and FDI prospective. *Forum of the World Economy and Politics* 4: 27.

5 China's External Position: Simulations with a Global Macroeconomic Model

Lukas Vogel

5.1 Introduction

The Chinese economy has transformed and developed remarkably during the past twenty years. Real output has grown at annualized two-digit rates. Per capita income has risen from 5 to 20 percent of EU-15 levels. At the same time China has accumulated large external surpluses and has become the world's largest international creditor.

The chapter focuses on the link between China's economic transition and integration, on the one side, and its position as large net capital exporter, on the other side. Contrary to the Chinese experience, the textbook open-economy model would suggest economic catch-up to coincide with net capital imports and a (transitory) international debtor position.

The chapter uses a multi-country version of the QUEST III macroeconomic model (Ratto et al. 2009). The four model regions are China, the United States, the euro area, and the rest of the world. I extent the standard QUEST structure by introducing (1) a portfolio approach that distinguishes gross/net and private/government sector foreign asset positions and accounts for limited cross-border capital mobility and (2) exchange rate management in the form of sterilized foreign exchange (Forex) intervention. The two extensions represent key elements of macroeconomic policy in China, namely the imposition of capital controls and exchange rate management. The rest of the model is fairly standard in that it includes only distortions/frictions in the China block that are standard also in the EU and US settings.

The chapter relates to previous research on global imbalances, especially from the angle of capital exporting countries, within multi-region DSGE models of the world economy, such as Cova et al. (2009), Faruqee et al. (2007), and Straub and Thimann (2009). These contributions do not include capital controls and Forex intervention in their models, however. The standard fix of augmenting the interest rate rule by exchange rate targets precludes a differentiated perspective on private versus government foreign asset positions and sterilized Forex interventions. Furthermore the present chapter puts more effort into a China-typical calibration of model parameters and exogenous shocks than previous DSGE-based analyses.

The chapter selects a set of shocks that cover important aspects of China's economic transition and integration in the world economy, namely TFP catch-up, labor supply growth, labor reallocation, precautionary savings, and export growth, and investigates their ability to match key stylized facts, namely the large-scale accumulation of net foreign assets (NFA) that combines increasing Forex reserves of the central bank with a net debtor position of the nongovernment sector, persistent surpluses in the trade balance and the current account, high real output growth, and declining (increasing) domestic demand shares of consumption (investment).

The simulations show the set of shocks to replicate China's external position quite well in the benchmark setting with limited capital mobility and Forex intervention, though the fit is less satisfactory for domestic demand shares. The results also highlight that effective capital controls, namely binding restrictions on cross-border capital flows, are crucial for the viability of China's exchange rate management. Finally the simulations suggest that enhanced flexibility of the RMB exchange rate would lead to RMB appreciation under the selected set of shocks, reduce China's NFA position and contribute to changing the composition of China's growth from exports toward domestic demand. Robustness checks indicate that a potential asymmetry of capital controls and alternative values for the elasticity of labor supply have little bearing on the results, while assumptions on expectation formation (perfect foresight versus simple extrapolation) are crucial.

The structure of the chapter is as follows. Section 5.2 provides a short review of the literature to place my analysis in context. Section 5.3 presents stylized facts on China's economic development that model simulations should replicate. Section 5.4 introduces the portfolio approach and Forex interventions into QUEST. Section 5.5 details the calibration of model parameters. Section 5.6 presents the simulation scenarios, results for alternative policy regimes and robustness checks. Section 5.7 summarizes the findings and concludes.

5.2 Review of the Literature

Emergence and persistence of the large current account imbalances have generated many policy statements and a large body of economic research (Gruber and Kamin 2007). Part of it focuses on net debtor countries as the demand side (e.g., Bems et al. 2007; Blanchard 2007; Bussière et al. 2005; Chinn and Prasad 2003; Chinn and Ito 2008; Corsetti and Mueller 2006); part deals with net creditors as the suppliers of savings (e.g., Blanchard and Giavazzi 2005; Bracke and Fidora 2008; Cova et al. 2009; Lee and McKibbin 2006; Mendoza et al. 2007; Yu 2007). Multi-country model simulations (e.g., Choi et al. 2008; Choi and Mark 2009; Faruqee et al. 2007; N'Diaye et al. 2010) often combine both sides.

China's large NFA and current account surplus reflects a persistent excess of domestic savings over domestic investment. The external surplus is difficult to reconcile with the neoclassical textbook model, given the country's position as emerging economy with TFP catch-up and growing labor supply. According to the standard model, TFP and labor supply growth increase the marginal productivity of capital and should lead to net capital inflows (e.g., Dollar and Kraay 2006; Ma and Haiwen 2009; Straub and Thimann 2009).

Economists have proposed several (not mutually exclusive) solutions to this paradox. A first group (e.g., Blanchard and Giavazzi 2005; Blanchard 2007; Chamon and Prasad 2010; Feng et al. 2009; Ma and Haiwen 2009; Modigliani and Cao 2004; Wei and Zhang 2009; Wen 2009) sees precaution, due to population aging, the decline of traditional families as old-age support, weak social security systems or even unbalanced gender ratios, as root cause for excess savings in the private sector. Choi and Mark (2009) and Choi et al. (2008) use state-dependent heterogeneity in discount rates to implement state-dependent saving and cross-country savings differentials in DSGE models. Patient economies lend to foreigners, impatient economies borrow from abroad. Gertler (1999) generates cross-country heterogeneity in savings rates in models with demographic change. Faruqee et al. (2007) impose regional differences in the calibration of the discount factor to generate a steady state with external imbalances. Straub and Thimann (2009) show that weak responses of domestic demand to permanent income shifts are able to generate positive correlation between output growth and the trade balance in reaction to technology and labor supply growth. The time-varying cost of money holding and the time-varying consumption tax that the authors use to proxy frictions in the adjustment of domestic demand are empirically not very intuitive, however.

A second group focuses on policies to promote exports and limit financial vulnerability as potential explanation. Exchange rate management and capital controls have received particular attention in this context. Exchange rate management has been labeled as protectionist measure to promote trade competitiveness and export growth (e.g., Dooley et al. 2007; Faruqee et al. 2007). Foreign reserve accumulation also provides the government with a war chest to defend its currency in speculative attacks (e.g., Cova et al. 2009; Prasad and Rajan 2008).

RMB undervaluation and the impact on external balances remain disputed. The meta-analysis by Korhonen and Ritola (2009) illustrates that most empirical studies (e.g., Cline and Williamson 2009) find the RMB (heavily) undervalued, but Cheung et al. (2007a, b) object that the evidence in those studies is no basis for strong verdicts. External balances depend ultimately on real effective exchange rates (REER), also affected by relative price and wage dynamics. Chinn and Wei (2009) find no strong, robust and monotonic link between nominal exchange rate flexibility and REER adjustment. Dooley et al. (2007), McKinnon (2006, 2007), McKinnon and Schnabl (2009), and Xiao (2008) stress that real appreciation is compatible with flexible and fixed nominal rates, provided that wage and price levels can adjust.

A third group explains saving-investment imbalances as the result of frictions/heterogeneity in financial markets. Caballero et al. (2008) argue that imbalances can be the equilibrium in a world in which regions differ in their capacity to generate financial assets for real investment. Mendoza et al. (2007) consider the impact of financial market development on saving and asset demand. Both papers focus on the US external deficit but do not explain why notably China has become a large international creditor. Real investment in China is high by international standards and has grown in the period of NFA accumulation, which gives limited plausibility to lacking investment opportunities as root cause of capital export.

Song et al. (2009) analyze financial frictions in the form of limited access to credit. Their model features high-productivity private firms that have poor access to capital markets, so that they must finance investment out of internal savings, and low-productivity state enterprises that have much better access to credit. The rising share of private firms implies that domestic saving for future investment is increasing and held in foreign assets. The model does not include the government's role as owner of foreign reserves, however, which dominates China's NFA surplus.

My chapter combines elements of the first and second group. I combine (1) economic "shocks" (economic transition, international integration) and (2) capital controls plus Forex intervention to investigate whether together these elements can explain the pattern of China's NFA accumulation.

5.3   Stylized Facts

The Chinese economy has developed rapidly during the last decades, with real output growth of around 10 percent per year and a steady convergence in per capita income toward industrialized countries (figure 5.1).

The moderate employment growth during the same period highlights the role of capital deepening and TFP growth in this process. The strength of investment in total demand growth also illustrates the importance of capital deepening. The output share of investment demand has increased, whereas the share of private consumption has fallen. The relative size of government consumption has remained fairly stable and net exports increased (figure 5.2).

China's economic transition and convergence coincide with the country's increasing integration in international goods and capital markets. Total trade as the sum of exports and imports and gross asset

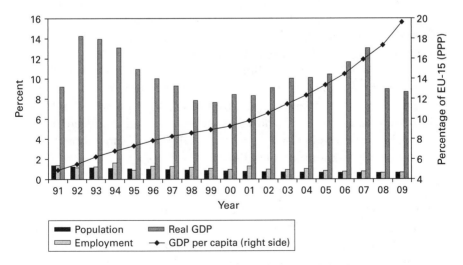

Figure 5.1
Output and per capita income growth. Sources: ECFIN AMECO and IMF IFS.

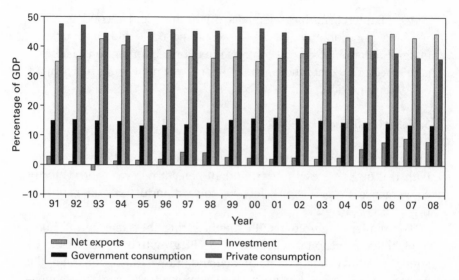

Figure 5.2
Composition of final demand. Source: IMF IFS.

positions as the sum of foreign assets and liabilities have risen relative to GDP (figure 5.3).

Despite strong investment, strong output growth and increasing integration in global markets, China has constantly run trade and current account surpluses since the mid-1990s. Its NFA position has increased accordingly. The government budget has been balanced or in small deficit during those years, implying that excess savings came from households and/or firms (Figure 5.4).

The large NFA position combines even larger Forex reserves of the central bank and a negative net position of the nongovernment (including state-owned companies) sector (figure 5.5). China is typical at least in its net inflow of FDI, which is standard in emerging economies. China has tilted capital inflows toward FDI. Portfolio investment has been less important up to now (Prasad and Rajan 2008).

Restrictions on cross-border capital flows have diminished in recent years. Currency inconvertibility ended in 1994, when the Chinese authorities abolished exchange rate controls on current account transactions, namely trade, interest, and dividend payments, and unified the exchange rate from a system in which multiple rates coexisted in fragmented markets (McKinnon and Schnabl 2009). The decision in 1994 to peg the RMB to the US dollar (figure 5.6) has forced the Chinese

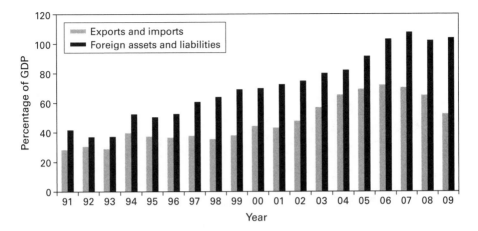

Figure 5.3
Growing economic openness. Sources: ECFIN AMECO, IMF IFS, and Lane and Milesi-Ferretti (2007).

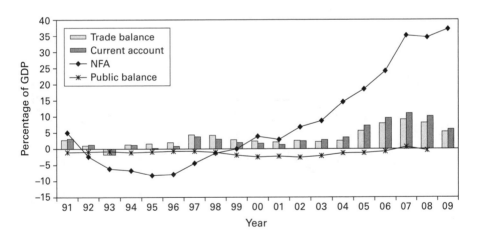

Figure 5.4
Foreign balances and net foreign asset position. Sources: China Statistical Yearbook, IMF IFS, and Lane and Milesi-Ferretti (2007).

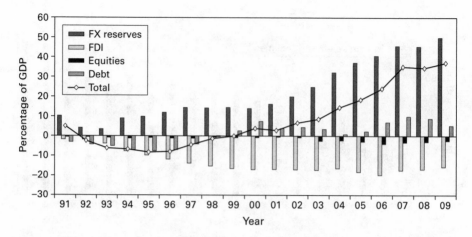

Figure 5.5
Net foreign asset position and components. Sources: IMF IFS for years 2004 to 2009, and
Lane and Milesi-Ferretti (2007) for years 1991 to 2003.

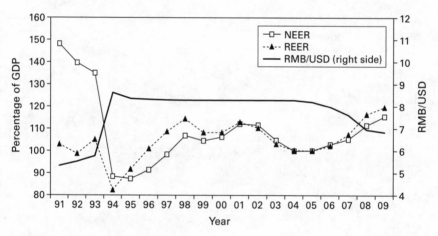

Figure 5.6
RMB exchange rates. Source: IMF IFS.

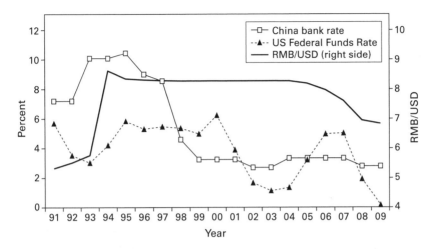

Figure 5.7
Short-term interest rate differential. Source: IMF IFS.

central bank (PBC) into large Forex operations and the accumulation of large Forex reserves in the context of growing capital mobility and pressure toward RMB appreciation. The PBC has sterilized the impact of Forex interventions on domestic money supply by offsetting sales/ purchases of domestic bonds in line with domestic inflation and output targets (e.g., Glick and Hutchinson 2008; Ouyang et al. 2008).

Continuing restrictions on the capital account remain effectively binding. Figure 5.7 shows China–US short-term interest rate differentials in a period of RMB–USD exchange rate stability. The deviation from uncovered interest rate parity (UIP) is a sign that barriers to capital mobility persisted after 1994.[1]

Ma and McCauley (2008) offer a more detailed and sophisticated analysis of the effectiveness of capital controls. They find deviations from UIP of 100 basis points and more in 1997 to 2005 and large, persistent yield differentials for identical assets in onshore versus offshore markets, indicating significant limitations to cross-border arbitrage.

5.4 Modeling Capital Controls and Forex Intervention

The analysis uses the QUEST macroeconomic model.[2] The model regions are populated by representative households and firms and have monetary and fiscal authorities committed to rules-based stabilization policies. Each region has tradable and nontradable goods sectors. Tradable goods produced in one region are imperfect substitutes for goods produced in other regions.

The model includes two types of households: (1) liquidity-constrained households that, in each period, consume the disposable wage and transfer income and (2) finitely lived but forward-looking households that have full access to financial markets and make optimal intertemporal choices. The optimizing households decide on financial and real capital investment and allocate wealth over domestic and foreign assets. Figure 5.8 shows the basic structure of the QUEST model.

I depart from the standard assumption of perfect international capital mobility and introduce imperfect substitutability between domestic and foreign assets to proxy legal and factual restrictions on cross-border capital flows. The portfolio decision is modeled as in Blanchard et al. (2005) and Breuss et al. (2009). In the model it applies to the China block and the decision between RMB and USD asset investment.

The second extension to QUEST is the modeling of Forex intervention as the PBC's instrument for exchange rate management. Forex intervention affects the domestic money supply and is sterilized in line with domestic objectives, notably low inflation and output stability.

The portfolio approach replaces the assumption of perfect substitutability between domestic and foreign assets of identical risk that gives rise to the standard UIP condition. Limited substitutability reduces the responsiveness of capital flows to cross-border return differentials and provides scope for Forex intervention to stabilize the exchange rate.

This chapter describes the portfolio approach and the modeling of Forex intervention in a two-country framework with domestic and foreign economies indexed d and f. Within the four-region model and given the focus on the RMB–USD portfolio decision and RMB–USD exchange rate stabilization, China becomes the domestic economy and the United States the foreign counterpart.

The modeling of goods and labor demand and supply corresponds to the standard QUEST specification. The equations for consumption, employment, productive investment and international trade remain therefore unchanged.

5.4.1 Household Portfolio Decision
Domestic and foreign households diversify portfolios across borders and hold both shares in domestic and foreign capital stocks. Part of the

total value of domestic firms (V^d) is in domestic ownership (V^{dd}), the other part in foreign ownership (V^{df}). The same applies to shares of foreign firms (V^f):

$$V_t^d = V_t^{dd} + V_t^{df}, \tag{5.1}$$

$$V_t^f = V_t^{ff} + V_t^{fd}. \tag{5.2}$$

The values are expressed in real terms as measured in the country in which the firms are located.

For a given expected yield differential, the domestic demand for domestic/foreign assets depends on the home bias (b^d) of investors, the elasticity of portfolio decisions with respect to yield differentials (σ^d) and domestic household wealth (F^d):

$$V_t^{dd} = \left[b^d + \sigma^d \left(r_t^d - r_t^f - E_t \frac{\Delta e_{t+1}}{e_t} \right) \right] \left(F_t^d - \frac{B_t^{dd}}{P_t^d} \right), \tag{5.3}$$

$$e_t \frac{P_t^f}{P_t^d} V_t^{fd} = \left[(1 - b^d) - \sigma^d \left(r_t^d - r_t^f - E_t \frac{\Delta e_{t+1}}{e_t} \right) \right] \left(F_t^d - \frac{B_t^{dd}}{P_t^d} \right). \tag{5.4}$$

The portfolio decision of foreign households is analogous:

$$V_t^{ff} = \left[b^f - \sigma^f \left(r_t^d - r_t^f - E_t \frac{\Delta e_{t+1}}{e_t} \right) \right] \left(F_t^f - \frac{B_t^{ff}}{P_t^f} \right), \tag{5.5}$$

$$\frac{1}{e_t} \frac{P_t^d}{P_t^f} V_t^{df} = \left[(1 - b^f) + \sigma^f \left(r_t^d - r_t^f - E_t \frac{\Delta e_{t+1}}{e_t} \right) \right] \left(F_t^f - \frac{B_t^{ff}}{P_t^f} \right). \tag{5.6}$$

Capital controls can translate into strong home bias (b), namely little steady-state portfolio diversification, and/or low substitution elasticity (σ), namely little adjustment to expected yield differentials.

Real household wealth is the sum of government bond (B) and productive asset (V) holdings. I assume, for simplicity, that private investors hold government debt only of their respective country ($B^{fd} = 0$, $B^{df} = 0$):

$$F_t^d = \frac{B^{dd}}{P_t^d} + V_t^{dd} + e_t \frac{P_t^f}{P_t^d} V_t^{fd}, \tag{5.7}$$

$$F_t^f = \frac{B^{ff}}{P_t^f} + V_t^{ff} + \frac{1}{e_t} \frac{P_t^d}{P_t^f} V_t^{df}. \tag{5.8}$$

In equilibrium the relative supply of domestic/foreign assets must equal the relative demand for domestic/foreign assets (see Blanchard et al. 2005; Breuss et al. 2009):

$$V_t^d - e_t \frac{P_t^f}{P_t^d} V_t^f = V_t^{dd} + V_t^{df} - e_t \frac{P_t^f}{P_t^d} V_t^{ff} - e_t \frac{P_t^f}{P_t^d} V_t^{fd} . \tag{5.9}$$

Combining this equilibrium condition with the demand functions (5.3) to (5.6) establishes a link between the expected yield differential and the aggregate asset allocation:

$$r_t^d - r_t^f - E_t \frac{\Delta e_{t+1}}{e_t}$$
$$= \frac{1}{2} \frac{V_t^d - e_t \frac{P_t^f}{P_t^d} V_t^f + (1 - 2b^d)\left(F_t^d - \frac{B_t^{dd}}{P_t^d}\right) - (1 - 2b^f) e_t \frac{P_t^f}{P_t^d}\left(F_t^f - \frac{B_t^{ff}}{P_t^f}\right)}{\sigma^d \left(F_t^d - \frac{B_t^{dd}}{P_t^d}\right) + \sigma^f e_t \frac{P_t^f}{P_t^d}\left(F_t^f - \frac{B_t^{ff}}{P_t^f}\right)} . \tag{5.10}$$

Equation (5.10) can be seen as generalized interest parity condition and has important policy implications. Low values of the elasticity of substitution (σ) limit the impact of interest rate differentials on exchange rate adjustment, so that capital controls that are effective in restricting yield arbitrage permit the coexistence of exchange rate targeting and monetary policy independence.

5.4.2 Forex Intervention

Current government debt (B) is the sum of past debt, debt service and the primary deficit as the difference between government consumption (G), investment (IG), transfers and subsidies (TR), on the one side, and tax revenues (T) plus central bank profit, on the other side:

$$B_t^d = (1 + r_{t-1}^d) B_{t-1}^d + P_t^{cd} (G_t^d + IG_t^d) + TR_t^d - T_t^d - profit_t^{CBd} . \tag{5.11}$$

Government debt is entirely hold by residents and domestic/foreign central banks:

$$B_t^d = B_t^{dd} + B_t^{dCBd} + B_t^{dCBf} , \tag{5.12}$$

$$B_t^f = B_t^{ff} + B_t^{fCBf} + B_t^{fCBd} . \tag{5.13}$$

Defining China the domestic economy, I simplify further and set foreign central bank stocks of domestic government debt to zero ($B^{dCBf} = 0$).

Changes in the stock of outstanding money must be backed by domestic or foreign bonds on the central bank's balance sheet:

$$B_t^{dCBd} + e_t B_t^{fCBd} = \Delta M_t . \tag{5.14}$$

Central bank profit is the net return on its asset portfolio:

$$profit_t^{CBd} = r_{t-1}^d B_{t-1}^{dCBd} + r_{t-1}^f e_t B_{t-1}^{fCBd} . \tag{5.15}$$

As specified in the budget constraint (5.11), the central bank transfers the profit to the government budget.

Policy objectives determine the portfolio of the central bank in a two-stage process. In the first step, Forex interventions are implemented to stabilize the exchange rate at the target level (γ_e) or the status quo ($\gamma_{\Delta e}$):

$$B_t^{fCBd} = B_{t-1}^{fCBd} - \gamma_e \left(\frac{e_t}{\bar{e}-1} \right) - \gamma_{\Delta e} \left(\frac{e_t}{e_{t-1}-1} \right). \tag{5.16}$$

The Forex interventions determine the central bank's foreign reserve position.

In the second step, the central bank sterilizes the effect of Forex interventions on domestic money supply. It sells/purchases domestic bonds to keep domestic interest rates at levels compatible with inflation and output targets:

$$r_t^d = (1-\rho)(\bar{r}+\bar{\pi}) + \rho r_{t-1}^d + (1-\rho)\gamma_\pi \left(\pi_t^{cd} - \bar{\pi} \right) + (1-\rho)\gamma_y \left(y_t^d - \bar{y} \right). \tag{5.17}$$

The policy interest rate from rule (5.17) and the balance sheet identity (5.14) jointly determine the domestic money supply and the net holding of domestic currency bonds by the central bank.[3]

Accounting for limited capital mobility and Forex intervention departs from the modeling in Faruqee et al. (2007), N'Diaye et al. (2010), and Straub and Thimann (2009), where capital markets are fully integrated and exchange rate targets included in the central bank's interest rate rule. The two-stage modeling of exchange rate and monetary policy approximates the practice of sterilized Forex intervention (Obstfeld and Rogoff 1996). Explicit modeling of the balance sheet (5.14) is also necessary to account for the crucial role of Forex reserves in China's NFA portfolio.

5.4.3 NFA Position

The NFA position in real terms is the difference between foreign assets in domestic ownership and domestic assets in foreign ownership:

$$BWR_t^d = e_t \frac{B_t^{fCBd}}{P_t^d} + e_t \frac{P_t^f}{P_t^d} V_t^{fd} - V_t^{df} , \tag{5.18}$$

$$BWR_t^f = -\frac{1}{e_t}\frac{P_t^d}{P_t^f}BWR_t^d. \tag{5.19}$$

The NFA position (5.18) combines the foreign asset positions of the central bank and the nongovernment sector, while the NFA position of the foreign country is the mirror image of the domestic economy's NFA position.

The NFA position evolves as function of the past NFA position, the net interest income and the trade balance:

$$BWR_t^d = \left(1+r_{t-1}^f\right)e_t\left(\frac{B_{t-1}^{fCBd}}{P_t^d}+\frac{P_t^f}{P_t^d}\frac{P_{t-1}^f}{P_t^f}V_{t-1}^{fd}\right)-\left(1+r_{t-1}^d\right)\frac{P_{t-1}^d}{P_t^d}V_{t-1}^{df}$$

$$+\frac{P_t^{xd}}{P_t^d}X_t^d-\frac{P_t^{md}}{P_t^d}IM_t^d. \tag{5.20}$$

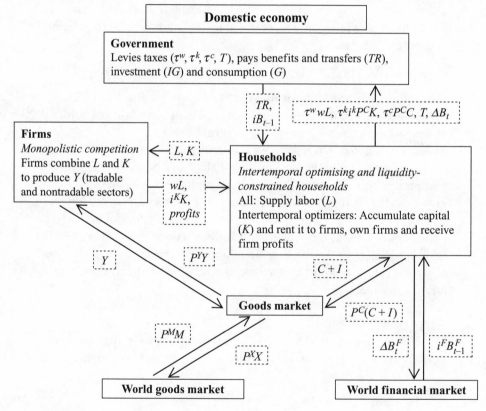

Figure 5.8
QUEST III country block

Net interest inflows and a trade surplus increase the stock of NFA for given outstanding NFA positions.

5.5 Model Calibration

The simulations use an annualized version of QUEST with four model regions, namely China, the United States, the euro area, and the rest of the world (RoW). Table 5.1 summarizes the calibration of the model parameters for the different regions. The regions' economic size, trade

Table 5.1
Calibration of the global model

Parameter	China	United States	Euro area	RoW
Domestic ownership share of domestic capital (b)	0.93	0.99	—	—
Elasticity of portfolio decisions (σ)	0.60	0.60	—	—
Taylor rule interest rate persistence (ρ)	0.45	0.45	0.45	0.45
Taylor rule coefficient on CPI inflation (γ_π)	1.15	1.50	1.50	1.50
Taylor rule coefficient on output gap (γ_y)	0.51	0.05	0.05	0.05
Share of liquidity-constrained consumers	0.70	0.40	0.40	0.40
Habit persistence	0.24	0.24	0.24	0.24
Household planning horizon (years)	30.0	30.0	30.0	30.0
Inverse of elasticity of labor supply	5.00	3.00	5.00	5.00
Size of tradable sector (2004, output share)	0.46	0.22	0.32	0.28
Steady-state trade openness (2004, exports to GDP)	0.42	0.14	0.18	0.18
Price elasticity of exports and imports	1.50	1.50	1.50	1.50
Elasticity of substitution between tradable and nontradable goods	0.50	0.50	0.50	0.50
Share in world output (2004, nominal USD)	0.05	0.29	0.23	0.44
Capital adjustment cost	15.0	6.25	7.50	7.50
Investment adjustment cost	10.0	2.50	3.75	3.75
Labor adjustment cost	6.25	5.00	6.25	6.25
Price adjustment cost for tradable goods	10.0	5.00	6.25	6.25
Price adjustment cost for nontradable goods	15.0	10.0	10.0	10.0
Exports goods price adjustment cost	0.00	0.00	0.00	0.00
Nominal wage adjustment cost	7.50	3.75	7.50	7.50
Degree of forward-looking in domestic pricing	0.90	0.90	0.90	0.90
Degree of forward-looking in export pricing	0.80	0.80	0.80	0.80
Degree of forward-looking in wage setting	0.90	0.90	0.90	0.90

openness, bilateral trade linkages, and sector structure (tradable, non-tradable) come from the GTAP 2004 database. The calibration of the US and euro area blocks draws on estimated US and euro area models presented in Ratto et al. (2009) and Ratto et al. (2010).

Although the RoW is a heterogeneous set of economies, including the rest of Asia, European countries outside the euro area, OPEC members, Latin America and Australia, euro area values are used to calibrate this block. The simplification parallels the practice in, for example, Cova et al. (2009), Faruqee et al. (2007), N'Diaye et al. (2010), and Straub and Thimann (2009), which apply identical values for many of the behavioral parameters and frictions to all model regions.

As limited availability of empirical evidence and estimates also complicates the calibration of the China block, I limit deviations from the US/euro area calibration to the portfolio composition, trade linkages, the sector structure and those parameters for which I could find supportive evidence.

The simulations start from a baseline with balanced trade and NFA positions and investigate the reaction of external balances to transition/integration shocks and policy settings. For simulations starting in the mid-1990s, the balanced baseline seems an admissible approximation.

Calibrating the portfolio structure requires an estimate for cross-border asset positions. I use the Lane and Milesi-Ferretti (2007) data on foreign asset positions in the early 1990s for the starting point. Gross foreign asset holdings of China's nongovernment sector equal 13 percent of GDP and Forex reserves 7 percent of GDP in the baseline. The numbers imply that Chinese households and firms initially hold 97 percent of the Chinese capital stock and 1 percent of worldwide USD assets.[4]

The efficiency of capital controls has arguably weakened over time, but the restrictions are still binding (Ma and McCauley 2008; Prasad 2009a), implying a limited reaction of portfolio decision to expected yield differentials. Direct empirical evidence on the value of σ, the decisive parameter to pin down the real impact of portfolio choices, is at best scarce. Blanchard et al. (2005) and Breuss et al. (2009) use $\sigma = 1$, implying that a 100 basis-point increase in the expected excess yield on foreign assets raises the desired foreign asset share in portfolios by one percentage point. Combining the estimates of RMB–USD yield differentials (1996 to 2006) by Cheung et al. (2008), and Ma and McCauley (2008) with equation (5.10) suggest $\sigma = 0.6$, which I will use in the baseline calibration. This value gives plausible magnitudes of NFA positions under the set of exogenous shocks discussed in section 5.6.

Potential asymmetry in the extent and timing of capital liberalization notwithstanding, the baseline assumes the elasticity for Chinese investment in USD and foreign investment in RMB assets to be equal ($\sigma^d = \sigma^f$).

The central scenario assumes a constant RMB–USD peg over the entire simulation horizon, corresponding to a high value of γ_e. I will then compare the central scenario to scenarios with higher capital mobility and floating RMB rates ($\gamma_e = 0$) to assess the impact of capital controls and Forex intervention on China's external position. Forex intervention targets the bilateral RMB–USD rate, not trade-weighted *effective* exchange rates. Additional weight on exchange rate smoothing is excluded ($\gamma_{\Delta e} = 0$).

The degree of sterilization depends on domestic policy targets expressed in rule (5.17) with $\gamma_\pi = 1.15$ and $\gamma_y = 0.51$ and intrinsic persistence $\rho = 0.45$, which corresponds to persistence of 0.82 at quarterly frequency. The values correspond to the Liu and Zhang (2007) estimate of a monetary policy rule for China (1990 to 2006) and put more weight on the output target than comparable estimates for the euro area and the United States.

On the fiscal side, lump-sum taxes react to deviations of government debt from target and ensure public finance sustainability.[5] Output shares of government consumption and investment are kept constant and public demand evolves in line with output as suggested by figure 5.2. Government investment augments the productivity of private capital and labor. The model does not distinguish between private and state-owned enterprises. All firms are considered part of the private sector and all firm-level investment as private investment.

The China blocks in Faruqee et al. (2007), N'Diaye et al. (2010), and Straub and Thimann (2009) set the share of liquidity-constrained households higher than in the United States and Europe. I follow this practice and use the Zhang and Wan (2004) estimate of 0.7 (1984 to 1998) compared to 0.4 for the other regions, even though the empirical support for tighter constraints in China is not unchallenged (e.g., Modigliani and Cao 2004). Given the lack of empirical evidence suggesting alternative values, consumer habit persistence is kept at 0.24 as for the other model regions and corresponds to 0.7 at quarterly basis. As in the other model regions, the planning horizon of intertemporal optimising households is set to 30 years.

The price elasticity of export/import demand is an important parameter in the context of external balances. Although one might expect the elasticity to be low on the import (commodities, investment goods) and

high on the export side (low product differentiation), empirical estimates lend little support and are often sensitive to alternative data
sources. Cheung et al. (2009) estimate Chinese imports to fall by 0.4 to
1.5 percent per percentage increase in import prices and exports to fall
by less than one to one, or even to rise, when export prices increase
(1993 to 2006). Estimates on US data for bilateral China–US trade
suggest an elasticity of 1.0 to 1.3 for Chinese imports (insignificant with
Chinese data) and 0.8 to 1.3 for exports (1.6 to 2.0 with Chinese data).
Recent estimates by Ahmed (2009) find a price elasticity of Chinese
exports of around 1.5 (1961 to 2009). In the light of this evidence, the
calibration uses a price elasticity of 1.5 for Chinese trade as for the other
world regions.[6] The elasticity of substitution between tradable and
nontradable goods is set to 0.5 as in Cova et al. (2008, 2009) and Faruqee
et al. (2007) and in the range of the estimates by Mendoza (1995) and
Stockman and Tesar (1995), so that tradable and nontradable goods are
complements rather than substitutes in domestic final demand.

The scarcity of comparable evidence on nominal and real rigidities
leads Cova et al. (2009), Faruqee et al. (2007), N'Diaye et al. (2010), and
Straub and Thimann (2009) to calibrate nominal and real product and
factor market rigidities in China and emerging Asia as for the other
world regions. This chapter introduces some differentiation. Comparable
evidence on product and factor market rigidities is certainly scarce and
sketchy but not nonexistent. The OECD indicators of product market
regulation (PMR) and employment protection legislation (EPL) provide,
for example, some indications (Herd et al. 2010; Woelfl et al. 2009).

Product markets in China seem still tightly regulated. The overall
PMR score is 3.3, on a scale 0 to 6 where high values indicate strong
regulation, compared to 0.8 in the United States and 1.3 in the euro
area. The sub-indicator "State involvement in business operations"
has score 3.9 (0.9 in the United States, 1.3 in the euro area) and "Barriers to entrepreneurship" score 2.9 (1.2 in the United States, 1.3 in
the euro area). Price controls, command and control regulation, and
the administrative burden on start-ups seem particularly pronounced.
China's overall EPL score of 2.8 on the 0 to 6 scale is above the US
score (0.9) and close to the euro area values, although limited enforcement of labor laws and minimum wage requirements may increase
de facto flexibility.

Based on China's relative position in the PMR and EPL rankings, I
set the parameter values for price, investment and capital adjustment
costs above and parameter values for wage and employment adjust-

ment costs equal to the euro area calibration. As the concepts of PMR and EPL dos not coincide with the concept of adjustment costs in QUEST, the choice is an informal guess.

The elasticity of labor supply is set to 0.33 in the United States and 0.2 in China, Europe, and the RoW. The value for China, which may look surprisingly low given priors on the flexibility of Chinese workers, corresponds to the firm-level estimates (1984 to 1990) by Fleisher and Wang (2004).

Regarding inflation and output persistence, Mehrotra et al. (2007) estimate New Keynesian Phillips curves for China that indicate roughly equal weight for lags and leads of inflation. Liu and Zhang (2007) find lagged output and inflation to dominate the output and inflation equations of a small estimated model of the Chinese economy. These reduced-form estimates are not very informative for calibration, however. Inflation and output persistence may capture inertia in shocks and other variables rather than backward-looking expectations. Many reduced-form estimates for the United States and Europe find similar weights on lagged inflation and output. Given the persistence embodied in adjustment costs and the lack of further evidence, the degree of forward-looking is kept at the level of the other regions.

5.6   Simulations

Simulations with the global model illustrate the impact of exogenous shocks and economic policies (capital controls, Forex intervention) on China's external position and allow comparison with the stylized facts of section 5.3. I focus on a set of shocks with major impact on China's economic transition that may explain the country's external position. The domestic/transition and foreign/globalization shocks are as follows:

• TFP growth: Bosworth and Collins (2008) estimate an annualized TFP growth rate of 3.9 (3.6) percent in the period 1993 to 2004 (1978 to 2004). Li (2009) finds a similar annual rate of 4.3 percent for the period 1984 to 2006. I use the Bosworth and Collins (2008) estimate of 3.9 percent and decompose it into 2.4 percent TFP convergence toward the leading countries and the 1.5 percent world trend TFP growth that is incorporated in the model. TFP convergence is tilted toward the tradable sector, where 3/4 of the TFP convergence occurs, as opposed to the nontradable sector, which contributes 1/4.[7]

• Labor force growth: China's labor force has grown moderately compared to real output growth. I rely on data from the National Bureau of Statistics of China that record an average annual growth rate of 1.2 percent since the early 1990s. Bosworth and Collins (2008) report the same annual rate for the period 1993 to 2004.

• Labor migration: The migration of workers from rural areas to urban centers and from agriculture and subsistence to manufacturing and services is characteristic for China's economic transition and a major source of measured income growth. According to data from the National Statistical Office, the share of agriculture in total employment has fallen from 54 to 40 percent and the share of manufacturing (services) risen from 23 (23) to 27 (33) percent between 1994 and 2008. I use these numbers that imply an average annual increase in the share of nonagriculture official employment of 1.1 percentage points. Labor reallocation toward industry and services increases the labor supply in the more productive parts of the economy. It also relaxes the liquidity constraints on private households and improves their access to capital markets. The workers that move from informal/subsistence work to manufacturing and service sectors have zero initial wealth. According to the estimate of saving/borrowing constraints in section 5.5, 70 percent of the migrant households will remain liquidity constrained, whereas 30 percent obtain access to financial markets and the opportunity to accumulate positive wealth.

• Household savings: Many authors attribute China's capital exports to the rise in private savings, which is certainly correct. The external surplus reflects an excess of domestic savings over domestic investment. Investment rates have been high and growing in recent years, and the government budget is close to balance or in moderate deficit. Song et al. (2009) attribute the high savings to borrowing constraints that force private firms to finance future investment out of internal savings. Many others (e.g., Blanchard and Giavazzi 2005; Chamon and Prasad 2010; Feng et al. 2009; Prasad 2009b) link the surplus to precautionary saving in the context of poorly developed social security and pension systems. Wei and Zhang (2009) even establish a link between household savings and regional gender imbalances. I include increasing private savings rates as shock to the rate of time preference, namely a decline in the preference for the present. The shock is calibrated to replicate the average annual 0.4 percentage-point increase in the private savings rate (1994 to 2008) reported by the National Bureau of Statistics of China, which is somewhat lower than the annualized 0.6 percentage-point increase (1995 to 2005) in Chamon and Prasad (2010). In line with the econometric evidence in Horioka and Wan (2007), the savings rate is assumed to remain high in the foreseeable future.

• Export demand growth: China has increasingly integrated in world trade, amplified by its WTO accession in 2001. Growing world trade has therefore also increased the demand for Chinese exports. I calibrate the path of world trade to the 8 percentage-point increase of the world import-to-GDP share, from 20 percent in 1994 to (estimated) 28 percent in 2010. The calibration implies a comparable increase in Chinese export demand. Rising demand for Chinese exports may be linked to the removal of trade barriers, growing quality and increasing product differentiation.

This set of five shocks is certainly not exhaustive, but it captures important elements of China's economic transition.[8] Strict exogeneity of the shocks may be challenged, however. FDI inflows and factor reallocation may explain significant parts of aggregate TFP growth. Labor migration is a response to the real wage growth and widening regional and sectoral wage differentials. The increase in household saving rates is not only a consequence of exogenous precaution but also of personal income growth.[9] Treating transition/integration trends as exogenous shocks is a simplification. It may exaggerate or understate actual disturbances, depending on whether the shocks tend to reinforce or offset each other in their impact on measured TFP growth, labor supply and savings. In the future, an estimated model for China would ideally provide a more rigorous distinction between the roles of exogenous shocks and endogenous adjustment.

Simulations start with the "second phase" (McKinnon and Schnabl 2009) of Chinese exchange rate policy in 1995, with RMB convertibility for current account operations and a RMB–USD peg. Capital controls and the fixed RMB–USD exchange rate are the policy baseline. This policy baseline is also applied to the years since 2005 during which the RMB has gradually revalued vis-à-vis the USD. I extrapolate trends in the exogenous shocks up to 2019 as a hypothetical, but implausible completion of economic transition in 2010 would distort the simulation results. Shortening the extrapolation horizon to 2014 would not change the results in qualitative terms and only marginally affect the quantitative outcomes. The core scenarios assume perfect foresight of the exogenous shocks/trends. The robustness checks include scenarios in which agents update their beliefs about the future path of the exogenous shocks, or in which departures from status quo are continuous surprises.

The simulations first use the policy baseline of limited capital mobility and fixed exchange rates (section 5.6.1) and then turn to an analysis of how capital mobility and exchange rate flexibility would affect the results, notably with respect to China's current account and NFA position (section 5.6.2).

5.6.1   Capital Controls and Fixed Exchange Rates

I first look at the policy baseline of limited capital mobility and RMB–USD exchange rate fixation, for which figure 5.9 shows the impact of the five shocks. The figure provides a fairly accurate description of China's NFA accumulation, with circa 30 percent of GDP in the simulations and 37 percent of GDP in the data for 2009, and also replicates the coincidence of massive Forex reserves, circa 54 percent of GDP in the simulations and 50 percent of GDP in the data for 2009, with (after some initial increase) negative net private sector positions. The REER

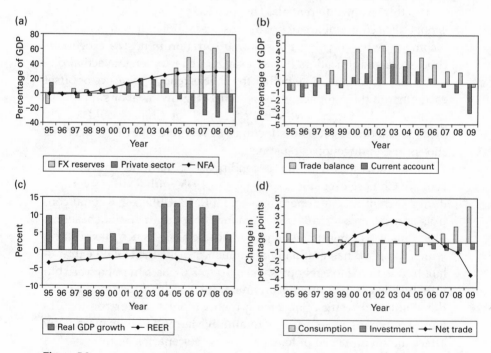

Figure 5.9
Adjustment with RMB pegged to the USD. Note: A fall in the REER indicates real effective appreciation.

appreciation implies pressure on the RMB–USD revaluation. To avoid an appreciation of the RMB, the PBC sells RMB and buys USD assets, leading to the accumulation of large Forex reserves at the central bank.

Figure 5.9 also replicates the surplus in the current account and the synchronized movement of the current account and the trade balance. Average annual output growth is lower than reported in the data, but the time paths have similar shape. Contrary to the more monotonous empirical trends (figure 5.2), the simulations provide alternating movements in the investment-to-output share, the consumption-to-output share, and the trade balance.

Separating the individual shocks illustrates the different impact of these components.[10] TFP and labor supply growth increase the return to productive investment and trigger net capital inflows, which manifest in negative current account and trade balances and negative NFA positions. The central bank intervenes to avoid RMB appreciation relative to the USD in the initial phase of real appreciation. The initial Forex reserve accumulation reverts into decumulation as REER appreciation comes to an end. Domestic households become wealthier and the consumption-to-output share increases.

Labor migration to manufacturing and service sectors and the growth of precautionary savings have opposite effects. The migrant workforce has zero initial assets and starts saving to accumulate positive wealth. Similarly higher precautionary saving increases private sector asset positions. External balances improve and the consumption-to-output share declines during the savings growth. Private foreign investment drives overall NFA accumulation. Rising supply of savings exerts pressure to depreciate on the RMB. The PBC would sell Forex reserves to avoid RMB devaluation. Only the reversal in the pressure to devalue in later years reverses the pattern to Forex reserve accumulation and declining nongovernment foreign asset holdings.[11]

The export demand shock, finally, comes closest to individual replication of the NFA pattern. Increasing export demand leads to strong REER appreciation. The central bank accumulates massive Forex reserves to maintain the RMB–USD peg. The shock leads to disconnect between the trade balance and the current account, however. Given the rise in the terms of trade and the positive wealth effect from REER appreciation, import growth exceeds export growth and the trade balance deteriorates. Thanks to the NFA yield, the current account remains in surplus.

External imbalances are, by definition, an equilibrium phenomenon. Current account surpluses/deficits require both supply of and demand for excess savings. Nevertheless, the imbalances may be driven by either excess savings or excessive savings demand. The first scenario is a situation in which global savings demand only follows from a general equilibrium response, without any additional savings demand shock. Excess savings supply reduces world interest rates, which in turn discourages saving and encourages borrowing and investment in other regions.

The NFA position in figure 5.9 suggests that China's external position may indeed be determined by excessive savings in the context of capital controls and RMB–USD fixation. The combination of domestic transition shocks and growing world trade, which does not result from an unsustainable expansion of world demand but from the general increase in openness, replicates the NFA dynamics fairly well, without any asset preference, investment bubble, or fiscal profligacy shocks abroad.

5.6.2 Capital Mobility and Exchange Rate Flexibility

I now turn to the contribution of macroeconomic policy to NFA accumulation, specifically to the impact of capital controls and exchange rate fixation.

Figure 5.10 shows adjustment to the same set of shocks as in figure 5.9, but with higher capital mobility. The elasticity of cross-border capital flows is increased from $\sigma = 0.6$ in the baseline to $\sigma = 10$. The higher elasticity implies more extreme asset positions of private and government sectors, whereas the total NFA, the current account and trade balances, and the demand composition remain largely unaffected.[12]

The NFA decomposition suggests that relatively low values of σ are appropriate to replicate past developments. It also illustrates the limits of successful Forex intervention. Defending the RMB–USD peg under growing capital mobility requires a massive Forex accumulation that goes far beyond the current and, arguably, beyond viable levels.

Figure 5.11 shows adjustment to the same set of shocks under hypothetical RMB floating, keeping capital mobility low at $\sigma = 0.6$. The RMB gradually appreciates by circa 30 percent vis-à-vis the USD. REER appreciation is stronger than under the RMB–USD peg in figure 5.9. China becomes a net foreign debtor as capital flows into the country to profit from growth in TFP and complementary factor supply and from expected RMB appreciation. The trade balance deteriorates with relative price adjustment and the positive wealth effect from RMB appreciation, but the current account moves to positive territory in the medium term as net interest payments to foreigners decrease with

(a)

(b)

(c)

(d)

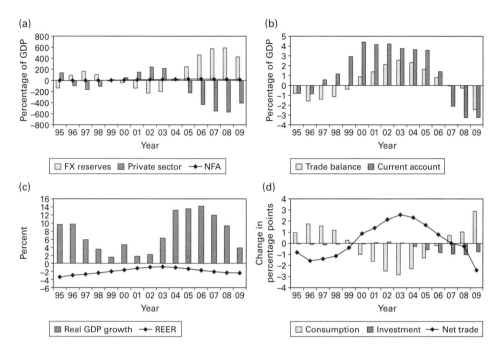

Figure 5.10
Adjustment with high capital mobility. Note: A fall in the REER indicates real effective appreciation.

falling domestic interest rates. The volume of NFA positions is much smaller than for adjustment under the currency peg.

Real output growth in figure 5.11 is almost identical to the scenario with RMB–USD peg, but the composition of demand markedly differs. Domestic consumption increases and net exports fall, suggesting that higher exchange rate flexibility is indeed a major policy lever for rebalancing growth toward the domestic sector.

The rebalancing toward domestic demand comes with a shift in production from tradable to nontradable goods. The positive wealth effect of real effective appreciation raises domestic consumption, and the expansion of domestic demand at the expense of lower export growth increases the demand for nontradables due to the complementarity between tradable and nontradable goods in final domestic demand.

Production factors can move from the tradable to the nontradable sector in the model. Sectoral reallocation is subject to quadratic adjustment costs on sectoral labor, investment and capital, and a time-to-build constraint on the sector-specific capital stock. The adjustment

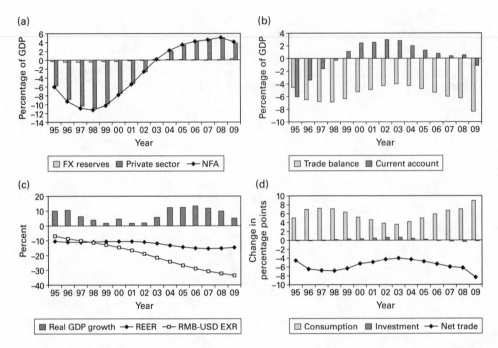

Figure 5.11
Adjustment with RMB floating. Note: A RMB–USD EXR (REER) fall indicates (real effective) appreciation.

costs dampen short-term fluctuations and delay/smooth the adjustment to permanent changes.

The reallocation of production factors in the model is supported by estimates by Guo and N'Diaye (2009) about the response of sectoral employment shares to income growth, technology, and relative prices. In this context Guo and N'Diaye (2009) emphasize that structural reforms facilitating sectoral factor reallocation support the rebalancing toward domestic demand.

Combining perfect capital mobility and full exchange rate flexibility boils down to the standard QUEST model without portfolio approach in which the NFA position reflects solely investment decisions of the nongovernment sector. Standard QUEST results for external balances and growth rebalancing under the set of transition/integration shocks are very close to figure 5.11. The standard model lacks the negative valuation effect on gross asset positions, which results in stronger medium-term NFA positions. After 15 years, the NFA surplus is twice as high as in figure 5.11.

Figure 5.11, indeed, also highlights the negative valuation effect, namely the loss of value on foreign assets in domestic currency terms under RMB appreciation, as potent political obstacle to RMB flexibility and an argument for gradual approaches.

5.6.3 Robustness Checks

This section delivers robustness checks to test the sensitivity of the simulation results with respect to core assumptions. The checks address three aspects of the calibration, namely the symmetry of capital controls, the relatively low elasticity of labor supply and the perfect-foresight assumption.

Contrary to the baseline calibration, capital controls may display some asymmetry. While the Chinese government has encouraged FDI inflows early on, it has been more reluctant to allow domestic firms and household to invest abroad (e.g., Glick and Hutchinson 2008). Figure 5.12 shows that asymmetry in the cross-border mobility of capital does not alter the aggregate dynamics. Exchange rate fixation

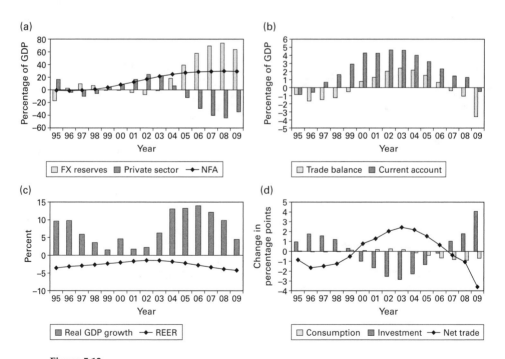

Figure 5.12
Adjustment with asymmetric capital mobility. Note: A fall in the REER indicates real effective appreciation.

with lower outward ($\sigma^d = 0.3$) and higher inward ($\sigma^f = 0.9$) capital mobility generates almost identical adjustment, only with somewhat stronger Forex reserve accumulation at the central bank and somewhat higher net foreign debt in the private sector.

There is a widespread prior that Chinese households display a high elasticity of labor supply, coming close to the Lewis model with unlimited labor supply at fixed wages (Fields 2004; Lewis 1954). Despite this prior, Fleisher and Wang (2004) estimate a rather low elasticity of labor supply with respect to wages of around 1/5. Neither does the fact that post-1994 wage growth in Chinese manufacturing has followed the growth in labor productivity (McKinnon, 2006), which corresponds to the simulation results, support the idea of infinite labor supply at given wages in the official economy.

Nevertheless, figure 5.13 shows simulation outcomes for more elastic labor supply. I increase the elasticity from 0.2 to 0.33, which is the value used for the US economy. The simulation results for external stock and

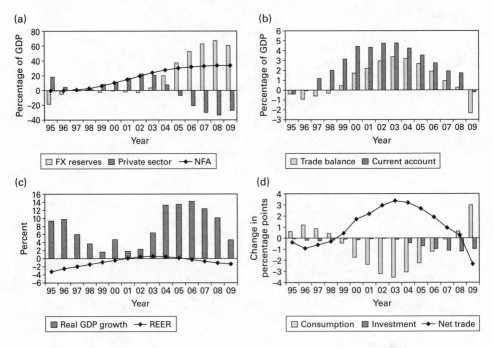

Figure 5.13
Adjustment with more elastic labor supply. Note: A fall in the REER indicates real effective appreciation.

flow balances, output growth, and demand composition are practically identical to figure 5.9 with the baseline calibration.

The final variants replace the assumption of perfect foresight with regard to the exogenous shocks that underlies the previous simulations. An intermediate scenario combines some forecasting of future changes with a regular updating of beliefs. The extreme alternative assumes that changes in exogenous variables in each period come as surprise and that agents expect the exogenous variables to remain at their status quo values thereafter.

Figure 5.14 presents the intermediate scenario. At each period of time agents do not know ex ante the actual size of the shocks. But, although the actual shocks are surprises, agents forecast the future path of the exogenous variables. Specifically, I assume that agents extrapolate the current change over the subsequent three years and, lacking reliable long-term information, assume the exogenous variables to remain constant thereafter.

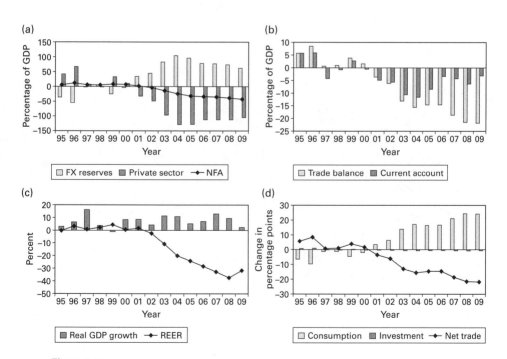

Figure 5.14
Surprise shocks and three-year extrapolation of growth rates. Note: A fall in the REER indicates real effective appreciation.

Backward-looking expectation formation has considerable impact on the adjustment dynamics. It generates higher net creditor and debtor positions of government and nongovernment sectors compared to figure 5.9. The central bank intervenes to prevent RMB appreciation, but the NFA turns negative in the medium term. Domestic interest rates start rising sharply after six years as inflation rises, implying large net interest payments to the rest of the world and deteriorating external balances.

The simple extrapolation of status quo levels after surprise shocks in each period (figure 5.15) generates a net creditor position of the private sector together with a decumulation of Forex reserves by the central bank. In the absence of positive expectations about future TFP and factor supply growth that would enhance the profitability of domestic investment, households export their savings. Equally, capital inflows from abroad are more modest than with higher expected profitability. Contrary to the benchmark scenario of figure 5.9, the central bank intervenes to avoid depreciation, instead of appreciation, of the RMB.

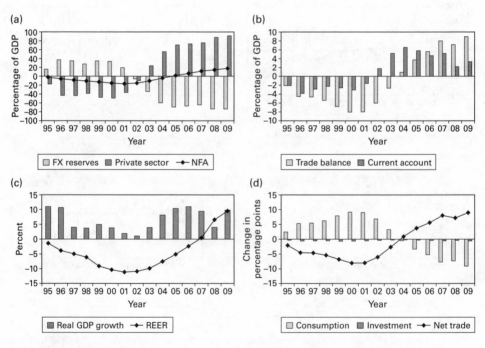

Figure 5.15
Surprise shocks and extrapolation of status quo. Note: A fall in the REER indicates real effective appreciation

Taken together, figures 5.14 and 5.15 show that the nature of exogenous shocks/expectations (foresight versus extrapolation) influences simulation results significantly. At the same time, it seems plausible to assume that households and firms have rather realistic expectations about the long-term trends of economic transition and globalization.

5.7   Conclusions

The chapter uses a multi-region DSGE model of the world economy (China, United States, euro area, RoW) to look at China's particular role as rapidly growing emerging economy and large international creditor.

The model features two key elements of Chinese macroeconomic policy, namely a portfolio approach that distinguishes gross/net and private/public foreign asset positions and includes limited capital mobility as modeling device for cross-border capital controls, and exchange rate management in the form of sterilized Forex intervention. The rest of the model is fairly standard in that it includes only distortions/frictions in the China block that are standard also in the EU and US settings.

The chapter selects a set of shocks that cover important aspects of China's economic transition and integration in the world economy, namely TFP catch-up, labor supply growth, labor reallocation, precautionary savings, and export growth, and investigates its ability to match key stylized facts, namely the large-scale NFA accumulation that combines even higher Forex positions of the central bank with a debtor position of the nongovernment sector, persistent surpluses in the trade balance and the current account, high real output growth, and declining (increasing) domestic demand shares of consumption (investment).

The simulations show the set of shocks to replicate China's external position quite well in the benchmark setting with limited capital mobility and Forex intervention, though the fit is less satisfactory for domestic demand shares. The fact that the set of domestic and trade shocks replicates the large NFA and Forex positions supports the hypothesis that China's surplus represents shifts in domestic saving supply, rather than exogenous shifts in foreign savings demand.

The simulations also highlight the importance of effective capital controls, namely binding restrictions on cross-border capital flows, for the viability of China's exchange rate management. Increasing cross-border capital mobility (i.e., financial liberalization) would require the central bank to accumulate Forex reserves well beyond current and, arguably, beyond viable levels.

Finally, the analysis suggests that greater flexibility of the RMB exchange rate could reduce China's net creditor position and contribute to a change in China's growth composition from exports to domestic demand. Rebalancing requires a factor reallocation from tradable to nontradable production to meet increasing nontradable demand, underlining that sectoral labor and capital mobility is a precondition for a successful transition.

Robustness checks indicate that neither the potential asymmetry of capital controls nor alternative values for the elasticity of labor supply affect the results in significant ways. Assumptions on expectation formation (perfect foresight versus simple extrapolation) appear crucial, however. Specifically, the good performance of the model in replicating China's external position is conditional on the assumption that agents have fairly accurate expectations about the long-term nature of transition and globalization trends.

The analysis leaves ample space for improvement, refinement and further research. Additional work on the empirical validation of the model structure, the parameter and the shock calibration would certainly increase the analytical value of the results. Future studies would ideally be based on a coherently estimated model of the Chinese economy.

Notes

Disclaimer: The views in the chapter are those of the author and should not be attributed to the European Commission. I thank Yin-Wong Cheung, Jakob de Haan, Ulrich Jochheim, Guonan Ma, Robert McCauley, Heikki Oksanen, James Reade, Werner Roeger, Andreas Steiner, István Székely, Jan in't Veld, and participants of the CESifo Summer Institute 2010 for valuable comments and suggestions.

1. This statement requires some qualification. Perfect capital mobility implies interest rate convergence if, and only if, the RMB–USD peg is credible and differentials in country risk premia narrow or disappear over time.

2. See Ratto et al. (2009) for a detailed description of QUEST III.

3. Money supply rules could be used as an alternative mechanism to relate domestic monetary conditions to stabilization objectives. Money supply rules leading to identical interest rate levels as the Taylor-type rule (5.17) would imply identical monetary conditions.

4. Given that capital exports to Hong Kong, Macau and Taiwan are partly redirected and reinvested, Li (2009) cautions against overestimation of mainland China's gross foreign asset position.

5. Using an alternative setting in which labor income taxes are adjusted to guarantee the sustainability of public debt has little impact on the results in section 6.

6. Export and import price elasticities have possibly increased over time, especially in the context of China's WTO accession in 2001. The simulations do not consider parameter

drift, however, but instead include growing world trade as a push to Chinese export demand.

7. It should be mentioned that the annual TFP growth estimate of 3.9 percent is at the upper end of available numbers. Based on a critical review of official Chinese statistics, other authors have provided more modest estimates. Hu (2010) finds annual TFP growth of only 1.5 percent (1988 to 2008) on the basis of revised output and factor input data. Young (2003) estimates annual TFP growth of 1.4 percent (1978 to 1998) with strong variation across sectors. Dollar and Wei (2007), and Hsieh and Klenow (2009) find widespread misallocation of production factors across firms and industries. Hsieh and Klenow (2009) estimate that factor reallocation within industries alone could raise Chinese TFP by 30 to 50 percent.

8. Additional elements include, for example, investment incentives. The availability of cheap credit from state-owned banks and cheap complementary factors (land, energy) supports investment and capital deepening. The government has also granted significant tax breaks to foreign and joint venture investors to attract FDI and related know-how (Prasad 2009a, b). I do not include simulations for such investment incentives, however, since changes in their net size since the mid-1990s are not obvious, and since constructing a time profile of investment incentives is beyond the reach of this chapter.

9. The general finding by Gruber and Kamin (2007) that higher youth and elderly population ratios lower the current account balance supports a role for exogenous savings shocks. Economies with the prospect of population aging and increasing dependency ratios have an incentive to accumulate wealth and dissave in future periods.

10. See the working paper version (Vogel 2010) for graphic and more extensive presentation of the results for the individual shocks.

11. Results for the savings shock are compatible with econometric evidence that the current account balance reacts negatively to dependency ratios (Cheung et al. 2010; Chinn and Ito 2008; Chinn and Prasad 2003; Ma and Haiwen 2009). Economies with lower dependency ratio have higher savings rates. Precautionary households save income to accumulate wealth and decumulate wealth when their average incomes decline.

12. The small impact of higher elasticity values on total NFA and current account positions harmonises with the inconclusiveness of econometric evidence on the issue. Chinn and Ito (2008) find the impact of financial openness on current account balances to be insignificant or, in emerging economies, negative. Chinn and Prasad (2003) find a positive impact of capital controls on the current account balance in industrial countries. Chinn and Wei (2009) find a positive impact of financial openness on current account positions for fixed and floating exchange rates but not for intermediate regimes of exchange rate management. The impact of the exchange rate regime on external balances, which is insignificant in Chinn and Wei (2009), should depend on the underlying shocks, namely on whether exchange rate management prevents or moderates either appreciation or depreciation of the currency.

References

Ahmed, S. 2009. Are Chinese exports sensitive to changes in the exchange rate? Discussion paper 987. Board of Governors of the Federal Reserve System International Finance.

Bems, R., L. Dedola, and F. Smets. 2007. US imbalances: The role of technology and policy. *Journal of International Money and Finance* 26 (4): 523–45.

Blanchard, O. 2007. Current account deficits in rich countries. *IMF Staff Papers* 54 (2): 191–219.

Blanchard, O., and F. Giavazzi. 2005. Rebalancing growth in China: A three-handed approach. Discussion Paper 5403. CEPR, London.

Blanchard, O., F. Giavazzi, and F. Sa. 2005. International investors, the US current account, and the dollar. *Brookings Papers on Economic Activity* 36 (1): 1–49.

Bosworth, B., and S. Collins. 2008. Accounting for growth: Comparing China and India. *Journal of Economic Perspectives* 22 (1): 45–66.

Bracke, Th., and M. Fidora. 2008. Global liquidity glut or global savings glut? Working Paper 911. ECB, Frankfurt.

Breuss, F., W. Roeger, and J. in 't Veld. 2009. Global impact of a shift in foreign reserves to euros. *Empirica* 36 (1): 101–22.

Bussière, M., M. Fratzscher, and G. Mueller. 2005. Productivity shocks, budget deficits and the current account. Working Paper 509. ECB, Frankfurt.

Caballero, R., E. Farhi, and P. Gourinchas. 2008. An equilibrium model of global imbalances and low interest rates. *American Economic Review* 98 (1): 358–93.

Chamon, M., and E. Prasad. 2010. Why are saving rates of urban households in China rising? *American Economic Journal, Macroeconomics* 2 (1): 93–130.

Cheung, C., D. Furceri, and E. Rusticelli. 2010. Structural and cyclical factors behind current-account balances. Economics Department Working Paper 775. OECD, Paris.

Cheung, Y.-W., M. Chinn, and E. Fujii. 2007a. The fog encircling the renminbi debate. *Singapore Economic Review* 52 (3): 403–18.

Cheung, Y.-W., M. Chinn, and E. Fujii. 2007b. The overvaluation of renminbi undervaluation. *Journal of International Money and Finance* 26 (5): 762–85.

Cheung, Y.-W., D. Tam, and M. Yiu. 2008. Does the Chinese interest rate follow the US interest rate? *International Journal of Finance and Economics* 13 (1): 53–67.

Cheung, Y.-W., M. Chinn, and E. Fujii. 2009. China's current account and exchange rate. Working Paper 14673. NBER, Cambridge, MA.

Chinn, M., and E. Prasad. 2003. Medium-term determinants of current accounts in industrial and developing countries: An empirical exploration. *Journal of International Economics* 59 (1): 47–76.

Chinn, M., and H. Ito. 2008. Global current account imbalances: American fiscal policy versus East Asian savings. *Review of International Economics* 16 (3): 479–98.

Chinn, M., and S. Wei. 2009. A faith-based initiative: Do we really know that a flexible exchange rate regime facilitates current account adjustment? Working Paper 14420. NBER, Cambridge, MA.

Choi, H., and N. Mark. 2009. Trending current accounts. Working Paper 15244. NBER, Cambridge, MA.

Choi, H., N. Mark, and D. Sul. 2008. Endogenous discounting, the world saving glut and the U.S. current account. *Journal of International Economics* 75 (1): 30–53.

Cline, W. and Williamson, J. 2009. New estimates of fundamental equilibrium exchange rates. *Policy Brief 09–10*. Washington, DC: Peterson Institute for International Economics.

Corsetti, G., and G. Mueller. 2006. Twin deficits: Squaring theory, evidence and common sense. *Economic Policy* 21 (48): 597–638.

Cova, P., M. Pisani, N. Batini, and A. Rebucci. 2008. Productivity and global imbalances: The role of nontradable total factor productivity in advanced economies. *IMF Staff Papers* 55 (2): 312–25.

Cova, P., M. Pisani, and A. Rebucci. 2009. Global imbalances: The role of emerging Asia. *Review of International Economics* 17 (4): 716–33.

Dollar, D., and A. Kraay. 2006. Neither a borrower nor a lender: Does China's zero net foreign asset position make economic sense? *Journal of Monetary Economics* 53 (5): 943–71.

Dollar, D., and S. Wei. 2007. Das (wasted) Kapital, firm ownership and investment efficiency in China. Working Paper 07/09. IMF, Washington, DC.

Dooley, M., D. Folkerts-Landau, and P. Garber. 2007. Direct investment, rising real wages and the absorption of excess labor in the periphery. In R. Clarida, ed., *G-7 Current Account Imbalances: Sustainability and Adjustment*. Chicago: Chicago University Press, 103–30.

Faruqee, H., D. Laxton, D. Muir, and P. Pesenti. 2007. Smooth landing or crash? Model-based scenarios of global current account rebalancing. In R. Clarida, ed., *G-7 Current Account Imbalances: Sustainability and Adjustment*. Chicago: Chicago University Press, 377–455.

Feng, J., L. He, and H. Sato. 2009. Public pensions and household saving: Evidence from China. BOFIT Discussion Paper 2/2009. Bank of Finland, Helsinki.

Fields, G. 2004. Dualism in the labour market: A perspective on the Lewis model after half a century. *Manchester School* 72 (6): 724–35.

Fleisher, B., and X. Wang. 2004. Skill differentials, return to schooling, and market segmentation in a transition economy: The case of mainland China. *Journal of Development Economics* 73 (1): 315–28.

Gertler, M. 1999. Government debt and social security in a life-cycle economy. *Carnegie-Rochester Conference Series on Public Policy* 50 (1): 61–110.

Glick, R., and M. Hutchinson. 2008. Navigating the trilemma: Capital flows and monetary policy in China. Working Paper 2008–32. Federal Reserve Bank of San Francisco.

Gruber, J., and S. Kamin. 2007. Explaining the global pattern of current account imbalances. *Journal of International Money and Finance* 26 (4): 500–22.

Guo, K., and P. N'Diaye. 2009. Employment effects of growth rebalancing in China. Working Paper 09/169. IMF, Washington, DC.

Herd, R., V. Koen, and A. Reutersward. 2010. China's labour market in transition: Job creation, migration and regulation. Economic Department Working Paper 749. OECD, Paris.

Horioka, Ch., and J. Wan. 2007. The determinants of household saving in China: A dynamic panel analysis of provincial data. *Journal of Money, Credit and Banking* 39 (8): 2077–96.

Hsieh, Ch., and P. Klenow. 2009. Misallocation and manufacturing TFP in China and India. *Quarterly Journal of Economics* 124 (4): 1403–48.

Hu, H. 2010. Accounting for China's growth in 1952–2008. Paper presented at the 2010 AEA Meeting, January 2–5, 2010, Atlanta.

Korhonen, I., and M. Ritola. 2009. Renminbi misaligned: Results from meta regressions. BOFIT Discussion Paper 13/2009. Bank of Finland, Helsinki.

Lane, Ph., and G. Milesi-Ferretti. 2007. The external wealth of nations mark II. *Journal of International Economics* 73 (2): 223–50.

Lee, J. and McKibbin, W. 2006. Domestic investment and external imbalances in East Asia. Brookings Discussion Papers in International Economics 172. Brookings Institution, Washington, DC.

Lewis, A. 1954. Economic development with unlimited supply of labour. *Manchester School* 22 (2): 139–91.

Li, K. 2009. China's total factor productivity estimates by region, investment sources and ownership. *Economic Systems* 33 (3): 213–30.

Liu, L., and W. Zhang. 2007. A New Keynesian model for analysing monetary policy in mainland China. Working Paper 18/2007. Hong Kong Monetary Authority.

Ma, G., and R. McCauley. 2008. Efficacy of China's capital controls: Evidence from price and flow data. *Pacific Economic Review* 13 (1): 104–23.

Ma, G., and Z. Haiwen. 2009. China's evolving external wealth and rising credit position. Working Paper 286. BIS, Basel.

McKinnon, R. 2006. China's exchange rate trap: Japan redux? *American Economic Review* 96 (2): 427–31.

McKinnon, R. 2007. Why China should keep its dollar peg. *International Finance* 10 (1): 43–70.

McKinnon, R., and G. Schnabl. 2009. The case for stabilizing China's exchange rate: Setting the stage for fiscal expansion. *China and World Economy* 17 (1): 1–32.

Mendoza, E. 1995. The terms of trade, the real exchange rate, and economic fluctuations. *International Economic Review* 36 (1): 101–37.

Mendoza, E., V. Quadrini, and J. Rios-Rull. 2007. Financial integration, financial deepness and global imbalances. Working Paper 12909. NBER, Cambridge, MA.

Mehrotra, A., T. Peltonen, and A. Santos Rivera. 2007. Modelling inflation in China: A regional perspective. BOFIT Discussion Paper 19/2007. Bank of Finland, Helsinki.

Modigliani, F., and S. Cao. 2004. The Chinese savings puzzle and the life-cycle hypothesis. *Quarterly Journal of Economics* 42 (1): 145–70.

N'Diaye, P., P. Zhang, and W. Zhang. 2010. Structural reform, intra-regional trade, and medium-term growth prospects of East Asia and the Pacific: Perspectives from a new multi-region model. *Journal of Asian Economics* 21 (1): 20–36.

Obstfeld, M., and K. Rogoff. 1996. *Foundations of International Macroeconomics*. Cambridge: MIT Press.

Ouyang, A., R. Rajan, and T. Willett. 2008. Managing the monetary consequences of reserve accumulation in emerging Asia. *Global Economic Review* 37 (2): 171–99.

Prasad, E. 2009a. Is the Chinese growth miracle built to last? *China Economic Review* 20 (1): 103–23.

Prasad, E. 2009b. Rebalancing growth in Asia. Working paper 15169. NBER, Cambridge, MA.

Prasad, E., and R. Rajan. 2008. A pragmatic approach to capital account liberalisation. *Journal of Economic Perspectives* 22 (3): 149–72.

Ratto, M., W. Roeger, and J. in 't Veld. 2009. QUEST III: An estimated DSGE model of the euro area with fiscal and monetary policy. *Economic Modelling* 26 (1): 222–33.

Ratto, M., W. Roeger, and J. in 't Veld. 2010. Using a DSGE model to look at the recent boom-bust cycle in the US. European Economy Economic Paper 397.

Song, Z., K. Storesletten, and F. Zilibotti. 2009. Growing like China. Discussion Paper 7149. CEPR, London.

Stockman, A., and L. Tesar. 1995. Tastes and technology in a two-country model of the business cycle: explaining international comovements. *American Economic Review* 83 (1): 473–86.

Straub, R., and Ch. Thimann. 2009. The external and domestic side of macroeconomic adjustment in China. Working Paper 1040. ECB, Frankfurt.

Vogel, L. 2010. China's external surplus: Simulations with a global macroeconomic model. European Economy Economic Paper 430.

Wei, S., and X. Zhang. 2009. The competitive saving motive: Evidence from rising sex ratios and savings rates in China. Working Paper 15093. NBER, Cambridge, MA.

Wen, Y. 2009. Saving and growth under borrowing constraints: Explaining the high savings rate puzzle. Working Paper 2009–045B. Federal Reserve Bank of St. Louis.

Woelfl, A., I. Wanner, T. Kozluk, and G. Nicoletti. 2009. Ten years of product market reform in OECD countries: Insights from a revised PMR indicator. Economic Department Working Paper 695. OECD, Paris.

Xiao, G. 2008. China's exchange rate and monetary policies: Structural and institutional constraints and reform options. *Asian Economic Papers* 7 (3): 31–49.

Young, A. 2003. Gold into base metals: Productivity growth in the People's Republic of China during the reform period. *Journal of Political Economy* 111 (6): 1220–61.

Yu, Y. 2007. Global imbalances and China. *Australian Economic Review* 40 (1): 3–23.

Zhang, Y., and G. Wan. 2004. Liquidity constraint, uncertainty and household consumption in China. *Applied Economics* 36 (19): 2221–29.

II Chinese Savings and Investment

6 How Much Do We Know about China's High Saving Rate?

Guonan Ma and Wang Yi[1]

6.1 Introduction

China saves more than half of its GDP and its marginal propensity to save approached 60 percent during the 2000s. Such high saving rate has attracted much attention (Zhou 2009; ADB 2009; IMF 2009), as it may have important implications both for China's own internal balance and for the external balance (Bernanke 2005).

This chapter has three aims: to highlight the stylized facts of Chinese saving, to review the debate over factors shaping the saving dynamics, and to explore its medium-term outlook and policy implications. Our review combines an international comparison of gross national saving and a breakdown of this aggregate by the components of household, corporate and government saving. Building on a growing body of research, we hope to take stock of the progress in understanding Chinese saving behavior, put the debate in perspective, and shed new light on the forces behind high Chinese saving.

The main findings of the chapter are as follows: First, China's saving rate is high by historical experience, international standards and model predictions and also has been rising (especially in the 2000s). Second, saving by each of the three sectors is also high but not exceptional. What sets China apart from the rest of the world is that it ranks near the top globally across all three components.

Third, adjusting for the effect of inflation alters the path of sectoral saving trends, as China swung from double-digit inflation to outright deflation within one decade. Fourth, we question some of the more recent wisdom about the principal drivers of high Chinese saving. In particular, the evidence does not support the proposition that distortions and subsidies have been the principal causes of China's rising corporate profits or high saving rate.

Fifth, we argue that three major economic factors seem to have been key but their roles have been much underappreciated: (1) major institutional reforms including tough corporate restructuring, pension reform, and the spread of private home ownership; (2) a marked Lewis model transformation process as labor left the subsistence sector where its marginal product was less than its average wage; and (3) the prospect of a rapid aging population.

Finally, structural factors point to a peak in the Chinese saving rate in the medium term. Policy measures promoting job creation and a stronger social safety net would contribute to the transition to more balanced domestic demand.

The chapter is organized as follows: Section 6.2 discusses the data issues, highlights China's gross national saving in an international perspective, and provides a broad backdrop to the Chinese saving trend. Section 6.3 examines saving of the corporate, household and government sectors and reviews some of the explanations advanced in the literature. Section 6.4 briefly outlines the structural factors shaping the medium-term outlook for the Chinese saving and explores two policy initiatives, before section 6.5 concludes.

6.2 Measurements and Stylized Facts of Chinese Saving

This section summarizes the main data issues in measuring the Chinese saving rate, highlights some of its most salient stylized facts and provides some backdrop to the evolving Chinese saving.

6.2.1 Data and Measurement Issues

We follow the SNA93 definition of gross national saving (GNS) as gross national disposable income (GNDI) less final consumption expenditure. For a given final consumption, there are two possible GNS estimates, depending on whether GNDI is derived from expenditure-based or production-based GDP (graph 1). The GNS estimated using expenditure-based GDP is equivalent to the sum of gross capital formation and current account balance. The GNS estimated using production-based GDP is consistent with the GNS based on the flow-of-funds statistics, which allows for breakdowns by sector.[2]

Both estimates of GNS may be inflated by the following three measurement problems (Ma and Wang 2010): a pattern of positive inventory accumulation of at least 1 to 2 percent of GDP every year, the low imputed housing rent given a high home ownership and a possible understatement of retained earnings at foreign firms operating in China. In sum, China's gross national saving rate could be overstated by a likely range of 2 to 4 percent of GDP.

6.2.2   Stylized Facts

First, there is little doubt that the Chinese national saving rate is high by international standards. It exceeded 53 percent of GDP in 2008, far above all the OECD economies and overtaking Singapore which has traditionally been among the highest savers globally (table 6.1).

Second, the reported Chinese saving rate is also high relative to predictions by models based on macroeconomic and structural fundamentals. Cross-country empirical panel regression studies have often identified China as a clear outlier with a saving rate one quarter higher than what might have been predicted (Kuijs 2006; Ferrucci 2007; Park and Shin 2009). In other words, China's saving/GDP ratio of 53 percent in 2008 could be 10 to 13 percentage points above what might be inferred from the empirical studies.

Table 6.1
Gross national saving as a percentage of GDP

	1990	1992	1995	2000	2005	2006	2007	2008
China	39.2	38.8	42.1	36.8	51.2	54.1	54.1	54.3
China	35.6	36.4	38.1	37.3	48.2	49.5	51.8	53.2
India	23.0	21.4	24.5	23.8	34.3	35.8	37.6	33.6
Japan	33.2	33.2	29.3	27.5	26.8	26.9	27.0	—
Korea	37.7	36.9	36.2	33.6	32.7	31.2	30.6	31.9
Mexico	23.6	18.6	21.1	23.8	23.3	25.5	—	—
Singapore	43.6	45.8	49.3	46.9	48.7	49.9	51.7	48.3
Australia	18.6	18.0	18.7	19.7	21.6	21.8	22.5	—
Canada	17.3	13.4	18.3	23.6	23.8	24.4	23.7	—
France	20.8	19.6	19.1	21.6	18.5	19.3	19.9	18.9
Germany	25.3	22.3	21.0	20.2	22.2	23.9	25.9	26.0
Italy	20.8	19.1	22.0	20.6	19.5	19.6	20.0	18.2
Switzerland	33.1	28.6	29.6	34.7	36.9	35.5	31.2	—
United Kingdom	16.4	14.3	15.9	15.0	14.6	14.2	15.6	—
United States	15.3	14.2	15.5	17.7	14.6	15.8	14.0	12.1

Sources: Asian Development Bank (ADB), National Bureau of Statistics of China (NBS), OECD, and authors' own estimates.
Note: For China, the first row is gross national saving estimated using expenditure-based GDP while the second row shows the estimate using production-based GDP. The latter is consistent with national gross saving based on the flow-of-funds statistics to be employed hereafter unless otherwise specified.

Third, the Chinese saving rate is not only high but has also been rising, from more than 30 percent in the early 1980s to above 50 percent in 2008 (figure 6.1). The marginal propensity to save reached 54 percent over the period of 1982 to 2008. Such a rapid rise in the national saving rate is rare but by no means unique to China. Fast-growing Asian economies in their transition phases also experienced large and sustained rises in their saving rates (Ma and Wang 2010).

Fourth, China has seen three distinct phases in its evolving saving rate—a steady increase from 30 to 35 percent of GDP to 40 to 45 percent between 1982 and 1994 followed by a decline to around 37 percent by 2000 and a resurgence thereafter to reach over 50 percent. During this last phase China's saving rate on average went up two percentage points of GDP per year, implying a marginal propensity to save of nearly 60 percent.

Fifth, a rising saving rate may also have interacted with a high investment rate. During 1998 to 2008 China's investment surged from 37 percent of GDP to 45 percent, while that of India went up from 24 to 40 percent. What sets China apart from the experiences of Japan, Korea, and India, though, is its large current account surplus during this transition, as the Chinese saving far outpaced its already high investment. This is a principal factor behind the nation's swing from a net debtor of 10 percent of GDP to a net creditor of 37 percent within one decade (Ma and Zhou 2009).

Sixth, another key feature of the Chinese saving rate is that the household, corporate and government sectors each have contributed to the rise in gross national saving. In terms of each component, China's saving is high but not exceptional. As a share of GDP, China's corporate saving at best rivals Japan's, its household saving is below India's, and its government saving is less than Korea's (figure 6.2). However, what really distinguishes China from other economies is that its three saving components have all ranked near their global tops.

In sum, these stylized features point to two central observations. First, there is a need to better understand the saving dynamics of the corporate, household and government sectors and their interactions. Attempts to identify any single explanation for China's exceptionally high aggregate saving rate will almost surely be less than convincing. Second, a challenge lies in a need to better understand not only the high but also rapidly rising saving rate in China, particularly during the 2000s. Explaining some "average" Chinese saving rate is unlikely to offer useful insight.

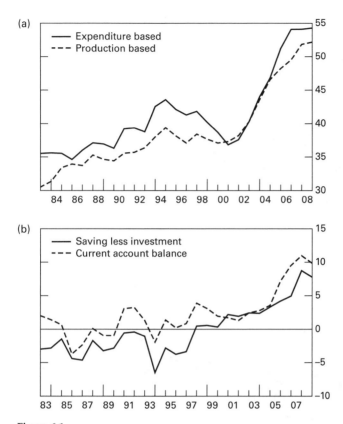

Figure 6.1
China's gross national saving as a percentage of GDP. (a) Gross national saving; (b) saving–investment balance and current account. Note: Gross national saving is estimated using either expenditure-based GDP or production-based GDP. Saving less investment here is calculated using national gross saving estimated by production-based GDP, which is consistent with the flow-of-funds statistics and will be employed for the rest of this chapter unless otherwise specified. Sources: National Bureau of Statistics of China (NBS) and authors' own estimates.

(a)
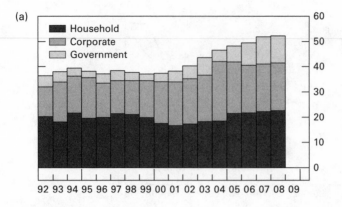

(b)
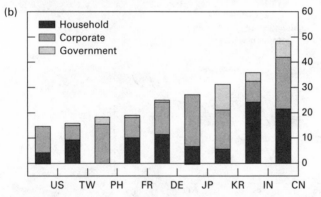

Figure 6.2
Gross national saving by institutional sector as a percentage of GDP. (a) China's gross
national saving; (b) 2005 to 2007 average, by market. Note: CN = China; DE = Germany;
FR = France; IN = India, JP = Japan; KR = Korea; PH = Philippines; TW = Chinese Taipei;
US = United States. Sources: Asian Development Bank (ADB), NBS, OECD, and authors'
own estimates.

Such a high and rising saving rate will inevitably have implications
for China's growth model and its profile of internal and external balances. First, a high saving has financed strong economic growth, with
low inflation and manageable exposures to adverse external shocks.
Over the past decade China's GDP growth registered 10 percent plus per
annum, while its inflation averaged below 2 percent. Second, it helped
shape China's internal and external balances. In particular, a rising
saving rate implies a falling consumption share in GDP and hence a
highly investment-intensive internal demand structure. Over those ten
years China's private consumption declined from 47 percent of GDP to
36 percent, the lowest among the world's major economies.[3]

6.2.3   A Backdrop to the Chinese Saving Behavior

Before we get into the detailed breakdowns of gross national saving, it is useful to first sketch some of the major forces influencing the whole Chinese economy. These forces may have been an important but often neglected and underappreciated part of the explanation for the high Chinese saving rate and fall into two broad categories: (1) major economic and demographic trends and (2) key institutional changes.

At least three sets of secular forces could have important bearing on China's high saving rate (Ma and Wang 2010). First, China has experienced rapid structural changes, as its agriculture share in GDP fell from 30 to 10 percent during 1980 to 2008. Second, underpinning this transformation has been the large-scale rural–urban labor migration and urbanization—the agriculture share of the total employment shrank from 70 to 40 percent while the urban population share rose from 20 to 45 percent. Third, China's demographic transition has been very compressed, in part owing to the one-child policy. China's dependence dropped from 68 to 38 percent within a generation, resulting in a surge of the working-age share of the population from 60 to 74 percent. As a consequence China's labor supply growth has been strong but is expected to slow sharply in ten years from now.

These three secular forces interacted to generate a sustained and large-scale labor migration from farms to factories. This dynamics can be best summarized as a dualism transformation process described by the Lewis model (Lewis 1954). In this model the modern sector with rising productivity draws surplus labor from the traditional sector at a relatively low wage rate. The Lewis model predicts a rising profit share in income, accelerated capital accumulation and faster economic growth during the transformation process, therefore a higher saving rate. This process, while not unique, could have been more accentuated in China's case because of its very compressed demographic transition and thus may help explain its recent high saving and investment rates.

A number of major institutional reforms since the 1990s could also have significantly influenced the Chinese saving trends (Ma and Wang 2010). First, China went through its toughest corporate restructuring, leading to large-scale labor retrenchment between 1995 and 2005, with employment at state companies being halved. As a result the enterprise-based cradle-to-grave social safety net shrank. Such corporate restructuring directly boosts corporate efficiency and reduces job security, thus lifting both corporate and household savings.

Second, the 1997 pension reform transformed the previous pay-as-you-go system to a partially funded three-pillar scheme. The new scheme reduced pension benefits, increased contributions, and introduced pre-funded individual pension accounts.[4] This institutional change, together with the anticipation of rapid population aging, may have induced additional accumulation of capital through increased saving and investment, which is sometimes called the second demographic dividend (Wang and Mason 2008).

The third institutional reform relates to private home ownership. The concomitant introduction of private home ownership and property market interacted with the "second demographic dividend" effect to provide additional incentives to build up pension assets, ushering in a housing boom. China's home ownership may exceed 85 percent today, following a substantial buildup of residential housing assets over the past twenty years (Ma and Wang 2010). The implied housing investment has been enormous. Thus sharply increased demand for housing assets has been a key driver for both high economic growth and high saving in China over the past decade.

6.3   Composition of Gross National Saving

To better understand the sources of and factors behind the high Chinese saving, it is useful to examine the breakdown of China's gross national saving by its components: corporate, household and government saving (Kuijs 2006; Li and Yin 2007; Wiemer 2008; Jha et al. 2009). This approach allows us to trace the composition of the Chinese saving, taking advantage of the following simple framework:

$$\frac{S}{Y} = \frac{\sum S_i}{Y} = \sum \frac{S_i}{Y_i} \cdot \frac{Y_i}{Y}, \quad S = \sum S_i, \quad \text{and} \quad Y = \sum Y_i, \quad i = e, h, \text{or } g, \quad (6.1)$$

where Y and S are gross national disposable income and gross national saving, respectively; and subscripts e, h, and g denote the corporate (enterprise), household or government sector, respectively. Simply, the equation says that an economy's aggregate saving rate is an income-weighted average of all sectors' average propensities to save. In other words, the sector i's contribution to the aggregate saving rate (S_i/Y) depends on two factors: its income share in the economy (Y_i/Y) and its average propensity to save from its own income (S_i/Y_i).

Three observations of China's saving composition are worth highlighting (table 6.2 and figure 6.2). First, according to official statistics, the household sector is the largest saver today, to be followed by the corporate sector. Second, the corporate and government sectors have been the principal drivers behind the rise in the aggregate saving rate over the past 17 years, contributing more than four-fifths of the 17-percentage point rise in China's saving/GDP ratio. Third, the year 2000 appears to be a turning point when the aggregate Chinese saving rate started its relentless climb of 16-percentage points of GDP. Half of this hike so far in the 2000s has come from the government sector.

6.3.1 Corporate Saving

China's corporate saving doubled from 12 percent of GDP in 1992 to a peak of 24 percent in 2004, but has since trended down to 19 percent in 2008 when China's current account surplus surged (table 6.2 and figure 6.2). Over the past fifteen years, it has been the biggest contributor to the increase in the Chinese aggregate saving.

Corporate saving consists two parts: depreciation and retained earnings. Depreciation as a share of GDP has probably risen over time, given that depreciation is positively linked to the higher capital stock and newer vintages of capital. According to Bai et al. (2006), China's capital stock as a ratio to GDP rose from 130 to 170 percent between the early 1990s and the mid-2000s.

More controversial have been the various hypotheses about the other element of corporate saving—retained earnings. Low dividend payments by Chinese firms could in part help explain the high net earning retained at firms, for two proposed and exaggerated reasons: financial underdevelopment and poor corporate governance (Jha et al. 2009; ADB 2009; IMF 2009).

First, limited access to external finance may force firms to hoard cash to hedge uncertainties or to use internal funds to finance expansion. Yet, while China's financial system remains underdeveloped, it may have advanced in recent years (Ma 2007). Moreover Chinese companies seem to have hoarded less, not more, cash at firm level, qualifying the importance of "precautionary corporate saving" (figure 6.3). Even private firms seem to have improved their access to external finance somewhat. This factor does not explain well the markedly higher corporate saving in the past fifteen years.

Second, poor corporate governance may result in low dividend payments. However, there is little evidence suggesting that the dividend behavior of listed Chinese firms differs systematically from those in the rest of the world (Zhang 2008; Bayoumi et al. 2009). Indeed the

Table 6.2
Contributions to China's national gross saving as a percentage of GDP

	National gross saving				Adjusted saving	
	Corporate	Household	Government	Total	Corporate	Household
	(1)	(2)	(3)	(1) + (2) + (3)		
1992	11.7	20.3	4.4	36.4	15.6	16.4
1993	15.7	18.2	4.1	38.0	21.4	12.5
1994	14.5	21.7	3.2	39.4	21.1	15.1
1995	16.0	19.6	2.5	38.1	21.0	14.6
1996	13.5	19.9	3.7	37.1	16.9	16.5
1997	13.0	21.4	4.0	38.4	14.8	19.6
1998	13.3	21.1	3.3	37.7	13.4	20.9
1999	14.6	19.9	2.6	37.1	14.1	20.4
2000	16.5	17.5	3.3	37.3	16.6	17.4
2001	17.4	16.6	4.2	38.2	18.1	15.9
2002	18.0	17.2	5.1	40.3	18.5	16.8
2003	18.3	18.3	7.0	43.6	18.9	17.7
2004	23.5	18.5	4.6	46.6	24.9	17.0
2005	20.4	21.5	6.4	48.2	21.7	20.2
2006	18.8	21.7	8.9	49.5	19.8	20.8
2007	18.8	22.2	10.8	51.8	20.0	21.0
2008	18.8	23.4	11.0	53.2	21.0	20.4

Table 6.2
(continued)

	National gross saving				Adjusted saving	
	Corporate	Household	Government	Total	Corporate	Household
	(1)	(2)	(3)	(1) + (2) + (3)		
Memo: changes						
1992–2008	7.1	3.1	6.6	16.8	5.9	4.3
1992–1999	4.7	-2.7	-1.1	0.9	1.1	1.0
2000–2008	2.3	5.9	7.7	15.9	4.4	3.0
MPS: 92–08	1.00	0.41	0.46	0.54	1.00	0.40

Sources: NBS and authors' own estimates.

Notes: (1) The adjusted corporate saving is corporate saving allowing for the erosion in real corporate debt arising from inflation, which is approximated as a product of expected inflation and net corporate debt. Expected inflation is measured by the two-year moving average of the GDP deflator. Net corporate debt is estimated as corporate loans less the sum of corporate deposits and half of the currency in circulation. Corporate loans are taken as the sum of short-, medium- and long-term loans minus loans to the households. The household loans before 2000 are computed backward by the 2000 outstanding level and the flow-of-funds statistics. The adjusted household saving is calculated on the assumption that adjustments in corporate saving are fully accommodated by household saving. (2) MPS stands for marginal propensity to save.

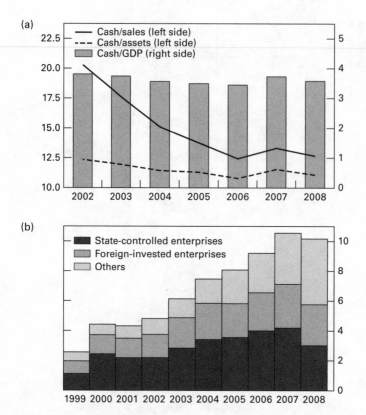

Figure 6.3
Corporate sector's cash balance and industrial profit in China. (a) Cash balance, in percent; (b) industrial profit, as a percentage of GDP. Notes: The cash balance is calculated based on a sample of 1,333 Chinese companies listed in China and Hong Kong. Foreign-invested enterprises include foreign, Chinese Taipei or Hong Kong SAR invested and controlled enterprises operating in China. Others are the non–state-controlled joint shareholding companies, collectives, private companies, and other joint ventures. Sources: Credit Suisse, NBS, and authors' own estimates.

dividend payout ratio (common dividend over EBIT) averages 16 percent for Chinese listed firms compared to less than 13 percent for those from the rest of the world.

In our view, blaming poor corporate governance could risk barking up the wrong tree, since it was a government policy that state companies were not required to pay dividends to the government. This policy could add to retained earnings, since the bulk of the dividend payouts by listed Chinese state companies might go to their nonlisted parent holding companies (direct majority shareholders) instead of the government (the ultimate owner) and thus is still retained within the corporate sector (Zhou 2005).

An even more controversial question is about the possible sources of higher corporate profits (figure 6.3). Many explanations have been advanced (Dollar and Wei 2006; Bai et al. 2006; Hofman and Kuijs 2008). For exposition purposes, we group some of these arguments into two hypotheses.

One hypothesis argues that high Chinese corporate saving, and indeed fast economic growth, is mostly the consequence of government distortions designed to subsidize the corporate sector in order to promote growth and exports. Two arguments have been advanced (Tyers and Lu 2008; Jha et al. 2009; ADB 2009). First, monopolies boost corporate profits of mostly state firms, owing to a lack of competition policy or its weak enforcement. Second, subsidies and factor price distortions (e.g., financial repression, restrictions on rural labor migration, subsidies for energy inputs, and below-market prices of land) inflate corporate earnings, again mostly benefiting state firms. In short, China's rapid economic growth and high saving rate are principally a function of government distortions and subsidies.

An alternative hypothesis emphasizes the broader forces discussed earlier as the more important factors leading to higher corporate saving. First, efficiency gains from corporate restructuring and an expanding indigenous private sector have intensified competition, raised productivity, and helped drive fast economic growth and lift corporate profits. Second, accentuated by a very compressed demographic transition and a large pool of surplus rural labor, the prolonged Chinese rural–urban labor migration has capped wage growth, thus boosting corporate profits in the transition process.[5]

These two hypotheses are not mutually exclusive and may well coexist. While the truth likely lies somewhere in between, an interesting question is which set of the two explanations matters more. In particular, it would be useful to find out whether the identified distortions have become more significant over time so as to help explain the higher corporate saving rate and whether the available evidence broadly confirms the main predictions of these two hypotheses. After presenting the pros and cons of these two hypotheses, we highlight the controversial roles of exchange rates and interest rates.

A central prediction of the distortion-and-subsidy hypothesis is that as the principal beneficiary, state companies should be the major driver of the observed higher Chinese corporate profits, since they are more likely to enjoy greater market power, receive more government subsidies, and gain from easier access to cheaper credit. Yet it has been China's less advantaged and more efficient local non-state firms that have been gaining profit shares (figure 6.3). Their share in China's industrial profits more than doubled from 20 to 43 percent during the 2000s. This questions the theory that the Chinese corporate earnings are mainly inflated by distortions and subsidies.[6]

Our analysis also provides some clues about the evolving relative trends of corporate profits at state and non-state (both foreign and indigenous) companies. For the manufacturing sector at least, the state companies' share in the total profit declined from two-thirds in 1999 to one-quarter in 2008. For the whole economy, we suspected that the share of state companies could be higher given their predominance in some monopoly sectors such as telecoms. Nevertheless, the trend decline for the state companies over this period should be similar.

Other evidence on the distortion-and-subsidy hypothesis is also mixed. First, although a case can be made for the presence of monopoly power in the Chinese banking industry, the market share of the big state-controlled banks has fallen over time. With the 2001 WTO accession, any oligopolistic rents may have waned on balance. In sum, while distortions and subsidies may inflate earnings at the state companies, they are unlikely a primary factor behind China's higher overall corporate saving over time.

Second, the effect of any residual energy subsidies on China's overall corporate profitability is ambiguous. Indeed, given China as a growing net energy importer, energy subsidies may worsen the country's current account balance. Related, low royalties may inflate earnings of resources industries. Yet little is known about the effect of resources taxes on both corporate and aggregate saving.

Third, limited access to credit by small firms may weaken demand for labor, giving rise to additional downward pressure on wages and thus boosting the profit share in income (Aziz and Cui 2007). But this factor too should not be overstated, as financing problems facing small firms in China may be no better or worse relative to other economies with high or low corporate saving.

Fourth, entry barriers and high tax burden could disadvantage the labor-intensive service sector, resulting in excessive expansion of more capital-intensive industries in the manufacturing sector and hence a higher income share of profits at the expense of labor (Guo and N'Diaye 2010).

Finally, there is also controversy about the role of both the exchange rate and interest rate in shaping corporate saving. Regarding the exchange rate, one view is that an undervalued exchange rate boosts relative competitiveness and thus corporate profits in the manufacturing sector, which often results in current account surpluses (Turner 1988; Eichengreen 2006; Goldstein and Lardy 2009). Another view suggests a minor and uncertain role of the exchange rate in the Chinese saving and current account balance (Chinn and Wei 2009; Cheung et al. 2009; Ma and Zhou 2009), as China's real effective exchange rate has fluctuated over time and strengthened vis-à-vis most major emerging market currencies (figure 6.4).

Low interest rates could play a role lifting corporate profits. Between 1992 and 2007 net interest payments by the nonfinancial corporate sector more than halved as a share of GDP, contributing to 30 percent of the rise in corporate saving (figure 6.5). While one may attribute this to financial repression that depresses funding cost of and hence subsidizes Chinese (state) firms, we think that corporate deleveraging and inflation volatility could be two greater forces behind the declining net corporate interest payments.

First, net corporate debts—the difference between corporate loans and deposits—as a share of GDP more than halved between 1992 and 2008, reducing net corporate interest payments at any prevailing interest rate (figure 6.5). Corporate deleveraging could reflect strong corporate cash flows. Second, as argued by Modigliani and Cohn (1979), in times of high inflation, a big part of the interest payments represents inflation premium compensating creditors for the reduction of their real debt claims and thus should be considered repayments of the loan principal. Hence corporate profits may be understated in high-inflation years, and vice versa in times of deflation. The Chinese economy swung from double-digit inflation in the early 1990s to outright deflation in the late 1990s, potentially giving rise to a gap between the economic profits and reported accounting profits.

We estimate this gap by taking into account the gains to shareholders accruing from the depreciation of the real corporate debt burden.[7] Our preliminary estimation shows that corporate profits are understated in the high-inflation years of 1992 to 1996 and overstated in the deflationary years of 1998 to 2000 (table 6.2 and figure 6.6), with two interesting insights. First, the adjusted series indicates that the rise in corporate profits has become smaller than that suggested by the official flow-of-funds statistics. While the official data indicate much of the rise in

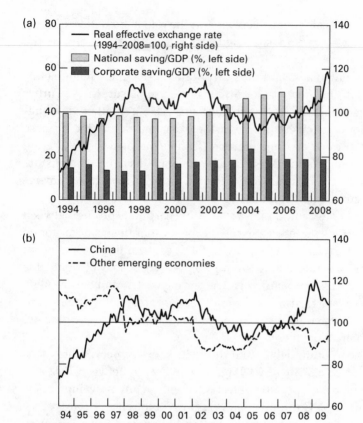

Figure 6.4
Real effective exchange rate and saving. (a) China's real effective exchange rate and saving; (b) real effective exchange rate (1994–2008 = 100). Note: The rate of other emerging economies is the simple average of the real effective exchange rates of ten major emerging economies (Argentina, Brazil, Chile, India, Indonesia, Korea, Malaysia, Mexico, Thailand, and Turkey). Sources: NBS, BIS, and authors' own estimates.

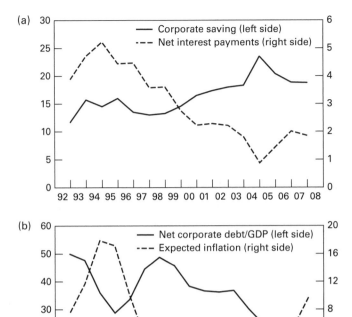

Figure 6.5
Inflation, interest payment, and corporate saving. (a) As a percentage of GDP; (b) in percent. Note: Expected inflation is measured by two-year moving average of GDP deflator. Net corporate debt is estimated by the difference between corporate loans, on the one hand, and corporate deposit and cash held by the corporate sector, on the other. Sources: NBS, People's Bank of China (PBC), and authors' own estimates.

corporate saving took place in the 1990s, our adjusted series shows that most of the smaller increase occurred in the 2000s. Second, the corporate sector has supplanted the household sector as the largest saver in China today but has not been the biggest driver of the rise in the national saving rate over the past fifteen years. Both point to a need of caution in interpreting the dynamics of corporate saving.

6.3.2 Household Saving

Household saving first fell from 20 percent of GDP in 1992 to a low of 16 percent in 2001 before staging a marked comeback to 23 percent by 2008 (table 6.2 and figure 6.2). During 1992 to 2008 the household sector

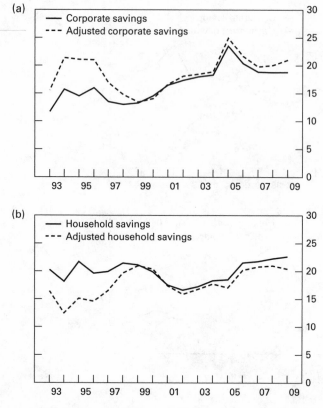

Figure 6.6
Corporate and household saving: before and after adjustment as a percentage of GDP.
(a) Corporate saving; (b) household saving. See the note in table 6.2. Sources: NBS, PBC,
and authors' own estimates.

has contributed three percentage points of the 17 percentage point rise
in the aggregate saving rate.

This modest contribution to the rising aggregate saving rate has
been the consequence of two competing influences: a 10 percentage
point decline in the household income share and a 10 percentage point
rise in its average propensity to save from its disposable income (table
6.3). Both have led to the marked decline in China's private consumption share in GDP over the past fifteen years (Aziz and Cui 2007; Guo
and N'Diaye 2010; Baker and Orsmond 2010).

The big drop in the household share in gross national disposal
income over the past fifteen years (figure 6.7) can be attributable to a
fall in the labor share in national income, a decline in investment
income and diminished net income transfers.

Table 6.3
Disposable income and saving propensity as a percentage of GDP

	Disposable income share					Average propensity to save		
	Corporate	Household	Government	Adjusted corporate	Adjusted household	Household	Adjusted household	Government
1992	11.7	68.3	20.0	15.5	64.5	29.5	25.4	22.0
1993	15.7	64.6	19.7	21.4	59.0	28.1	21.2	21.0
1994	14.5	67.0	18.5	21.1	60.4	32.4	25.0	17.1
1995	16.0	67.2	16.5	21.3	62.1	29.6	23.8	15.5
1996	13.5	68.4	17.9	17.1	65.0	29.4	25.7	20.7
1997	13.0	68.6	18.3	14.9	66.8	31.4	29.6	21.9
1998	13.3	68.4	18.1	13.6	68.3	31.2	31.1	18.3
1999	14.6	67.2	18.1	14.2	67.7	29.8	30.3	14.7
2000	16.5	64.2	19.2	16.7	64.1	27.5	27.3	17.2
2001	17.4	62.0	20.5	18.3	61.2	27.0	26.1	20.8
2002	18.0	61.0	21.0	18.5	60.5	28.3	27.7	24.2
2003	18.3	59.8	22.0	18.8	59.2	30.4	29.8	31.4
2004	23.5	57.8	18.9	24.7	56.4	31.6	29.9	24.0
2005	20.4	59.4	20.5	21.3	58.1	35.6	34.2	30.4
2006	18.8	58.7	22.8	19.5	57.8	36.4	35.4	38.6
2007	18.8	57.5	24.1	19.7	56.3	37.9	36.6	44.2
2008	18.8	57.6	23.9	20.6	55.5	39.9	36.1	45.3

Sources: NBS and authors' own estimates.
Note: See note to table 6.2.

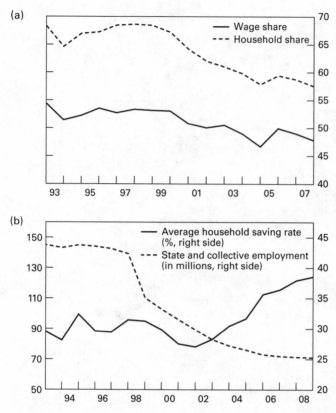

Figure 6.7
Income share and labor downsizing in China. (a) Labor and household income (as a percentage of gross national disposable income); (b) labor downsizing. Note: State and collective employment refers to that of the urban area, as there was little state sector employment to speak of in the rural area. Source: NBS, World Bank, and authors' own estimates.

It is first and foremost the consequence of a declining labor share in the economy, given that wages constitute 80 percent of the Chinese household disposal income. The decline in the labor share accounts for 60 percent of the observed decline in the household income share. This may have been the combined consequence of a compressed demographic transition, a prolonged process of absorbing surplus rural labor, a lagging labor-intensive service sector and difficult financing conditions for small firms (Bai and Qian 2009).

The household income share has also been dragged down by its shrinking net interest income.[8] As a share of GDP, the net interest income halved in the past fifteen years, accounting for a quarter of the decline in the household income share. As the household sector is a net creditor in the economy, this is not surprising. Another reason for the falling net interest income is the rising household debt in the past decade, to be discussed below.

A third factor behind a falling household income share is increased contributions required to fund the large future pension benefits and other welfare obligations related to the expected population aging. Such contributions made by the household sector are a deduction to its disposable income and tripled between 1992 and 2007, from 1.4 percent of GDP to 4.2 percent.

Despite this drop in household income share, household saving still rose as a share of GDP, owing to the much higher personal saving propensity. The household average propensity to save rose by 10 percentage points, mostly during the 2000s (table 6.3). The high and rising household saving propensity has been a subject of intense research. Four sets of interpretations have been advanced.

First, as life-cycle, permanent-income, and habit-formation hypotheses suggest, interactions among economic growth, income level and demographic changes may influence the personal saving rate. Record economic growth, a sharp decline in the Chinese youth dependency rate, the expected rapid aging of the population and saving/consumption habit persistence all have contributed to a high personal saving propensity.[9] A related factor is a flatter earning profile over the life cycle in recent years, which in part explains a high average household saving rate that displays a U-shape pattern across cohorts (Song and Yang 2010).

Second, precautionary saving motives also help explain the higher personal saving rate. The large-scale corporate restructuring and downsizing between 1995 and 2005 increased both income and expenditure uncertainties and weakened the enterprise-based social safety net, reinforcing the precautionary motives to save.[10] The new social welfare system has been taking shape but has not expanded fast enough and so far remains limited and fragmented (figures 6.7 and 6.8).

Third, liquidity or borrowing constraint is another often cited factor accounting for the high personal saving (Wen 2010). But bank loans to the Chinese household sector reached 15 percent of the total outstanding bank loans in 2009 from less than 1 percent in the late 1990s (figure 6.8). In other words, the availability of consumer credit does not appear

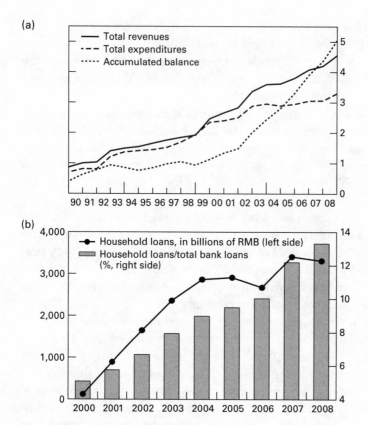

Figure 6.8
Social security and household loans in China. (a) Social security as a percentage of GDP;
(b) household loans. Sources: Credit Suisse, NBS, PBC, and authors' own estimates.

to be a major binding constraint to consumption smoothing for the
period under study and is unlikely an important cause behind the
rising personal saving propensity in the past ten years.[11]

Finally, institutional changes may have significantly influenced personal saving behavior. The 1997 pension reform led to reduced pension
wealth. This helped trim the large implicit pension debts but might
have lifted the current household saving rate (Feng et al. 2009). Also
scandals associated with local pension funds might weaken confidence,
thus limiting any substitution between mandatory and voluntary personal saving. Another important institutional change is the introduction of private home ownership that has triggered significant demand
for housing assets, thus boosting household saving.

6.3.3 Government Saving

The government has been the smallest saver in China but a major contributor to the rise in national saving. As a share of GDP its saving more than doubled, from less than 5 percent in 1992 to 11 percent in 2008 (table 6.2 and figure 6.2). During the 2000s it has accounted for half of the 16 percentage point rise in China's gross national saving rate.

The marked increase in government saving largely reflects higher government income. The government share in disposable income first declined from 20 to 16 percent in the first half of the 1990s, before recovering steadily to 24 percent by 2008 (table 6.3). Meanwhile the government consumption has averaged about 15 percent of GDP since the early 1990s. Thus rising government disposable income and steady government consumption together resulted in higher government saving and more government investment, especially in the 2000s (figure 6.9). The Chinese government's marginal propensity to save exceeded 50 percent during the 2000s, compared to less than 20 percent in the 1990s.

The government disposable income has risen briskly since the mid-1990s (figure 6.9). This has been the combined result of high economic growth, the 1994 tax reform, increased land sales, and greater social welfare contributions from both the corporate and household sectors. Over the years government disposable income tends to closely track government revenues.[12] China's government revenues dropped from around 40 percent of GDP in the late 1970s to only 15 percent in the early 1990s. The 1994 tax reform under Premier Zhu Rongji aimed to lift both the share of government revenues in GDP and share of the central government in the overall fiscal revenues. Both goals have apparently been met.

The government consumption and expenditure, however, diverged noticeably from each other, especially in the 2000s (figure 6.9). The government consumption has been more stable over time, at some 15 percent of GDP; but total expenditure swung from 11 to 12 percent of GDP in the 1990s to 18 to 20 percent lately. One main difference between the two measures is investment spending undertaken by the government, which is part of government expenditure but not part of government consumption. Therefore, at the margin, much of the government income gain has been invested and saved rather than consumed in the 2000s. Yet, by international standards, China's government consumption of 15 percent of GDP is not low: it is above the historical average of the emerging market economies of 13 percent but below the mean of 20 percent for the advanced economies. It indeed ranks among the highest in emerging Asia (figure 6.10).

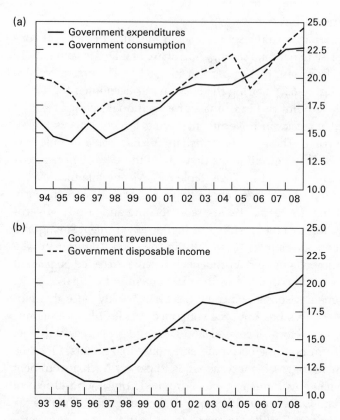

Figure 6.9
Government revenue/income and expenditure/consumption in China as a percentage
of GDP. (a) Revenues and disposable income; (b) expenditures and consumption. Note:
Government revenues and expenditures are based on the fiscal and budgetary statistics,
including both budgetary and extra-budgetary revenues and expenditure. Government
disposable income and consumption are based on the flow-of-fund statistics. Sources:
NBS and authors' own estimates.

Why does the Chinese government save and invest but not consume
most of its rising income? Three different but related explanations can
be advanced. It appears that all of these forces have been at work at
the same time in China, jointly contributing to higher government
saving in the 2000s.

First, the anticipation of rapid population aging and the 1997 pension
reform prompted increased pension contributions by the corporate and
household sectors. These contributions are intended to partially prefund
future pension benefits and treated as a source to the government disposable income, as they are parked under various pension funds administered

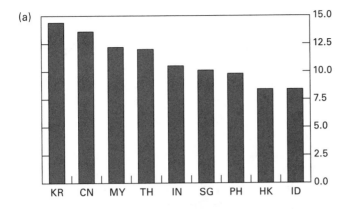

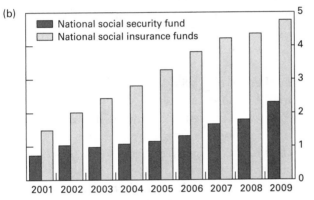

Figure 6.10
Government consumption and social welfare funds as a percentage of GDP. (a) Government consumption in Asia (average of 2005–2007); (b) balances of welfare funds in China. Notes: CN = China; HK = Hong Kong SAR; IN = India, ID = Indonesia; KR = Korea; MY = Malaysia; PH = Philippines; SG = Singapore; TH = Thailand. The national social security fund covers only the net assets directly managed by the central government while the insurance funds are balances pooled and managed at both the national and provincial levels in China. Sources: IMF, NBS, and the National Social Welfare Fund of China.

by the government. These funds have been invested in financial and physical assets at home or abroad. As a ratio to GDP the net asset balances of China's National Social Security Fund and other social welfare funds tripled between 2001 and 2009 (figure 6.10). Both suggest that the higher government saving could in part relate to pension asset buildup.

Second, local Chinese government officials have incentives to start new investment projects, as promotions have been mainly determined by performance indicators such as economic growth in their jurisdictions. Hence there is an innate tendency to invest more rather than to provide additional public services for a given rise of government revenues, thus boosting government saving. However, high investment spending on public facilities and infrastructure by the Chinese government today should eventually generate a greater stream of future government consumption.

Third, there is a so-called federal fiscal imbalance issue in China: while a rising share of fiscal revenue is appropriated by the central government, the lion's share of the social expenditure burden remains on the shoulder of the less well-funded local governments (Ma and Wang 2010). Transfers through the central government are considered far from adequate in addressing the financing pressures facing local governments. This tends to put the local governments under funding pressure, in turn depressing social spending.

In sum, higher government saving has largely been attributable to both rising government income and steady government consumption. The resultant higher government saving propensity in the 2000s may relate to a combination of three factors: the need to accumulate pension assets in anticipation of rapid population aging, the incentives for local governments to invest rather than providing public services, and a large burden of social spending on the local governments that have come under increased funding pressures.

6.4   Medium-Term Outlook and Policy Implications

6.4.1   Medium-Term Outlook
The medium-term outlook for China's saving rate matters not only for its future economic growth path but possibly also for rebalancing of the global economy. Although private consumption expenditure has been growing 8 to 9 percent per annum in recent years, China's saving rate remains considerably higher than its investment rate, resulting in a sub-

stantial current account surplus. Going forward, given the outlook of a relatively weak global recovery and an already high domestic investment rate in China, private consumption may play an increased role in sustaining nation's high economic growth. One key challenge for Chinese policy makers is thus to maintain robust internal demand while rebalancing the economy more toward consumption. Both domestic structural factors and policy measures could influence such a transition.

Of the structural factors discussed earlier, three can be highlighted. First, it is reasonable to assume that the large-scale labor retrenchment observed during 1995 to 2008 has by and large been behind us. Going forward, such one-off efficiency gains for the corporate sector would likely be more limited, and the associated income and expenditure uncertainties of the Chinese households should become less pronounced. Thus the incentives for private saving of both the household and corporate sectors should weaken.

Second, China is projected to enter a phase of accelerated population aging within a decade, which may suggest two things. On the one hand, growth of labor force will decline, possibly along with a declining household saving rate and a slower pace of investment spending, likely resulting in lower potential output growth. On the other hand, we may continue witnessing strong infrastructure investment for years to come, to build up the physical capital stock and pension assets in preparation for the aging of the population and to accommodate urbanization.

Third, the rural–urban labor migration away from agriculture is likely to continue in the years ahead, as the urban share of the population is projected to rise within a decade from the current 45 to 60 percent, a threshold level of peaking personal saving rate based on the experiences of other Asian economies. By contrast, there may be some early and tentative signs that China could get closer to the Lewis turning point, which predicts a rise in the labor share of income, lower corporate saving and a greater role of personal consumption in future (Garnaut 2006 and Cai 2007).

Taken together, a key implication from these medium-term forces is that China's saving rate is likely to plateau before long and may ease off noticeably from the current 53 percent or even higher levels over the next ten years. The marked U-shaped experience of China's saving rate over the past twenty-five years also suggests that the prospective Chinese saving rate can fall meaningfully in the years ahead.

6.4.2 Policy Options

During this process, policy can assist the transition to a more balanced growth model. Of many possible policy options widely debated, this chapter touches on two broad and largely complementary sets of issues: measures to promote urban job creation and policies to enhance the social safety net. While strong investment is still needed to accommodate the urbanization process, deregulations that facilitate labor mobility between the urban and rural areas, support small companies and reduce entry barriers to the labor-intensive services sector, may help job creation, ease downward pressure on wages, and stabilize the labor income share. They would also support resource reallocation to nontradable sectors while facilitating consumer demand growth. This is a promising area of policy initiatives.

A strengthened social safety net is another option, since the current public welfare system remains fragmented and its coverage is limited. This policy option will become even more valuable with the continued rural labor migrants into the urban areas. The recent moves to transfer some of the listed state company shares to beef up pension assets and improve the portability of welfare benefits therefore go in the right direction. But there are challenges and pitfalls to any state-welfare solution.[13] One risk is that a poorly designed social insurance system could backfire. Another risk is the sustainability of any social welfare scheme, especially in the context of the expected rapid population aging and likely slower economic growth. Finally, reforms to social welfare systems could have unintended side effects. In any case, the priority should ideally be to aim for a more integrated and broader based social safety net, with a focus on the low-income segments of the population and with an enhanced funding role by the central government.

6.5 Summary

This chapter explores the stylized facts and explanations about the Chinese corporate, household, and government saving. They have all added substantially to China's high and rising saving rate, especially during the 2000s. What really distinguishes China from the rest of the world is that the saving of each of these three sectors as a share of GDP has ranked near the top worldwide, making China's aggregate saving rate exceptionally high.

No single theory or model will likely provide a simple explanation to this pattern of the high Chinese saving. On the one hand, the evidence appears mixed for the proposition that China's fast economic growth and high saving rate are principally a function of subsidies and distortions. On the other hand, some of the structural forces may not have received sufficient attention. Such forces include those associated with rapid economic growth, structural transformation, a compressed demographic transition, large-scale corporate restructuring, and household and government responses to institutional changes and to the expected acceleration of population aging.

Notes

1. Guonan Ma is from the Bank for International Settlements (BIS) and Wang Yi from the People's Bank of China (PBC). The views expressed here are those of the authors only and do not necessarily reflect those of the BIS or the PBC. The chapter has benefited from comments by participants at seminars at the BIS and Hong Kong Institute of Monetary Research, the 21st Annual Conference of the Chinese Economic Association (UK) at Oxford University, and the CESifo Summer Workshop in Venice. We thank Claudio Borio, Vincent Chan, Ben Cohen, Andrew Filardo, Robert McCauley, Madhusudan Mohanty, Ramon Moreno, Thomas Rawski, and Philip Turner. We also thank Lillie Lam for her able assistance.

2. The Chinese time series on GDP at the aggregate level starts with 1982, but the official flow-of-funds statistics begins from 1992.

3. As a comparison, India's consumption share fell from 64 to 55 percent in the same period. But a falling consumption share should not be confused with anemic consumer demand growth—China's private consumption grew at near double-digit paces in recent years.

4. For more details of China's pension system, see Feldstein (1998), Salditt et al. (2007), Song and Yang (2010), and Herd et al. (2010).

5. Since 2006 there has been a lively debate over whether China has reached a so-called Lewis turning point, whereby the pool of surplus labor starts drying up, as parts of its economy for the first time witnessed accelerated real wage growth and reported "labor shortage." For more details, see Cai (2007), Meng and Bai (2007), and Islam and Yokota (2008).

6. Using an asymmetric credit friction model, Song et al. (2009) suggest that the high-productivity and credit-constrained firms finance investment by internal saving and thus tend to generate high corporate saving while maintaining high return to capital by attracting more resources to themselves. This interesting insight differs importantly from the proposition that high corporate profit and saving come mostly from state-sponsored subsidies and distortions.

7. Erosion in the real corporate debts arising from inflation may be approximated as the product of expected inflation and net corporate debt outstanding. Expected inflation is measured by the two-year moving average of the implicit GDP deflator. Net corporate debt is estimated as corporate loans less the sum of corporate deposits and half of the currency in circulation. Corporate loans are taken as the sum of short-, medium-, and long-term loans minus loans to the households. The data on household loans before 2000 are computed backward by the 2000-level outstanding and the flow-of-funds statistics.

8. More generally, the household income from other investment income sources has fallen as well. At least two causes can be suggested. First, the ownership of stock shares is not sufficiently broad-based. Second, imputed rent and income from owner-occupied homes could have been underrecorded (Ma and Wang 2010).

9. While Kraay (2000) report no conclusive evidence on the role of growth and demographics, Modigliani and Cao (2004) confirm their effects. Horioka and Wan (2008) find mixed supports for these hypotheses but highlight the important role of habit persistence. Wei and Zhang (2009) argue that China's rising sex ratios led to increased competition in the marriage market and thus drove wealth accumulation. Ma and Zhou (2009) suggest that a sharp fall in the youth dependence could raise saving across the household, corporate, and government sectors.

10. See Meng (2003), Blanchard and Giavazzi (2005), and Chamon and Prasad (2008). In addition this chapter has not covered other potentially important factors influencing personal saving propensity such as income inequality and consumption risk sharing across regions. These are promising areas of further research.

11. Certainly there is room for further expanded access to consumer credit, as Chinese households remain lightly leveraged and their aggregate balance sheet seems strong.

12. Government revenue and expenditure, based on the fiscal and budgetary statistics, are conceptually distinct from government disposable income and consumption based on the flow-of-funds statistics. For instance, a government can run a fiscal/budget deficit while yielding a positive saving, owing to its investment spending.

13. An enhanced social safety net should first and foremost serve the purposes of social equity and risk pooling under long-term fiscal sustainability and should not be taken as a makeshift tool to lift personal consumption growth beyond the recent 8 to 10 percent pace.

References

Asian Development Bank (ADB). 2009. *Asian Development Outlook 2009: Rebalancing Asia's Growth*. Manila: ADB Publishing.

Aziz, J., and L. Cui. 2007. Explaining China's low consumption: The neglected role of household income. Working Paper WP/07/181. IMF, Washington DC.

Bai, C., C. Hsieh, and Y. Qian. 2006. Return to capital in China. Working Paper 12755. NBER, Cambridge, MA.

Bai, C., and Z. Qian. 2009. Factor income share in China: The story behind the statistics. *Economic Research* 2009 (3): 27–40.

Bayoumi, T., H. Tong, and S. Wei. 2009. China's corporate savings is not a key driver for its current account surplus: A cross-country firm-level comparative perspective. Draft paper presented at the HKMA conference "Financial Reform, macro policy and currency Internationalisation: The Case of China." Hong Kong.

Bernanke, B. 2005. The global saving glut and the US current account deficit. Speech at the Homer Jones Lecture, St Louis, April 14.

Blanchard, O., and F. Giavazzi. 2005. Rebalancing growth in China: A three-handed approach. Working Paper 05–32. MIT Department of Economics.

Cai, F. 2007. The coming Lewis turning point and its policy implications. In F. Cai, ed., *Reports on China's Population and Labour,* no 8. Beijing: Social Science Academic Press.

Chamon, C., and E. Prasad. 2008. Why are saving rates of urban households in China rising? Working Paper WP/08/145. IMF, Washington DC.

Cheung, Y., M. Chinn, and E. Fujii. 2009. China's current account and exchange rate. In R. Feenstra and S.-J. Wei, eds., *China's Growing Role in World Trade.* Chicago: University of Chicago Press, 231–71.

Chinn, M., and S. Wei. 2009. A faith-based initiative meets the evidence: Does a flexible exchange rate regime really facilitate current account adjustments? Draft. University of Wisconsin, Madison.

Dollar, D., and S. Wei. 2007. Das (wasted) Kapital: Firm ownership and investment efficiency in China. Working Paper WP/07/9. IMF, Washington DC.

Eichengreen, B. 2006. Global imbalance, demography and China. In M. Balling, E. Gnan, and F. Lierman, eds., *Money, Finance and Demography: The Consequences of Ageing.* A volume for the 26th SUERF Colloquium. Vienna: SUERF, 31–48.

Feng, J., L. He, and H. Sato. 2009. Public pension and household saving: Evidence from China. BOTIT Discussion Paper 2009/02. Bank of Finland, Helsinki.

Ferrucci, G. 2007. Saving behaviour and global imbalances: The role of emerging market economies. Working Paper 842. ECB, Frankfurt.

Feldstein, M. 1998. Social security pension reform in China. Working Paper 6794. NBER, Cambridge, MA.

Garnaut, R. 2006. The turning point in China's economic development. In R. Garnaut and L. Song, eds., *The Turning Point in China's Economic Development.* Canberra: Australian National University Press, 1–11.

Goldstein, M., and N. Lardy. 2009. The future of China's exchange rate policy. *Policy Analyses in International Economics Series,* no. 87. Washington, DC: Peterson Institute for International Economics.

Guo, K., and P. N'Diaye. 2010. Determinants of China's private consumption: An international perspective. Working Paper 10/93. IMF, Washington, DC.

Herd, R., Y. Hu, and V. Koen. 2010. Providing greater old-age security in China. Economics Working Paper 750. OECD, Paris.

Hofman, B., and L. Kuijs. 2008. Balancing China's growth. In M. Goldstein and N. Lardy, eds., *Debate China's Exchange Rate Policy.* Washington, DC: Peterson Institute for International Economics, 119–30.

Horioka, Y., and J. Wan. 2008. Why does China save so much? In B. Eichengreen, C. Wyplosz, and Y. Park, eds., *China, Asia, and the New World Economy.* New York: Oxford University Press, 371–91.

International Monetary Fund (IMF). 2009. *Asia and Pacific Regional Economic Outlook: Building a Sustained Recovery.* Washington DC: IMF.

Islam, N., and K. Yokota. 2008. Lewis growth model and China's industrialisation. Working Paper 2008–17. East Asian Development, Kitakyushu.

Jha, S., E. Prasad, and A. Terada-Hagiwra. 2009. Saving in Asia and issues for rebalancing growth. Economics Working Paper 161. ADB, Manila.

Kraay, A. 2000. Household saving in China. *World Bank Economic Review* 14 (3): 545–70.

Kuijs, L. 2006. How will China's saving-investment balance evolve? Policy Research Working Paper 3958. World Bank, Washington, DC.

Lewis, W. 1954. Economic development with unlimited supplies of labour. *Manchester School* 22 (2): 139–91.

Li, Y., and J. Yin. 2007. An exploration of the high Chinese saving. *Economic Research* (6): 1–18.

Ma, G. 2007. Who pays China's bank restructuring bill? *Asian Economic Papers* 6 (1): 46–71.

Ma, G., and Y. Wang. 2010. China's high saving rate: Myth and reality. Working Paper 312. BIS, Basel.

Ma, G., and H. Zhou. 2009. China's evolving external wealth and rising creditor position. Working Paper 286. BIS, Basel.

Meng, X. 2003. Unemployment, consumption smoothing and precautionary saving in urban China. *Journal of Comparative Economics* 31 (3): 465–85.

Meng, X., and N. Bai. 2007. How much have the wages of unskilled workers in China increased? In R. Garnaut and L. Song, eds., *China: Linking Markets for Growth*. Canberra: Australian National University Press, 151–96.

Modigliani, F., and L. Cao. 2004. The Chinese saving puzzle and the life-cycle hypothesis. *Journal of Economic Literature* 42 (March): 145–70.

Modigliani, F., and R. Cohn. 1979. Inflation, rational valuation and the market. *Financial Analysts Journal* 35 (2): 24–44.

Park, D., and K. Shin. 2009. Saving, investment and current account surplus in developing Asia. Economics Working Paper 158. ADB, Manila.

Salditt, F., P. Whiteford, and W. Adema. 2007. Pension reform in China: Progress and prospects. Social, Employment and Migration working paper 53. OECD, Paris.

Song, Z., K. Storesletten, and F. Fzilibotti. 2009. Growing like China. Discussion Paper DP7149. CEPR, London.

Song, Z., and D. Yang. 2010. Life cycle earnings and the Chinese household saving puzzle in a fast-growing economy. Presented at the Hong Kong Institute of Monetary Research.

Turner, P. 1988. Saving and investment, exchange rates and international imbalances: A comparison of the United States, Japan and Germany. *Journal of the Japanese and International Economies* 2 (3): 259–85.

Tyers, R., and F. Lu. 2008. Competition policy, corporate saving and China's current account surplus. Draft mimeo. Australian National University, Canberra.

Wang, F., and A. Mason. 2008. The demographic factor in China's transition. In L. Brandt and T. Rawski, eds., *China's Great Economic Transformation*. New York: Cambridge University Press, 136–66.

Wei, S., and X. Zhang. 2009. The competitive saving motive: Evidence from rising sex ratios and saving rates in China. Working Paper 15093. NBER, Cambridge, MA.

Wen, Yi. 2010. Saving and growth under borrowing constraints: Explaining the "high saving rate" puzzle. Working Paper 2009-045C. Federal Reserve Bank of St. Louis.

Wiemer, C. 2008. The saving story behind China's trade imbalance. Working paper 08/08. Lee Kuan Yew School of Public Policy, National University of Singapore.

Zhang, H. 2008. Corporate governance and dividend policy: A comparison of Chinese firms listed in Hong Kong and in the mainland. *China Economic Review* 19 (3): 437–59.

Zhou, X. 2005. Remarks about the return to capital of state-owed enterprises. Speech at the 2005 Annual Meeting of China Enterprise Leaders and the 20th Anniversary of *China Entrepreneurs Magazine*.

Zhou, X. 2009. Some observations and analyses on savings ratio. Speech at the High Level Conference Hosted by Bank Negara Malaysia on February 10, 2009, Kuala Lumpur.

7 Why Is China's Saving Rate So High? A Comparative Study of Cross-Country Panel Data

Juann H. Hung and Rong Qian

7.1 Introduction

China's extraordinarily high national saving rate has been at the center of much concern and analysis in recent years. In March 2005 Chairman Ben Bernanke of the Board of Governors of the Federal Reserve System proposed that the saving glut (i.e., more saving than needed for domestic investment) in parts of the world—notably China and some oil-exporting countries—has contributed to the large US current account deficit and global imbalance. Since then, concerns about the mounting global imbalance—and more recently, the conviction in some quarters that the large saving glut was a main culprit of the 2008 to 2009 financial meltdown and the accompanying great recession—have drawn even more attention to China's high saving rate.

China's saving rate is higher than the average of other high-saving countries, such as its East Asian neighbors and OPEC countries (figure 7.1). Its national saving rate was 54.4 percent of gross national income in 2007, more than twice of the average saving rate of OECD countries (table 7.1). Moreover high saving, not weak investment, is responsible for China's large excess saving. China's investment/GDP ratio averaged 41 percent from 2000 through 2008, more than double that in the United States (20 percent) over the same period. However, China's national saving rate was even higher: it averaged 48 percent from 2000 to 2008, compared to 15 percent in the United States.

Many hypotheses have been advanced to make sense of China's extraordinarily high saving rate, but it remains unclear to what extent each of those hypothetical factors contributed to making China's saving rate higher than most other countries. In particular, whether China's exchange rate policy has played a significant role in driving its high saving rate has been subject to much debate. Many analysts have

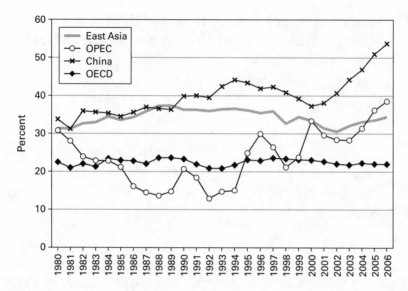

Figure 7.1
National saving rate by region (percent). Sources: World Bank National Accounts Data and OECD National Accounts.

Table 7.1
Real GDP per capita and national saving rate (annual average)

	High income	Upper middle income	Lower middle income	low income	OECD	United States	China
Real GDP per capita (constant 2005 international dollar based on PPP rates)							
1980–1990	13,280	6,158	3,156	1,049	20,875	28,420	807
1991–2000	18,313	7,686	3,367	1,037	25,123	34,796	1,920
2001–2006	21,501	9,125	4,070	1,140	29,343	40,588	3,613
2007	25,990	11,665	5,019	1,368	30,533	43,102	5,084
National saving rate (%)							
1980–1990	20.5	20.7	19.8	9.0	22.6	17.8	35.6
1991–2000	23.8	18.8	18.0	11.0	22.5	16.7	41.1
2001–2006	30.3	18.8	23.1	14.9	22.1	15.0	45.8
2007	29.5	20.0	26.7	19.8	23.0	14.3	54.4

Sources: World Development Indicators and Survey of Current Business.
Note: Countries' income-level classifications are based on World Bank classification.

argued that China's policy of undervaluing its currency is a major reason for its high saving rate.[1] However, other economists have argued that a revaluation of the yuan would not necessarily eliminate China's surplus saving because that saving is mainly rooted in complicated structural factors.[2]

Indeed most analysts would agree that saving is driven by various motives, opportunities, incentives, and constraints. An extensive literature has suggested that there are several structural and economic factors that could have played a part in its high saving for the past two decades: a weak social safety net, an underdeveloped consumer credit market, a low degree of urbanization, a relatively young population, and rapid economic growth.[3] It may be important to take those factors into account in any attempt to assess the effect of exchange rate policy—or other types of policies—on China's saving.

Against this backdrop, this chapter investigates two related empirical questions. First, to what extent does China's saving rate exceed the projections of credible models of saving rates? That is, if we include most traditional and newly formed theoretical determinants (or their proxies/instruments) of saving rates in a model, how much of China's saving rate is left unexplained? Second, what are the factors primarily responsible for China's extraordinarily high saving rate? That is, how much of China's high saving rate is attributable to structural factors, as opposed to variables that can be significantly influenced by macroeconomic policies in the short run—such as the exchange rate, the government budget balance, the real interest rate, and inflation?

Our empirical method consists of two stages. At stage one we estimate models of national saving, using a large panel dataset of about 70 countries over the time span from 1980 through 2007. At this stage we are mainly interested in identifying plausible models of national saving. We consider several explanatory variables, including variables that are traditionally considered as macroeconomic policy instruments (e.g., the budget balance, interest rates, inflation, and the exchange rate) and those that are not (e.g., real per capita income, income growth, demography, social safety net, and financial development). Following Loayza, Schmidt-Hebbel, and Serven (2000), we use a dynamic two-step system generalized method of moments (GMM) method of estimation. That method has been used by many researchers to address many issues in the estimation of equations that include lagged dependent variables as well as explanatory variables that are potentially endogenous.[4] On the whole, our coefficient estimates on the traditional list of variables are not too far off from those of Loayza et al. (2000).

In the second stage we use our estimated models to make in-sample predictions of national saving rates for individual countries and to measure the extent to which a country's national saving deviates from models' predictions for that country. Overall, our estimated models do a very decent job of explaining national saving rates of the 70 countries in the sample. Thus they provide a useful benchmark to assess the extent to which China's saving behavior differs from that of the average country and the relative contributions of different explanatory variables to China's high saving rate.

We find that China's lower *old dependency* (the population ages 65 and older relative to the population ages 15 to 64) than that of other countries is the most important factor responsible for China's higher saving. To a lesser extent China's *weaker social safety net, stronger economic growth, lower urbanization, and larger currency undervaluation* are also significant factors responsible for China's higher saving rates. Despite the attention given to the role of China's currency policy, China's currency undervaluation does not appear to be a predominat contributor to its high saving.[5] Other variables either contribute little or have a negative contribution to China's saving rate. Overall, China's national saving rate is higher than the predictions of our benchmark model by about 10 to 12 percentage points, depending on whether China is included in the dataset.

By including *the East Asia dummy* in some of our models, we find that factors proxied by that dummy variable also contribute to China's higher saving rate, and that most of those factors are those underlying the high-saving, high-growth strategy of East Asian economies. However, it is beyond the scope of this chapter to disentangle the many complex factors that are likely to be proxied by that dummy.

The remainder of the chapter is organized as follows. Section 7.2 presents existing theories of China's high saving rate. Section 7.3 reports the choice of explanatory variables, empirical strategy, and the regression results. Section 7.4 chooses the benchmark model and compares China's national saving rate to the long-term forecast of the benchmark model. Section 7.5 uses our estimated models to account for the gap between saving rates of China and the United States. Section 7.6 discusses the relationship between China's high saving and the East Asia model of economic growth. Section 7.7 concludes.

7.2 Related Literature

This chapter is related to three strands of economic literature. One strand is concerned with the causes and consequences of global imbalances—for example, Chinn and Prasad (2003), Eichengreen (2004), Dooley et al. (2003, 2004), Obstfeld and Rogoff (2005), Roubini and Setser (2005), Hung and Kim (2006), Congressional Budget Office (2004, 2005, 2007), and Caballero (2009). Nearly all those papers argue the large global imbalance is not sustainable, though some are more optimistic than others in how the imbalance will be resolved. Another set of papers attempts to explain why countries have vastly different saving rates—for example, Edwards (1996), Masson et al. (1998), Loayza et al. (2000), and International Monetary Fund (2005). Those papers generally use a large multiple-country dataset to estimate the marginal effect of various structural and nonstructural determinants on national or private saving rates.

More directly related to this chapter is the third set of papers, which focuses on addressing why China's national saving rate is much higher than the saving rate of most countries. Those papers' explanations can be roughly summarized as follows:

1. The Chinese have a higher demand for saving in part because of their frayed social safety net and an underdeveloped financial sector (Chamon and Prasad 2010; Blanchard and Giavazzi 2006; Kuijs 2006). The declining public provision of education, health, and housing services and the lack of pension programs (or, the breaking of "the iron rice bowl") creates a strong motive for the Chinese to save. An underdeveloped banking/financial sector adds to that precautionary demand for saving, since it is difficult for consumers to borrow from banks to tide them over hard times. China's small firms, which generally do not receive the preferential treatment that large state-owned enterprises do, also tend to retain earnings because they need them to finance their ventures and to provide a cushion for bad times.

2. China's policies favor industry at the cost of jobs and consumer spending (Kuijs 2006).[6] This policy bias has led to higher national saving in two ways. First, it has led household disposable income to decline relative to national income. Thus, even if the consumption share of disposable income stays constant, the consumption share of national income will decline, and the national saving rate will increase, as the economy grows.[7] Second, those policies not only have helped keep corporate profits high; they have also allowed or encouraged those

profits to be retained in the companies (rather than distributed to shareholders), thereby adding to national saving.[8]

3. China has a high rate of economic growth (Modigliani and Cao 2004). According to the life-cycle hypothesis, people save when they are wage earners in order to finance their negative saving after they retire. When the economy is growing, workers' saving will increase relative to retirees' dissaving, thereby raising aggregate saving. This channel may even be stronger for countries such as China where the social safety net is weak for retirees.

4. China has an undervalued currency (Goldstein 2007; Wolf 2010).[9] An undervalued currency undercuts the abilities of Chinese consumers to purchase foreign goods and services while it improves the price competitiveness of its exports, thereby keeping China's saving rate high.

This third set of papers suggests that part of the root cause of China's high saving are the poverty and underdevelopment of the country and its haste to grow and catch up. Indeed China was a destitute country when its pro-market economic reform started in late 1978. Despite its rapid economic growth over the past three decades, China's real per capital GDP in 2007 was still lower than one half of an average upper middle income country's level and no higher than an average lower middle country's level (table 7.1 and figure 7.2).[10]

However, each of those papers tends to focus on a small set of factors alone, and thus is susceptible to the problems caused by omitted variables. It's difficult to know a priori whether each of those factors would still play a significant role in China's high saving when most of them are included in the same model, along with other traditionally important variables such as demography and urbanization. This chapter supplements this third strand of literature—by estimating a model of national saving rates that includes variables from a broad range of theories, and by using that estimated model to assess the relative contribution of each included variable on China's saving rate.

7.3 Estimating Models of National Saving Rates

We estimate models of national saving, not private saving. This is largely because we are primarily interested in shedding light on whether the global imbalance can be largely accounted for by the vast differences in preexisting economic and institutional conditions among

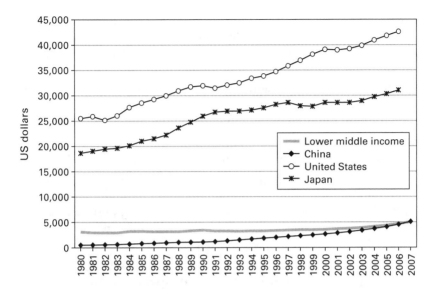

Figure 7.2
Real GDP per capita (constant 2005 US dollars based on PPP rates). Source: World Development Indicators 2008.

countries. It is also partly because data on household saving are much more limited than data on national saving.

7.3.1 Explanatory Variables
Following Loayza et al. (2000), our specifications are reduced-form linear equations, drawing on a broad range of theories for explanatory variables. We include several "traditional" variables—those that have been included in previous studies—as well as four "new" variables: *an income-adjusted growth rate, the amount of government social spending, the degree of currency undervaluation,* and *an East Asia dummy.*[11] The constructions of these new variables are described in the data appendix at the end of this chapter.

Real Income Per Capita   In a standard Keynesian model, saving is a positive function of income because people's ability to save begins to rise after their income exceeds subsistence level of consumption.[12] Lower income people tend to consume a larger share of their income than higher income people. The national saving rate is expected to rise as per capita income rises within a country or between countries, since most wage earners in poor countries tend not to have much left to save for retirement after spending on necessities.

Growth of Real Income Per Capita   While standard growth models typically posit that an increase in the saving rate leads to higher economic growth, a growing body of empirical studies has concluded that the causality from growth to saving is much more robust than that from saving to growth.[13] Theoretical channels for growth-to-saving causality include the life-cycle hypothesis and the habit-formation hypothesis.[14] The life-cycle hypothesis posits that individuals maximize utility over their lifetime through optimal allocation of their time resources. Thus people are dissavers when they are young (before they begin to work or when their income is too low to cover their expenses) and when they are old and retired; the working population (those between the young and the old) are those who save. When the economy is growing, the income and saving of the working population will increase relative to the non-working population's income and dissaving, causing aggregate saving to rise. The habit-formation hypothesis posits that when the economy is growing, people's habits tend to pull their consumption toward the level compatible with their past habits and away from the steady-state level compatible with the higher level of income. Thus, if an economy receives a shock that boosts its growth rate, its saving will rise during the transition to the new steady state. The more powerful are habits, the larger and longer-lived are these transitional effects.

Income-Adjusted Growth Rate   Saving rate may also be a positive function of the growth rate of real GDP because poor countries have an added incentive to save: to reach the Golden Rule steady state by increasing capital accumulation.[15] Poor countries that have the motivation to grow by saving may not be able to do so if they are mired in a poverty trap. However, given a poor country's desire to grow and move to a higher income and consumption steady state (i.e., the Golden Rule state), if somehow that country's growth rate picks up due to lucky exogenous shocks, that growth rate's effect on its saving rate may be stronger than that on a richer country's rate because of the poorer country's added incentive to save.[16] Because this "catch-up" or "Golden Rule" motivation for saving is likely to be positively correlated with the degree of poverty of a country, we include an income-adjusted growth rate in the model to capture that additional effect of growth on the saving rate.

Dependency Ratio   The life-cycle hypothesis argues that people are dissavers when they are young, savers when they are wage earners, and dissavers again after they have retired. Thus a country's saving declines (rises) when its dependency ratio increases (decreases). We include both the old dependency ratio and the young dependency ratio in our regressions.

Domestic Credit   A greater availability of credit could lead to a decline in saving. The extent to which individuals can smooth their consumption will depend on their ability to borrow to finance consumption. If the borrowing constraint is binding, households will be unable to increase their present consumption even if their expected lifetime income stream has increased, and they will have to lower consumption in response to negative transitory shocks to income. Moreover stringent borrowing constraints mean that households need to save a large sum before they can think of buying a house or other big-ticket items, and that firms need to rely more on retained earnings to fund their investment. This chapter uses the *domestic credits/GDP ratio* as an indicator for the availability of domestic credit. The higher is this ratio, the less stringent is the borrowing constraint.

Social Safety Net (Government's Social Spending)   An important implication of the life-cycle framework of saving is that private saving will be affected by the extent and coverage of the social safety net provided by the government. The more generous the social safety net (unemployment benefits, medical assistance to the poor, etc.), the less individuals are likely to save for precautionary purposes. We use government social spending (as a percentage of GDP) as an indicator of the generosity of the social safety net.

Urbanization (Urban Population/Total Population)   Rural households, which depend heavily on agricultural income, tend to save a larger proportion of their income than city households because precautionary saving tends to be higher for households subject to higher income volatility. According to this theory, industrial countries that have a higher degree of urbanization than developing countries will also have a lower saving rate than the latter. In our view, another likely reason for the negative effect of urbanization on saving rates is related to the fact that in developing countries dual economy is the norm. In a duel economy, even as city dwellers' living standards rise to be close to those of industrial economies, households in many villages still do not have even most basic services such as running water, electricity, and easy access to buying goods. Income inequality would rise as the economy grows if the rural population trapped in poverty does not decline. Thus a rise in urbanization amounts to a decline in income inequality. Since the saving rate tends to be positively correlated with income inequality—the richest are the ones that save most, it will also tend to be negatively correlated with urbanization.

Real Interest Rate   The effect of a higher real interest rate depends on the relative strength of substitution and income effects. The substitution effect is positive: An increase in the real interest rate will increase saving by increasing the rate of return on saving in the current period relative to that in the next period. The income effect is negative: An increase in the real interest rate will lower saving because it increases income (an increase in wealth), and thus consumption, in the current period. In many developing countries, governments are known to have kept their real interest rates low as a means of financial repression to force the national saving rate to rise—providing cheap credit to industries to promote production while suppressing consumption through lower interest income.

Inflation   In many developing countries, consumer price inflation means the amount of consumer goods that wage earners can afford will fall. Inflation thus may increase saving by redistributing wealth from workers (who tend to have a lower saving rate) toward capital owners (who tend to have a higher saving rate). Many researchers have also included inflation in a saving equation as a proxy for macroeconomic uncertainty, an increase of which is expected to have a positive effect on precautionary saving.[17]

The Government Budget Balance   In the hypothetical world of Ricardian equivalence (RE), change in the government budget balance has no effect on national saving. In that world any decrease in the budget balance is completely offset by an increase in private saving because taxpayers view government spending as a substitute of their own spending and an increase in the government deficit as an increase in their future tax liabilities. However, most analysts believe that the taxpayers' offset is smaller than predicted by the RE hypothesis, and that a decrease in the budget balance will decrease the national saving rate to some extent.

The Real Exchange Rate   The mercantilist view that a country can boost its net exports—and thus its national income and national saving—by undervaluing its currency is a long-held one. Its presumption is that a country, to the extent it succeeds in devaluing its currency and keeping it undervalued, can boost and preserve the price competitiveness of its tradables. Of course, that is not a consensus view among economists.[18] Nevertheless, the mercantilist view is popular among contemporary commentators in reaction to China's large trade surplus and high saving rate.

There is also a growing literature that shows that an undervalued currency has a positive effect on saving through nonmercantilist channels. For example, Levy-Yeyati and Sturzzenegger (2007) show that an undervalued currency boosts output growth by increasing savings and capital accumulation. Korinek and Serven (2010) claim that currency undervaluation can raise growth through learning-by-doing externalities in the tradable sector that was otherwise underdeveloped.

We include two exchange rate variables as explanatory variables: a measure of real currency depreciation and an index of currency undervaluation.

East Asia Dummy   It is well known that countries in East Asia—namely Japan, South Korea, Taiwan, China, Hong Kong, and Singapore—on average have a higher national saving rate than do other regions (table 7.1). Some attribute this to East Asian cultural factors, while others attribute it to the "East Asian growth model," which includes various policies designed to promote growth through capital accumulation. We include an *East Asia dummy* to capture any marginal effect that "being an East Asian country" has on the saving rate.

7.3.2   Data and the Estimation Method

The main source of data used to estimate the benchmark model is the World Bank's World Development Indicators 2009. We also used data from IMF's International Financial Statistics, and data from the Asian Development Bank and the United Nations. After the removal of outliers, we ended up with a sample of 70 countries, from 1980 to 2007. The data appendix at the end of this chapter reports the definition and construction of variables, data sources, and the criteria used for removing outliers.

The empirical analysis is based on generalized method of moments (GMM) estimators applied to a dynamic system of saving rates. More specifically, GMM is used to estimate a system of two equations:

$$s_{i,t} = \alpha s_{i,t-1} + \theta' X_{i,t} + \delta_i + \varepsilon_{i,t}, \tag{7.1}$$

$$s_{i,t} - s_{i,t-1} = \alpha(s_{i,t-1} - s_{i,t-2}) + \theta'(X_{i,t} - X_{i,t-1}) + (\varepsilon_{i,t} - \varepsilon_{i,t-1}), \tag{7.2}$$

where s is the saving rate, X is a set of explanatory variables, δ is the country-specific effect, and ε is the error term. The subscript i represents country and t stands for time period. A detailed description of the estimation method used in this paper, and its assumptions and advantages, is provided in section III of Loayza, Schmidt-Hebbel, and Serven (2000).

7.3.3 Regression Results

We report the estimation results in two sets of tables. The first set of tables, tables 7.2 and 7.3, report results of regressions that do not include *the income-adjusted growth rate* as a regressor. Table 7.2 reports results that include China in the dataset and table 7.3 those that exclude China. The second set of tables, tables 7.4 and 7.5, reports results of regressions that include *the income-adjusted growth* as a regressor. Table 7.4 reports results that include China in the dataset and table 7.5 those that do not.

The results of the specification tests generally support the use of GMM system panel estimates.[19] Thus, in the subsequent discussion, we will interpret our estimates under the assumption that we have succeeded in isolating the effects of the exogenous component of the explanatory variables on the saving rate.

To facilitate discussion—purely for the purpose of convenience and by no means a scientific assertion, we will henceforth refer to variables that are conventionally considered as policy instruments or targets—that is, *the real interest rate, the budget balance, inflation,* and *the exchange rate variables*—as policy variables.

General Observations of Results Presented in All Four Tables

1. All explanatory variables, except *inflation,* are statistically significant at the 95 percent confidence level in at least two tables. They also have the expected, or theoretically justifiable, sign. Coefficient estimates in

tables 7.4 and 7.5 are more stable across models than those in tables 7.2 and 7.3, especially coefficients on *urbanization* and *social spending*.

2. The national saving rate is estimated to be a positive function of *(real) per capita GDP, the growth rate of per capita GDP, the income-adjusted growth rate, the budget balance, real currency depreciation, and currency undervaluation;* and a negative function of *domestic credit/GDP, old dependency, young dependency, social safety net, and urbanization.*[20] *The real interest rate* has a negative coefficient, suggesting that its income effect outweighs the sum of its substitution and wealth effects.[21] One-percentage point increase in *government saving* leads to about 0.3 percentage points increase in national saving, suggesting that there is a partial Ricardian equivalence effect.

3. The coefficient estimates on both exchange rate variables are statistically significant with similar magnitudes in both tables 7.2 and 7.3 and in both tables 7.4 and 7.5. This suggests that the marginal impact of the real exchange rate on China's saving rate is not markedly different from that in other countries. In each table the magnitudes of those exchange rate coefficients are also stable regardless of whether the *East Asia dummy* is included in the regression, suggesting that the net effect of factors captured by that dummy—be it a culture of thrift, industrial policies, or something else—is largely independent of the exchange rate.

4. The coefficient estimates on the lagged dependent variable are around 0.5 in all four tables, impling that the long-run effects (on the saving rate) of other explanatory variables are about twice as large as their respective short-run effects, if all changes in these variables were permanent.

Comparing Table 7.2 to Table 7.4   The coefficient estimate on *income-adjusted growth rate* is statistically significant, with an expected sign and a reasonable magnitude, in all six regressions of table 7.4. This supports the "catch-up effect" hypothesis, which argues that the marginal effect of economic growth on the saving rate tends to be higher for poorer countries. The coefficient estimates on *urbanization* and on *social spending* in regressions in table 7.4 are also more statistically significant and lie within a narrower range than their counterparts in table 7.2.

Comparing Table 7.4 to Table 7.5:   1. The coefficient estimates on *income-adjusted growth* are somewhat larger in table 7.4 than in table 7.5. This suggests that the catch-up effect is more powerfully at work in China than in other countries.

Table 7.2
Dynamic panel regressions of national saving rates, including China in dataset (estimation method: two-step system GMM; *P*-values are below coefficient estimates)

Variable	Model A1	Model A2	Model A3	Model A4	Model A5	Model A6
Lagged saving rate	**0.51**	**0.499**	**0.535**	**0.5**	**0.564**	**0.532**
	0.0	0.0	0.0	0.0	0.0	0.0
Ln(real GDP per capita)	**0.036**	**0.038**	**0.032**	**0.035**	**0.03**	**0.027**
	0.0	0.0	0.0	0.0	0.0	0.0
Growth of real GDP per capita	**0.11**	**0.129**	**0.153**	**0.1**	**0.213**	**0.183**
	0.0	0.0	0.0	0.0	0.0	0.0
Domestic credit/GDP	-0.038	-0.024	-0.04	-0.033	-0.013	-0.025
	0.0	0.0	0.0	0.0	0.0	0.0
Old dependency	**-0.522**	**-0.579**	**-0.44**	**-0.477**	**-0.47**	**-0.464**
	0.0	0.0	0.0	0.0	0.0	0.0
Young dependency	**-0.161**	**-0.154**	**-0.118**	**-0.107**	**-0.148**	**-0.141**
	0.0	0.0	0.0	0.0	0.0	0.0
Urbanization	-0.04	-0.077	-0.001	-0.084	-0.049	-0.002
	0.1	0.0	0.9	0.0	0.2	1.0
Social spending	**-0.194**	**-0.144**	**-0.209**	-0.047	-0.051	-0.03
	0.0	0.0	0.0	0.2	0.4	0.6
Inflation		0.001				
		0.9				
Real interest rate			-0.146			
			0.0			

Table 7.2
(continued)

Variable	Model A1	Model A2	Model A3	Model A4	Model A5	Model A6
Government budget balance				**0.283** 0.0		
Change in real exchange rate					**0.038** 0.0	**0.031** 0.0
Undervaluation					**0.014** 0.0	**0.013** 0.0
East Asia dummy						**6.761** 0.0
P-Values of Wald test of joint significance and other tests for consistency of estimators						
Wald test	0.00	0.00	0.00	0.00	0.00	0.00
Sargan test	1.00	1.00	1.00	1.00	1.00	1.00
First-order serial correlation	0.01	0.01	0.02	0.02	0.01	0.01
Second-order serial correlation	0.19	0.19	0.24	0.30	0.17	0.17
Third-order serial correlation	0.15	0.15	0.19	0.23	0.14	0.14
Number of observations	1,188	1,188	1,092	1,110	1,170	1,170
Number of countries	70	70	69	67	69	69

Table 7.3
Dynamic panel regressions of national saving, excluding China from dataset (estimation method: two-step system GMM; *P*-values are below coefficient estimates)

Variable	Model A1	Model A2	Model A3	Model A4	Model A5	Model A6
Lagged saving rate	0.487	0.471	0.546	0.488	0.535	0.511
	0.0	0.0	0.0	0.0	0.0	0.0
Ln(real GDP per capita)	0.035	0.036	0.029	0.034	0.031	0.029
	0.0	0.0	0.0	0.0	0.0	0.0
Growth of real GDP per capita	0.089	0.095	0.140	0.065	0.174	0.170
	0.0	0.0	0.0	0.0	0.0	0.0
Domestic credit/GDP	-0.034	-0.027	-0.038	-0.034	-0.012	-0.026
	0.0	0.0	0.0	0.0	0.0	0.0
Old dependency	-0.492	-0.568	-0.411	-0.428	-0.518	-0.447
	0.0	0.0	0.0	0.0	0.0	0.0
Young dependency	-0.149	-0.160	-0.113	-0.104	-0.154	-0.154
	0.0	0.0	0.0	0.0	0.0	0.0
Urbanization	-0.024	-0.038	0.010	-0.092	-0.051	-0.016
	0.5	0.1	0.7	0.0	0.3	0.7
Social spending	-0.218	-0.149	-0.177	-0.023	-0.040	-0.057
	0.0	0.0	0.0	0.6	0.5	0.1
Inflation		0.002				
		0.8				
Real interest rate			-0.156			
			0.0			

Table 7.3
(continued)

Variable	Model A1	Model A2	Model A3	Model A4	Model A5	Model A6
Government budget balance				**0.289** 0.0		
Change in real exchange rate					**0.036** 0.0	**0.033** 0.0
Undervaluation					**0.012** 0.0	**0.010** 0.0
East Asia dummy						**4.248** 0.0
P-Values of Wald test of joint significance and other tests for consistency of estimators						
Wald test	0.00	0.00	0.00	0.00	0.00	0.00
Sargan test	1.00	1.00	1.00	1.00	1.00	1.00
First-order serial correlation	0.01	0.01	0.02	0.02	0.01	0.01
Second-order serial correlation	0.19	0.19	0.24	0.31	0.17	0.18
Third-order serial correlation	0.15	0.15	0.19	0.23	0.14	0.14
Number of observations	1,170	1,170	1,074	1,096	1,152	1,152
Number of countries	69	69	68	66	68	68

Table 7.4
Dynamic panel regressions of national saving, including China in dataset (estimation method: two-step system GMM; *P*-values are below coefficient estimates)

Variable	Model B1	Model B2	Model B3	Model B4	Model B5	Model B6
Lagged saving rate	**0.555**	**0.536**	**0.567**	**0.532**	**0.545**	**0.491**
	0.0	0.0	0.0	0.0	0.0	0.0
Ln(real GDP per capita)	**0.032**	**0.035**	**0.03**	**0.031**	**0.033**	**0.032**
	0.0	0.0	0.0	0.0	0.0	0.0
Growth of real GDP per capita	**0.089**	**0.069**	**0.103**	**0.065**	**0.144**	**0.138**
	0.0	0.0	0.0	0.0	0.0	0.0
Adjusted growth rate	**0.01**	**0.012**	**0.005**	**0.008**	**0.008**	**0.007**
	0.0	0.0	0.0	0.0	0.0	0.0
Domestic credit/GDP	**-0.033**	**-0.022**	**-0.034**	**-0.032**	-0.002	**-0.019**
	0.0	0.0	0.0	0.0	0.7	0.0
Old dependency	**-0.492**	**-0.549**	**-0.459**	**-0.48**	**-0.547**	**-0.458**
	0.0	0.0	0.0	0.0	0.0	0.0
Young dependency	**-0.157**	**-0.171**	-0.1	**-0.117**	**-0.164**	**-0.154**
	0.0	0.0	0.0	0.0	0.0	0.0
Urbanization	**-0.029**	**-0.057**	-0.027	**-0.047**	-0.05	-0.07
	0.0	0.0	0.1	0.0	0.0	0.0
Social spending	**-0.126**	**-0.115**	**-0.111**	-0.003	**-0.122**	**-0.042**
	0.0	0.0	0.0	0.9	0.0	0.3
Inflation		**0.013**				
		0.2				

Table 7.4
(continued)

Variable	Model B1	Model B2	Model B3	Model B4	Model B5	Model B6
Real interest rate			**-0.144** 0.0			
Government budget balance				**0.287** 0.0		
Change in real exchange rate					**0.035** 0.0	**0.041** 0.0
Undervaluation					**0.011** 0.0	**0.013** 0.0
East Asia dummy						**6.648** 0.0
P-Values of Wald test of joint significance and other tests for consistency of estimators						
Wald test	0.00	0.00	0.00	0.00	0.00	0.00
Sargan test	1.00	1.00	1.00	1.00	1.00	1.00
First-order serial correlation	0.01	0.01	0.02	0.02	0.01	0.01
Second-order serial correlation	0.18	0.18	0.25	0.29	0.18	0.18
Third-order serial correlation	0.17	0.17	0.20	0.24	0.15	0.14
Number of observations	1,188	1,188	1,092	1,110	1,170	1,170
Number of countries	70	70	69	67	69	69

Table 7.5
Dynamic panel regressions of national saving, excluding China from dataset (estimation method: two-step system GMM; P-values are below coefficient estimates)

Variable	B1	B2	B3	B4	B5	B6
Lagged saving rate	0.502 0.0	0.493 0.0	0.530 0.0	0.484 0.0	0.506 0.0	0.520 0.0
Ln(real GDP per capita)	0.037 0.0	0.034 0.0	0.030 0.0	0.035 0.0	0.035 0.0	0.034 0.0
Growth of real GDP per capita	0.072 0.0	0.069 0.0	0.085 0.0	0.042 0.1	0.137 0.0	0.133 0.0
Domestic credit/GDP	-0.033 0.0	-0.016 0.0	-0.038 0.0	-0.035 0.0	-0.004 0.5	-0.021 0.0
Adjusted growth	0.006 0.0	0.007 0.0	0.003 0.2	0.003 0.1	0.006 0.0	0.007 0.0
Old dependency	-0.525 0.0	-0.519 0.0	-0.320 0.0	-0.519 0.0	-0.586 0.0	-0.532 0.0
Young dependency	-0.176 0.0	-0.152 0.0	-0.103 0.0	-0.128 0.0	-0.171 0.0	-0.165 0.0
Urbanization	-0.050 0.0	-0.062 0.0	-0.043 0.0	-0.059 0.0	-0.054 0.0	-0.072 0.0
Social spending	-0.149 0.0	-0.084 0.0	-0.116 0.0	-0.021 0.6	-0.129 0.0	-0.050 0.3
Inflation		0.014 0.2				

Table 7.5
(continued)

Variable	B1	B2	B3	B4	B5	B6
Real interest rate			**-0.130** 0.0			
Government budget balance				**0.304** 0.0		
Change in real exchange rate					**0.030** 0.0	**0.032** 0.0
Undervaluation					**0.011** 0.0	**0.007** 0.0
East Asia dummy						**1.756** 0.6
P-Values of Wald test of joint significance and other tests for consistency of estimators						
Wald test	0.00	0.00	0.00	0.00	0.00	0.00
Sargan test	1.00	1.00	1.00	1.00	1.00	1.00
First-order serial correlation	0.01	0.01	0.02	0.02	0.01	0.01
Second-order serial correlation	0.19	0.19	0.26	0.31	0.18	0.18
Third-order serial correlation	0.16	0.16	0.20	0.23	0.15	0.14
Number of observations	1,170	1,170	1,074	1,096	1,152	1,152
Number of countries	69	69	68	66	68	68

2. The coefficient on the *East Asia dummy* in model B6 in table 7.5 is statistically insignificant and quantitatively much smaller than that in table 7.4. Because the former is estimated without China in the dataset, this result suggests that there are other factors proxied by the *East Asia dummy* that are at work more powerfully in China than in other East Asian economies.

Comparing Our Results to the Literature   To our knowledge, IMF (2005) is the only study of national saving rate using a large cross-country panel dataset since Loayza et al. (2000).[22] A comparison between coefficient estimates in table 7.2 (the regression closest to those two papers in regression specification and the construction of explanatory variables) and those two papers are presented in table 7.6. Despite the considerable differences in regression models used in this and those two papers, our long-term coefficient estimates on comparable explanatory variables are either reasonably close, or qualitatively compatible, to estimates in those two studies.[23]

7.4   Choosing the Benchmark Model

Which of our estimated models is most appropriate as the benchmark model for our purpose? Since we have already established that models with *the income-adjusted growth rate* perform better than those without, we narrow our comparison to the models in tables 7.4 and 7.5. Unsurprisingly, the extent of each country's unexplained saving—the difference between the national saving rate and the long-term model forecast—varies across the six models and depends on whether China is included in the dataset (table 7.7).[24] By the standard of the average rate of unexplained saving of all OECD countries and that of China, the best choice is model B6—the model that includes *the East Asia dummy* and *the two exchange rate variables*. However, model B6 should be ruled out since we already established that the *East Asia dummy* largely reflects China-specific factors—may it be its unique industrial policy mix, its government's ability to command those policies through the state-owned enterprises and other means, or something else. Having ruled out model B6, the unambiguous winner is model B5 as it has the best fit to China's and OECD's average saving rates. Moreover its ability to fit national saving rates remains relatively unchanged regardless of whether it is estimated with or

Table 7.6
Comparisons of short-term and long-term coefficient estimates

Dependent variable: saving rate	This chapter	IMF	LHS	Implied long-term estimates This chapter	IMF	LHS
Lagged saving rate	0.51	0.62	0.38			
Growth rate of per capita GDP or GNDI	0.11	0.17	0.45	0.22	0.45	0.73
Real per capita GDP or GNDI	0.04		0.10	0.07		0.16
Domestic credit/ GDP or GNDI	−0.04	−3.47	−0.36	−0.08	−9.13	−0.58
Old dependency	−0.52	−0.44	−0.77	−1.07	−1.16	−1.24
Young dependency	−0.16		−0.16	−0.33		−0.26
Urbanization	−0.04		−0.50	−0.08		−0.81
Real interest rate	−0.15		−0.14	−0.30		−0.22
Government saving	0.28	0.27		0.58	0.71	
Real exchange rate change	0.04	0.08	0.06	0.08	0.21	0.09
Inflation	0.00		0.18	0.00		0.29

Note: The comparison needs to be taken in perspective mainly for the following reasons:
1. LHS refers to Loayza et al. (2000). Both LHS and IMF (2005) include terms of trade growth, not real exchange rate change.
2. LHS data were from 1965 to 1994, the IMF data were from1972 to 2004, and this paper's data were from 1980 to 2007.
3. This chapter's coefficient estimates are taken from table 7.2. Estimates of inflation, real interest rate, and government saving are taken from models A2, A3, and A4 respectively. Other coefficients are from model A5.
4. The dependent variable is somewhat different in the three papers: it is private saving/ gross national disposable income (GNDI) in LHS; national saving/gross national income (GNI) in this chapter, and national saving/GDP in IMF.

without China in the dataset, in contrast to that of model B6 (figures 7.3 and 7.4).

Using model B5 as the benchmark model, China's average unexplained saving from 1990 to 2007 was about 10.3 percentage points (24 percent of its saving rate) if China is included in the dataset, and 12.2 percentage points (28 percent of its saving rate) if China is excluded. China had a higher level of unexplained saving rate on average than all other countries in the sample except Bhutan, Singapore, and Brunei (table 7.8).

Table 7.7
Unexplained saving rates by model (percent; average of sample period) (unexplained saving = national saving − long-term forecast) (% deviation = national saving/long-term forecast − 1)

Regression	China		OECD		All Countries	
	Unexplained saving	Percent deviation	Unexplained saving	Percent deviation	Unexplained saving	Percent deviation
Models estimated with the full dataset (table 7.2)						
B1	16.1	59%	−0.1	0%	−1.1	−5%
B2	13.7	46%	−0.3	−1%	−1.1	−5%
B3	15.8	57%	−0.3	−1%	−1.4	−6%
B4	19.8	83%	−0.3	−1%	−1.3	−5%
B5	10.3	31%	−0.1	0%	−0.8	−3%
B6	3.7	9%	1.1	5%	0.5	2%
Models estimated without Chinese data (table 7.4)						
B1	17.6	68%	0.1	0%	−0.5	−2%
B2	16.5	62%	−0.3	−1%	−0.6	−3%
B3	19.1	79%	−0.3	−1%	−0.3	−1%
B4	21.3	95%	0.3	1%	−0.6	−3%
B5	12.2	39%	0.4	2%	−0.3	−1%
B6	11.9	38%	0.5	2%	−0.1	0%

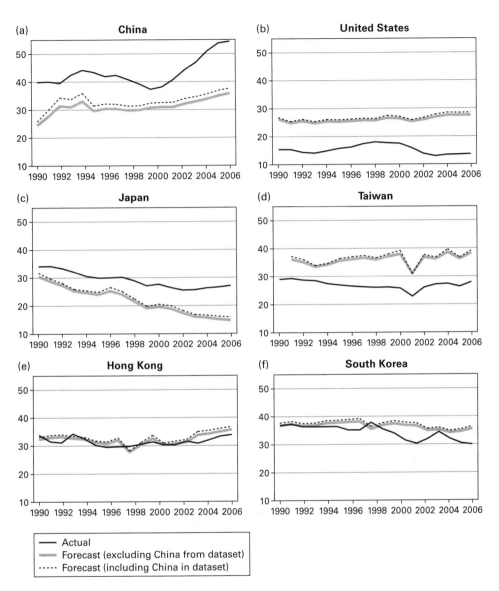

Figure 7.3
National saving rate: Actual versus long-term forecast of the benchmark model (percent).

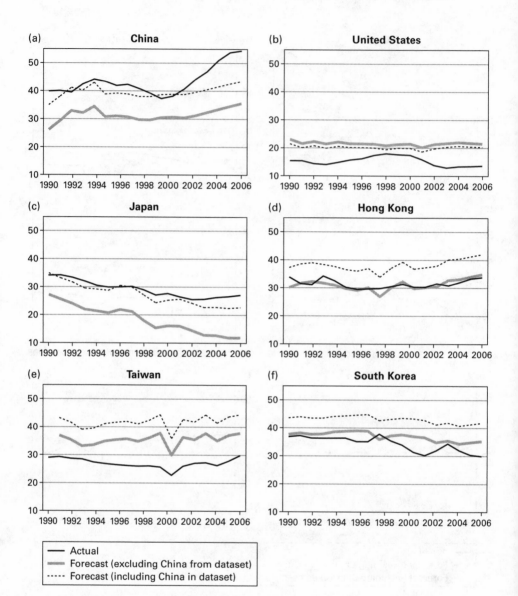

Figure 7.4
National saving rate: Actual versus long-term forecast of the benchmark model plus East Asia dummy (percent).

7.5 What Factors Are Responsible for China's High National Saving Rate?

The preceding analysis suggests that about three-quarters of China's high saving rate is attributable to explanatory variables included in the benchmark model (model B5 in table 7.4). This section assesses the relative importance of each model variable in China's high saving rate by estimating its contribution to the gap between China's and OECD countries' saving rates. It then discusses the factors outside the model that may have been responsible for the sharp rise in the unexplained portion of China's saving rate after 2001.

The contribution of each variable to the China–OECD saving gap depends on the difference in the magnitude of that variable as well as the elasticity of the saving rate with respect to that variable. Table 7.9 shows that the magnitudes of most variables in China are quite different from those in the OECD economies. The levels of *old dependency, social spending,* and *urbanization* in China are much lower than their average levels in OECD, while *the growth rate* (including *the income-adjusted growth rate*) and the degree of *currency undervaluation* are much higher in China than that in OECD. To provide some degree of sensitivity analysis, table 7.10 presents the contribution of each explanatory variable using coefficient estimates in the benchmark model as well as those in other models reported in table 7.4.

Table 7.10 shows that, regardless of which model's coefficient estimates are used, China's much *lower level of old dependency* stands out as most responsible for the explained portion of China's much higher saving rate. The rankings of other factors are somewhat model-dependent. Based on our benchmark model, the other important factors are China's *higher growth rate of real GDP per capita* (including *the adjusted growth*), *weaker social safety net,* and *lower urbanization ratio*. Relative to those factors, the exchange rate variables (i.e., *undervaluation* and *depreciation*) appears to be a modest contributor to China's higher saving rate.

The preeminence of *old dependency* in accounting for the China–OECD saving gap remains unchanged when we use coefficient estimates without China in the dataset (table 7.11). That preeminence stemmed from both the large elasticity of saving in response to *the old dependency ratio* and the fact that the ratio is much higher in OECD than in China (by 12 percentage points). The relatively modest marginal contribution of China's *currency undervaluation*, however, mainly reflected the small elasticity of saving in response to currency undervaluation.

Table 7.8
Actual and model forecasts of national saving rates (percent) (unexplained saving = national saving − long-term forecast) (% deviation = national saving rate/long-term forecast − 1). Model = model B5 of table 7.4, estimated with China in dataset

Country	Saving rate	Unexplained saving rate	Percent deviation	Country	Saving rate	Unexplained saving rate	Percent deviation
Brunei	49.9	4.4	10%	Dominican Republic	21.6	−0.9	−4%
Bhutan	49.1	21.2	76%	Fiji	21.6	−3.7	−15%
Singapore	46.6	6.5	16%	Australia	21.4	−3.9	−15%
China	43.3	10.3	31%	Italy	21.3	0.4	2%
South Korea	34.3	−3.0	−8%	Sri Lanka	21.2	−9.1	−30%
Luxembourg	34.1	5.9	21%	Denmark	21.1	3.1	17%
Thailand	32.5	−2.5	−7%	Mexico	20.7	−4.8	−19%
Hong Kong, China	31.5	−1.5	−5%	Sweden	20.7	10.0	93%
India	30.5	5.0	20%	Germany	20.4	1.3	7%
Switzerland	30.2	5.0	20%	Canada	20.2	−7.6	−27%
Japan	30.1	4.8	19%	Hungary	19.7	−2.2	−10%
Mongolia	29.9	10.1	51%	France	19.4	1.7	10%
Venezuela	28.7	4.1	17%	New Zealand	18.9	−2.9	−13%
Norway	28.0	8.4	43%	Poland	18.6	−4.2	−18%
Indonesia	27.2	−0.6	−2%	Georgia	18.3	−2.7	−13%
Taiwan	27.0	−9.9	−27%	Argentina	17.8	1.4	9%
Trinidad and Tobago	26.6	−11.4	−30%	Greece	17.2	−4.9	−22%
Papua New Guinea	26.5	6.0	30%	Colombia	16.9	−7.9	−32%
Netherlands	25.3	0.4	2%	Iceland	16.6	−6.6	−29%

Table 7.8
(continued)

Country	Saving rate	Unexplained saving rate	Percent deviation	Country	Saving rate	Unexplained saving rate	Percent deviation
Czech Republic	25.2	0.3	1%	United Kingdom	16.1	-0.8	-5%
Panama	24.9	1.9	8%	Turkey	16.1	-10.1	-39%
Philippines	24.8	5.0	25%	United States	16.0	-11.1	-41%
Honduras	24.3	10.6	78%	Paraguay	15.9	-2.5	-13%
Finland	23.9	1.7	8%	Brazil	15.3	-7.7	-33%
Chile	23.8	-1.9	-7%	Tonga	15.3	-1.6	-9%
Jamaica	23.7	4.0	20%	Costa Rica	15.0	-10.5	-41%
Bangladesh	23.6	3.5	18%	Bolivia	14.9	0.7	5%
Ireland	23.3	-1.3	-5%	El Salvador	13.9	-6.7	-32%
Slovak Republic	23.3	-4.9	-17%	Uruguay	13.6	2.4	21%
Austria	22.5	0.8	4%	Guatemala	12.9	-1.2	-8%
Nepal	22.3	5.1	30%	Cambodia	12.8	-10.4	-45%
Belgium	22.2	6.1	38%	Nicaragua	12.4	-2.5	-17%
Portugal	22.0	-1.5	-6%	Vanuatu	11.9	-7.4	-38%
Spain	21.9	1.0	5%	Tajikistan	11.8	-11.1	-49%
Peru	21.9	-1.6	-7%	Kyrgyz Republic	10.6	-10.4	-50%
OECD					22.3	-0.1	0%
All 70 countries in sample					22.3	-0.8	-3%

Note: Each country's saving rate is the average over the years for which data are available for that country. The sample period is from 1980 to 2007, but some countries do not have data for the entire sample period.

Table 7.9
Determinants of national saving in China and OECD

Explanatory variable	China	OECD average	China–OECD gap
Annual average over 2001 to 2006; in percentage terms			
Ln(real GDP per capita)	8.2	10.3	−2.1
Growth of real GDP per capita	9.2	2.2	7.1
Adjusted growth rate	120.0	3.8	116.2
Domestic credit/GDP	138.4	132.2	6.2
Old dependency	10.6	22.1	−11.6
Young dependency	32.4	26.3	6.1
Urbanization	39.0	75.1	−36.1
Social spending	4.1	20.8	−16.7
Inflation	1.3	2.6	−1.2
Real interest rate	2.3	3.9	−1.6
Government budget balance	−1.8	−0.8	−1.0
Real exchange rate depreciation	0.7	−1.0	1.7
Undervaluation	47.4	−55.7	103.1
East Asia dummy	1.0	0.1	0.9
Annual average over 1990 to 2000; in percentage terms			
Ln(real GDP per capita)	7.5	10.1	−2.6
Growth of real GDP per capita	8.6	2.2	6.4
Adjusted growth rate	197.1	4.2	192.8
Domestic credit/GDP	99.7	106.3	−6.6
Old dependency	9.0	20.7	−11.7
Young dependency	39.3	28.7	10.6
Urbanization	31.5	74.1	−42.6
Social spending	1.8	20.3	−18.5
Inflation	7.1	4.2	2.9
Real interest rate	1.9	6.3	−4.3
Government budget balance	−2.5	−2.8	0.2
Real exchange rate depreciation	3.6	0.7	2.9
Undervaluation	47.1	−55.0	102.1
East Asia dummy	1.0	0.1	0.9

Notes: OECD comprises 27 countries, including two East Asian countries (Japan and South Korea); unlike other varaibles, Ln(real GDP per capita) is not reported in percentage terms.

Table 7.10
Contributions of explanatory variables to the China–OECD saving gaps (percent)

Explanatory variable	Model B1	Model B2	Model B3	Model B4	Model B5	Model B6
Based on coefficients estimated with China in the dataset 2001 to 2006						
Ln(real GDP per capita)	−14.9	−15.6	−14.4	−13.7	−15.0	−13.0
Growth of real GDP per capita	1.4	1.1	1.7	1.0	2.2	1.9
Adjusted growth rate	2.6	3.0	1.3	2.0	2.0	1.6
Domestic credit/GDP	−0.5	−0.3	−0.5	−0.4	0.0	−0.2
Old dependency	12.8	13.7	12.2	11.8	13.9	10.4
Young dependency	−2.2	−2.3	−1.4	−1.5	−2.2	−1.9
Urbanization	2.4	4.4	2.3	3.6	4.0	5.0
Social spending	4.7	4.1	4.3	0.1	4.5	1.4
Inflation		0.0				
Real interest rate			0.5			
Government budget balance				−0.6		
Change in real exchange rate					0.4	0.4
Undervaluation					2.5	2.6
East Asia dummy						12.0
Total contribution	6.3	8.1	6.1	2.3	12.3	20.2
China–OECD saving rate gap	23.6	23.6	23.6	23.6	23.6	23.6

Table 7.10
(continued)

Based on coefficients estimated with China in the dataset 1990 to 2000

Explanatory variable	Model B1	Model B2	Model B3	Model B4	Model B5	Model B6
Ln(real GDP per capita)	-18.7	-19.6	-18.0	-17.2	-18.8	-16.3
Growth of real GDP per capita	1.3	1.0	1.5	0.9	2.0	1.7
Adjusted growth rate	4.3	5.0	2.2	3.3	3.4	2.7
Domestic credit/GDP	0.5	0.3	0.5	0.4	0.0	0.2
Old dependency	13.0	13.9	12.5	12.0	14.1	10.6
Young dependency	-3.7	-3.9	-2.4	-2.6	-3.8	-3.2
Urbanization	2.8	5.2	2.7	4.3	4.7	5.9
Social spending	5.2	4.6	4.7	0.1	5.0	1.5
Inflation		0.1				
Real interest rate			1.4			
Government budget balance				0.2		
Change in real exchange rate					0.1	0.1
Undervaluation					2.5	2.6
East Asia dummy						12.1
Total contribution	4.7	6.6	5.1	1.4	9.2	17.9
China–OECD saving rate gap	18.4	18.4	18.4	18.4	18.4	18.4

Note: Marginal contribution of variable X = (X in China – X in OECD) × coefficient of $X/(1$ – coefficient of lag saving); the coefficients are taken from regressions in table 7.4, which includes China in the dataset.

Table 7.11
Marginal contributions of explanatory variables to the China–OECD saving gaps (percent)

Explanatory variable	Model B1	Model B2	Model B3	Model B4	Model B5	Model B6
Based on coefficients estimated without China in the dataset 2001 to 2006						
Ln(real GDP per capita)	-15.4	-13.9	-13.2	-14.1	-14.7	-14.7
Growth of real GDP per capita	1.0	1.0	1.3	0.6	2.0	2.0
Adjusted growth rate	1.4	1.6	0.7	0.7	1.4	1.7
Domestic credit/GDP	-0.4	-0.2	-0.5	-0.4	-0.1	-0.3
Old dependency	12.2	11.8	7.9	11.6	13.7	12.8
Young dependency	-2.2	-1.8	-1.3	-1.5	-2.1	-2.1
Urbanization	3.6	4.4	3.3	4.1	3.9	5.4
Social spending	5.0	2.8	4.1	0.7	4.4	1.7
Inflation		0.0				
Real interest rate			0.4			
Government budget balance				-0.6		
Change in real exchange rate					0.3	0.3
Undervaluation					2.3	1.4
East Asia dummy						3.4
Total contribution to saving gap	5.2	5.6	2.7	1.1	11.2	11.7
China–OECD saving rate gap	23.6	23.6	23.6	23.6	23.6	23.6

Table 7.11
(continued)

Based on coefficients estimated without China in the dataset 1990 to 2000

Explanatory variable	Model B1	Model B2	Model B3	Model B4	Model B5	Model B6
Ln(real GDP per capita)	-19.3	-17.4	-16.6	-17.6	-18.4	-18.4
Growth of real GDP per capita	0.9	0.9	1.2	0.5	1.8	1.8
Adjusted growth rate	2.3	2.7	1.2	1.1	2.3	2.8
Domestic credit/GDP	0.4	0.2	0.5	0.4	0.1	0.3
Old dependency	12.4	12.0	8.0	11.8	13.9	13.0
Young dependency	-3.7	-3.2	-2.3	-2.6	-3.7	-3.6
Urbanization	4.3	5.2	3.9	4.9	4.7	6.4
Social spending	5.5	3.1	4.6	0.8	4.8	1.9
Inflation		0.1				
Real interest rate			1.2			
Government budget balance				0.1		
Change in real exchange rate					0.1	0.1
Undervaluation					2.3	1.4
East Asia dummy						3.4
Total contribution to saving gap	2.8	3.5	1.7	-0.6	7.9	9.1
China–OECD saving rate gap	18.4	18.4	18.4	18.4	18.4	18.4

Note: Marginal contribution of variable $X = (X$ in China $- X$ in OECD) $\times$ coefficient of $X/(1 -$ coefficient of lag saving); the coefficients are taken from regressions in table 7.5, which excludes China in the dataset.

The other variables—*domestic credit/GDP, the young dependency ratio,* and *real GDP per capita*—made either little or negative contributions to the China–OECD saving gap. In particular, everything else being equal, the higher income level of the OECD countries meant China's saving rate should have been lower than OECD's rate by 15 percentage points during 2000 to 2006. From this perspective those positive factors together contributed over 27 percentage points to the China–OECD saving rate gap during that period.

All those positive factors' contributions to the saving gap declined somewhat in recent years. The contribution of China's *lower old dependency ratio* declined from 77 percent in 1990 to 2000 to 59 percent in 2001 to 2006; that of China's *higher growth rate* from 29 to 19 percent; that of its *weaker social safety net* from 27 to 19 percent; and that of its *lower urbanization* from 26 to 17 percent. The combined contribution of *currency undervaluation and currency depreciation* was 14 percent in 1990 to 2000 and 12 percent in 2001 to 2006.[25] Indeed the benchmark model has become less able to account for China's saving rate in recent years (figure 7.3). Even model B6, which includes *the East Asia dummy* and tracks China's saving rate remarkably well before 2001, becomes less able to explain China's saving after 2001 (figure 7.4)

Clearly, some factors not included in our models have become increasingly important in driving China's saving rate in recent years. The literature suggests three possibilities.

The first is the possible effect of the 1997 to 1998 Asian crisis on boosting both private and government precautionary saving. In one of his speeches in 2009, Zhou Xiaochuan, the governor of the People's Bank of China, claimed that one factor behind East Asian countries' high saving rates and large foreign reserves is "defensive reactions against predatory speculation" that had led to the Asian financial crisis.[26] Park and Shin (2009) also argue that the Asian crisis has had a positive effect on precautionary saving in East Asian economies, boosting their current account surpluses. When we add an *Asian Crisis dummy* to our regressions, we find that it has a positive effect on national saving in several specifications. However, that dummy is not significant in all the specifications that include the exchange rate variables, suggesting that the exchange rate may be an important tool used to reach the higher level of precautionary saving in response to the Asian crisis.[27]

The second possibility is the widening gender imbalance, as hypothesized by Wei and Zhang (2009). According to the authors, China's one-child policy and Chinese partiality favoring boys over girls have resulted in a surplus of men. This in turn has generated a highly competitive marriage market, driving up China's saving rates as households with sons were forced to raise their saving to increase the chance of winning a bride. The authors presented evidence to show that the saving rate started to shoot up around 2002 largely because that was when the gender ratio for the marriage-age cohort began to be seriously out of balance, enhancing incentives of households with sons to increase saving for the sake of winning a bride.

The third possible factor is the increase in the transfer of income away from the household sector to banks and businesses as a result of policy makers' efforts to resolve the crisis posed by the surge in non-performing loans (NPLs) that began in the late 1990s. The government began to implement a variety of measures to reduce the NPLs in 1998; those efforts began to speed up in earnest in 2001 as the government stepped up the country's transition from a centrally planned economy to a market-oriented one.[28] According to Pettis (2010), the government's measures to resolve the bad-loan crisis all resulted in passing the bailout costs on to bank depositors.[29] Thus, he argues, household income share, already a low share of domestic income by international standards, declined further. Regardless of Pettis' hypothesis is valid, China's household income share did begin to decline significantly in 2002 (figure 7.5). As pointed out by Aziz and Cui (2007), that decline has in turn contributed to the rise in China's national saving rate unexplained by our models in recent years.

7.6   China's High Saving and the East Asian Economic Growth Model

The finding that model B6, which includes the *East Asia dummy*, explained nearly 92 percent of China's saving rate from 1990 to 2006 begs this question: How much of China's high saving rate is attributable to factors that are shared by East Asian economies but different from the rest of the world? This section discusses this issue by drawing from empirical findings of this chapter, stylized facts, and the literature.

The fact that the coefficient estimate on *the East Asia dummy* becomes statistically insignificant when model B6 is re-estimated without China in the dataset would seem to suggest that the dummy mainly captures China-specific factors. However, that the dummy remains statistically significant in model A6—the model that excludes *the income-adjusted*

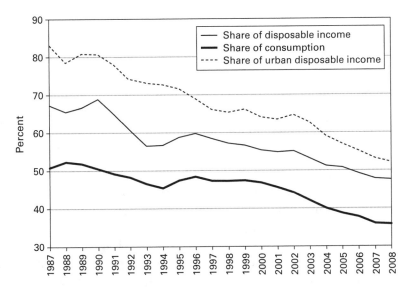

Figure 7.5
Disposable income and consumption as share of GNI (percent). Source: CEIC Data.

growth rate—even when China is excluded, the dataset suggests that one cannot easily dismiss *the East Asia dummy* as merely a proxy for China's fixed effects. More plausible is the interpretation that there is a significant overlap of the factors captured by *the East Asia dummy* and those by the *income-adjusted growth rate*. Thus, when China is excluded from the dataset, the *East Asia dummy* becomes insignificant in a model that already includes *the adjusted growth rate* but remains significant in the model that does not. The question is: What are those common factors captured by both *the East Asia dummy* and *the income-adjusted growth rate*?

Volumes have been written about why East Asian economies have managed to grow much more rapidly than other developing economies. In that literature the East Asian growth model can be loosely described as a "high saving–high investment–high growth" strategy modeled after Japan's economic growth and development.[30] Although the specific policy mix varies across East Asian economies, that growth model basically relies on heavy government interventions that favor industrialization via capital formation, generally by various policies that effectively force savings from consumers to keep the cost of financing low for investment.[31] For example, some countries—including Japan, South Korea, and Taiwan—provided affordable credit to business by allowing inflation to effectively curtail consumer spending in some periods during their years of industrialization. Until recent years consumers generally had more difficulty obtaining credit than did business entities in those countries. Even in Japan, which grew to become a rich and industrialized country roughly three decades ago, policies that favor business investment at the expense of consumer demand have only begun to fade or be reversed in recent years. Haggard (1988) argues that a key element underlying those East Asian governments' ability to implement those policies with success is their political systems "in which economic policy-making process was relatively *insulated* from direct political pressures and compromises" and "legislatures are historically weak or nonexistent and other channels of political access and representation tightly controlled, even under nominally democratic regimes."

There is plenty of evidence that China has adopted its neighbors' strategies of achieving rapid growth through high saving and investment. For example, China's policies are known to favor capital-intensive investment, which arguably is less effective in creating jobs to absorb its large pool of excess labor than labor-intensive investment is. Partly as a result of that, profits have outpaced wage income and household consumption has declined relative to national income (figure 7.5). Capital-intensive production has been encouraged by low interest rates and by the fact that most state-owned firms do not pay any dividends, which allowed them to reinvest all their profits. Furthermore the government has also favored manufacturing over services by policies such as holding down the yuan exchange rate and suppressing the prices of land and energy.

Indeed, as pointed out by Kuijs (2005, 2006) and Ma and Yi (2010), much of the sharp rise in China's national saving is attributable to the rise in corporate saving saving (the sum of retained earnings and depreciation) and in government saving (figure 7.6). Ma and Yi (2010) attribute the rise in corporate saving to two related factors. The first is a very tough corporate restructuring during 1995 to 2005 that consequently boosted corporate efficiency and profitability.[32] The second is a government policy that state companies were not required to pay dividends to the government.[33] In addition to those two factors, one may add this: some smaller private firms' need to fund investment with retained earnings because they tend not to have easy access bank loans—which are mainly reserved for large state-owned enterprises. The rise in government saving from 2001 to 2007 was even larger than

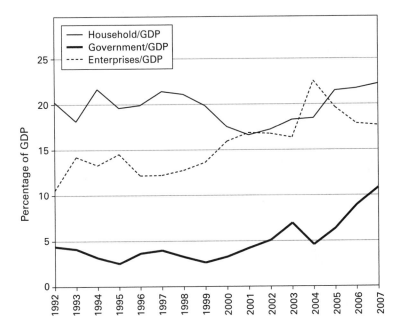

Figure 7.6
Compositions of gross saving in China (percent of GDP). Source: CEIC.

that in corporate saving (figure 7.6). That rise mainly stemmed from the fact that much of the increase in government revenue went to government investment (which is considered government saving) as opposed to consumption (unemployment benefit, medical care for the poor, etc.).[34] The Chinese central government actually ran a small budget deficit during that period, because its total spending (the sum of investment and consumption) exceeded its total revenue. The household saving/GDP ratio, despite the decline in the share of national income going to households, has again surpassed the enterprise saving/GDP ratio after 2004 (figure 7.6). In part this is due to the continuing rise in household saving rate since the early 1990s, which reached nearly 30 percent by 2008 (figure 7.7).[35]

Clearly, all three players—the household sector, the corporate sector (both private-owned and state-owned enterprises), and the government—have been responsible for China's high saving rate. This is consistent with what one would expect from a country that has adopted the East Asian growth model, especially if the first two groups' high savings are in part induced by government policies.

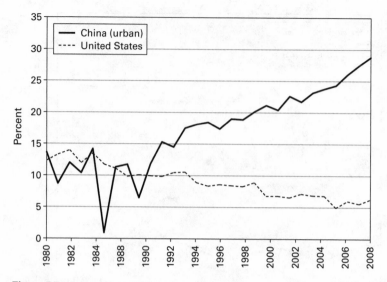

Figure 7.7
Household saving rates in China and the United States (percent). Sources: CEIC and US Bureau of Economic Analysis.

The evolution of national saving and economic growth in Japan, the grandfather of the East Asian growth model, suggests that we are likely to see a gradual normalization of China's saving rate as the Chinese economy continues to develope and converge toward rich countries in terms of real income per capita. Given that China's real GDP per capita in 2007 was still slightly below that of Japan in the early 1960s, however, it is unlikely that China's saving will decline to a more "normal" level within the next decade.[36] Nevertheless, there are signs that that process of "normalization" has begun. For example, the government allowed its currency to rise against the US dollar by over 17 percent from June 2005 to July 2008 (the beginning of the 2008 to 2009 global financial turmoil). That trend is likely to continue once the global recovery is on a more solid footing. The government has also begun to strengthen the social safety, especially after 2005 (figure 7.8).

7.7 Conclusions

In this chapter, we estimate models of national saving rates to gauge the extent to which China's high saving rate can be accounted for by models that explain other countries' saving rates reasonably well on average. We find that our benchmark models explain about 72 to 76 percent of China's national saving rate during 1990 to 2007, depending

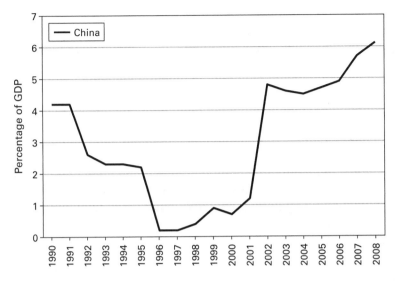

Figure 7.8
Government social spending in China (percent of GDP). Sources: Asian Development Bank and US Bureau of Economic Analysis.

on whether China is included in the dataset. On average, China's national saving rate exceeded the predictions of those models by about 10 to 12 percentage points.

Many traditional determinants of saving indeed have a statistically and quantitatively significant effect on national saving rates. The predominant drivers of China's higher saving rates are its relatively *low old dependency ratio*, and, to a lesser extent, its *strong growth rate, weak social safety net, low urbanization*, and large *currency undervaluation*. Our results also suggest that some factors shared by East Asian economies have contributed to China's higher saving rate, and that those factors are mainly those underlying the high-savings–high-growth strategy of East Asian economies. However, it is beyond the scope of this chapter to disentangle the many complex factors that are likely to be proxied by that dummy.

Our results imply that, as the Chinese population becomes older and China's national income reaches its potential, its saving rate will also begin to decline.

Acknowledgments

This chapter is an updated and shortened version of "Why Is China's Saving Rate so High—A Comparative Study of Cross-Country Panel

Data, " CBO working paper 2010–07. The authors thank colleagues in the Congressional Budget Office—especially John Peterson, Bob Dennis, Kim Kowalewski—and participants in the CESifo Workshop at Venice Summer Institute—especially Galina Hale, Menzie Chinn, Bob McCauley, and Ying-Wong Cheung—for helpful comments and suggestions. Priscila Hammett's valuable research assistance is deeply appreciated.

Data Appendix. Definition of Variables and Sources of Data

Data are obtained from the World Bank's *World Development Indicators 2009*, except otherwise indicated. Outliers removed from the sample include (1) Domestic Credit/GDP greater than 1000, (2) real interest rates greater than 50 or less than −50, and (3) inflation rates greater than 500.

Asian-Crisis dummy equals zero before 1999 and one beginning in 1999.

Adjusted growth rate of real GDP per capita of country i is the product of the growth rate of real GDP per capita of country I and the income-adjustment factor, which is measured by [moving average of $(Y^{us}_{t-1,t-3}/Y^{i}_{t-1,t-3})] \times [(Y^{i}_{t}/Y^{i}_{t-1}) - 1]$, where Y^{us} is the real GDP per capita of the United States.

Currency undervaluation is constructed following Rodrik (2008). The real exchange rate for country i in year t (RER_{it}) is constructed as $\ln(RER_{it}) = \ln(XRAT_{it}/PPP_{it})$, where $XRAT$ is the exchange rate and PPP the conversion factor from Penn World Table 6.3. Then we adjust for the Balassa–Samuelson effect by estimating the equation $\ln(RER_{it}) = \alpha + \beta \ln(RGDPCH_{it}) + f_t + \varepsilon_{it}$ (where $RGDPCH$ is the real GDP per capita, and f_t accounts for the time fixed effect), and use the fitted value of $\ln(RER^*_{it})$ as the adjusted real exchange rate. The degree of currency undervaluation ($UNDERVAL$) is measured as equal to $\ln(RER_{it}) - \ln(RER^*_{it})$.

Domestic credit is the percent share of domestic credit of GDP.

East Asia dummy is set to equal one for China, Japan, South Korea, Taiwan, Singapore, and Hong Kong; it is set to zero for all other countries.

Government budget balance is the central government budget balance as a percent share of GDP. Data are obtained from OECD, the United Nations Economic Commission for Latin America and the Caribbean (ECLAC), and the Asian Development Bank.

Growth rate of real GDP per capita is measured by $100 \times ((Y^i_t/Y^i_{t-1}) - 1)$, where Y^i_t is real GDP per capita of country i in year t.

Inflation is the annual percentage change in the consumer price.

National saving rate is gross national saving as a percent share of GNI.

Old dependency is the ratio of the old-age population (ages 65 and older) relative to the working-age population (ages 15 to 64), in percent terms.

Real interest rate is the bank lending rate adjusted for the annualized inflation rate, in percent terms.

Real exchange rate (2000 = 100) is the index of the bilateral real exchange rate of a country's currency relative to the dollar. For the United States, the real exchange rate is the Federal Reserve Board's broad index of its trade-weighted real exchange rate relative to its major trading partners.

Real GDP per capita is a country's real GDP per capita, expressed in terms of constant 2005 international dollars. An international dollar has the same purchasing power as the US dollar does in the United States.

Social spending is government social spending as a percentage of GDP. Social spending includes expenditure on unemployment benefit, social security, health care, and education. Data are obtained from OECD, the United Nations Economic Commission for Latin America and the Caribbean (ECLAC), and the Asian Development Bank.

Urbanization is measured by urban population as percent of total population.

Young dependency is the ratio of the youth population (ages 14 and younger) relative to the working-age population (ages 15 to 64), in percent terms.

Notes

1. For example, see Wolf (2010) and papers cited in that article.

2. For example, Spence (2010) argues that China's exchange rate undervaluation is one facet in the complexity of its transition toward a middle-income economy, and that revaluing the yuan is unlikely to get rid of China's surplus saving because China's high savings are embedded in its overall economic structure—such as the government's extensive control of income (directly and through ownership of the state-owned enterprises). Similarly Rodrik (2009) maintains that China's exchange rate policy is designed mainly as a second-best solution to reduce the distortions and inefficiencies in its economic/financial infrastructure that retard its economic growth. Thus, pressuring China to revalue its currency may do more harm than good.

3. See section 7.2 for more detail discussion.

4. The GMM estimation was proposed by Chamberlain (1984); Holtz-Eakin, Newey, and Rosen (1988); Arellano and Bond (1991); and Arellano and Bover (1995). It has been applied to cross-country studies by, among others, Easterly, Loayza, and Montiel (1997) and Rodrik (2008).

5. A country's currency undervaluation boosts its saving rate not only *directly* via reducing consumption on imports but also *indirectly* via spurring economic growth (which has a positive effect on the saving rate). However, our tally based on avaiable estimates suggests that the indirect effect of currency undervaluation on saving is even smaller than its direct effect. If we take literally Rodrik's (2008) estimate—a 1 percent currency undervaluation, though has a neglible effect on industrial countries' growth rates, increases the growth rate of developing countries by 0.027 percentage points, and apply it to this chapter's estimate—a one-percentage point increase in economic growth raises the saving rate by about 0.31 percentage points (in the long run), then we get the estimate that a 1 percent currency undervaluation increases the saving rate by 0.8 percentage points (= 0.027 × 0.31) through the indirect effect. That in turn suggests that China's currency undervaluation during 2001 to 2006 (about 47 percent) contributed only 0.4 percentage points (= 0.008 × 47) to its saving rate, considerably smaller than its direct contribution (2.5 percentage points).

6. This point is particularly emphasized by Kuijs (2006). Several studies have found that the rapid growth in total factor productivity (TFP) is a main pillar of China's real GDP growth in the reform era, second only to capital formation. For example, Kuijs and Wang (2006) found that capital accumulation contributed over 50 percent, and TFP growth about 33 percent, to China's output growth between 1978 and 2004, with employment growth contributing the modest remainder. Bosworth and Collins (2007) also have similar findings.

7. Partly as a result of China's pro-industry policy, the share of wages and other household income in GDP fell from 72 percent in 1992 to 55 percent in 2007. See Aziz and Cui (2007).

8. See Kuijs (2006). An article in *the Economist* (October 1st, 2009) with the title "The hamster-wheel" also reports that China's state-owned enterprises now provide a modest payout to the government, but until 2008 they paid nothing at all. In 2008 almost 45 percent of listed companies in China did not pay a dividend.

9. Whether a country's currency is undervalued depends on the concept of the yardstick (i.e., the fundamental equilibrium exchange rate) used to measure its undervaluation. Cheung et al. (2007) provides a brief review of some of those concepts and discusses the difficulty in measuring the equilibrium exchange rate and the uncertainty surrounding those measurements. Most analysts have concluded that the Chinese currency has been significantly undervalued.

10. For example, China's real GDP per capita was only 38 percent of that in Mexico (an upper middle income country) in 2007.

11. Some variables, such as measures of income inequality and degree of financial openness, are not included in our study because of the limited availability of good-quality data across countries over the sample period.

12. This can be shown if we derive the saving equation from a typical Keynesian consumption equation, $C = C_0 + \alpha Y$, where C is consumption, C_0 is the subsistence consump-

tion, Y is income, and α is the propensity to consume. The corresponding saving equation would be $S = -C_0 + (1 - \alpha)Y$, implying that

$$\frac{S}{Y} = (1 - \alpha) - \frac{C_0}{Y}$$

Thus

$$\frac{d(S / Y)}{dY} > 0$$

the saving/income ratio is a positive function of income.

13. For example, see Bosworth (1993), Carroll and Weil (1994), Edwards (1996), , Loayza et al. (2000), and Sinha and Sinha (2008).

14. See Modigliani (1970) and Modigliani and Cao (2004) for the life-cycle hypothesis, and Carroll et al. (2000) for the habit-formation model.

15. See Phelps (1961, 1965).

16. See Easterly et al. (1997) for stylized facts and empirical findings that suggest shocks are important relative to country characteristics in determining long-run growth. Relatedly, in their attempt to interpret the experience of the East Asian countries in the context of the habit-formation model, Carroll et al. (2000) write "The evidence in William Easterly et al. (1997) suggests that the best way to model the growth experiences in the East Asian countries is as a series of positive shocks. Thus we might interpret the East Asian experience as a sequence of exogenous increases in the 'broad capital' embodied in k in our model. . . . One prediction of our model is that saving rates in the East Asian countries should decline once those economies stop their technological convergence with more advanced economies." (p. 351)

17. See Loayza, Schmidt-Hebbel, and Serven (2000).

18. For example, the Harberger–Laursen–Metzler hypothesis postulates that a real devaluation, which causes a decline in real income, will lead to a decrease in savings via the Keynesian channel. See Harberger (1950) and Laursen and Metzler (1950).

19. In all regressions the Sargan test of overidentifying restrictions cannot reject the null hypothesis that the instruments are uncorrelated with the error term. Likewise the tests of serial correlation reject the hypothesis that the error term is either second-order or third-order serially correlated, giving additional support to the use of lagged explanatory variables as instruments in the regression.

20. The real exchange rate is the price of the US dollar in foreign currency terms, adjusted for relative prices. Thus an increase in a country's real exchange rate means a depreciation of its currency.

21. Loayza et al. (2000) point out that in view of the strong negative correlation between inflation and the real interest rate, the real interest rate measure may reflect more the action of nominal interest-rate controls and financial repression than the intertemporal rate of substitution of consumers.

22. IMF (2005) applies the method used in Loayza et al. (2000) to a smaller set of variables.

23. The differences include those in model specification, measurement of independent and explanatory variables, number of countries and sample periods. For example, this

paper uses data from 1980 to 2007, and measures national saving as gross national income (GNI) minus consumption. In comparison, Loayza et al. (2000) uses data from 1965 to 1994 and measures national saving as gross national disposable income (which equals to GNI plus all net unrequited transfers from abroad) minus consumption .

24. The long-term model forecasts are obtained by ignoring fixed effects of each country, summing up only the long-term marginal effects of all explanatory variables in each model, where the marginal effect of variable X = (level of variable X) × coefficient of variable $X/(1 - \text{coefficient of lagged saving})$.

25. The contribution of China's *lower old dependency ratio* is calculated as equal to 14.1/18.4 in 1990 to 2000 and 13.9/23.6 in 2001 to 2006. Those of other variables are calculated in the same fashion.

26. See Zhou (2009).

27. These results are reported in Hung and Qian (2010).

28. See Xu (2005).

29. According to Pettis (2010), the government used three tools to reduce NPLs. First, the central bank kept lending rates low, making it easier for struggling businesses to roll over the debt while the growth of the economy reduced the real value of debt payments. Second, policy makers infused the banks with additional equity,financing those infusions by borrowing at artificially low rates, thereby passing the repayment burden on to lenders. Finally, the central bank mandated a wide spread between the lending and the deposit rates, which helped recapitalize banks by increasing their profitability. All three tools required that bank depositors subsidize the bailout of the banking industry.

30. For example, see Hirono (1988). A study by the World Bank (1993) also emphasizes that a "virtuous circle" —going from higher growth to higher savings, to even higher growth—has played a central role in successful development experiences in East Asia.

31. Foreign credit tended to be too expensive or too scant during the early stage of industrialization in those countries after World War II. For more discussion of the similarities and differences between China's development model and those of the East Asian model, see Baek (2005) and Boltho and Weber (2009).

32. Net corporate profits in China rose from about 4 percent of GNI in 2001 to 10 percent in 2007. Data on depreciation is not available. But Ma and Yi (2010) argue that depreciation as a share of GDP has probably risen over time because (1) depreciation is positively linked to the higher capital stock and newer vintages of capital and (2) the capital stock per worker in the industrial sector has at least doubled in the past decade as a result of rapid industrialization.

33. The dividend policy allowed the bulk of the dividend payouts by listed Chinese state companies to go to their nonlisted parent-holding companies (direct majority shareholders) instead of the government (the ultimate owner) and thus is still retained within the corporate sector.

34. See Ma and Yi (2010) for possible reasons for the Chinese government's decision to invest rather than consume most of its rising income.

35. This may stem from the fact that, due to the rapid growth in national income, households' disposable income has continued to rise even though their share in national

income declines, which in turn increases their saving rate through the mechanism proposed by the habit-formation hypothesis.

36. Japan's real GDP per capita, in PPP-adjusted 2005 dollars, was $5,698 in 1960. In comparison, China's real GDP per capital was $5,084 in 2007. (China's data are taken from World Economic Indicators of the World Bank; Japan's data are from the US Bureau of Labor Statistics.).

References

Arellano, M., and S. Bond. 1991. Some tests of specification for panel data: Monte Carlo evidence and an application to employment equations. *Review of Economic Studies* 58 (2): 277–97.

Arellano, M., and O. Bover. 1995. Another look at the instrumental variable estimation of error-component models. *Journal of Econometrics* 68 (1): 29–51.

Aziz, J., and L. Cui. 2007. Explaining China's low consumption: The neglected role of household income. Working Paper 07/181. IMF, Washington, DC.

Baek, S.-W. 2005. Does China follow the East Asian development model? *Journal of Contemporary Asia* 35 (4): 485–98.

Blanchard, O., and F. Giavazzi. 2006. Rebalancing growth in China: A three-handed approach. *China and World Economy* 14 (4): 1–20.

Boltho, A., and M. Weber. 2009. Did China follow the East Asian development model? *European Journal of Comparative Economics* 6 (2): 267–86.

Bosworth, B.. 1993. *Saving and Investment in a Global Economy*. Washington, DC: Brookings Institution.

Caballero, R. 2009. The "other" imbalance and the financial crisis. Working Paper 15636. NBER, Cambridge, MA.

Carroll, C. D., and D. N. Weil. 1994. Saving and growth: A reinterpretation. *Carnegie–Rochester Conference Series on Public Policy* 40: 133–92.

Carroll, C. D., J. Overland, and D.N. Weil. 2000. Saving and growth with habit formation. *American Economic Review* 90 (3): 341–55.

Chamberlain, G. 1984. Panel data. In Z. Griliches and M. D. Intriligator, eds., *Handbook of Econometrics*. vol. 2. Amsterdam: Elsevier, 1247–1313.

Chamon, M., and E. Prasad. 2010. Why are saving rates of urban households in China rising? *American Economic Journal: Macroeconomics* 2 (1): 93–130.

Cheung, Y.-W., M. D. Chinn, and E. Fujii. 2007. The overvaluation of renminbi undervaluation. *Journal of International Money and Finance* 26 (5): 762–85.

Chinn, M. D., and E. S. Prasad. 2003. Medium-term determinants of current accounts in industrial and developing countries: An empirical exploration. *Journal of International Economics* 59 (1): 47–76.

Congressional Budget Office. 2004. The decline in the U.S. current-account balance since 1991. Economic and Budget Issue brief.

Congressional Budget Office. 2005. Recent shifts in financing the U.S. current account deficit. Economic and Budget Issue brief.

Congressional Budget Office. 2007. Will the U.S. current account have a hard or soft landing? Economic and Budget Issue brief.

Dooley, M., D. Folkerts-Landau, and P. Garber. 2003. An essay on the revived Bretton Woods system. Working Paper 9971. NBER, Cambridge, MA.

Dooley, M., D. Folkerts-Landau, and P. M. Garber. 2004. The U.S. current account deficit and economic development: Collateral for a total return swap. Working Paper 10727. NBER, Cambridge, MA.

Edwards, S. 1996. Why are Latin America's savings rates so low? An international comparative analysis. *Journal of Development Economics* 51 (1): 5–44.

Easterly, W., N. Loayza, and P. Montiel. 1997. Has Latin America's post-reform growth been disappointing? *Journal of International Economics* 43 (3/4): 287–312.

Eichengreen, B. 2004. Global imbalances and the lessons of Bretton Woods. Working Paper 10497. NBER, Cambridge, MA.

Goldstein, M. 2007. A (lack of) progress report on China's exchange rate policies. Working Paper 07–5. Peterson Institute for International Economics, Washington, DC.

Haggard, S. 1988. The politics of industrialization in the Republic of Korea and Taiwan. In H. Hughes, ed., *Achieving Industrialization in East Asia*. New York: Cambridge University Press, ch. 9: 260–82.

Harberger, A. C. 1950. Currency depreciation, income, and the balance of trade. *Journal of Political Economy* 58 (1): 47–60.

Holtz-Eakin, D., W. Newey, and H. Rosen. 1988. Estimating vector autoregressions with panel data. *Econometrica: Journal of the Econometric Society* 56 (6): 1371–95.

Hung, J. H., and R. Qian. 2010. Why is China's saving rate so high? A comparative study of cross-country panel data. Working Paper 2010–07. Congressional Budget Office, Washington, DC.

Hirono, R. 1988. Japan: Model for East Asian industrialization? In H. Hughes, ed., *Achieving Industrialization in East Asia*. New York: Cambridge University Press, ch. 8: 241–59.

Hung, J. H., and Y. J. Kim. 2006. Implications of past currency crises for the U.S. current account adjustment. Working Paper 2006–07. Congressional Budget Office, Washington, DC.

International Monetary Fund. 2005. Global imbalances: A saving and investment perspective. In *World Economic Outlook*. Washington, DC: IMF, 91–124.

Korinek, A., and L. Serven. 2010. Undervaluation through foreign reserve accumulation: Static losses, dynamic gains. Policy Research Working Paper 5250. World Bank, Washington, DC.

Kuijs, L. 2005. Investment and saving in China. Policy Research Working Paper 3633. World Bank, Washington, DC.

Kuijs, L. 2006. How will China's saving–investment balance evolve? Policy Research Working Paper 3958. World Bank, Washington, DC.

Kuijs, L., and T. Wang. 2006. China's patten of growth: Moving to sustainability and reducing inequality. *China and World Economy*, no.1: 1–14.

Laursen, S., and L. A. Metzler. 1950. Flexible exchange rates and the theory of employment. *Review of Economics and Statistics* 32 (4): 281–99.

Levy-Yeyati, E., and F. Sturzenegger. 2007. Fear of appreciation. Policy Research Working Paper 4387. World Bank, Washington, DC.

Loayza, N., K. Schmidt-Hebbel, and L. Serven. 2000. What drives private saving across the world? *Review of Economics and Statistics* 82 (2): 165–81.

Ma, G., and W. Yi. 2010. China's high saving rate: Myth and reality. Working Paper 312. BIS, Basel.

Masson, P. R., T. Bayoumi, and H. Samiei. 1998. International evidence on the determinants of private saving. *World Bank Economic Review* 12 (3): 483–501.

Modigliani, F. 1970. The life cycle hypothesis of saving and intercountry differences in the saving ratio. In W. A. Eltis, M. F. Scott, and J. N. Wolfe, eds., *Induction, Growth and Trade: Essays in Honor of Sir Roy Harrod*. Oxford: Clarendon Press, 197–226.

Modigliani, F., and S.L. Cao. 2004. The Chinese saving puzzle and the life cycle analysis. *Journal of Economic Literature* 42 (1): 145–70.

Obstfeld, M., and K. Rogoff. 2005. The unsustainable U.S. current account revisited. Working Paper 10864. NBER, Cambridge, MA.

Park, D., and K. Shin. 2009. Saving, investment and current account surplus in developing Asia. Economics Working Paper 158. Asian Development Bank, Mandaluyong City, Philippines.

Pettis, M. 2010. Bad loans could take their toll on China's growth. *Financial Times*, April 22, p. 11. Also available at: http://www.ft.com/intl/cms/s/0/9d2a0448-4d77-11df-9560-00144feab49a.html#axzz1pIWWwU8q.

Phelps, E. S. 1961. The Golden Rule of accumulation: A fable for growth men. *American Economic Review* 51 (4): 638–43.

Phelps, E. S. 1965. Second essay on the Golden Rule of accumulation. *American Economic Review* 55 (4): 793–814.

Rodrik, D. 2008. The real exchange rate and economic growth. *Brookings Papers on Economic Activity* 2: 365–412.

Rodrik, D. 2010. Making room for China in the world economy. *American Economic Review: Papers and Proceedings* 100: 89–93. .

Roubini, N., and B. Setser. 2005. The sustainability of the U.S. external imbalances. *Ifo Institute for Economic Research, CESifo Forum* 1: 8–15.

Sinha, D., and T. Sinha. 2008. Relationships among household saving, public saving, corporate saving and economic growth in India. *Journal of International Development* 20 (2): 181–86.

Spence, M. 2010. The West is wrong to obsess about the renminbi. *Financial Times*, January 22, p.11. Also available at: http://www.ft.com/intl/cms/s/0/00f770a8-06cb-11df-b058-00144feabdc0.html#axzz1pIWWwU8q.

Wei, S.-J., and X. Zhang. 2009. The competitive saving motive: Evidence from rising sex ratios and saving rates in China. Working Paper 15093. NBER, Cambridge, MA.

Wolf, M. 2010. Evaluating the renminbi manipulation. *Financial Times*, April 7, p. 7. Also available at: http://www.ft.com/intl/cms/s/0/dbc9fa4c-41af-11df-865a-00144feabdc0 .html#axzz1pIWWwU8q.

World Bank. 1993. *The East Asian Miracle: Economic Growth and Public Policy.* New York: Oxford University Press.

Xu, Min. 2005. Resolution of non-performing loans in China. Manuscript. Leonard N. Stern School of Business, New York University.

Zhou, X. 2009. On savings ratio. Governor's speech. The People's Bank of China, Beijing.

8 If You Try, You'll Get By: Chinese Private Firms' Efficiency Gains from Overcoming Financial Constraints

Galina Hale[1] and Cheryl Long

8.1 Introduction

The importance of finances in economic development has long been postulated and empirically tested in the economic literature. As early as 1911 Schumpeter linked availability of financial services to firms' capacity for technological innovation and thus a country's economic development. Much later, country-level analyses by King and Levine (1993) provided evidence that multiple indicators of financial development are not only positively correlated with the present levels of multiple economic indicators but also their future values. Using industry-level data for a large number of countries, Rajan and Zingales (1998) showed that industries with higher external finance requirements tend to grow faster in countries with more developed capital markets.

Thus a big puzzle in China's rapid economic growth over the past three decades relates to the financial sector. The Chinese economy has experienced one of the fastest growth rates in the world continuously since the late 1970s, largely driven by the rapid development of the private sector, which has substantially outpaced the growth rate of the state sector. However, the vast majority of researchers believe that the formal financial sector in China performs poorly by international standards, especially in a failure to provide finances to the private sector. How did the private sector in China manage to grow so rapidly with limited access to external finance? There are two possible explanations: either alternative financing helped overcome a limited supply of external funds from the formal financial sector or firms found new ways to reduce their demand for external funds.

Previous studies addressing the puzzle have focused mainly on alternative financing sources, including internal funds, informal loans (from family, friends, and acquaintances), foreign direct investment (FDI), and trade credit among private firms themselves and from other types of firms. While there is evidence that the first three alternative sources (internal funds, informal loans, and FDI) have been important in alleviating private firms' financial constraints (Allen et al. 2005 Hèricourt and Poncet 2009; Lardy 1998, 2004; Poncet et al. 2010), trade credit from other sectors (e.g., state-owned or foreign-invested sector) has been shown to play an insignificant role (Cull et al. 2009) or to be non-existent since the late 1990s (Hale and Long 2010).[2]

In this chapter we focus on the second explanation and consider the ways in which Chinese private firms are able to lower their demand for external financing; we study whether their methods lead to increased or decreased efficiency and productivity. To the best of our knowledge, only one other paper explores the finances of Chinese private firms from the demand side of finances: Long and Zhang (2010) point out that organizational innovations such as clustering may lead to a lower level of financial needs for Chinese firms by reducing the fixed capital requirement and facilitating inter-firm credit. In this chapter we go further and investigate two other channels, namely the management of inventory and of accounts receivable, which allow firms to reduce the demand for operating costs.

Various studies provide evidence that private firms have been discriminated against in the financial market. Brandt and Li (2003) provide direct evidence that between 1994 and 1997 private firms were discriminated against by township branches of the Agricultural Bank of China and the local Rural Credit Cooperatives, compared to township enterprises. Dollar and Wei (2007) show that, on average, Chinese domestic private firms have significantly higher returns to capital than stateowned enterprises (SOEs), implying more funds going to the SOEs, an inefficient allocation of financial resources. Liu and Siu (2006) similarly show that the "implied" cost of capital derived from their estimated structural parameters is substantially higher for private firms and foreign invested firms than for SOEs in China. Hale and Long (2010) further demonstrate that even if internal and informal sources of financing are accounted for, private Chinese firms are barely making their ends meet. More generally, Hsieh and Klenow (2009) estimate that Chinese manufacturing sector could potentially improve its total factor productivity by 30 to 50 percent through more efficient capital allocation.

Using balance-sheet data from Chinese Industrial Surveys of Medium-Sized and Large Firms for 2000 to 2006 (the NBS survey) and survey data from the Large-Scale Survey of Private Enterprises in China that was conducted in five waves between 1997 and 2006, we first confirm the conventional wisdom, that private firms still had more limited access to external finance during the period of rapid economic growth prior to the global recession. However, we find substantial variations among private firms: the small private firms face more financial constraints, while the more established large private firms seem to have access to finances more equal to their state-owned counterparts.

We then proceed to our main analysis of the channels through which private firms reduce their demand for operating funds. Using the NBS survey data as well as the Survey of Private Enterprises data, we study the relationship between firms' access to external finances and the ratios of inventories and accounts receivable to sales. Because inventories make up a large part of daily working capital, a lower level of inventory implies fewer funds required for working capital, and thus less need for finances. Likewise lower average level of accounts receivable means that firms recover their revenues and use them for working capital financing more quickly, thus relying less on external financing.

First of all, we find that the ratios of inventory to sales and accounts receivable to sales are substantially lower in private firms than in firms of other ownership types, even after controlling for various firm characteristics, industry, and location. Next, we show that these ratios depend on our measures of access to external finance both in a cross-sectional and in the fixed effects panel. This suggests that not only firms with less access to credit have lower ratios of inventories and accounts receivable to sales (cross-sectional results) but also that firms make greater adjustments in their inventories and accounts receivable when credit gets tighter (fixed effects panel results). These results are robust to adjusting measures of inventory and accounts receivable to sector averages and using lagged values of our measures of access to financing. Moreover we find that for firms in sectors that are more dependent on external financing the relationships between access to finance and inventory and accounts receivable ratios are stronger.

An important question is whether the low levels of inventories and accounts receivable due to a firm's limited access to external finances are below the levels necessary to guarantee optimal sales. In other words, are the low ratios of inventories and accounts receivable observed in Chinese private firms just another indicator of detrimental effects of limited access to external finances? One warning sign is that these ratios for private firms are even lower than those for the majority of foreign-invested firms, which are thought to be the most efficient among Chinese firms. We address this question by fitting nonlinear regressions of the various measures of firm profitability on inventory and accounts receivable ratios, and we find that firm profitability monotonically decreases in these ratios. In other words, there is no evidence that low ratios of inventories and accounts receivable to sales in private firms are associated with lower profitability.

We further find that lower levels of inventory and accounts receivable are actually associated with higher levels of productivity, and more so in industries with higher shares of final goods inventory in total inventory and in sectors that use more trade credit. The results for inventory are consistent with the findings of Lieberman and Demeester (1999) for Japanese car manufacturers. Here the argument is that a lower inventory level makes it easier to expose and subsequently resolve problems throughout the production process, leading to higher productivity. However, the higher productivity in firms with lower accounts receivable/sales ratios may be explained by a firm's greater ability to fully utilize its production capacity (Fisman 2001), to better coordinate activities among various employees, and to finance processes, products, or technology development that help enhance productivity. Thus lower levels of inventory and accounts receivable increase firms' profitability through both higher productivity and lower financial costs.

Nevertheless, we should like to make it clear that our results do not mean that there are no costs associated with limited access to financing by private firms. It is quite likely that restricted access to credit is impeding the development of Chinese private firms by limiting fixed assets investment and growth. We do indeed show that private firms in China have found ways of coping with day-to-day shortage of finances through becoming more cost effective in ways that do not harm their profitability. Such efficiency improvements also make private firms in China more competitive compared to their state-owned counterparts in China and potentially more competitive compared to less constrained firms in other countries. In fact another way to see our findings is that the extraordinarily easy access to credit of SOEs can lead them to accumulate inefficiently high levels of inventory and accounts receivable.

The rest of the chapter is organized as follows: Section 8.2 discusses the data we use to demonstrate that private firms are more financially constrained compared to state-owned firms. Section 8.3 shows that firms respond to constrained financial access by reducing their levels of inventories and accounts receivable. Section 8.4 analyzes the effects of such mechanisms on profitability and productivity, and section 8.5 concludes.

8.2   Do State-Owned Firms Have Easier Access to External Financing?

Our data come from two sources. First, we use balance sheet and ownership information from the Chinese Industrial Surveys of Medium-Sized and Large Firms for 2000 to 2006, which includes all state-owned firms and firms of other ownership types that are in excess of a certain scale. This dataset is commonly referred to as the National Bureau of Statistics (NBS) manufacturing census, and it consists of an unbalanced panel with a total of 496,738 firms for 2000 to 2006.[3] For short, we will refer to this dataset as the "census" data. We use two versions of these data—the cross section of firms in the last year of our sample (297,665 firms) and a balanced panel that only includes firms that were in our data in each of the years during 2000 to 2006 (48,382 firms, 338,674 observations).[4]

Second, we use survey data from the Large-Scale Survey of Private Enterprises in China jointly conducted by the All China Federation of Industrial and Commerce (ACFIC) and the United Front of the Chinese Communist Party in 1997, 2000, 2002, 2004, and 2006, often with help from the Bureau of Industry and Commerce. This survey is a repeated cross section in which firms are not matched across years. A total of 18,527 firms are surveyed over all the years, and only private firms are included. For short, we will refer to this dataset as the "survey" data.

The census data cover firms of all ownership types, including those with foreign capital share. We classify firms by ownership types in two ways: by the registration type, and by the type of investor holding the majority share of the paid-up capital. While the first measure may be outdated, as the registration of the firm may not change as soon as the firm's capital structure changes, it is possible that the registration type, rather than the de facto ownership structure determines the access to financing. We will refer to the two classifications as the de jure ownership type (by registration) and the de facto ownership type (by actual shares).

Table 8.1 shows that in the 2006 cross section most often there is a good match between the two classifications. Note that one exception is the set of firms with the majority share held by "legal person," and

Table 8.1
Firm distribution by de facto and de jure ownership type in the 2006 census cross section

De facto ownership	De jure ownership						
	State	Private	Collective	FRN*	HMT*	Other	Total
State	12,309	37	46	325	262	2,807	15,786
Private	104	111,610	862	2,054	1,600	27,843	144,073
Collective	100	378	10,556	354	344	4,324	16,056
FRN[a]	2	112	3	21,976	251	173	22,517
HMT[a]	3	102	9	380	21,220	155	21,869
Legal person	2,754	35,962	2,736	5,898	5,081	23,590	76,021
Other[b]	55	136	48	304	237	563	1,343
Total	15,327	148,337	14,260	31,291	28,995	59,455	297,665

Number of firms reported in each cell

Balanced panel De facto ownership	De jure ownership						
	State	Private	Collective	FRN[a]	HMT[a]	Other	Total
State	47,702	105	475	1,116	1,373	6,119	56,890
Private	614	36,098	3,532	1,489	1,700	28,094	71,527
Collective	847	1,114	21,924	1,262	1,852	7,684	34,683
FRN[a]	20	55	67	23,169	2,400	124	25,835
HMT[a]	20	126	146	1,955	24,117	129	26,493
Legal person	6,457	10,576	5,014	5,223	6,478	18,976	52,724
Other[b]	229	143	320	605	616	1,661	3,574
Total	55,889	48,217	31,478	34,819	38,536	62,787	271,726

Notes: Number of observations reported in each cell. Number of firms = number of observations/7.
a. FRN = owned by foreign company with headquarters outside greater China area; HMT = owned by a company with headquarters in Hong Kong, Taiwan, or Macao
b. Firms where no single ownership category holds more than 50 percent shares

these firms are mostly registered as private firms but could also be in other categories. In what follows, we analyze results using both classifications, but to spare the reader from all the details, we only report results from the de facto classification analysis and point to the differences wherever they arise.

We would like to point out that in the three datasets we consider—the 2006 cross section of the census, the balanced panel from the census, and the private firm survey—the samples of firms are quite different. The manufacturing census has a minimum size threshold for including private firms, which was revised and simplified in 2004. Consequently many of the smaller private firms that appear in the 2006 cross section are not included in the balanced panel that extends back to 2000. The firms covered in private firm surveys, however, are almost exclusively small firms. As a result the balanced panel data includes mostly SOEs and large private firms, the 2006 census cross section additionally includes smaller private firms, while the private firm survey includes only private firms, which are mostly small.

As we noted previously, our main indicator of how efficiently the financial system operates in China is whether banks treat firms of different ownership types differently when extending loans to them. Thus we first study how SOEs differ in their access to formal loans as compared to private firms. We observe that state-owned firms indeed have easier access to external financing: they tend to have slightly higher leverage (debt/total assets) and a higher share of financial expenses out of total expenses, but what they pay is half as much per unit (RMB) of their external financing compared to what private firms pay (see table 8.2).[5]

For the balanced panel of the firms, with the sample held constant, we see that while the leverage level was more or less unchanged during our sample period for SOEs, it declined for private firms. Moreover, for older and larger private firms that were in our balanced panel since 2000, the leverage is a bit higher than for the SOEs and is declining. If we include new firms, as in our 2006 cross section, the average leverage of the private firms is substantially lower than that in the balanced sample, suggesting that new entrants have more restricted access to financing than older private firms and SOEs. In addition, smaller private firms, the ones included in our survey data, have less than half the leverage of the private firms in the census, indicating that access to finance is particularly hard for young small private firms.

Looking at the share of financial expense in total expense, we find that even in the balanced panel the share is a lot lower for private firms

Table 8.2
Mean leverage, financial and interest expense ratios

Mean (leverage = total debt/total asset)

	Ownership						Legal
Year	Other	State	Private	Collective	FRN	HMT	person
Census full 2006 cross section							
2006	0.527	0.560	0.554	0.539	0.470	0.476	0.529
Balanced panel (census)							
2000	0.571	0.567	0.622	0.597	0.473	0.496	0.572
2001	0.554	0.561	0.614	0.587	0.454	0.481	0.567
2002	0.545	0.561	0.610	0.581	0.450	0.476	0.567
2003	0.550	0.559	0.610	0.577	0.451	0.475	0.564
2004	0.530	0.566	0.609	0.568	0.468	0.465	0.574
2005	0.528	0.568	0.597	0.562	0.453	0.470	0.562
2006	0.540	0.565	0.590	0.560	0.446	0.470	0.556

Survey data (private firms only)			
Year	Debt/asset	Debt/asset1
2000	0.171	—
2002	0.177	0.211
2004	0.184	0.223
2006	0.217	0.248

Where asset does not include accounts receivable, but asset1 includes AR (which was not available for 2000).

Mean (financial expense/total expense)

	Ownership						Legal
Year	Other	State	Private	Collective	FRN	HMT	person
Census full 2006 cross section							
2006	0.026	0.046	0.015	0.018	0.015	0.012	0.020
Balanced panel (census)							
2000	0.045	0.063	0.028	0.032	0.030	0.019	0.040
2001	0.041	0.062	0.027	0.030	0.028	0.017	0.038
2002	0.041	0.059	0.024	0.029	0.024	0.014	0.037
2003	0.034	0.057	0.023	0.026	0.022	0.014	0.032
2004	0.034	0.055	0.023	0.022	0.018	0.013	0.032
2005	0.029	0.050	0.022	0.023	0.016	0.013	0.030
2006	0.030	0.050	0.022	0.020	0.016	0.015	0.027

Table 8.2
(continued)

Mean (interest expense/total debt)

Year	Ownership						
	Other	State	Private	Collective	FRN	HMT	Legal person
Census full 2006 cross section							
2006	0.027	0.016	0.031	0.025	0.015	0.012	0.029
Balanced panel (census)							
2000	0.032	0.022	0.033	0.036	0.023	0.017	0.032
2001	0.032	0.021	0.032	0.033	0.020	0.016	0.030
2002	0.027	0.020	0.030	0.032	0.017	0.015	0.031
2003	0.025	0.019	0.029	0.030	0.015	0.014	0.029
2004	0.023	0.017	0.029	0.026	0.014	0.013	0.027
2005	0.023	0.017	0.030	0.027	0.015	0.014	0.027
2006	0.026	0.016	0.031	0.025	0.016	0.013	0.026

than for the SOEs. It gets even lower once we include all firms as in our 2006 cross section. At the same time interest rate as a ratio to total debt is almost twice as high for private firms as it is for SOEs, in both the cross section and the balanced panel. This suggests that when private firms access external finance, they pay substantially more for it than SOEs. In addition we see that total financial expenses and interest expenses have declined, on average, for SOEs during our sample period, while they remained basically unchanged for private firms.

As private firms in China are, on average, younger and smaller than state-owned firms, and therefore lack credit history and reputation, one potential reason for the latter's easier access to finances could be their better creditworthiness rather than prejudice against private firms in the formal financial sector. We address this difficulty in interpretation by estimating the effects of ownership, controlling for size and measures of creditworthiness (e.g., liquidity and profitability), using the regression analysis.

Table 8.3 reports the results of the regression analysis for the 2006 cross section. We see that at least in terms of leverage power, size matters as well: once we control for the log of assets, the coefficient on the SOE dummy falls by about half, indicating that half of the difference in leverage between private firms and SOEs in the 2006 census cross section is due to the fact that state firms tend to be larger. We find

Table 8.3
OLS regressions in the 2006 NBS census cross section

Dependent variable is leverage (= total debt/total asset)

	(1)	(2)	(3)	(4)	(5)
State	0.027***	0.015***	0.027***	0.024***	0.015***
	(0.002)	(0.002)	(0.002)	(0.002)	(0.002)
log(asset)		0.013***			0.011***
		(3.4E-04)			(3.4E-04)
pretaxROE			−1.2E-05		−2.0E-05
			(4.0 E-05)		(3.9E-05)
liquidity				−4.0E-06***	−4.1E-06***
				(6.2E-07)	(6.2E-07)
Observations	286,993	286,993	286,894	279,662	279,628
Adjusted R^2	0.001	0.006	0.001	0.001	0.004

Dependent variable is LT debt/LT assets

	(1)	(2)	(3)	(4)	(5)
state	0.11***	0.094***	0.11***	0.11***	0.095***
	(0.001)	(0.001)	(0.001)	(0.001)	(0.001)
log(asset)		0.019***			0.019***
		(2.1E-4)			(2.2E-04)
pretaxROE			2.9E-6		−3.9E-06
			(2.5E-5)		(2.5E-05)
liquidity				−2.8E-07	−4.9E-07
				(4.0E-07)	(4.0E-07)
Observations	289,883	289,883	289,780	282,840	282,802
Adjusted R^2	0.021	0.045	0.021	0.021	0.047

Dependent variable is financial expenses/total expenses

	(1)	(2)	(3)	(4)	(5)
state	0.029***	0.024***	0.029***	0.029***	0.024***
	(4.2E-04)	(4.2E-04)	(4.2E-04)	(4.3E-04)	(4.2E-04)
log(asset)		0.006***			0.006***
		(6.2E-05)			(6.3E-05)
pretaxROE			3.2E-06		1.5E-06
			(7.2E-06)		(7.1E-05)
liquidity				−7.9E-08	−1.5E-07
				(1.4E-07)	(1.3E-07)
Observations	265,672	265,670	265,630	258,509	258,472
Adjusted R^2	0.018	0.052	0.018	0.018	0.053

Table 8.3
(continued)

Dependent variable is interest expense/total debt

	(1)	(2)	(3)	(4)	(5)
state	−0.012***	−0.010***	−0.012***	−0.011***	−0.010***
	(0.001)	(0.001)	(0.001)	(0.001)	(0.001)
log(asset)		−0.003***			−0.003***
		(8.9E-05)			(8.9E-05)
pretaxROE			4.1E-06		4.7E-06
			(1.0E-05)		(1.0E-05)
liquidity				8.2E-07	8.4E-07
				(5.9E-07)	(5.9E-07)
Observations	274,884	274,884	274,841	269,382	269,344
Adjusted R^2	0.002	0.004	0.002	0.002	0.004

Notes: Liquidity = (short-term asset − short-term debt)/short-term debt. * Significant at 10 percent, ** significant at 5 percent, *** significant at 1 percent.

that state-owned firms have significantly higher leverage, a larger ratio of financial to total expenses, and a lower share of accounts payable in total debt, even after controlling for size, profitability, and liquidity measures. These findings confirm that state-owned firms have easier access to formal external finance and rely less on informal finance than other firms.

We repeat this analysis for the balanced panel to see what the trends were between 2000 and 2006 (or between 2003 and 2006 in the case of accounts payable over debt). To this end, we correlate the indicator for the majority of state-owned firms with the time trend and estimate a panel regression by GLS with random effects (see table 8.4). We find that although in our balanced panel sample the leverage is roughly the same for private firms and SOEs, the other two measures indicate that even for this sample, which only includes larger and older private firms, the private firms have more difficult access to credit. While these differences between state-owned and other firms diminish over our sample period, the rate of convergence is very slow for the share of financial and interest expenses. Moreover, if we consider the ratio of long-term debt to long-term assets, we find that state-owned firms had larger, and growing, ratio throughout the sample period. As a result there is evidence for more limited financial access by Chinese private firms as late as 2006, shortly before the outbreak of the recent financial crisis.

Table 8.4
Balanced panel census GLS RE regressions

	(1)	(2)	(3)	(4)
	Leverage	LT debt/ LT assets	finexp	int_rate
state	−0.039***	0.039***	0.019***	−0.003***
	(0.002)	(0.002)	(0.001)	(4.7E-04)
state*time trend	0.011***	0.003***	−0.001***	−0.000***
	(3.4E-04)	(3.0E-04)	(1.1E-04)	(9.3E-05)
log(asset)	0.018***	0.022***	0.007***	−0.002***
	(5.3E-04)	(4.0E-04)	(1.5E-04)	(1.0E-04)
pretaxROE	−2.6E-06	1.6E-05	3.3E-06	5.2E-06
	(1.9E-05)	(1.9E-05)	(6.1E-06)	(5.0E-06)
Liquidity	−2.4E-07	−1.4E-07	4.8E-09	5.8E-09
	(1.9E-07)	(1.9E-07)	(6.0E-08)	(5.2E-08)
Time trend	−0.005***	−0.007***	−0.003***	−0.001***
	(1.5E-04)	(2.0E-04)	(5.1E-05)	(4.2E-05)
Observations	250,261	254,770	230,893	237,803
Number of firms	38,320	38,691	37,978	38,312
Within R^2	0.130	0.009	0.190	0.040

Notes: Liquidity = (short-term asset − short-term debt)/short-term debt. * Significant at 10 percent, ** significant at 5 percent, *** significant at 1 percent.

8.3 Reducing Financing Needs through Inventory and Accounts Receivable

Given the preceding findings, how is it possible that private firms in China have been growing so fast? We suggest a couple of ways that private firms might have proceeded to lower their demand for external financing, which, to the best of our knowledge, haven't been explored in the literature. Table 8.5 shows that in our 2006 census cross section, private firms have substantially lower inventory/sales ratios than their SOE counterparts: 14 versus 31 percent. They also have lower accounts receivable/sales ratios than SOEs: 13 versus 16 percent. Among firms of all ownership types, both of these ratios are the lowest for the subsample of private firms.

As all the industrial firms exceeded a certain size, the huge differences in the inventory/sales ratio and the accounts receivable/sales ratio most likely indicate much more efficient management of inventories and accounts receivable, and thus less need for working capital in private firms as compared to SOEs. To test the hypothesis that the low

Table 8.5
Average inventory/sales and AR/sales ratios by ownership in the 2006 census cross
section

Ownership	Mean (inventory/sales)	Mean (AR/sales)
Census (2006 cross section)		
State	0.306	0.161
Private	0.138	0.131
Collective	0.171	0.165
FRN	0.195	0.166
HMT	0.222	0.173
Legal person	0.172	0.134
Other	0.221	0.172
Survey (2006)		0.158

levels of inventory and accounts receivable reflect the attempt of financially constrained firms to reduce their need for working capital funds,
we regressed the inventory and accounts receivable ratios on our measures of credit constraint, namely leverage, financial expense/total
expense, and interest expense/debt ratios. The results are presented in
table 8.6, with panel A giving the 2006 cross-sectional results and panel
B giving the firm fixed effects results for the balanced panel. As
expected, we find statistically significant correlations for all three measures of access to external financing in both the cross section (with
ownership and industry dummies included) and in the panel (with
firm and year fixed effects).

The cross-sectional results show that firms with easier access to
external financing, reflected by higher leverage, higher ratio of financial to total expenses, or lower ratio of interest expenses to total debt,
tend to have higher level of inventories and accounts receivable. Fixed
effect panel results further show that when access to external finance
gets tighter for an individual firm, as reflected in this firm's lower
leverage, lower ratio of financial to total expenses, or higher ratio of
interest expenses to total debt, it lowers its inventory and accounts
payable ratios.

To address a potential concern that these results are driven by the
changes in the denominator of both inventory and accounts payable
ratios, namely sales, over time, we add to our panel estimation the
growth rate of sales as a control variable. The results are reported in
the fifth column of table 8.6B, with all the main results preserved. In

Table 8.6
Relationship between inventory/sales and ar/sales ratios and measures of financial constraints

A. 2006 Cross section; 2-digit industry and ownership dummies included but not reported (39 industries)

Dependent variable: inventory/sales ratio

	(1)	(2)	(3)	(4)
Leverage	0.130***			0.091***
	(0.002)			(0.003)
finexp_tot~p		1.270***		1.220***
		(0.014)		(0.015)
int_rate			−0.290***	−0.290***
			(0.010)	(0.009)
Observations	257,719	239,551	247,052	226,218
Adjusted R^2	0.047	0.068	0.042	0.075

Dependent variable: AR/sales ratio

	(1)	(2)	(3)	(4)
Leverage	0.084***			0.070***
	(0.001)			(0.001)
finexp_tot~p		0.370***		0.400***
		(0.008)		(0.008)
int_rate			−0.230***	−0.200***
			(0.005)	(0.005)
Observations	254,494	236,546	243,788	223,612
Adjusted R^2	0.094	0.086	0.085	0.110

B. Balanced panel with firm and year fixed effects

Dependent variable: inventory/sales ratio

	(1)	(2)	(3)	(4)	(5)
Leverage	0.100***			0.057***	0.062***
	(0.004)			(0.005)	(0.005)
Financial expense/		1.140***		1.160***	1.130***
total expense		(0.015)		(0.016)	(0.018)
Per unit			−0.170***	−0.360***	−0.310***
borrowing cost			(0.018)	(0.016)	(0.018)
Growth rate of					9.9E-07
sales					(2.8E-06)
Observations	257,304	237,809	243,552	220,436	187,955
Number of firms	38,315	37,989	38,298	37,180	36,772
Within R^2	0.030	0.030	0.004	0.030	0.030

Table 8.6
(continued)

Dependent variable: AR/sales ratio

	(1)	(2)	(3)	(4)	(5)
Leverage	0.058***			0.041***	0.044***
	(0.002)			(0.002)	(0.002)
Financial expense/ total expense		0.300***		0.340***	0.330***
		(0.007)		(0.008)	(0.008)
Per unit borrowing cost			−0.110***	−0.140***	−0.130***
			(0.007)	(0.007)	(0.008)
Growth rate of sales					2.02E-06
					(1.4E-06)
Observations	251,338	231,876	237,267	215,400	183,922
Number of firms	38,175	37,834	38,145	37,004	36,559
Within R^2	0.020	0.020	0.010	0.030	0.030

C. Repeated cross section using survey data; year, 1-digit industry, and ownership dummies included but not reported (19 industries)

Dependent variable: AR/sales ratio

	(1)	(2)	(3)
Leverage	0.130***		0.240**
	(0.024)		(0.100)
int_rate		−0.004	−0.004
		(0.004)	(0.004)
Observations	6,287	727	658
Adjusted R^2	0.019	0.082	0.200

Note: * Significant at 10 percent, ** significant at 5 percent, *** significant at 1 percent.

particular, coefficients on the variables of interest remain largely unchanged, even though we now have one less year of data for each firm.

In terms of the economic effects we find in the cross-sectional sample that firms had access to finance the same as an average private firm (55 percent leverage, 1.6 percent ratio of financial to total expenses, and 3 percent ratio of interest expenses to total debt) will have an inventory to sales ratio that is 4.3 percentage points lower and an accounts receivable to sales ratio that is 1.6 percentage points lower than a firm with access to finance equal to an average state-owned firm (56 percent leverage, 4.7 percent ratio of financial to total expenses, and 1.6 percent ratio of interest expenses to total debt). These differences explain a large fraction, 28 and 61 percent, of the differences in the inventory to sales and accounts receivable to sales ratios, respectively, between an average private firm and an average SOE.

In the panel we find that if access to external finances improves for the average level of private firms (leverage of 60 percent, financial to total expense of 2.7 percent, and interest expense to total debt of 3 percent) to the average level of state-owned firms (5.6, 5.7, and 1.9 percent, respectively), the inventory to sales ratio would increase by 3.6 percentage points, which would explain just over a quarter of the difference in the ratio between private- and state-owned firms. The same change would lead to an increase in the accounts receivable to sales ratio by 1 percentage point, explaining a third of the difference between private and state-owned firms. These magnitudes are large, given that they are identified by variation over time in the relevant variables for individual firms, and that private firms in the balanced panel sample are older and larger and thus tend to be more similar to state-owned companies.

We also study the patterns using the private firm survey data, which provides information on small private firms. While, unfortunately, this survey does not provide information on inventory, we can still analyze the effects of financing constraints on accounts receivable to sales ratio. Moreover, as financial costs are not available in the survey data, we only use leverage and interest rate as measures of credit constraints. Finally, the repeated cross-sectional nature of the data precludes us from conducting firm fixed effects estimation, but we do control for industry, province, and year fixed effects in the analysis.

As panel C in table 8.6 shows, leverage power has positive and significant effects on the accounts receivable to sales ratio. Thus the results obtained are largely in line with those for the census data, suggesting that the positive correlation between access to external finances and the level of working capital applies to small Chinese firms as well as to large and medium-sized firms. Furthermore the estimated effect of leverage on accounts receivable is larger than what we obtained for the large and medium-sized firms, suggesting greater sensitivity of small private firms' accounts receivable ratio to the availability of external funds.[6]

A natural concern with the results described above is potential endogeneity. There may be some other factors—unobserved to researchers—that cause firms to face more financial constraints and at the same time carry lower levels of inventory and accounts receivable. To address this issue, we conducted a few robustness tests using our balanced panel data. First, we computed the inventory/sales ratio and accounts receivable/sales ratio relative to the sector averages, and we reran the estimates. This adjustment allowed us to make sure that our results are not driven by differences in inventory and sales technologies across industries. Panel A of table 8.7 presents the results from this analysis. We can see that not only our results remain qualitatively the same but also the magnitudes of the coefficients are essentially unchanged.

Next we repeated the analysis with all three measures of access to external finances lagged by one year. Since our estimation was conducted with firm fixed effects, the coefficients are identified by variations over time in our dependent and independent variables. Lagging independent variable by one year allowed us to test whether our main results were driven by reverse causality. Panel B in table 8.7 shows the results of this test. With the exception of a lagged leverage in the accounts receivable regressions, our results remain qualitatively unchanged, although coefficients are somewhat smaller in magnitude. This suggests that we cannot reject the causal relationship between the limited access to external financing and lower levels of inventories and accounts receivable.

We adopted the Rajan–Zingales approach to study how the relationship between financial constraints and inventory or the accounts receivable levels differ across sectors with different degrees of reliance on external finances. If our argument is correct that the lower level of inventory or accounts receivable is a result of financial constrains faced by firms, then such an effect should be larger in sectors that have a greater reliance on external finances. To test this possibility, we included in the preceding estimation some additional explanatory variables: the index of external finance reliance (based on US data from 1980 from Rajan and Zingales 1998) and its interactions with the various financial constraint measures.[7] The results presented in panel C of table 8.7 show that firms in sectors more dependent on external finances reduce their inventory and accounts payable levels more in response to an increase in financial constraints. These findings are consistent with our hypothesis that financially constrained firms reduce their financial needs by adjusting their inventory and accounts payable levels.

Table 8.7
Robustness tests for relationship between financial constraints and inventory (AR) ratios

A. Using sector-adjusted inventory and AR ratios

Dependent variable: sector-adjusted inventory/sales ratio

	(1)	(2)	(3)	(4)
Leverage	0.100***			0.056***
	(0.004)			(0.005)
Financial expense/		1.081***		1.100***
total expense		(0.015)		(0.016)
Per unit			−0.173***	−0.349***
borrowing cost			(0.018)	(0.016)
Observations	257,304	237,809	243,552	220,436
Number of fmid1	38,315	37,989	38,298	37,180
Adjusted R^2	−0.172	−0.161	−0.186	−0.170

Dependent variable: sector-adjusted AR/sales ratio

	(1)	(2)	(3)	(4)
Leverage	0.057***			0.0416***
	(0.002)			(0.002)
Financial expense/		0.271***		0.304***
total expense		(0.007)		(0.008)
Per unit			−0.102***	−0.133***
borrowing cost			(0.007)	(0.007)
Observations	251,338	231,876	237,267	215,400
Number of fmid1	38,175	37,834	38,145	37,004
Adjusted R^2	−0.174	−0.185	−0.190	−0.191

B. Lagged independent variables

Dependent variable: inventory/sales ratio

	(1)	(2)	(3)	(4)
Leverage (1 year lag)	0.024***			0.010*
	(0.005)			(0.005)
Financial expense/		0.380***		0.410***
total expense (1 year lag)		(0.017)		(0.018)
Per unit			−0.043**	−0.120***
borrowing cost (1 year lag)			(0.019)	(0.018)
N	221,001	204,252	208,785	189,834
Number of firms	38,241	37,827	38,194	36,920
Within R^2	0.002	0.006	0.003	0.006

Table 8.7
(continued)

Dependent variable: AR/sales ratio

	(1)	(2)	(3)	(4)
Leverage (1 year lag)	0.003			−0.004
	(0.002)			(0.002)
Financial expense/		0.140***		0.150***
total expense (1 year lag)		(0.007)		(0.008)
Per unit			−0.015**	−0.049***
borrowing cost (1 year lag)			(0.007)	(0.008)
N	216,091	199,396	203,659	185,671
Number of firms	38,085	37,630	38,009	36,729
Within R^2	0.010	0.015	0.012	0.014

C. Interacting with sector dependence on external financing

Dependent variable: inventory/sales ratio

	(1)	(2)	(3)	(4)
Reliance on	−0.046	−0.074**	−0.072**	−0.046
external financing (1)	(0.030)	(0.035)	(0.036)	(0.034)
Leverage (2)	0.093***			0.054***
	(0.011)			(0.012)
(1) * (2)	0.033			0.035
	(0.020)			(0.023)
Financial expense/		1.789***		1.967***
total expense (3)		(0.054)		(0.059)
(1) * (3)		0.256***		−0.002
		(0.091)		(0.100)
Per unit			−0.132***	−0.262***
borrowing cost(4)			(0.044)	(0.039)
(1) * (4)			−0.045	−0.319***
			(0.097)	(0.087)
Observations	116,145	107,120	110,398	98,445
Number of firms	26,988	26,662	27,003	25,588
Within R^2	0.004	0.048	0.002	0.048

Table 8.7
(continued)

Dependent variable: AR/sales ratio

	(1)	(2)	(3)	(4)
Reliance on	−0.037***	−0.008	−0.003	−0.011
external financing (1)	(0.012)	(0.013)	(0.013)	(0.014)
Leverage (2)	0.048***			0.040***
	(0.005)			(0.005)
(1) * (2)	0.047***			0.024**
	(0.008)			(0.010)
Financial expense/		0.359***		0.432***
total expense (3)		(0.022)		(0.026)
(1) * (3)		0.053		0.148***
		(0.038)		(0.045)
Per unit			−0.070***	−0.070***
borrowing cost(4)			(0.015)	(0.016)
(1) * (4)			−0.070**	−0.176***
			(0.034)	(0.036)
Observations	113,780	104,673	107,763	96,493
Number of firms	26,829	26,470	26,799	25,418
Within R^2	0.010	0.016	0.006	0.025

Notes: We are able to estimate the level effects because some firms change their industries over time. * Significant at 10 percent, ** significant at 5 percent, *** significant at 1 percent.

8.4   Do Low Ratios of Inventories and Accounts Receivable Harm Profitability?

We have demonstrated that firms with more limited access to external finances tend to have lower inventory and accounts receivable ratios. We also have shown, in the fixed effects regression, that a given firm lowers these ratios in response to worsening financing conditions. A natural question that arises is whether these effects of limited access to external finance may be harmful to firms because inventory and accounts receivable ratios of financially constrained firms are so low as to prevent them from operating at an optimal level of sales. In fact both ratios in private firms are even lower than those in foreign-invested firms. If we assume that foreign-invested firms are both unconstrained financially and efficient at managing their inventory, this may imply that private firms are reducing their inventory below the optimal level, so as to confirm the suspicion noted above.

Table 8.8
Comparing Chinese firms with OECD firms in inventory level (days)

Firms	2000 to 2006	Finished goods inventory	Goods inventory
Private	53.3	26.1	27.2
HMT	92.7	36	56.7
Foreign	82.3	31.1	51.2
SOE	189	89.9	99.9
Mixed	110.6	54.2	56.5
	1994 to 2004		
Canada	74	36	38
France	103	61	42
Germany	92	58	34
Britain	78	41	37
Japan	56	31	25
Korea	42	19	23
Switzerland	93	41	52
Netherlands	83	51	32
United States	82	36	46
Total	63	34	29

Sources: Inventory days for Chinese firms are the authors' own calculations based on the NBS data (2000–2006), where inventory days = inventory/ sales * 365 days; those for the OECD country firms during the period 1994 to 2004 are from Roumiantsev and Netessine (2007, tab. 1), which are in turn summary statistics of active companies from 9 OECD countries that are included in the COMPUSTAT Global database and that operate in the manufacturing, wholesale and retail, and minerals and mining sectors excluding construction.

Table 8.8 shows that this fear may not be justified, as the total and the component inventory days for Chinese private firms (inferred from the inventory data) are all comparable to the average levels in OECD firms in 1994 to 2004. In contrast, most other types of Chinese firms have longer inventory days, particularly in raw material and intermediate goods inventories. The Chinese private firms are even closer to firms in Japan and Korea, China's two Asian neighbors. If one uses Korea as a benchmark, the Chinese private firms still have room to further reduce their inventory level. In other words, although much lower than other types of Chinese firms in inventory levels, especially Chinese SOEs, Chinese private firms seem to operate within the normal range of inventory levels by international standards. The time coverage

difference between the Chinese data and the OECD data further
strengthens this argument, as improvements in inventory technologies
have led to declining inventory levels over time.

Table 8.9 compares Chinese firms with US firms in terms of the
accounts receivable/sales ratio. For large firms, Chinese firms have
slightly lower account receivables ratios than their American counterparts. Given that US data are from the late 1980s while the Chinese data
are for this century, and that the accounts receivable/sales ratios tend
to decrease over time due to more advanced payment methods, it is
reasonable to argue that large firms in the two countries have similar
accounts receivable/sales ratios. For small firms, Chinese firms have
higher average accounts receivable/sales ratios than the US firms yet
lower median ratios, implying more variation among small Chinese
private firms in their ability to recoup sales revenue from customers.
As we saw before, among large and medium-sized firms, Chinese
private firms maintain lower levels of accounts receivable than Chinese
SOEs. Overall, there is no clear evidence that Chinese private firms
have to maintain overly low accounts receivable/sales ratios.

To further address the possibility of Chinese private firms carrying
levels of inventory and accounts payable that are too low, we studied
the potential nonlinear effects of inventory and accounts receivable
ratios on profitability and productivity of the firms. In table 8.10 we
show the estimation results of regressing the profitability measure
(before-tax or after-tax returns on assets) or the total factor productivity
measure on the ratios of inventory and accounts receivable to sales and
the squares of these ratios.[8] If reducing inventories below a certain level
has a detrimental effect on profitability, we should see a negative coefficient on the square term and positive coefficient on the linear term.
As columns 1, 2, 4, and 5 of table 8.10 show, for both inventory and
accounts receivable the pattern is reversed—the coefficient is positive
on the square term and negative on the linear term. Furthermore the
magnitudes of these coefficients indicate that for the entire range of
values for both ratios, lower ratios are associated with higher profitability—the minima of both quadratic functions are above the highest
value of the ratios in our data.[9] The findings related to inventory levels
are consistent with Lieberman and Demeester (1999) who studied Japanese car manufacturers, while the results on accounts receivable are in
line with those in Fisman (2001).

Columns 3 and 6 of table 8.10 show that productivity is associated
with inventory and accounts receivable ratios in the same way as prof-

itability—for the values of these ratios in our sample, lower ratios are usually associated with higher productivity. The theoretical argument in support of the findings on inventory is outlined in Lieberman and Demeester (1999): for firms that have lower inventory levels, problems related to various steps in the production process are more easily exposed and thus are more likely to be resolved by managers and workers, which then leads to increases in firm productivity. As for trade credit, Fisman (2001) argues that greater supplier credit helps firms more fully utilize their capacity. By reducing working capital requirement, a lower accounts receivable level will have similar effects in helping firms reaching their full capacity and thus enhancing productivity. Additionally the extra funds available may help make new process and technology more afford-able, which further enhances productivity. It is worth noting that such an advantage is in addition to the channel of lower financial costs, which is the usually the focus of research.

Therefore, for large and medium-sized Chinese firms, we find that (1) in controlling for industry and ownership type, firms with lower inventory and accounts receivable ratios tend to have higher profit-ability and higher total factor productivity in the cross section, and (2) in controlling for firm fixed effects, firms become more profitable and more productive as inventories and accounts receivables fall. To explore the patterns for small private firms, we again turn to the private firm survey data. Panel B presents the corresponding results using the survey data. As before, industry, province, and year dummies are con-trolled for in the analysis of the repeated cross-sectional data.

Columns 1 to 3 give estimation results using before-tax and after-tax return on assets and a crude measure of total factor productivity as the dependent variable, respectively.[10] As can be seen, just as the results from analyzing the data for the larger firms, the linear term always has a negative effect, whereas the effect of the quadratic term is always positive. For the before-tax return on the asset, the coefficient on the linear term of the accounts receivable/sales ratio is the only significant effect, implying a monotonically negative correlation between accounts receivable and profitability: the lower accounts receivable is to the sales ratio, the higher is the profitability. Likewise the results suggest that the relationship between accounts receivable and the total factor pro-ductivity (TFP) is exclusively monotonic: the lower accounts receivable is to the sales ratio, the higher is the firm's TFP.[11] In addition the effects of accounts receivable on both profitability and productivity are larger than those obtained for the larger firms. This suggests that small private

Table 8.9
Comparing Chinese firms with OECD firms in accounts receivable to sales ratio (percent)

A. Large firms

	US firms (1988–1989)		Chinese firms (2006 cross section)					
	Private		Private		SOE		All	
	Mean	Median	Mean	Median	Mean	Median	Mean	Median
Mining	28.7	21.7	7.7	2.2	12.6	6.1	8.8	2.8
Construction	15.8	16.4						
Manufacturing	19.1	17	13.1	7.6	18	11.1	14.1	8.3
Transportation/Utilities	16.2	14.1	11.3	5.6	12.2	5.1	12.3	7.8
Wholesale trade	15.5	14						
Retail trade	7.3	2.3						
Services	22.4	19.4						
Total	18.5	16.1	12.8	7.2	15.6	8.5	13.8	7.9

Table 8.9
(continued)

B. Small firms

	US firms (1988–1989)		Chinese firms (2006 cross section) private	
	Mean	Median	Mean	Median
Mining	9.9	6.9	14.8	0.05
Construction	10.4	7.8	19.6	0.09
Manufacturing	11.8	10	16.3	0.07
Transportation/utilities	8.1	6.5	16	0.02
Wholesale trade	8.1	7		
Retail trade	3	0.4	6.7	0
Services	8	3.5	9	0
Total	4.4	1.8	13.6	0.03

Source: Information on Chinese firms is from the authors' own calculations based on the NBS data (2000–2006, for the large firm sample) and the private firm survey data (2002–2006, for the small firm sample), while that on US firms is from Petersen and Rajan (1997, table 1), which in turn summarizes data from the National Survey of Small Business Finances in 1988–1989 for small firms and the Compustat for the large firms.

Table 8.10
Relationship between inventory and AR ratios and firm performance

A. Census data

	2006 Cross section			Balanced panel		
	Industry and ownership dummies			Firm and year FEs		
	(1)	(2)	(3)	(4)	(5)	(6)
	pretaxROA	aftertaxROA	TFP	pretaxROA	aftertaxROA	TFP
inventory/sales	−0.220***	−0.190***	−0.310***	−0.070***	−0.062***	−0.340***
	(0.003)	(0.003)	(0.005)	(0.002)	(0.002)	(0.006)
(inventory/sales)^2	0.037***	0.032***	0.039***	0.009***	0.008***	0.024***
	(0.001)	(0.001)	(0.001)	(0.000)	(0.000)	(0.001)
AR/sales	−0.560***	−0.490***	−0.300***	−0.150***	−0.130***	−0.320***
	(0.008)	(0.007)	(0.014)	(0.006)	(0.006)	(0.018)
(AR/sales)^2	0.590***	0.520***	0.320***	0.130***	0.110***	0.180***
	(0.012)	(0.011)	(0.022)	(0.007)	(0.007)	(0.022)
Observations	263,477	263,477	148,239	263,543	263,543	130,392
Adjusted R2	0.074	0.068	0.039			
Number of firms				38,670	38,670	22,434
Within R2				0.010	0.010	0.070

Notes: 2-digit industry dummies (39 industries in ROA and 31 industries in TFP regressions) are included in cross-section regression, but not reported. * Significant at 10 percent, ** significant at 5 percent, *** significant at 1 percent.

Table 8.10
(continued)

B. Repeated cross section using survey data; year, 1-digit industry, and ownership dummies included but not reported (19 industries)

	(1)	(2)	(3)
	pretaxROA	aftertaxROA	log(sales)
AR/sales	−0.360*	−0.120	−1.100***
	(0.210)	(0.098)	(0.050)
(AR/sales)^2	0.033	0.010	0.078***
	(0.026)	(0.012)	(0.006)
log(employment)			0.480***
			(0.014)
log(asset)			0.540***
			(0.012)
Observations	4,633	5,887	6,188
Adjusted R^2	0.002	0.009	0.700

Note: * Significant at 10 percent, ** significant at 5 percent, *** significant at 1 percent.

firms benefit from managing their working capital more efficiently. As small private Chinese firms are the most constrained in their access to external finances, these findings provide more critical support for the argument that more efficient management of working capital (inventory and accounts receivable) can lead to better firm performance, both through lower financial costs and real productivity gains.

We performed one more robustness test to support the argument that lower inventory levels can lead to higher productivity or profitability. As is well known, among the different types of inventories, final products inventories are the easiest to change into sales, and thus the best source for higher profitability or productivity (measured on the basis of sales). Thus firms in sectors with a higher proportion of inventories in final products will find it easier to increase productivity and profitability by reducing the level of inventory. We were not aware of any existing indexes that rank sectors by their inventory composition, so we constructed our own sector level inventory measures (at CIC 2 digit level averaged over 2000 to 2006) by focusing on foreign-invested firms in China. These firms provide a reasonable standard for how firms allocate inventories without financial constraints. We then added two explanatory variables to the analysis above using the balanced panel data: the sector level ratio between final products inventory and total inventory, as well as its interaction with the firm level inventory/sales ratio. As panel A in table 8.11 shows, firms in sectors with more of their inventories in final products indeed find it easier to increase both their profit rate (ROA) and their productivity (TFP), as evidenced by the interaction term having the same negative sign as the inventory/sales ratio.[12]

Similarly, to study whether a similar story applies to accounts receivable, we included the sector average reliance on trade credit (i.e., the accounts payable/total asset ratio) using data from US firms in the 1980s (Fisman and Love 2003) as well as the interaction of trade credits with accounts receivable/sales as the additional explanatory variables. Our logic was the following: if firms can improve productivity or profitability by reducing accounts receivable, then the sectors with a greater reliance on trade credit overall should find it easier to do so, as there are more opportunities to do so. Thus we expected a negative sign for the coefficient of the interaction term, same as that of the accounts receivable/sales ratio itself. The results in panel B of table 8.11, as expected, give negative estimates for the effects of the interaction terms, although only the estimates for TFP are very close to being significant. Finally, panel C in table 8.11 presents the results when both interaction terms are included, with the previous findings preserved.

Table 8.11
Robustness tests for relationship between inventory and AR ratios and firm performance

	(1)	(2)	(3)
Variables	pretaxROA	aftertaxROA	TFP
Panel A			
Inventory/sales (1)	−0.015***	−0.014***	−0.193***
	(0.004)	(0.003)	(0.010)
AR/sales (2)	−0.062***	−0.052***	−0.207***
	(0.003)	(0.002)	(0.008)
Finished goods inventory/	0.002	0.002	0.054**
total inventory (3)	(0.008)	(0.007)	(0.021)
(1) * (3)	−0.045***	−0.038***	−0.109***
	(0.009)	(0.009)	(0.025)
Observations	261,697	261,697	128,969
Number of firms	38,568	38,568	22,338
Within R^2	0.009	0.007	0.061
Panel B			
Inventory/sales (1)	−0.025***	−0.022***	−0.231***
	(0.002)	(0.002)	(0.005)
AR/sales (2)	−0.063**	−0.051*	−0.108
	(0.028)	(0.027)	(0.070)
Accounts payable/	−0.285	−0.259	0.046
asset (4)	(0.267)	(0.251)	(0.864)
(2) * (4)	−0.025	−0.042	−1.273
	(0.326)	(0.307)	(0.809)
Observations	119,948	119,948	73,349
Number of firms	27,543	27,543	17,837
Within R^2	0.007	0.006	0.059
Panel C			
Inventory/sales (1)	−0.010	−0.009	−0.148***
	(0.006)	(0.006)	(0.015)
AR/sales (2)	−0.064**	−0.051*	−0.111
	(0.029)	(0.027)	(0.071)
Finished goods inventory/	0.036**	0.026*	0.151***
total inventory (3)	(0.017)	(0.016)	(0.045)
(1) * (3)	−0.042**	−0.037**	−0.234***
	(0.017)	(0.016)	(0.040)
Accounts payable/	−0.295	−0.266	0.004
asset (4)	(0.268)	(0.252)	(0.867)
(2) * (4)	−0.024	−0.040	−1.242
	(0.328)	(0.308)	(0.813)
Observations	119,324	119,324	72,801
Number of firms	27,440	27,440	17,742
Within R^2	0.007	0.006	0.060

Notes: We are able to estimate the level effects because some firms change their industries over time. * Significant at 10 percent, ** significant at 5 percent, *** significant at 1 percent.

8.5　Conclusion

It has long been noted in the literature that private firms in China have more limited access to external financing and that such credit constraints are harmful for the development of the private sector in China. Nevertheless, despite limited access to financing, the private sector in China has experienced a long period of strong growth. While we cannot fully reconcile these two apparently conflicting observations, we provide evidence that may help explain some of the puzzle. In particular, we show that Chinese private firms respond to financing constraints by lowering inventory and accounts receivable and thus limiting their need for working capital. We further show that even at the low levels of inventory and accounts receivable, reductions in these ratios are associated with higher productivity and profitability. In other words, facing and overcoming financing constraints seems to have forced Chinese private firms to become more efficient, especially compared to their state-owned counterparts for which easy access to financing seems instead to lead to inefficiently high levels of inventory and trade credit.

Our findings do not necessarily contradict the argument that limited access to external funding is likely slowing down the development of the private sector in China. In fact, because private firms are able to manage working capital very efficiently (by maintaining low levels of inventory and accounts receivable), our results imply that easier access to external finance should lead to more expansion and long-term investment projects by private firms. Hence financial market reforms, by allowing further growth of the private sector through more credit availability, may well be the next engine of sustained economic growth in China.

Notes

1. The views expressed in this chapter are those of the authors and do not necessarily represent the views of the Federal Reserve Bank of San Francisco or Federal Reserve System. Part of this work was conducted while Hale was visiting the Hong Kong Institute of Monetary Research, for whose hospitality she is most grateful. We thank participants at the 2010 CESifo Summer Institute and 2010 NBER China Working Group Meeting, especially Li Jin and Gunther Schnabl for their comments, and Hirotaka Miura for excellent research assistance.

2. Using a small sample of private firms and SOEs for 1994 to 1999, Ge and Qiu (2007) provide evidence that private firms use trade credit as a net source of credit (i.e., incur higher accounts payable than accounts receivable), while SOEs on average are a net sup-

plier of trade credit. However, in the more recent years we are focusing on (2000 to 2006), this channel appears to have dried out.

3. While the raw data includes 622,424 firms, after we drop observations with missing values for year, location, industry code, duplicates or near duplicates, as well as observations with key variables that appear erroneously reported or missing, we are left with 496,738 firms in the unbalanced panel dataset.

4. One may be concerned with the survivorship bias in our balanced panel regression. However, our results also hold in the cross section, a snapshot of 2006 data, where they cannot be driven by survivorship bias.

5. Note that the per unit cost for external financing computed here is different from average interest rate for at least two reasons: (1) a firm's total debt may include liabilities not bearing interest payments such as various accounts payable, and (2) even if the firm's total debt comprises only interest-bearing bank loans, the year-end total debt may not correspond to the amount of bank loans that incurred the interest payment in that year. However, this ratio still gives a proxy for the average cost of obtaining finances faced by firms of different types.

6. If we repeat table 8.6 using LT debt/LT assets instead of leverage, theresults in both the cross section and the panel analysis are largely preserved, with the only exception of a small negative effect of state dummy for AR in the cross-sectional results.

7. We are able to estimate the level effect because some firms have changed their industries over time.

8. Total factor productivity (TFP) for the panel analysis here is measured as a residual from estimating an industry-by-industry system GMM model of production function. For the detailed description of how these TFP measures are obtained, see Hale et al. (2010).

9. To be precise, there are 129 observations in the cross-sectional data and 153 observations in the panel data for which inventory to sales ratio is in the increasing range of the estimated quadratic function. For the accounts receivable there are no observations in the increasing range of the quadratic function.

10. Because raw material usage is unknown for firms in the survey data, we construct estimate TFP by running a regression of log sales on log assets and log labor, in addition to variables of interest.

11. There are only 17 firms in our sample of small private firms for which the accounts receivable to sales ratio is in the increasing range of the estimated quadratic function.

12. The following alternative specifications give similar results, testifying to the robustness of the results: The finish goods/inventory ratio is also computed at the sector-year level, or the inventory/sales ratio and the accounts receivable/sales are computed relative to the sector averages.

References

Allen, F., J. Qian, and M. Qian. 2005. Law, finance, and economic growth in China. *Journal of Financial Economics* 77 (July): 57–116.

Brandt, L., and H. Li. 2003. Bank discrimination in transition economies: Ideology, information or incentives? *Journal of Comparative Economics* 31 (September): 387–413.

Cull, R., and L. C. Xu. 2000. Bureaucrats, state banks, and the efficiency of credit alloca-tion: The experience of Chinese state-owned enterprises. *Journal of Comparative Economics* 28 (March): 1–31.

Cull, R., L. C. Xu, and T. Zhu. 2009. Formal finance and trade credit during China's transition. *Journal of Financial Intermediation* 18: 173–92.

Dollar, D., and S. Wei. 2007. Das (wasted) Kapital: Firm ownership and investment effi-ciency in China. Working Paper 13103. NBER, Cambridge, MA.

Fisman, R. 2001. Trade credit and productive efficiency in developing countries. *World Development* 29 (2): 311–21.

Fisman, R., and I. Love. 2003. Trade credit, financial intermediary development, and industry growth. *Journal of Finance* 58 (1): 353–74.

Ge, Y., and J. Qiu. 2007. Financial development, bank discrimination and trade credit. *Journal of Banking and Finance* 31 (2): 513–30.

Hale, G., and C. Long. 2010. What are the sources of financing of the Chinese firms? In Yin-Wong Cheung, ed., *The Evolving Role of Asia in Global Finance*. Bingley, UK: Emerald Group Publishing, 313–41.

Hale, G., C. Long, T. Moran, and H. Miura. 2010. Where to find positive productivity spillovers from FDI in China: Disaggregated analysis. Working Paper 142010. HKIMR, Hong Kong.

Hèricourt, J., and S. Poncet. 2009. FDI and credit constraints: Firm level evidence from China. *Economic Systems* 33 (1): 1–21.

Hsieh, C.-T., and P. J. Klenow. 2009. Misallocation and manufacturing TFP in China and India. *Quarterly Journal of Economics* 124 (4): 1403–48.

King, R., and R. Levine. 1993. Finance and growth: Schumpeter might be right. *Quarterly Journal of Economics* 108: 717–37.

Lardy, N. R. 2004. State-owned banks in China. In G. Caprio, J. L. Fiechter, R. E. Litan, and M. Pomerleano, eds., *The Future of State-Owned Financial Institutions*. Washington, DC: Brookings Institution.

Lardy, N. 1998. *China's Unfinished Economic Revolution*. Washington, DC: Brookings Institution.

Lieberman, M. B., and L. Demeester. 1999. Inventory reduction and productivity growth: Linkages in the Japanese automotive industry. *Management Science* 45 (4): 466–85.

Liu, Q., and A. Siu. 2006. Institutions, financial development, and corporate investment: Evidence from an implied return on capital in China. Available at SSRN: http://ssrn .com/abstract=965631.

Long, C., and X. Zhang. 2010. Industrial clusters and firm financing in China. Discussion Paper. International Food Policy Research Institute, Washington, DC.

Poncet, S., W. Steingress, and H. Vandenbussche. 2010. Financial constraints in China: Firm-level evidence. *China Economic Review* 21 (3): 411–22.

Rajan, R. G., and L. Zingales. 1998. Financial dependence and growth. *American Economic Review* 88 (3): 559–86.

III China's Monetary Policy and Capital Controls

9 Chinese Monetary Policy and the Dollar Peg

J. James Reade and Ulrich Volz

9.1 Introduction

China's reinstitution of its dollar peg in July 2008 in the wake of the global financial crisis has stirred a heated discussion about China's alleged currency manipulation and beggar-thy-neighbor policy. Proponents of a reform of China's currency regime have argued that the dollar peg not only has negative effects on China's trading partners, it also has detrimental effects on the Chinese economy since it impedes an independent monetary policy by the People's Bank of China (PBC), China's central bank (e.g., Roberts and Tyers 2003; Eichengreen 2004; Prasad et al. 2005; Goldstein and Lardy 2006, 2009).

The theoretical implications of a fixed exchange rate peg on the conduct of monetary policy are clear. The "impossible trinity" stipulates that a country is unable to maintain an open capital account, a fixed exchange rate, and an independent monetary policy simultaneously. Policy makers are thus obliged to choose between two of the three goals. Since Chinese policy makers have opted for a fixed exchange rate against the dollar and a fairly closed capital account, this policy choice should theoretically provide room for an independent conduct of monetary policy. However, the validity of the impossible trinity hypothesis has been contested. On the one hand, the isolation property of floating exchange rates has been questioned and the empirical evidence has been mixed (e.g., Rose 1996; Calvo and Reinhart 2002; Frankel et al. 2004; Shambaugh 2004; Obstfeld et al. 2005). On the other hand, in practice, it is difficult to maintain effective capital controls over time, especially for economies that are open to trade. The empirical evidence suggests that capital controls can be circumvented and that they are not very effective in achieving a higher degree of monetary policy independence (Edwards 1999).

Surprisingly, there has been relatively little empirical research on the impact of the Chinese dollar peg on the conduct of and constraints on Chinese monetary policy so far. Ma and McCauley (2007) examine price and flow evidence to determine the effectiveness of China's capital controls. Looking at onshore and offshore renminbi yield differentials, as well as gaps in the dollar/renminbi interest rate differentials, they find that China's capital controls remain substantially binding. Although the Chinese capital controls have not been watertight, Ma and McCauley conclude that they have allowed the Chinese authorities to retain some degree of short-term monetary autonomy, despite the fixed exchange rate.

Cheung et al. (2007) focus on the link between US and Chinese interest rates. Using multiple-equation cointegration analysis, they investigate the interaction between US and Chinese money market rates. According to their findings, China does not meet the assumptions of a perfect interest rate pass through since the effect of US interest rates on Chinese rates that they find is rather weak. Like Ma and McCauley, Cheung et al. conclude that China has had alternative means in place to de-link its interest rates from the US rates.

Glick and Hutchison (2009) scrutinize to what extent China's current account surpluses, foreign direct investment (FDI) inflows, and occasionally large non-FDI capital inflows compromise China's monetary policy goal of limiting inflation in the presence of a fixed or tightly managed exchange rate regime. They estimate a vector error correction model that links foreign exchange reserve accumulation to developments in China's reserve money, broad money, real GDP, and price level to explore the inflationary implications of different policy scenarios. Under a scenario of limited exchange rate flexibility, rapid foreign exchange reserve accumulation, and limited effectiveness of sterilization operations, their model predicts a rapid increase in inflation. They see a temporary yet limited effect of increasing reserve requirements in dampening inflationary pressures. Glick and Hutchison conclude that as long as China continues to place a higher priority on exchange rate stability than on using monetary policy as a tool for macroeconomic management, China's scope for an autonomous monetary policy is constrained.

Prasad (2008) concurs that when constrained by a tightly managed exchange rate, monetary policy can at best play a very limited role for China in responding to economic shocks, be they internal or external. However, he points out that although the huge accumulation of foreign exchange reserves—a consequence of Chinese foreign exchange market intervention to counter the appreciation of the yuan—added to the liquidity of the banking system and further complicated the control of credit growth, the PBC was able to sterilize the capital inflows rather well. Unlike in most other emerging market economies, where sterilization policies usually run into limits quickly, the PBC encounters a great demand for its bills even at relatively low interest rates, a result of both high savings rates in the private and corporate sectors as well as limited diversification alternatives in the closed Chinese capital market. Still, Prasad insists that the PBC's inability to use interest rates as a primary tool of monetary policy implies that monetary growth has to be controlled by blunter and non–market-oriented instruments such as targets or ceilings for credit growth as well as "nonprudential administrative measures."

In this chapter we attempt to shed more light on China's monetary and exchange rate policy by conducting a number of empirical analyses. The difficulty of carrying out empirical analysis on China, and Chinese monetary policy in particular, is common knowledge: data availability is limited, the quality of the available data is often questionable, and the economy is undergoing dramatic and rapid structural change. Also research is complicated by the fact that the PBC uses a host of unconventional measures in its conduct of monetary policy.[1] When the recent global financial crisis is taken into consideration, one might be tempted to abandon all hope of learning anything from Chinese economic data. However, we believe this is not the best course of action. Economic data are only interesting and informative when they contains variation because only then can we begin to discover the constancies that remain beneath the variation and start to test whether economic theories of steady states and relationships between variables exist in the data. Naturally, by definition, structural change can make any such steady-state relationships difficult to detect because they can change dramatically. However, co-breaking is known to exist where multiple data series break at the same point, and hence steady-state relationships continue to exist before and after a break (Hendry and Massmann 2007). Hence structural change need not force us to abandon all hope of finding steady-state relationships.

Our approach is empirical in nature, building from economic theory. We seek to detect steady-state relationships using the multiple-equation cointegration approach of Johansen (1995). By this approach we are able to model macroeconomic variables without a priori assuming exogeneity of many of the variables in our model. Given the complex nature of macroeconomies, this is highly desirable, as we are able to avoid an endogeneity bias. The expected steady-state relationships of economic theory can be represented by cointegrating relationships, or vectors, in this framework. The multiple-equation framework allows us to detect for many possible steady-state relationships, again corresponding to the complex nature of macroeconomies: We can test for standard textbook macroeconomic relationships, and we can learn whether different policy tools can exist together.

We try to address two questions in this chapter. First, following Cheung et al. (2007), we want to know how much monetary policy independence the PBC enjoys with monetary independence understood in a narrow sense as the PBC's ability to conduct its own interest rate policy without having to follow any outside influences (most notably not having to follow interest rate policy conducted in the United States). To investigate this, we conduct a detailed analysis of interest rates in China. In particular, we investigate international parity linkages via relationships with nondeliverable forward and the spot exchange rate, and also internal interest rate relationships to ascertain whether via administrative interest rates the PBC is able to conduct policy that is effective (i.e., impacts interest rates).

Second, we want to know how effective the PBC's interest rate policy and the other monetary policy tools it has used (i.e., changes in the reserve requirement ratios and open market operations) have been in managing monetary growth and containing inflation. For this purpose we estimate a monetary model for China that includes the PBC's policy rate, the required reserve ratio, a measure of the PBC's open market operations, as well as macroeconomic indicators that policy might be expected to respond to, namely inflation, economic activity, growth in broad money, and growth in foreign currency reserves. Via this analysis we can shed light on how policy tools have been used in the context of the macroeconomy, and how effective these tools have been.

Our results indicate that China has been able to largely insulate its monetary policy from international monetary movements. However, in terms of monetary instruments, the interest rate tool does not seem to exert particularly much influence on the macroeconomy. Rather, the PBC has made more extensive use of less market-based policy tools like reserve ratio requirement. Money growth targeting appears to be important alongside inflation targeting and GDP growth targeting.

The reminder of this chapter is organized as follows: Section 9.2 provides a brief overview of Chinese monetary and exchange rate policy. Section 9.3 introduces our econometric methodology, and section 9.4 presents our econometrics results in two parts: in section 9.4.1 we consider China's monetary policy independence; in section 9.4.2 we investigate China's monetary policy in terms of policy tools and target macroeconomics variables. Section 9.5 concludes.

9.2   Brief Overview of China's Monetary and Exchange Rate Policy

The PBC's objective of monetary policy is "to maintain the stability of the value of the currency and thereby promote economic growth."[2] According to the PBC, "[t]he monetary policy instruments applied by the PBC include reserve requirement ratio, central bank base interest rate, rediscounting, central bank lending, open market operation and other policy instruments specified by the State Council."[3]

In practice, as pointed out by Koivu (2009), the foundations of China's monetary policy have been a fixed exchange rate, strict controls on capital flows and a wide selection of administrative and quantitative policy tools. Figure 9.1 displays the exchange rate of the Chinese yuan against the US dollar. China fixed its exchange rate at 8.28 yuan to the dollar from 1994 to July 21, 2005, when it abandoned the tight dollar peg and adopted an undisclosed basket exchange rate regime under which it allowed a small and tightly controlled appreciation of the yuan against the dollar. Between July 2005 and July 2008, the yuan appreciated by 21 percent against the dollar. In July 2008, in the face of the global financial crisis, China returned to the tight peg against the dollar, now at 6.8 yuan to the dollar. In June 2010 the PBC relaxed the peg, although the permitted change in the exchange rate has been negligible thus far.

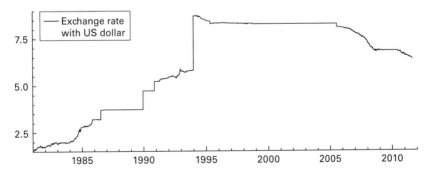

Figure 9.1
Exchange rate between the Chinese renminbi and the US dollar between 1981 and 2010. Source: Datastream.

Throughout this time China has administered tight capital controls. According to the Chinn–Ito index for financial openness, which measures a country's international financial openness on a scale from −2.54 to 2.54 (with −2.54 indicating a completely closed capital account and 2.54 full liberalization), China's degree of capital account openness has remained unchanged at −1.13 since 1993.[4]

As noted above, the PBC uses various instruments to achieve its monetary objective. However, as will be shown later in our empirical analysis, not all instruments have been effectively made use of. In particular, several studies observe the absence of a major role for interest rates in the Chinese economy, as compared to advanced economies (Laurens and Maino 2007; Mehrotra 2007; Prasad 2008; Geiger 2008; Koivu 2009; Koivu et al. 2009). Although the PBC sets several interest rates (central bank lending rate, rediscount rate, and benchmark rates for different maturities of deposits and loans), in practice, the role of interest rates has been limited in pursuing the objective of monetary policy. Laurens and Maino (2007) maintain that there are several potential obstacles to the effectiveness of interest rates as an operating target for monetary policy conduct in China. First, they point out that some of the characteristics of China's financial sector may limit the effectiveness of the interest rate transmission channel for monetary policy. In particular, the effectiveness of the transmission channel is hampered due to insufficient progress in establishing a commercially driven financial sector as well as market segmentation of the banking sector and money markets.[5] Moreover Laurens and Maino argue that the PBC does not yet have in place the monetary framework and instruments to conduct full-fledged market-based monetary policy.

However, as pointed out by Yi (2008), the PBC's approach to financial macromanagement has gradually changed since the 1990s and the PBC has been trying to advance the reform of the interest rate system and strengthen the role of interest rates. For instance, the band of deposit and lending rates has been widened and the lending rate ceiling and deposit rate floor have been abolished. Yi maintains that with this improvement of the central bank interest rate system, the PBC is now better able to guide the market interest rate and that market participants have become more sensitive to interest rate changes. In any case, while the PBC has been generally reluctant to use the interest rate as a policy tool, it did increase the use of the interest rate instrument when trying to contain accelerating inflation in 2006 to 2007 (Koivu 2009) and slumping output in the face of the global financial crisis.

While the PBC has been making efforts to shift from direct to indirect control—for example, through the abolition of credit ceilings on January 1, 1998—the transmission mechanism continues to rely on measures affecting the quantity of loans and money supply, instead of prices such as interest rates (Nagai and Wang 2007). The PBC sets annual intermediate and operational targets for money supply growth (M1 and M2) and base money; in recent years it has also announced a target for credit growth. The money supply is then controlled by setting the reserve requirement ratio and deciding on central bank lending.[6]

Koivu (2009) points out that since summer 2003, expanding capital inflows have increased liquidity in China's financial markets and have made the conduct of domestic monetary policy more complicated. A particular challenge was the growth of reserve money, a consequence of frequent intervention in the foreign exchange market in order to maintain the dollar peg. The PBC responded by raising bank reserve requirements and imposing lending restrictions in an attempt to decouple reserve money growth from broad money growth (Glick and Hutchison 2009). The PBC has also tried to control market liquidity via open market operations (OMO) by selling central bank bills to commercial banks.[7] According to Yi (2008), the role of OMO has been strengthened in the daily adjustment of base money and they have become a major instrument.

Last but not least, the PBC continues to use administrative policy tools to guide financial market developments. Even after the abolishment of credit plans, which formed the basis of bank lending until the end of 1997, the PBC continues to issue lending guidelines for commercial banks. The so-called window guidance policy, which involves the issuance of direct guidelines and orders to commercial banks, was intensified due to rapid credit growth in 2003 and again in 2007 (Koivu et al. 2009).[8] With this brief outline of Chinese monetary policy, we now move on to econometrically examine what is driving Chinese interest rates and the role of the various monetary policy instruments in actual Chinese monetary policy making.

9.3 Empirical Methodology

The approach taken in this chapter, as indicated in the introduction, is empirical. Shaped as much as possible by economic theory and institutional knowledge regarding China, we attempt to understand more about the Chinese economy by investigating the data. We are under no illusions regarding the difficulty of this task: lack of data, quality of available data, and massive structural change inside and outside of China complicate our task. Nonetheless, we see value in adopting such an approach, hopefully to augment the discussion and analysis taking place elsewhere with regard China's monetary system.

We seek a methodology that can as best as possible cope with the types of data available for China: nonstationary time series that are dynamically connected through the macroeconomy. By using cointegration methods (Engle and Granger 1987), we can cope with nonstationarity and other degrees of high persistence while still retaining economic theory coherence, and by using multiple-equation methods (Johansen 1995), we can cope with the endogeneity inherent in the macroeconomy.

We specify a $p \times 1$ data vector X_t, which contains p variables measured at time t. The VAR model with K lags is written as

$$X_t = \Pi_0 + \sum_{k=1}^{K} \Pi_k X_{t-k} + \varepsilon_t, \qquad \varepsilon_t \sim N(0, \Sigma), \tag{9.1}$$

where Π_k are $p \times p$ matrices of regression coefficients, and ε_t is a $p \times 1$ vector of residuals. The data vector is assumed to contain variables that are at most integrated of order one, so have unit roots. Some variables in X_t can be stationary, although for this exposition we will assume that all variables have unit roots hence $X_t \sim I(1)$.[9] The VAR model can be reformulated into a vector error-correction form:

$$\Delta X_t = \Pi_0 + \Pi X_t + \sum_{k=1}^{K-1} \Gamma_k \Delta X_{t-k} + \varepsilon_t, \tag{9.2}$$

where Δ is the difference operator such that $\Delta X_t = X_t - X_{t-1}$, $\Pi = \sum_{k=1}^{K} \Pi_k$ and $\Gamma_k = -\Pi_k$. Because we assume $X_t \sim I(1)$, then $\Delta X_t \sim I(0)$, and since the error term ε_t is also assumed to be stationary, then for (9.2) to balance, we need Δ to be of reduced rank. If we denote the reduced rank of Π by r, then there exist two $p \times r$ matrices and such that $\Pi = \alpha\beta'$ and so

$$\Delta X_t = \Pi_0 + \alpha\beta'^{X_t} + \sum_{k=1}^{K-1} \Gamma_k \Delta X_{t-k} + \varepsilon_t. \tag{9.3}$$

In (9.3), the $r \times 1$ vector $\beta' X_{t-1}$ contains the r cointegrating vectors, or steady-state relationships, implied by the reduced rank r of the economic system.

Our procedure in this chapter is that recommended by Johansen (1995) and Juselius (2007), to start generally by modeling the VAR model in (9.1) and ensuring that the model satisfies the independent normality assumption placed on the error term. From Rahbek and Mosconi (1999) it is known that only autocorrelation and nonnormality in the residuals (so not heteroskedasticity) affect the trace test for cointegrating rank and subsequent coefficient estimates, and hence we focus only on these two tests. Next we conduct the trace test for cointegration rank to determine r, before imposing the rank and analyzing the resulting cointegrating vectors $\beta'X_{t-1}$ and the adjustments of each variable to the cointegrating vectors, described in the matrix.

The important thing to emphasize is that as much as possible we let the data speak freely. It may be considered somewhat foolish to even attempt to enter into the murky depths of the economic data of China; questions can be raised not just about its accuracy but also about its generation, since China is not a market economy and much appears to happen as a result of what are euphemistically referred to as "administrative measures." It may be asserted by some that in this kind of context, only "expert judgment" can possibly provide any useful insight. We disagree with this stance. The judgmental forecasting literature has adequately revealed the subjective biases that even "expert" forecasters exhibit when altering the forecasts provided before them, and in particular noted their inability to recognize longer term time trends in economic data in making errors. We do not reject expert advice, it must also be asserted; we are fully dependent on this in forming our econometric models. Our standpoint, however, is what we see as constructive; we wish to augment the existing analysis of the Chinese monetary system with some hard-edged numbers, where possible. We recognize this is not an easy task with the aforementioned administrative measures, but we nonetheless believe it to be a useful task. It can help us gain some idea of how the system fits together, about marginal effects, about the endogeneity and exogeneity of variables, and about the efficacy of policy.

Juselius (2007) is transparent and clear about the difficulties of empirical work. The assumptions we make on our error terms are often violated, which naturally raises the difficult question of what can really be learned from empirical investigations. This difficulty is all the greater given the object of our empirical interest is China; the potential difficulties of the integrity and quality of data collection, allied with the length of time series collected, makes the task yet more difficult. As mentioned, some model misspecifications do not result in problems for subsequent analysis, but others do. Many more subtle misspecifications are often ignored in empirical papers, such as structural uncertainty. Again, given the immense speed at which China is industrializing, the likelihood of structural breaks and instability in the data is multiplied on a grand scale. Our aim in this chapter is thus not to present an empirical analysis as the definitive insight on how Chinese monetary policy operates. This would be difficult in a more stable, Western-style economy, let alone China. Instead, we simply seek to shed some light on what may be taking place in China, and to some extent present a cautionary note on attempting to read too much into patterns that might be seemingly apparent from the data in that country. It is our hope that this analysis is one further step on the road toward a better understanding of Chinese monetary policy.

Our methodology allows us to uncover constancies if they exist in the data. An economy undergoing such dramatic structural change as in China may be expected to display little if any steady-state, stationary relationships. If this is so, our econometric methods will show this. We now proceed to answer our two questions regarding the independence of monetary policy and its internal nature, and in each section we will describe the data we are using, and what we expect to find. Our strategy for investigating monetary policy arrangements in China is similar to that of Johansen and Juselius (2003) who consider inflation targeting in the United States; they first establish the link between the policy tool (the Federal Funds Target Rate) and the interbank interest rate (the Effective Federal Funds Rate) before analyzing the effective rate's influence on macroeconomic outcomes. Here we first consider whether Chinese policy tools (administratively set interest rates) are able to exert a dominant influence on the market-orientated interest rates before considering the impact of those monetary policy tools more generally on economic activity.

9.4 Empirical Output

9.4.1 Policy Independence and Interest Rates in China

Economic Theory Background As with any economy, state administered or market based, there are plenty of interest rates that might be used to investigate monetary policy. Some naturally will be more useful and informative than others, and as such we seek to understand which rates should be considered most informative. We attempt to do this by considering some of the major administratively set interest rates, and some of the most important market-determined interest rates. In a standard Western market economy, the interbank interest rate is the obvious choice to consider monetary policy because such rates reflect macroeconomic and liquidity conditions, and also naturally because monetary policy makers seek to influence these interest rates to particular ends. Porter and Xu (2009) provide a description of the interaction between administratively set interest rates and more market-orientated rates in China, and note that the market-determined interbank and repo rates are strongly influenced by the administratively set retail interest rates for savings and deposits.

Thus we have at least two objectives in this subsection. We wish to consider the extent to which the Chinese interbank rate is insulated from world events via its fixed exchange rate peg and capital controls, and also the extent to which it is determined internally via these administratively controlled interest rates. A standard consideration of the Chinese interbank rate and its international movements, via uncovered interest rate parity among other things, may provide a somewhat distorted impression of how the interest rate moves, particularly if internal movements are more important. Hence we combine the two possible analyses in order to yield a clearer picture of monetary dynamics in China. This preempts our analysis of monetary policy tools by yielding insight on which tools, if any, are more appropriate for use. Porter and Xu (2009) investigate their hypothesis of influence from one interest rate to another using a single-equation GARCH model and find that the interbank interest rate is influenced, as expected, by the savings and deposit interest rates. In this section we investigate the same question using the multiple-equation methods of the cointegrated VAR model; although we do not explicitly model the ARCH likely present in the interest rate series, we are able to capture any endogeneity between the interest rate series via these methods, and we can investigate which interest rates exert the most influence via the adjustments to cointegrating vectors found.

We are at first interested in the policy dependence, or otherwise, that China exhibits in its monetary policy-making; such information helps paint the picture of Chinese monetary policy-making. A reasonably standard mechanism for establishing independence among market-based industrial economies is to consider interbank interest rates;

relative to some other economy, say economy B, how do domestic interbank interest rates vary? If domestic rates merely follow the rates in this economy B, then domestic monetary policy cannot be described as being independent: it is following the monetary movements in economy B. The domestic economy could simply be reacting to common macroeconomic shocks. Yet, if the economy systematically follows economy B in responding to these shocks, it implies the argued dominance. Were the economy to display independence, we would expect not to find cointegrating relationships between the economies. This approach has been taken by Edison and MacDonald (2003) and Reade and Volz (2011) for pre-EMU Europe and searches for cointegrating relationships between the interbank interest rates of Germany and each individual European nation. The uncovered interest rate parity (UIP) condition is

$$(1+R_{s,t}) = \frac{E_t(S_{t+s})}{S_t}(1+R_t^*) = \frac{F_t}{S_t}(1+R_{s,t}^*), \tag{9.4}$$

where $R_{s,t}$ is the domestic interest rate on assets with maturity after s time periods, $R_{s,t}^*$ is the overseas interest rate on the same maturity of assets, S_t is the spot exchange rate of the domestic currency in terms of the overseas currency, and F_t is the forward exchange rate, equal to the expectation at time t of the spot exchange rate at time $t + s$.

Taking logs of (9.4) and using the approximation that $\log(1 + x) \approx x$ for small x, we get

$$R_{s,t} = f_t - s_t + R_{s,t}^*, \tag{9.5}$$

where lowercase letters denote the logarithm of a variable. Often investigations of interest rate comovements in the context of fixed exchange rate systems will use the assumption that the fixed exchange rate implies that $E_t(S_{t+s}) = S_t$ and hence the exchange rate terms cancel out of (9.4). However, figure 9.2 plots spot and forward exchange rates for China, a country that for most of its recent economic history has implemented a fixed exchange rate system.[10] From the plot, long before the RMB was allowed to appreciate in July 2005 there was an expectation that it would. The exchange rate was no longer credible and as such the forward and spot exchange rate terms in (9.4) will not cancel out for our sample.

Given economic theory, we might expect that (9.5) be satisfied in the economic data, yet repeated empirical studied have shown a

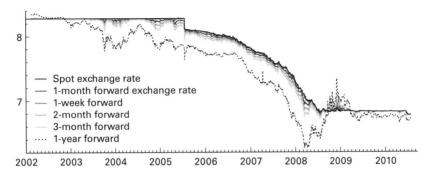

Figure 9.2
Spot and forward exchange rates for RMB/USD. Source: Datastream.

failure of the condition, apart from estimation over very short time horizons (Chaboud and Wright 2005) or very long ones (Chinn 2006). Nonetheless, the important question we are concerned about is whether interest rates in China are forced to follow such a relationship, or whether some deviation is possible. Considering UIP instead of a simple interest rate parity condition that excludes exchange rates gives a richer picture of policy dependence; it may be that China's interest rates don't react to the US interest rate, but that may be because of capital controls. When running a fixed exchange rate system, economic theory tells us that the interest rate must be used to defend the exchange rate peg. Including the exchange rate and expectations regarding that exchange rate, we have a richer picture of interest rate movements. When combined with other domestic interest rates, that picture is yet richer! Is the interbank rate influenced by international, exchange-rate-related movements fundamentally, or by internal factors such as the administratively set interest rates? In considering these two possibilities together, we can get some idea of what impacts interbank rates most, and fundamentally whether China has any degree of monetary policy independence (defined as the ability to conduct one's own monetary policy unencumbered by the policies of other countries, notably the United States).

Naturally, a criticism of this approach is that China does not operate a market economy and hence its interbank market is not really a market. Naturally, if this is the case, then we would not expect China's interbank rates to follow anything even closely resembling UIP; hence our analysis is still relevant and appropriate for investigating China's

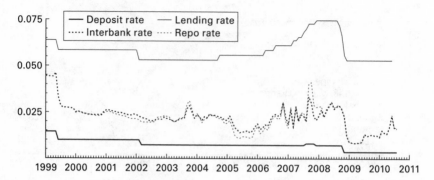

Figure 9.3
Market-orientated (interbank and repo) and administratively set (deposit and lending) interest rates for China. Source: PBC.

monetary policy-making framework.[11] Furthermore, by modeling UIP within the context of a range of Chinese interest rates, we can conduct a number of interesting analyses regarding Chinese insulation from international movements.

We denote the interbank interest rate as $r_{i,t}$, the repo interest rate $r_{r,t}$, the lending rate $r_{l,t}$, the deposit rate as $r_{d,t}$, the US interbank interest rate as $r^*_{i,t}$, the spot exchange rate as s_t, and the forward exchange rate as f_t. Hence our data vector is

$$X_t = \begin{pmatrix} r_{i,t} \\ r_{r,t} \\ r_{l,t} \\ r_{d,t} \\ r^*_{i,t} \\ f_t \\ s_t \end{pmatrix}. \tag{9.6}$$

Based on the discussion of internal Chinese interest rates, we expect to find one cointegrating vector pertaining to this, and we expect the coefficients of that cointegrating vector to be homogeneous of degree zero so that all the rates move together. We may also expect to find a cointegrating vector relating to the UIP condition, with a coefficient of something in excess of unity using previous studies as a guide. We may also find that each Chinese interest rate enters into some kind of UIP relationship with the United States, and this will be a test of the policy independence of China. Then again, identifying a cointegrating vector

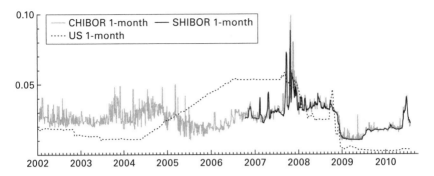

Figure 9.4
Interbank interest rates for the US and China. Note: CHIBOR is the China interbank rate, and SHIBOR is the Shanghai interbank rate (the latter employs market makers and hence is smoother). Source: PBC.

for domestic monetary movements, and one for international ones, will give some idea over which set of influences are most important for interest rate determination in China.

Data The Chinese and US interbank interest rates are plotted at a one-month horizon in figure 9.4, and the four domestic interest rates mentioned in the previous section are plotted in figure 9.3. It would appear that the comovement between the Chinese and US interest rates is limited to the latter part of the sample, postfinancial crisis. Considering the domestic interest rates, we again aim for a one-month horizon that is simple for the interbank and repo rates, but for the administrative rates we have to take the 3-month time deposit interest rate and the 0- to 6-month lending rate due to availability. The market rates generally lie in-between the two administratively set rates. The period over which data are available for all series is 2000:5 to 2010:6, yielding 122 observations.

Turning to exchange rates (figures 9.1 and 9.2), we immediately meet with difficulties. The change in exchange rate policy in 2005 between a fixed exchange rate and a managed floating exchange rate and the subsequent re-establishment of a fixed exchange rate in mid-2008 are very apparent in figure 9.2. Modeling the entire period will not cause problems if all the variables also break at the same time (Hendry and Massmann 2007); it is clear from figure 9.2 that the forward exchange rates also break at this time, although from the plot of interbank interest rates in figure 9.4 it is not clear that the interest rates also exhibit breaks at these points.

The next difficulty is which interbank rate to employ for China; the China interbank rate (CHIBOR) or the Shanghai interbank rate (SHIBOR); the latter only began in late 2006 but that market employs market makers and hence yields a smoother interbank series.[12] Both are plotted in figure 9.4 However, the short time period is a constraint to conducting analysis using the series; although we have daily data and hence hundreds of observations, it still remains that the actual time period covered is short, and potentially too short in which to detect long-run relationships. We conducted unreported cointegration analysis on the CHIBOR and SHIBOR interest rates and found that the two are strongly cointegrated, and hence we use the longer CHIBOR series in the models in this chapter.

Econometric Output Estimating each model individually (a UIP model and a domestic rates model) yields two models that roughly accord to prior expectations: China is somewhat isolated from world events and its interbank rate is dictated by administrative interest rates.

We'll first briefly cover the two individual models and draw out their implications, before attempting to bring the two analyses together to put each into its own context.

Considering China in the wider world, we attempt to construct a UIP model. Modeling with 10 lags, we find that a rank of two is appropriate.[13] The resulting system is

$$
\begin{pmatrix} \Delta r_t \\ \Delta r_t^* \\ \Delta f_t \\ \Delta s_t \end{pmatrix} \cdot = \begin{pmatrix} -0.046 & -0.087 \\ {\scriptstyle(0.009)} & {\scriptstyle(0.020)} \\ 0 & 0 \\ -0.004 & -0.024 \\ {\scriptstyle(0.002)} & {\scriptstyle(0.006)} \\ 0 & -0.023 \\ & {\scriptstyle(0.003)} \end{pmatrix} \begin{pmatrix} r_t - r_t^* + 4.17\, f_t - 3.89\, s_t - 0.56 \\ {\scriptstyle(0,68)} \quad {\scriptstyle(0.67)} \quad {\scriptstyle(0.06)} \\ s_t - f_t + 0.38\, r_t - 0.01 \\ {\scriptstyle(0.07)} \quad {\scriptstyle(0.002)} \end{pmatrix}.
\tag{9.7}
$$

The parity relationships found are distinctly odd—which to a large extent conforms to findings in the literature at this short time horizon (e.g., Froot and Thaler 1990). Various different attempts at identification only supported this initial observation. The first cointegrating vector (the top row in the right-hand vector) is the most similar to UIP with a $(1, -1)$ restriction imposed on the two interest rates, and a near $(1, -1)$ relationship for the spot and forward exchange rates (although these coefficients cannot be restricted to be equal to each other). However, as has often been found in the most spectacular of UIP failures, we find that the sign on the exchange rate differential $(f_t - s_t)$ is of the wrong sign and significantly larger than zero. The second relationship, where a (1, −1) relationship is imposed on the two exchange rate variables, has an insignificant overseas (US) interest rate effect, and hence that coefficient is restricted to be zero. Neither of these relationships makes particularly much economic sense other than as fragments of parity relationships, perhaps highlighting the Chinn (2006) story of confounding shorter term macroeconomic policy impacts. Nonetheless, both relationships do show that the Chinese interbank interest rate is involved in international monetary movements. Without considering the adjustment coefficients, however, we cannot tell whether China adjusts to these movements or exerts some influence over them.

From the adjustment coefficients (the first right-hand-side matrix in 9.7 where each column refers to a row in the matrix) China doesn't appear to exhibit particularly much independence, adjusting in a corrective manner to both relationships. The half-lives of adjustment may seem long, but we are modeling daily data and these half-lives are smaller than many pre-EMU European nations as found by Reade and Volz (2011).[14] Considering the other variables and their adjustment, the US interbank rate is weakly exogenous, and hence, as might be expected, the US interest rate drives the system; this is a sign of some degree of policy dominance that the United States is able to exert. The two exchange rate variables adjust to the second cointegrating vector, but the spot rate adjusts insignificantly to the first cointegrating vector. In figure 9.5 the two cointegrating vectors are plotted; they are zero in equilibrium, and hence we see that over the sample the two vectors are stationary. However, from the plot there are prolonged deviations from zero, hence long periods where the Chinese interest rate could deviate from these equilibrium relationships; in a fixed or managed

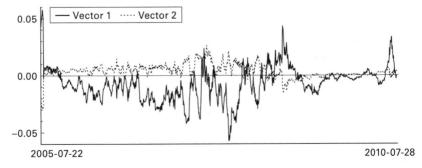

Figure 9.5
Cointegrating vectors for UIP model (9.7). Source: Authors' calculations.

exchange rate system, it is difficult to reconcile this possibility of deviation without the coexistence of capital controls. Hence we conclude that while there is some evidence for a lack of policy independence, it would appear that, in practice, Chinese monetary policy is insulated from global monetary movements, and US monetary policy in particular.

Naturally it is also important to consider China's domestic monetary arrangements. At first we do this individually without considering the international dimension. Modeling over our entire sample (we suspect that the series under consideration co-break, if any breaking at all happens, around the change in exchange rate regime; recursive analysis is unable to uncover evidence of a structural break around the time of the change), we employ 10 lags and find via the rank test that a rank of one is appropriate.[15] The resulting system is[16]

$$
\begin{pmatrix} r_{i,t} \\ r_{r,t} \\ r_{l,t} \\ r_{d,t} \end{pmatrix} = \begin{pmatrix} \underset{(0.03)}{-0.27} \\ 0 \\ 0 \\ 0 \end{pmatrix} \left(r_{i,t} - \underset{(0.05)}{0.89}\, r_{r,t} - \underset{(0.23)}{0.99}\, r_{l,t} + \underset{(0.08)}{0.04}\, r_{d,t} - \underset{(0.003)}{0.005} \right). \tag{9.8}
$$

As in equation (9.7) we show the estimated α and β' matrices in (9.8) on the right-hand side, and as a guide show the variables referred to on the left-hand side. The rank of the system is only one here; hence just one cointegrating vector appears, and there is only one column in α. The homogeneity of degree zero restriction is rejected by the data here, and moreover we can see that the deposit rate ($r_{d,t}$) is insignificant. The two other interest rate coefficients, on the repo rate and the lending rate, are near unity. This suggests that if both of these interest rates move by one percentage point, the interbank rate will need to move by almost two percentage points. However the more fundamental point is that indeed a steady-state cointegration relationship exists between the administratively set and market-orientated interest rates exists, as suggested by Porter and Xu (2009).

Using our multiple-equation approach, we can also investigate an adjustment to this vector via the matrix, and we see that only the interbank interest rate adjusts to this vector. Hence the administrative interest rates drive the system along with the repo rate.[17] This largely corresponds to the descriptions provided by Porter and Xu (2009), although they propose that the repo rate also adjusts as opposed to driving the system. Most important, perhaps, it displays the influence that the PBC has over the monetary system in China, and hence their ability to effect monetary outcomes using the tools available to them. The size of the adjustment in this domestic model (9.8) is greater than in the international model (9.7), suggesting that the interbank interest rate is influenced more by domestic monetary movements than international ones.

In order to make a direct comparison between the two cases, however, it is better to try and consider the two together. Juselius (2007) promotes such a "specific-to-general" approach when using cointegrated VAR models; a key property is that any cointegrating vectors found in individual systems should be found when combining the information sets of the two individual models. Hence we attempt to model the domestic and international component of the Chinese monetary system by bringing together our two models thus far. The most important comparison that can be made in this model is between how the interbank rate responds to the international, UIP-like condition we found earlier, and how it responds to the domestic component just found.

Modeling the entire system gives us a seven-variable VAR, and we estimate again only over the post-2005 period due to including the exchange rate variables in this model. Rank testing suggests a rank of four or five (although, confusingly, the only imposed rank that doesn't leave a near-unit next-largest root is rank one), and in order to enable us to identify the two vectors we found earlier, we impose a rank of four. The resulting system is

$$
\begin{pmatrix} r_{i,t} \\ r_{r,t} \\ r_{l,t} \\ r_{d,t} \\ r_{i,t}^* \\ f_t \\ s_t \end{pmatrix} = \begin{pmatrix} -0.36 \underset{(0.05)}{} & 0.09 \underset{(0.02)}{} & 0 & 0.005 \underset{(0.002)}{} \\ 0.05 \underset{(0.03)}{} & 0 & -0.07 \underset{(0.01)}{} & -0.02 \underset{(0.003)}{} \\ -0.03 \underset{(0.03)}{} & 0.04 \underset{(0.03)}{} & -0.03 \underset{(0.02)}{} & -0.005 \underset{(0.003)}{} \\ 0.05 \underset{(0.03)}{} & -0.04 \underset{(0.03)}{} & 0.03 \underset{(0.02)}{} & 0.002 \underset{(0.003)}{} \\ -0.20 \underset{(0.03)}{} & 0.19 \underset{(0.03)}{} & -0.13 \underset{(0.02)}{} & -0.02 \underset{(0.003)}{} \\ 0 & 0 & -0.02 \underset{(0.003)}{} & -0.004 \underset{(0.001)}{} \\ 0 & -0.01 \underset{(0.001)}{} & 0 & 0 \end{pmatrix} \begin{pmatrix} r_{i,t} - 0.70 \underset{(0.01)}{} r_{r,t} + 0.18 \underset{(0.04)}{} r_{l,t} - 0.35 \underset{(0.05)}{} r_{d,t} - 0.01 \underset{(0.002)}{} \\ r_{i,t} - 0.24 \underset{(0.12)}{} r_{i,t}^* - 1.95 \underset{(0.46)}{} f_t + 1.99 \underset{(0.46)}{} s_t - 0.09 \underset{(0.07)}{} \\ r_{r,t} + 0.01 \underset{(0.33)}{} r_{i,t}^* - 6.52 \underset{(1.25)}{} f_t + 6.46 \underset{(1.25)}{} s_t + 0.09 \underset{(0.18)}{} \\ r_{l,t} - 2.20 \underset{(1.34)}{} r_{i,t}^* + 30.3 \underset{(5.05)}{} f_t + 29.4 \underset{(5.04)}{} s_t - 1.66 \underset{(0.74)}{} \end{pmatrix}.
$$

$$(9.9)$$

With a rank-four system the α and β matrices are somewhat more complicated. As with (9.7), each column of α contains the adjustment coefficients for all variables to the cointegrating vector in the corresponding row of the β matrix. So the first column of β contains adjustment coefficients for the cointegrating vector in the first row of β. The first cointegrating vector is the domestic interest rate relationship found in (9.8), and the second is the interbank UIP relationship, akin to what was found in (9.7). In the remaining two vectors we attempt to identify UIP-style relationships with the other interest rates, to investigate whether they are influenced by international movements.

The coefficient sizes in the domestic rate relationship are considerably smaller, and despite summing up to around 0.87, the restriction of homogeneity of degree zero is again rejected in the data; as can be seen, the estimate for the repo rate is very precise indeed, and this likely contributes to the rejection of the homogeneity restriction. Nonetheless, the comovement of interest rates appears a little more sensible in this vector. Considering the adjustments, we have not restricted the coefficients to zero here, but the lending and deposit interest rates have insignificant adjustment coefficients, while the repo rate coefficient is borderline significant, and the interbank interest rate adjustment (top left) is strongly significant: the interbank rate corrects 36 percent of any disequilibrium each period. Hence the same findings as before are upheld.

The second vector, the international monetary movements vector (UIP), yields a small coefficient of borderline significance on the US interest rate (at 0.24), and on the expected exchange rate appreciation term the coefficient is smaller and of the right sign. Most important, when considering the adjustments to this vector, we see that although the interbank rate does adjust, it does not do so in a correcting manner: if there is a positive disequilibrium then the interbank rate will increase and worsen the disequilibrium. That the adjustment coefficient, at 9 percent of the disequilibrium, is much smaller than the domestic adjustment is irrelevant given that the adjustment is not correcting the disequilibrium. The forward exchange rate is not adjusting to disequilibria here, but the US interest rate and the spot exchange rate do appear to adjust.[18] We devote little attention to the last two cointegrating vectors because our focus is on the interbank interest rate and its relationships domestically and internationally, but we do note in these last two vectors that again the US interbank rate comes in very insignificantly, while the coefficient on the expected exchange rate appreciation term is large and for the lending rate of the wrong sign. In all these cases the important factor is again that the deposit and lending rates have insignificant coefficients of adjustment, and hence the administratively set interest rates do not appear to be adjusting to either the domestic or international monetary movements, arguing in favor of China's policy impendence.

As a result of these findings, we next proceed to model the Chinese monetary policy system focusing on the administratively set deposits interest rate alongside a number of other monetary policy tools.

9.4.2 Chinese Monetary Policy

Economic Theory Background   Having investigated the extent to which the PBC can conduct monetary policy insulated from external events we now move to consider monetary policy directly. We seek to determine how it is carried out by estimating policy rules, and we then investigate how effective it has been.

We can motivate the monetary policy maker with reference to some loss function:

$$L = \sum_{s=t}^{\infty} \beta_{s-t} W(\Delta p_t, \Delta y_t, \Delta e_t, \Delta m_t). \tag{9.10}$$

We might next specify that growth in the broad money supply, mechanistically, is a function of growth in the reserves held by the PBC and the credit expansion by banks (influenced negatively by the required reserve ratio) plus a constant amount printed by the PBC to accompany income growth. We also imagine that some kind of Phillips curve relationship exists between output growth and inflation: high growth is accompanied by high inflation, and vice versa. We treat the stock market and exchange rate as exogenous in this model; the former is a random walk, the latter a fixed constant.

Hence we tentatively specify the PBC's problem as

$$\min_{R_t, rrr_t, omo_t, res_t} L \text{ s.t.}$$

$$(m - p)_t^d = \delta_0 + \delta_1 (y - p)_t + \delta_2 R_t^d + \delta_3 R_t^f + \delta_4 \Delta p_t + \delta_4 \Delta e_t + \delta_4 \Delta s_t$$

$$\Delta m_t = \alpha_0 + \alpha_1 \Delta res_t + \alpha_2 rrr_t,$$
$$\Delta p_t = \beta_0 + \beta_1 \Delta y_t + \beta_2 R_t,$$
$$\Delta e_t = \gamma_0,$$
$$\Delta s_t = \varepsilon_t.$$

Solving this yields solutions for R_t, rrr_t, omo_t, and res_t that are linear functions, provided that the loss function is quadratic (so the policy maker suffers proportionately more the further realizations of variables are from their targets). We allow the policy maker to choose the values of these tools as functions of all the macroeconomic variables mentioned thus far. Given this basic theoretical framework, we proceed to model monetary policy. Our X_t vector of variables is

$$X_t = \begin{pmatrix} R_t \\ omo_t \\ rrr_t \\ \Delta res_t \\ \pi_t \\ \Delta y_t \\ \Delta m_t \\ \Delta e_t^e \end{pmatrix}. \tag{9.11}$$

The exchange rate variable is defined as RMB per US dollar, and hence an increase in e_t represents a depreciation of the RMB as more RMB are required to purchase a single US dollar. The actual variable included in the model is the expected exchange rate change, Δe_t^e, and this is the difference between a one-year nondeliverable forward in the RMB and the contemporaneous exchange rate value.

We expect four cointegrating vectors to be found, representing each policy variable that is theoretically at the policy maker's discretion, namely the interest rate, the required reserve ratio, open market operations, and reserve accumulation. We would also expect that each policy tool adjusts to its policy-identified cointegrating vector; in other words, once a shock has knocked the system out of equilibrium (where all vectors are at zero) we would expect that the policy tool would move in order to re-establish equilibrium. The Taylor rule of monetary policy is perhaps clearest about this: the real interest rate should increase in response to a rise in inflation in order to bring inflation back down. Hence additionally we expect that the economic variable being targeted (e.g., inflation) would respond to the cointegrating vector also; if not, then this indicates that the particular choice of tool is inappropriate since the tool will not, via any changes made, have any impact on the target variable.

Of course, neither of these conditions might be found; violation of the first suggests that perhaps policy is being carried out for other reasons, reasons that cannot be represented in economic variables, such as the Window Guidance that the PBC provides. Then, if the target variable does not respond, then this may indicate that the mechanisms that operate in more market-based Western economies may not function for China; that is, an interest rate does not convey the kind of price signals it might be expected to in a more market-orientated economy and hence policy does not have the desired effect.

Data   All the data for our monetary policy model was acquired using Datastream, and the original source of our data was either the PBC or the National Bureau of Statistics in China.

Figure 9.6 plots the Chinese monetary policy interest rate (the rediscount rate) alongside its one-month interbank on the left panel, and on the right panel the US target interest rate (the Federal Funds target rate) alongside both the actual Federal Funds rate and the interbank interest rate:[19] US market rates remain much closer to the target interest rate than is the case in China. This we suspect is related to the other tools that are used for monetary policy manipulation in China such as the required reserve ratio and open market operations to sterilize reserve accumulation.

Figure 9.7 plots the variables related to our investigation of Chinese monetary policy. Due to the types of data series we wish to use, we must use data of a monthly frequency here. In the top panel, the macroeconomic indicators we use are plotted: inflation, output growth (proxied by industrial output growth), and money growth; in the bottom panel, what might be described as monetary policy tools are

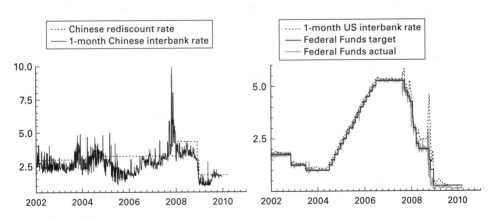

Figure 9.6
Monetary policy interest rates in China and the United States alongside their respective interbank rates. Source: Datastream.

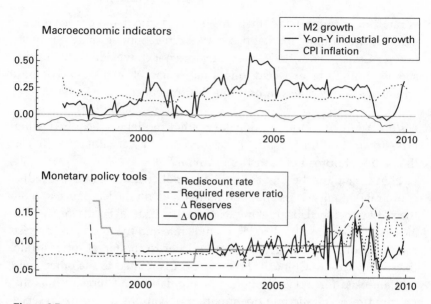

Figure 9.7
Data series included in the monetary policy model for China reported in section 9.4.2.
Source: Datastream.

plotted: the rediscount interest rate, the required reserve ratio, the change in open market operations, and the change in the level of foreign reserves.[20] As can be seen, some of the policy tools have periods with no variation. This makes these variables somewhat akin to dummy variables, which require particular attention when carrying out rank testing, but does not preclude them from our modeling exercise. We are seeking to understand the policy movements and hence policy rates such as the rediscount rate, and the required reserve ratio are more appropriate variables to include here.

Econometric Output   When we estimate the model, we include three lags to eradicate autocorrelation and yield a system in which only two of forty misspecification tests fail at the 1 percent significance and hence we can attribute those failures to statistic change and proceed. Although we expected a rank of four, as with the interest rate model in section 9.4.1 we find that the rank test suggests something different. The trace test output is given in table 9.1 and shows that rank two is the test outcome. Nonetheless, there are four eigenvalues (correlations between linear combinations of our variables and the first differences of them) above 0.25, which would appear to suggest reasonably strong correlation and hence cointegration. The decision is particularly difficult here because when a rank of four is imposed, the next largest root of the system is 0.97 suggesting that by allowing an extra stationary dimension in the system we have declined to impose a near-unit root to the unit circle (by choosing a lower rank). Nonetheless, if we impose rank of four we get the four cointegrating vectors plotted in figure 9.9 and none of the vectors look particularly distinct and as such it seems reasonable to assume that if one of these is deemed stationary that all might be. Finally, as will be seen below, when we impose a rank of four not only do we get some economically coherent cointegrating vectors, we also find that there are significant adjustment coefficients for all four vectors, another sign that rank four is the right choice.

Having chosen a rank of four, we need to identify the four cointegrating vectors. As mentioned above, we seek to identify one cointegrating vector for each policy tool and hence we normalize each vector on the relevant tool, but we must also impose three other restrictions on each vector in order to identify it. For the discount rate, required reserve ratio, and open market operations we exclude the other two tools from each cointegrating vector; however, for open market operations and the reserve ratio we do not wish to omit reserves immediately because these tools may be used to sterilize the reserve accumulation. For these two tools we instead omit the expected exchange rate change, while for the discount rate we omit reserves, and for reserves we omit the three main monetary policy-making tools to identify.

Before presenting the model and interpreting it, we consider the stability of the model and present some recursive plots in figure 9.8. From this plot, which considers the coefficients of the cointegrating vectors (yet to be identified), it seems that a reasonably stable model has been found: for essentially all the coefficients, the full-sample estimate lies within the confidence bounds of the first estimate (based on about a quarter of the full sample). Hence we can proceed to interpret the model with more confidence in the coefficient values it produces.

The resulting system yields a number of additional insignificant variables, which we omit where the likelihood ratio test of overidentifying restrictions allows. We also restrict adjustment coefficients to zero where they are insignificant, and the resulting system is[21]

Table 9.1
Trace test output for monetary policy model

r	Eigenvalue	Log-likelihood	Trace test	p-Value
0		2159.397	247.99	0.000**
1	0.61609	2203.435	159.91	0.001**
2	0.46632	2232.321	102.14	0.063
3	0.34725	2251.943	62.898	0.366
4	0.25778	2265.656	35.471	0.702
5	0.15212	2273.247	20.289	0.709
6	0.098566	2278.020	10.743	0.574
7	0.066027	2281.162	4.4583	0.360
8	0.047304	2283.391		

Source: Authors' calculations.

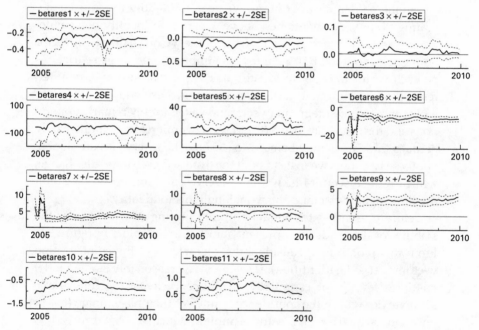

Figure 9.8
Recursive coefficient estimates for monetary policy model. Source: Authors' calculations.

$$
\begin{pmatrix} \Delta R_t \\ \Delta omo_t \\ \Delta rrr_t \\ \Delta^2 res_t \\ \Delta \pi_t \\ \Delta^2 y_t \\ \Delta^2 m_t \\ \Delta^2 e_t^e \end{pmatrix} =
\begin{pmatrix}
\underset{(0.021)}{-0.036} & \underset{(0.0001)}{0.0005} & \underset{}{-0.003} & 0 \\
\underset{(3.371))}{13.95} & \underset{(0.023)}{-0.062} & \underset{(0.122)}{-0.279} & 0 \\
0 & \underset{(0.003)}{0.014} & \underset{(0.020)}{-0.111} & \underset{(0.195)}{-0.515} \\
0 & 0 & 0 & 0 \\
0 & \underset{(0.001)}{-0.001} & \underset{(0.004)}{0.008} & 0 \\
0 & 0 & \underset{(0.024)}{-0.064} & \underset{(0.390)}{1.162} \\
0 & \underset{(0.001)}{0.004} & 0 & \underset{(0.054)}{-0.203} \\
\underset{(1.329)}{6.054} & \underset{(0.009)}{-0.040} & \underset{(0.065)}{0.221} & \underset{(0.627)}{-0.529}
\end{pmatrix}
$$

$$
\begin{pmatrix}
R_t - \underset{(0.07)}{0.38}\,\pi_t - \underset{(0.03)}{0.02}\,\Delta y_t - \underset{(0.04)}{0.09}\,\Delta m_t - \underset{(0.01)}{0.02}\,\Delta e_t^e + \underset{(0.011)}{0.005} \\
omo_t + \underset{(4.56)}{99.8}\,\Delta res_t - \underset{(51.7)}{180.3}\,\pi_t - \underset{(19.6)}{121.0}\,\Delta y_t - \underset{(11.0)}{34.96}\,\Delta m_t + \underset{(4.82)}{6.82} \\
rrr_t + \underset{(0.81)}{18.2}\,\Delta res_t - \underset{(9.45)}{39.9}\,\pi_t - \underset{(3.58)}{20.3}\,\Delta y_t - \underset{(1.71)}{5.07}\,\Delta m_t + \underset{(0.85)}{3.52} \\
\Delta res_t - \underset{(0.62)}{2.03}\,\pi_t - \underset{(0.23)}{1.49}\,\Delta y_t - \underset{(0.02)}{0.10}\,\Delta e_t^e + \underset{(0.05)}{0.07}
\end{pmatrix}.
$$

$$(9.12)$$

Hence we have our four cointegrating vectors, one for each policy tool. As mentioned earlier, a first check regarding these policy vectors is whether or not the policy tool adjusts to the cointegrating vector. This can be ascertained from the leading diagonal of the matrix. The discount rate weakly adjusts (coefficient of –0.036 and t-statistic of about 1.6), while open market operations and the reserve requirement adjust more strongly (coefficients of –0.062 and –0.111, respectively). Reserve accumulation is weakly exogenous for the whole system, as shown by the row of zeros corresponding to the adjustment of reserves, and as such reserves do not adjust to disequilibria in the reserves cointegrating vector. This calls into question the interpretation of the final vector as a reserves vector since the value of reserves is determined outside the system of reference (presumably by the level of demand for Chinese exports). We leave discussion of this vector until later.

We consider the vectors individually in turn, beginning with the discount rate vector:

$$
R_t = \underset{(0.07)}{0.38}\,\pi_t + \underset{(0.03)}{0.02}\,\Delta y_t + \underset{(0.04)}{0.09}\,\Delta m_t + \underset{(0.01)}{0.02}\,\Delta e_t^e - \underset{(0.011)}{0.005}. \tag{9.13}
$$

The discount rate weakly adjusts to this vector, suggesting that it is not being fully used in the standard, monetary policy-making manner.

Additionally the coefficient on inflation is less than unity, violating the Taylor principle and adding weight to the impression that the discount rate is not used for fighting inflation. The output coefficient, although of the right sign, is small and insignificant, while the money growth coefficient suggests a weak role in money aggregate targeting.

Next the vector for open market operations

$$omo_t = \underset{(4.56)}{-99.8}\,\Delta res_t + \underset{(51.7)}{180.3}\,\pi_t + \underset{(19.6)}{121.0}\,\Delta y_t + \underset{(11.0)}{34.96}\,\Delta m_t - \underset{(4.82)}{6.82}. \tag{9.14}$$

Open market operations do adjust to this vector, closing 6 percent of any disequilibrium each month. The first coefficient on reserve accumulation is somewhat surprising as it might be expected that bonds would be issued in greater numbers the greater are reserves accumulated in order to sterilize the impact on the money supply. However, indirectly it would appear that open market operations have an impact: in response to an increase in inflation there is a large increase in OMOs, as is the case if output growth increases, and if the money supply increases, so do OMOs. Hence, given one imagines reserve accumulation accompanies an increase in output, some of which is exported, and that this and the increased money supply via reserves will have some inflationary impact, it would appear that overall OMOs are used to attempt this delicate balancing act of the macroeconomy.

The next vector is for the required reserve ratio:

$$rrr_t = \underset{(0.81)}{-18.2}\,\Delta res_t + \underset{(9.45)}{39.9}\,\pi_t + \underset{(3.58)}{20.3}\,\Delta y_t + \underset{(1.71)}{5.07}\,\Delta m_t - \underset{(0.85)}{3.52}. \tag{9.15}$$

Again, this tool responds to its cointegrating vector, so we can consider it as a policy tool: each month it corrects 11 percent of any disequilibrium. Its coefficients are quite similar in sign and magnitude to those for the OMO vector. A seemingly wrong signed response to reserves is counteracted with appropriately signed coefficients on inflation, output, and money growth, suggesting that this tool is used to conduct monetary policy.

Finally we consider reserves

$$\Delta res_t = \underset{(0.62)}{2.03}\,\pi_t + \underset{(0.23)}{1.49}\,\Delta y_t + \underset{(0.02)}{0.10}\,\Delta e_t^e - \underset{(0.05)}{0.07}. \tag{9.16}$$

Reserves increase alongside inflation reflecting their inflationary potential, alongside output growth reflecting their use in facilitating the exporting of goods, and positively with an expected appreciation since they are purchased to create supply of the RMB to counter appreciation pressure on the currency. The reserve requirement adjusts to this relationship, from the alpha matrix in (9.12) and is the only tool to do so; reserves themselves drive the relationship. This would appear to imply that the reserve requirement is used as a tool against the inflationary consequences of reserve accumulation (as would be the case with unsterilized intervention), even if the reserve requirement vector has a seemingly wrong-signed response coefficient to reserve accumulation. The coefficient of 0.515 says that if reserves are too high for equilibrium (potentially driven by a shock to reserves), then the reserve requirement will increase to close half of this disequilibrium, hence restraining banks' ability to create extra credit. Output growth responds positively also, perhaps reflecting that reserve accumulation increases the money stock potentially raising demand for goods via cheaper credit (at home or abroad).

The cointegrating vectors are plotted in figure 9.9. These vectors are all zero when that relationship is in equilibrium, and hence it is informative to consider how often these vectors are at zero or cross the origin. It is also informative to consider the sign of the disequilibrium. We can think of each vector conceptually as

$$x_t - x_t^* = 0, \tag{9.17}$$

where x_t is the value of the monetary policy tool at time t, and x_t^* is the optimal value of the tool at that point, as dictated by the values of the other variables in each policy rule.

We can think of policy being tight if the policy tool is above what its optimal value is, that is, if $x_t > x_t^*$, and hence when its cointegrating vector is positive. Hence from figure 9.9 we learn that the discount rate (top left plot) has since 2005 generally been above what economic fundamentals would suggest it should be: policy as dictated by the discount rate is tight. It remained tight throughout the global economic crisis of 2007 to 2009 also, notably. Interestingly the required reserve ratio and open market operations tools only significantly loosened in early 2009 (presumably as a response to the global economic crisis) before tightening again in 2010.

Hence to attempt to sum up the results of this section, it would appear that monetary policy has made more extensive use of OMOs and reserve requirements based on the extent to which these tools are used to respond to disequilibria. It would appear that monetary targeting is important alongside inflation targeting and any form of GDP growth targeting. In terms of impact on targeting variables, it appears

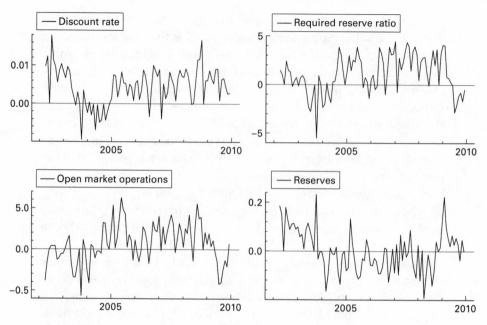

Figure 9.9
Cointegrating vectors for the monetary policy model. Source: Authors' calculations.

that growth responds to reserve requirements, money growth to OMOs and inflation to both of these. The interest rate tool does not appear to exert particularly much influence on the macroeconomy despite the influence we noted for it in (9.9) on the interbank market.

9.5 Conclusions

In this chapter we addressed two questions. First, we considered how much monetary policy independence the PBC has enjoyed. We understand monetary independence in a narrow sense as the PBC's ability to conduct its own interest rate policy without having to follow the Fed's lead. To this end, our analysis has investigated whether the Chinese money market rates are driven by US rates. We find evidence that China has been largely able to insulate its monetary policy from US policy.

Second, we investigated how effective the PBC's interest rate policy and the other monetary policy tools it has used have been in managing monetary growth and containing inflation. For this purpose we estimated a monetary model for China that included the PBC's policy rate, the required reserve ratio, a measure of the PBC's open market operations, as well as macroeconomic indicators that policy might be expected to respond to, namely inflation, economic activity, growth in broad money, and growth in foreign currency reserves. Our estimates suggested that the interest rate tool has not been effectively made us of. Rather, monetary policy has relied upon open market operations and the required reserve ratio for sterilizing foreign exchange intervention and changes in the reserve requirement ratio to affect output growth.

We conclude that through the maintenance of capital controls and the reliance on monetary instruments other than the interest rate China has been able to exert relatively autonomous monetary policy. We nonetheless believe that the PBC's current monetary policy mix is suboptimal, since the interest rate is not effectively made use of, which arguably is a direct consequence of the constraints resulting from the exchange rate peg.

Notes

We would like to thank Tamon Asonuma, Anindya Banerjee, Ansgar Belke, Yin-Wong Cheung, Menzie Chinn, Ettore Dorrucci, Jakob de Haan, John Fender, Galina Hale, Tuuli Koivu, Iikka Korhonen, Guonan Ma, Bob McCauley, Eswar Prasad, Daniel Santabárbara, Lukas Vogel, and Ming Zhang for helpful comments on earlier versions of this chapter. We also received useful comments from participants of the Macroeconomic and Econometrics Conference at the University of Birmingham, the CESifo Venice Summer Institute Workshop on "The Evolving Role of China in the Global Economy," the Columbia–Tsinghua International Conference on "Exchange Rates and New International Monetary System," the XVIth World Congress of the International Economic Association at Tsinghua University, the 2011 Meeting of the German Economic Association at Frankfurt University, the 9th ESCB Workshop on Emerging Markets, and presentations at the European Central Bank, BIS, DIW Berlin, and the School of Oriental and African Studies of the University of London.

1. See Shu and Ng (2010), who use a narrative approach to examine the PBC's monetary stance.

2. http://www.pbc.gov.cn/publish/english/970/index.html.

3. http://www.pbc.gov.cn/publish/english/979/index.html.

4. The index is available on the Chinn–Ito Index website: http://web.pdx.edu/~ito/Chinn-Ito_website.htm

5. China has a two-tier commercial banking system that features commercial banks, which are subject to prudential ratios and international standards of portfolio risks, as well as policy lending banks, which are not subject to similar regulations. The segmentation of the money market is another obstacle to greater reliance on interest rates as policy tools. China's money market consists of three main submarkets: the interbank market, the interbank bond market, and the bond repo market. The segmentation between these markets implies that monetary policy actions of the PBC in the interbank market cannot migrate to the other components of China's money market.

6. Koivu et al. (2009) use a McCallum rule based on money supply for modeling the implementation of Chinese monetary policy and come to the conclusion that such a rule is reasonably capable of modeling the PBC's focus on monetary aggregates as intermediate policy targets. Although Geiger (2008) maintains that the PBC has often missed its exact targets for monetary growth, Koivu et al. point out that monetary developments have closely followed the major trends in central bank targets and that the ultimate targets of China's monetary policy—low inflation and rapid growth—have been simultaneously achieved since the mid-1990s.

7. The OMO (open market operations) can be traced back to the interbank foreign exchange transactions that were started in 1996 (Nagai and Wang 2007). The OMO had for a long time been centered on purchases and sales of government and treasury bonds. However, it became increasingly difficult to carry out OMO with these securities because the variety of government bonds was limited and the outstanding amount of treasury bills was small. In April 2003 the PBC began to issue central bank papers as a new tool for OMO.

8. The window guidance policy is actually carried out by the PBC in conjunction with the China Banking Regulatory Commission (CBRC). See Geiger (2008).

9. Any stationary variables in X_t will be found as cointegrating vectors, thus ensuring that the overall VAR model is balanced.

10. We should write "forward" because China does not provide such markets in the RMB, meaning that investors wishing to hedge positions are forced to "unofficial" providers of forwards, also known as nondeliverable forwards (NDFs). Our forward rates are provided by Reuters and described as forward rates, although they are almost identical to the NDFs that we have access to via Tullett Prebon from 2006 onward.

11. Others, such as Cheung et al. (2007), have followed this methodology in previous studies investigating China.

12. Porter and Xu (2009) have a short section explaining the difference between the SHIBOR and the CHIBOR.

13. We are spartan with the details in modeling these data series here in order to save space. Some misspecification tests failed in our models, but appropriate additional information was incorporated to support the chosen rank, and further details are available on request.

14. Modeling over the entire sample including the pegged period pre-2005 leads to even stranger results, indicative of the strong influence the exchange rate regime has on this model.

15. Despite the trace test being inconclusive, imposing rank one yields a next highest root of the system of 0.88, so we feel confident that rank one is the appropriate choice.

16. The overidentifying restrictions included in this model are accepted with a likelihood-ratio test statistic of 2.04 and a p-value of 56.4 percent.

17. A similar conclusion is found if we use a three-month horizon, the only difference being that in that situation the repo rate appears to also adjust to the administrative rates. These results are available on request from the authors.

18. These last two effects are clearly implausible since they suggest that the US interbank rate moves dependent on the Chinese monetary stance.

19. As interest rates hit zero in 2008, the Federal Reserve target rate became a target zone between 0 and 0.25 percent. We take the target, for the sake of argument, in this period as 0.25 percent.

20. We use year-on-year changes for our growth variables (inflation, money growth and industrial output growth) despite our data being differenced to mop up any remaining seasonality and because year-on-year differences are predominantly used for economic analysis.

21. We include a slight abuse of notation here in that the delta-squared terms refer to the first difference of the growth rate of that particular variable, not the second difference.

References

Calvo, G. A., and C. M. Reinhart. 2002. Fear of floating. *Quarterly Journal of Economics* 117 (2): 379–408.

Chaboud, A. P., and J. H. Wright. 2005. Uncovered interest parity: It works, but not for long. *Journal of International Economics* 66 (2): 349–62.

Cheung, Y.-W., D. Tam, and M. S. Yiu. 2007. Does the Chinese interest rate follow the US interest rate? *International Journal of Finance & Economics* 93 (1): 52–67.

Chinn, M. D. 2006. The (partial) rehabilitation of interest rate parity in the floating rate era: Longer horizons, alternative expectations, and emerging markets. *Journal of International Money and Finance* 25 (1): 7–21.

Edison, H., and R. MacDonald. 2003. Credibility and interest rate discretion in the ERM. *Open Economies Review* 14 (4): 351–68.

Edwards, S. (1999), How Effective are Capital Controls? NBER Working Paper 7413. NBER, Cambridge, MA.

Eichengreen, B. 2004. Chinese currency controversies. Discussion Paper 4375. CEPR, London.

Engle, R. F., and C. W. J. Granger. 1987. Co-integration and error correction: Representation, estimation and testing. *Econometrica: Journal of the Econometric Society* 55 (2): 251–76.

Frankel, J., S. L. Schmukler, and L. Serven. 2004. Global transmission of interest rates: Monetary independence and currency regime. *Journal of International Money and Finance* 23 (5): 701–33.

Froot, K. A., and R. H. Thaler. 1990. Foreign exchange. *Journal of Economic Perspectives* 4 (3): 179–92.

Geiger, M. 2008. Instruments of monetary policy in China and their effectiveness: 1994–2006. Discussion Paper 187. UNCTD, Geneva.

Glick, R., and M. Hutchison. 2009. Navigating the trilemma: Capital flows and monetary policy in China. *Journal of Asian Economics* 20 (3): 205–24.

Goldstein, M., and M. Lardy. 2006. China's exchange rate policy dilemma. *American Economic Review* 96 (2): 422–26.

Goldstein, M., and M. Lardy. 2009. *The Future of China's Exchange Rate Policy.* Policy Analyses in International Economics 87. Washington, DC: Peterson Institute for International Economics.

Hendry, D. F., and M. Massmann. 2007. Co-breaking: Recent advances and a synopsis of the literature. *Journal of Business and Economic Statistics* 25 (1): 33–51.

Johansen, S. J. 1995. *Likelihood-Based Inference in Cointegrated Vector Autoregressive Models.* New York: Oxford University Press.

Johansen, S. J., and K. Juselius. 2003. Controlling inflation in a cointegrated vector autoregressive model with an application to US data. Discussion Paper. Department of Economics, University of Copenhagen.

Juselius, K. 2007. *The Cointegrated VAR Model: Methodology and Applications.* New York: Oxford University Press.

Koivu, T. 2009. Has the Chinese economy become more sensitive to interest rates? Studying credit demand in China. *China Economic Review* 20 (3): 455–70.

Koivu, T., A. Mehrotra, and R. Nuutilainen. 2009. An analysis of Chinese money and prices using a McCallum-type rule. *Journal of Chinese Economic and Business Studies* 7 (2): 219–35.

Laurens, B. J., and R. Maino. 2007. China: Strengthening monetary policy implementation. Working Paper 07/14. IMF, Washington, DC.

Ma, G., and R. N. McCauley. 2007. Do China's capital controls still bind? Implications for monetary autonomy and capital liberalization. Working Paper 233. BIS, Basel.

Mehrotra, A. 2007. Exchange and interest rate channels during a deflationary era—Evidence from Japan, Hong Kong and China. *Journal of Comparative Economics* 35 (1): 188–210.

Nagai, S., and H. Wang. 2007. Money market operations in China: Monetary policy or FX policy? Working Paper 07-E-13. Bank of Japan, Tokyo.

Obstfeld, M., J. C. Shambaugh, and A. M. Taylor. 2005. The trilemma in history: Tradeoffs among exchange rates, monetary policies, and capital mobility. *Review of Economics and Statistics* 87 (3): 423–38.

Porter, N., and T. Xu. 2009. What drives China's interbank market? Working Paper 189. IMF, Washington, DC.

Prasad, E., T. Rumbaugh, and Q. Wang. 2005. Putting the cart before the horse? Capital account liberalization and exchange rate flexibility in China. Policy Discussion Paper 05/1. IMF, Washington, DC.

Prasad, E. S. 2008. Monetary policy independence, the currency regime, and the capital account in China. In M. Goldstein and M. Lardy, eds., *Debating China's Exchange Rate Policy.* Washington, DC: Peterson Institute for International Economics, 77–108.

Rahbek, A., and R. Mosconi. 1999. The role of stationary regressors in the cointegration test. *Econometrics Journal* 2 (1): 76–91.

Reade, J. J., and U. Volz. 2011. Leader of the pack? German monetary dominance in Europe prior to EMU. *Economic Modelling* 28 (1/2): 239–50.

Roberts, I., and R. Tyers. 2003. China's exchange rate policy: The case for greater flexibility. *Asian Economic Journal* 17 (2): 155–84.

Rose, A. K. 1996. Explaining exchange rate volatility: An empirical analysis of "The Holy Trinity" of monetary independence, fixed exchange rates and capital mobility. *Journal of International Money and Finance* 15 (6): 925–45.

Shambaugh, J. C. 2004. The effect of fixed exchange rates on monetary policy. *Quarterly Journal of Economics* 119 (1): 300–51.

Shu, C., and B. Ng. 2010. *Monetary Stance and Policy Objectives in China: A Narrative Approach.* China Economic Issues 1/10. Hong Kong: Hong Kong Monetary Authority.

Yi, G. 2008. The monetary policy transmission mechanism in China. BIS Paper 35. BIS, Basel.

10 Offshore Markets for the Domestic Currency: Monetary and Financial Stability Issues

Dong He and Robert N. McCauley[1]

10.1 Introduction

The global financial crisis of 2007 to 2009 highlighted a potential benefit of the internationalization of emerging market currencies. As banks scrambled for liquidity, US dollar funding markets and foreign exchange swap markets seized up in late 2008 (Baba and Packer 2009; Hui et al. 2009). The resulting "dollar shortage" (McGuire and von Peter 2009a, b) threatened to stifle international trade. In response, more than one emerging market central bank found itself in the unaccustomed business of providing dollar funding to domestic banks and financing exports. This experience has highlighted the danger of relying excessively on one reserve currency in international trade and payments, and the possible benefits of using a wider array of currencies, including emerging market currencies, especially in transactions between emerging markets.

For some emerging market policy makers, the policy responses to the financial crisis in the countries that supply reserve currencies have also raised concerns. Expansion of central bank balance sheets amid fiscal expansion in the world's major economies has, in some views, called into question the major currencies' reliability as stores of value.

Whatever the grounds for such concerns, shifting to a situation in which emerging market countries' claims on the rest of the world are denominated in the domestic currency can offer advantages to the holders of such claims in the official, institutional investor or household sectors. Many fast-growing emerging market economies that are attractive to international investors now find their international balance sheets have large open positions in foreign currency: their liabilities (e.g., FDI by foreigners) tend to be denominated in domestic currencies while their claims on foreigners (e.g., official reserves) tend to be denominated in major reserve currencies. Allowing nonresidents to borrow in the domestic currency would shift this currency exposure from domestic residents to the rest of the world (Cheung et al. 2011). Just as there are welfare gains from an earthquake-prone economy sharing that risk with the rest of the world, there can be welfare gains from sharing this currently concentrated foreign exchange risk.

While keen to hedge the risks of relying on a single national money and to reap the benefits of denominating their external claims in domestic currency, emerging market policy makers remain leery of the potential risks arising from allowing their currencies to be internationalized. However, risks to monetary and financial stability in the internationalization of domestic currencies need to be articulated clearly. Drawing on the experience of the major currencies over the period since the inception of the euro markets in the 1950s and 1960s, this chapter identifies and analyzes the challenges posed to monetary and financial stability by offshore markets in domestic currency. It pays particular attention to the policy measures that were considered or used by policy makers in major currency countries in their attempts to control such risks.

This chapter is written for policy makers in emerging market economies who are contemplating allowing, or have begun to allow, their currencies to be used outside their economies. Currency internationalization is not likely to be a major policy objective in itself, but it can help frame the benefits, and affect the pace and sequencing, of removing impediments to the free flow of capital. While we pose the questions and set out the main arguments in general terms, we refer to developments in the extraterritorial use of China's currency, the renminbi, owing to the several measures recently taken to allow its use outside the mainland. Since 2004 Hong Kong, in particular, has progressively developed into a renminbi offshore center, with the scope of its renminbi banking business expanding from personal deposits to bonds and to trade credit.[2] This development is of particular analytical and policy interest because it has taken place notwithstanding the fact that the mainland authorities have by and large effectively maintained control over capital flows (Ma and McCauley 2008a, b; McCauley and Ma 2009; McCauley 2011).

Can authorities promote offshore use of their currencies while maintaining a significant degree of capital account control? Do they have policy options to manage potential risks to monetary and financial stability posed by the offshore markets of their currencies? Our answers to both questions are positive. Moreover the positive answers are

closely related. Some of the same measures applied to foreign currencies to maintain control of the capital account can serve to manage the
potential risks arising from the domestic currency trading offshore.

Thus in this chapter we argue that full capital account liberalization
is neither necessary nor sufficient for significant offshore use of a currency. To be sure, full internationalization of a currency may require
such liberalization, but it is less obvious that it is "premature to discuss
policies to promote currency internationalisation before it has been
decided that restrictions on capital account transactions should be
removed" (Genberg 2011).[3] After all, it should be recalled that significant controls on capital by the US authorities from the 1960s to the early
1970s (the interest equalization tax of 1963 and later "voluntary"
restraints on capital exports) did not undo the international role of the
dollar, and in some ways even gave a boost to the eurodollar market.

The rest of the chapter is organized as follows. In section 10.2 we
briefly describe the role of offshore markets in the international use of
major reserve currencies. Section 10.3 analyses how the offshore market
affects onshore monetary stability, through its influence on the quantity
of money and credit, on the yield curve and on the exchange rate.
Section 10.4 discusses risks of lending in domestic currency by both
domestic and foreign banks, and how such risks should be managed
through prudential policies. Section 10.5 concludes.

10.2   The Role of Offshore Markets

A useful observation to make at the outset of the discussion is that a
significant portion of international use of major reserve currencies,
such as the US dollar, takes place offshore. In particular, when non–US
residents use the US dollar to settle trade and make investments, they
need not transact onshore through banks and in financial markets in
the United States. Rather, they concentrate their transactions in international financial centers such as the eurodollar market in London. One
could even argue that without the offshore markets, the US dollar
would not have attained the dominant position in international trade
and payments that it occupies today.

We show that non–US residents reveal a strong preference for doing
their dollar business outside the United States. That is, they tend to
deposit US dollars in banks abroad and to buy US dollar bonds issued
by nonresidents outside the United States (and probably to hold them
in European depositories as well).

Table 10.1
US dollar in the global deposit market at end-2008 (billions of USD)

Nonbank depositor	Location of bank		Total
	Inside United States	Outside United States	
US resident	11,743[a]	1,520	13,263
Non–US resident	809	2,580	3,389
Total	12,552	4,100	16,652

Sources: Federal Reserve; BIS international locational banking statistics by residence (deposit liabilities of reporting banks vis-à-vis nonbank sector).
Note: Chi-squared statistic is 6,082, indicating a rejection of the null hypothesis of independence of residence of depositor and location of the bank at the 0.0001 level of significance.
a. US bank deposits estimated as M2 times M3/M2 in February 2006 (1.52) less outstanding currency.

10.2.1 The Global Dollar Deposit Market

The global market for dollar bank accounts shows that home is where the deposits are kept. US residents overwhelmingly favor domestic deposits, while depositors in the rest of the world somewhat less strongly favor offshore dollar deposits. As shown in table 10.1, the bulk of holdings lies on the northwest–southeast axis.

Depositing dollars offshore is nothing new for non–US residents, although this practice has been less pronounced in recent years. For the first 30 years of the eurodollar deposit market, Fed reserve requirements gave non–bank depositors an incentive to hold their dollars offshore to avoid what was in effect a tax (Aliber 1980, 2002; Kreicher 1982; McCauley and Seth 1992). There was no immediate response to the lowering by the Federal Reserve of the reserve requirement on domestic large-denomination deposits to zero in 1990. However, Bank for International Settlements (BIS) locational banking statistics show that, in the 2000s, non–US nonbanks raised the share of their US dollar deposits with banks located in the United States to over a quarter for the first time since the 1980s (figure 10.1).

Official reserve managers also prefer US dollar deposits outside the United States, although not quite so strongly. Official holders of US dollar reserves (mostly central banks) were prominent among early placers of dollars in the euro market (Bank for International Settlements 1965). Table 10.2 shows that in recent years more than 60 percent of official US dollar reserves are held in banks located outside the United States.

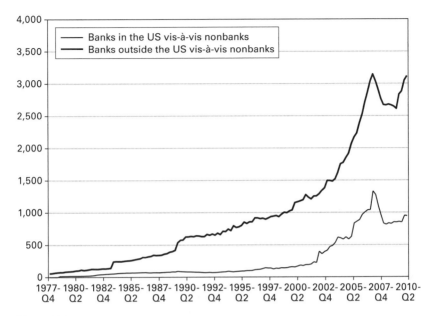

Figure 10.1
Amount outstanding in billions of US dollars

There are many reasons why both private and public investors choose to place dollar deposits outside the United States. One objective may be to separate currency risk from country risk. In other words, through offshore markets, investors can hold a currency without being subject to possibly adverse laws, policies and taxes of that currency's home country. For a depositor, such so-called country risk might at the limit prevent the use of funds placed in the currency's home jurisdiction. Historians of the eurodollar deposit market, the market for short-term dollar deposits outside the United States, have pointed to the Soviet Union's placement of dollar deposits in London, as an early offshore deposit (Einzig 1970, p. 30; Kindleberger 1973, p. 289). This practice, arising from cold war tensions, might have concealed dollar payments from US authorities and might have permitted dollars to be mobilized in the event of an all-out war. A chief consideration was that offshore holdings with non–US banks would have been harder for the US authorities to freeze.

That depositors seek low-risk venues for their dollar deposits is evident from the geography of dollar deposits outside the United States. At the end of 2008, London claimed the largest share, with 20

Table 10.2
Official dollar deposits by location and nationality of banks (billions of USD)

Nationality of banks	December 2004 Location of deposits			December 2007 Location of deposits			December 2008 Location of deposits		
	US	Off-shore	Total	US	Off-shore	Total	US	Off-shore	Total
United States	73.6	7.8	81.4	143.1	28.1	171.3	127.6	32.5	160.1
Others	73.0	268.2	341.2	73.1	475.0	548.1	59.7	269.4	329.1
Total	146.6	276.0	422.7	216.2	503.2	719.4	187.3	301.8	489.2

Source: BIS locational banking statistics by nationality.
Notes: Chi-squared statistics are 138.2, 306.2, and 172.7 for 2004, 2007, and 2008, respectively, indicating a rejection of the null hypothesis of independence of nationality of banks and location of official deposits at the 0.0001 level of significance.

percent of total offshore deposits. In the top 10 jurisdictions (accounting for 64 percent of all dollar deposits), over half were in jurisdictions with foreign currency ratings of Aaa, according to Moody's.

The choice of offshore deposits is strongly associated with the choice of non–US banks. Official investors place their onshore deposits disproportionately with US banks, but place offshore deposits disproportionately with non–US banks (table 10.2). This may in part reflect differences in the term of deposits, with deposits in US banks in the United States available at call for payment services while term deposits with non–US banks outside the United States serve as short-term investments.

The demand to separate currency risk from country risk may also be due to concerns over concentration of infrastructure or operational risk in one country. As central banks have lengthened their investment portfolios, their overall access to liquidity has become more dependent on the proper functioning of securities markets, including repurchase markets. Thus the interruption of trading of US Treasury securities in September 2001 owing to terrorist attacks reminded officials of the potential benefits of having diverse trading and custodial locations. McCauley (2005) observed that while normal operations with Treasury securities were interrupted, central banks with dollar securities held in European depositories were still able to carry out normal operations with them, since the US payment system continued to operate and thus banks could still make dollar payments.

It makes sense to separate country risk and currency risk, because the former need not lead to the latter. True, much country risk makes for currency risk. For instance, the US Gold Reserve Act of 1934 abrogating gold clauses in domestic contracts (a country risk) was associated with the dollar's 41 percent decline against gold-linked currencies. But US seizure of a given sovereign's assets in the United States or 9/11-style damage to US financial infrastructure would not necessarily be associated with dollar depreciation.

A second consideration in choosing between onshore and offshore markets is yield differentials. For most of the life of the eurodollar market, a substantial yield pickup was available to those willing to place a deposit in a bank in London or another center outside the United States (Kreicher 1982). This yield premium reflected in early days a sense of greater risk attached to offshore dollars. For most of the 1980s, however, higher yields on dollars deposited outside the United States approximated the cost of domestic reserve requirements and deposit insurance (McCauley and Seth 1992). (This suggested that US depositors paid the cost of the reserve requirement and deposit insurance "taxes.") As noted, the latter regulatory reason to hold dollar deposits offshore mostly disappeared with the Federal Reserve's reduction of the reserve requirement to zero in 1990. Whatever the cost of regulation had done to spur the growth of the eurodollar deposit market, its subsequent marked reduction did not close the market down.

A further consideration is the convenience factor: to some investors and fund-raisers, the regulatory environment, accounting standards, language and time zone of the location of the offshore markets make them more convenient than the onshore markets.

10.2.2   The Global Dollar Bond Market

The larger global dollar bond market also shows a bias, albeit a weaker one, of non–US investors for dollar bonds issued by non–US residents and bonds issued in the offshore market. Non–US resident investors in US dollar bonds disproportionately invest in obligations of issuers resident outside the United States (table 10.3).

This bias of non–US investors to hold the bonds of non–US obligors has shaped the pattern of issuance in the primary market for dollar bonds. Obligors from outside the United States issue the overwhelming majority of their paper offshore (table 10.4). Historically the offshore dollar bond market was boosted by US capital controls in the late 1960s into the 1970s[4] and by withholding taxes into the mid-1980s. The first gave non–US obligors an incentive to issue dollar bonds in Europe, while the second gave non–US investors an incentive to buy dollar

Table 10.3
US dollar in the global bond market by issuer and holder at end of 2008 (billions of USD)

	Residence of holder		
US dollar bond issuer	Inside United States	Outside United States	Total
US resident	18,117	5,656	23,773
Non–US resident	917	2,740	3,657
Total	19,034	8,396	27,430

Sources: Department of the Treasury, Federal Reserve Bank of New York and Board of Governors of the Federal Reserve System, Report on US portfolio holdings of foreign securities as of December 31, 2008, October 2009. Report on foreign portfolio holdings of US securities as of June 30, 2008, April 2009, p 23; BIS.
Notes: Non–US resident holdings of US dollar-denominated bonds issued by US residents are from June 2008 rather than end of 2008. US resident holdings of US dollar-denominated bonds issued by US residents estimated as a residual from total US dollar bonds issued by US residents as reported by the BIS and the June 2008 figure for non-resident holdings. US holdings of US dollar bonds issued by non–US residents are at market value while the total is at historical value. The chi-squared statistic is 3902, indicating a rejection of the null hypothesis of independence of residence of dollar bond issuer and dollar bond holder at the 0.0001 level of significance.

Table 10.4
US dollar in the global bond market by issuer and primary market at end of 2008 (billions of USD)

	Location of primary market		
US dollar bond issuer	United States	Offshore	Total
US resident	19,206	4,567	23,773
Non–US resident	466	3,191	3,657
Total	19,672	7,758	27,430

Sources: Dealogic; Euroclear; ISMA; Thomson Financial Securities Data; national authorities; BIS.
Note: Chi-squared statistic is 7, indicating a rejection of the null hypothesis of independence of residence of dollar bond issuer and location of primary market issuance at the 0.0001 level of significance.

Table 10.5
Holders and primary market of US dollar bonds issued by non–US obligors, December 2008

	Bond originally sold		
Investor	Onshore	Offshore	Total
United States	...	....	917
Non–United States	...	...	2,740
Total	466	3,191	3,657

Sources: Department of the Treasury, Federal Reserve Bank of New York and Board of Governors of the Federal Reserve System, Report on US portfolio holdings of foreign securities as of December 31, 2008, October 2009, p. 14; Dealogic; Euroclear; ISMA; Thomson Financial Securities Data; national authorities; BIS.
Note: US holdings of US dollar securities are at market value while the total is at historical value. "..." = not available.

bonds that were issued offshore. Indeed, until the repeal of the US withholding tax on bond interest, dollar bonds issued offshore by highly rated sovereigns and companies (e.g., Kingdom of Sweden, IBM) yielded less than US Treasury bonds of the same maturity owing to the desire of nonresident investors to avoid the US withholding tax.

Since the mid-1980s the onshore and offshore markets have become integrated in their pricing. Still, even given limited information on holdings of dollar bonds by primary market, it is evident that offshore investors are overrepresented among holders of bonds issued by non-residents offshore (table 10.5).

Thus, judging from the US dollar, global investors prefer to transact in a particular currency in its offshore markets. Non–US residents, private and official alike, keep the bulk of their US dollar deposits outside the United States and invest disproportionately in US dollar bonds issued by non–US residents.

That said, it should be clear that in the normal case the offshore market does not exist in isolation. In fact the payment flows associated with these accounts and investments ultimately pass through bank accounts in the United States, just as payment flows associated with non–bank financial intermediaries in the United States ultimately pass through banks in the United States. While the US authorities put in place capital controls from the late 1960s until the early 1970s, they never impeded the flow of payments through US banks to allow the settlement of offshore trade and investment transactions.

Thus offshore markets in a currency can flourish if offshore financial institutions are able to maintain and to access freely clearing balances in the currency with onshore banks (Dufey and Giddy 1994). In other words, nonresident convertibility of the currency is allowed at least for overseas banks. Once this condition is met, both long and short positions in the currency can be built up offshore even without a wholesale liberalization of capital account controls by the home country authorities. If offshore banks do not have access to clearing balances kept with onshore banks, then offshore markets can still exist, though in a more limited fashion, through nondeliverable contracts, as argued below.

10.3 Monetary Stability

The development of offshore markets in a given currency poses several challenges to a central bank's responsibility for maintaining monetary stability.[5] An offshore market in a given currency can increase the difficulty of defining and controlling the money supply in that currency. Equally, an offshore market in a given currency can pose a challenge to measuring and controlling bank credit. For example, domestic firms and households, perhaps through the aggregation of some non–bank financial institution (e.g., money market funds), can substitute offshore deposits in the domestic currency for onshore ones. If these in turn are lent back into the economy (so-called round-tripping), hard-to-measure and hard-to-control offshore deposits and credit can substitute for their domestic counterparts. If monetary policy is based to some extent on the control of money or credit, then the effect of offshore use of the currency on money or credit should be factored in when setting monetary or credit targets or monitoring ranges.

Offshore activity in the currency might also affect the shape of the yield curve or the exchange rate. If the central bank sets the overnight (or some other short-term) rate with a view to targeting inflation and growth, then policy makers would have to factor these effects into their inflation forecasts and set the short-term interest rate appropriately.

In what follows, we first consider the interactions of an offshore market with the control of money or credit, with a focus on the credit multiplier and the use of reserve requirements. We conclude that, as long as capital controls are maintained, the authorities can control offshore deposits unilaterally through reserve requirements. In the absence of capital controls, experience suggests that it is possible to impose reserve requirements on banks' net funding in domestic currency from offshore, albeit at the cost of some distortions across firms and banks. Banks not incorporated in the home country can circumvent such requirements by funding and booking loans offshore that are extended to domestic firms.

We then consider the issues that arise with regard to offshore investors' influence on the onshore yield curve. Here we emphasize that an offshore domestic currency yield curve has already come into existence on the back of the nondeliverable offshore currency market and that adding offshore deliverability may not represent a large change. We sketch the longer term implications for the yield curve of offshore activity in a currency, which depend on the impediments to foreign investment in the domestic market, and the relative size of the off- and onshore markets. If the influence of offshore money markets on the onshore interest rates is significant and warrants a response, it is possible for the home central bank to intervene in the offshore markets through private or public sector agents.

The implications of offshore activities for the exchange rate ultimately depend on how the long and short positions of the currency in offshore markets balance out. Capital controls may at present place restrictions on the ability of offshore market participants to take either long or short positions. In this context, offshore nondeliverable exchange markets already permit speculative bets on the currency that may increase pressure on the exchange rate given prevailing macroeconomic conditions. Greater integration of the onshore and offshore foreign exchange market would make these pressures more immediate. In the longer term, and under more liberalized capital account regimes, the influence on the exchange rate depends largely on the level of domestic interest rates relative to global levels. Relatively low interest rates would tend to make the currency a borrower's currency and its offshore use a net source of downward pressure on its exchange rate. Conversely, relatively high interest rates would tend to make the currency an investor's currency and its offshore use a net source of upward pressure on its exchange rate.

10.3.1 The Definition of Money

If the monetary policy strategy involves targeting or monitoring some monetary aggregate, then it is important to define that aggregate properly. Should the definition of money include offshore deposits in the domestic currency? Major central banks tended to answer this question in a manner that balanced principle with pragmatic considerations. In principle, offshore deposits held by domestic residents should be included in a monetary aggregate, because such deposits tend to have a high degree of substitutability with onshore deposits. The appropriate aggregate would tend to be M2 or M3, since these offshore accounts do not typically serve as transaction accounts.[6] Nevertheless, availability of data can be a major constraint. Comprehensive data on offshore deposits are typically available only at a quarterly frequency from sources such as the BIS. Policy makers who wish to make use of monthly or weekly data may need to rely on data that are made available by a subset of cooperating central banks.

10.3.2 The Credit Multiplier and Reserve Requirements on Offshore Deposits

When targeting or monitoring monetary aggregates, home central banks face the general question of whether credit extension in domestic currency in offshore centers significantly weakens the ability of onshore authorities to control such aggregates. The question arises because offshore banks operate in a different jurisdiction from that of onshore banks and therefore face different regulatory burdens and cost structures. This issue was extensively discussed and debated in the 1970s and the early 1980s, and box 10.1 profiles the discussion. It should be remembered that the monetary strategy of not only the Deutsche Bundesbank and the Swiss National Bank but also of the Federal Reserve put emphasis on the control of monetary aggregates and that other central banks on the European continent sought to control credit aggregates. In this context, reserve requirements served a broader purpose than they generally do in advanced economies these days, namely to stabilize the demand for bank reserves, or in some places to tax the banking system[7] (Borio 1997).

Perhaps the best formulation was that the offshore markets, like domestic non–bank financial institutions such as thrifts in the United States, decrease the effective reserve ratio, or equivalently increase the credit multiplier of a given sum of bank reserves (Aliber 1980). So whether they made monetary policy more difficult depended on whether the home central bank can impose unilateral reserve requirements on offshore deposits. As long as this ability is retained, even if offshore credit extension in domestic currency leads to a multiple expansion of deposits (taking into account any "leakage" to the domestic market), the home central bank would still be able to maintain control through setting the reserve requirement.

Box 10.1
The eurodollar multiplier

Working under James Tobin at Yale, Swoboda (1968) came up with the notion of a eurodollar multiplier, which was subsequently taken up by Friedman (1969). The question posed was by how much some monetary or credit aggregate would expand on the basis of another, say, million dollars deposited in London in the eurodollar market. On the basis of various proposed answers, the G10 central banks decided to cap and then gradually draw down their direct deposits in the euro markets (Toniolo (2005, pp. 465–66)).

Aliber (1980) argued that the euro market, like nonbank financial intermediation, served to economize on needed base money. Big banks operated in both the offshore market and the onshore market, and in major onshore jurisdictions they were required to hold reserves with the central bank well in excess of operational requirements. Thus offshore deposits could be serviced out of such required reserves. The result was that the effective reserve requirement was lower (or the effective credit multiplier was higher).

The implication is that, although the euro markets may make control of monetary aggregates more complicated or difficult, they do not make it impossible. "If one bluntly asked whether the Euromarkets are, in themselves, a source of unbridled credit growth, the answer of most professional writers on the subject would be unambiguously in the negative" (Swoboda 1980). As long as there is some degree of convergence of regulations and reserve requirements affecting domestic and offshore bank lending and borrowing, and a revision of appropriate monetary targets in view of the existence of offshore markets for domestic currency deposits, the offshore market would not pose a serious threat to the ability of the onshore central bank to control the money supply. This was thought to be the lesson of experience of the US Federal Reserve, even at the Federal Reserve Bank of St Louis, which then focused on the monetary base (Balbach and Resler 1980).

In retrospect, however, it is not so clear that adequate account was taken of the credit and liquidity growth in the euro markets. A view at the Federal Reserve Bank of New York was that inflation accelerated in the 1970s in part because the single digit growth of various measures of money in the United States seemed reassuring even as the eurodollar market expanded at rates like 20 to 30 percent a year. And two years after the views above were published, the developing country debt crisis would re-pose the question of whether the easy and excessive credit to Latin American borrowers was only incidentally raised in the euro markets (see below).

In major currencies the notion that reserve requirements might be placed on offshore deposits sounds strange to modern ears. Yet a generation ago, when the Federal Reserve had as an intermediate target some measure of money, the possibility was actively explored (Sub-group Studying the Establishment of Reserve Requirements on Euro-currency Deposits 1980; Frydl 1982).[8] An important threshold consideration was whether reserve requirements would be applied to one currency or to all currencies. If only to one currency, it was reasoned, then market participants could evade the requirements through use of forward contracts. Say, for instance, that offshore US dollars were subject to a reserve requirement, but offshore yen were not. In this case an investor could buy a yen deposit and sell the yen forward against the dollar, in effect holding a synthetic dollar deposit not subject to the reserve requirement.[9]

This reasoning would hold as long as covered interest rate parity held, so that offshore forward foreign exchange rates just reflect interest rate differentials. This condition is the same as the absence of effective controls on capital flows between the domestic and offshore money markets. It has generally been fulfilled, for example, for the yen/dollar ever since the early 1980s. An important result therefore is that effective reserve requirements on a single currency offshore ultimately depend on capital controls that succeed in splitting the onshore and offshore money markets. In other words, reserve requirements can be used unilaterally with some expectation of effectiveness if offshore investors are not able to deal in forward foreign exchange contracts that embody the difference between domestic and dollar money rates.

Such is the case for the Chinese renminbi and the Indian rupee. Thus there is, at least in a transition period, scope for the extension of monetary control to offshore deposits in these currencies. Given that, there are two dimensions to the technical choice of reserve requirement implementation. First, the required reserve can be payable to the host central bank or to the home central bank of the currency (table 10.6, cases A, C, E or B, D, F). Second, the required reserve can be remunerated at zero (table 10.6, cases E, F), or a fixed rate below market rates (table 10.6, cases C, D) or at a market rate (table 10.6, cases A, B).

In Hong Kong, renminbi deposits are not subject to any de jure reserve requirements. However, until recently the de facto reserve requirement had been set at 100 percent because all deposits had to be

Table 10.6
Reserve requirements on offshore deposits: a typology of possibilities

| Rate of remuneration paid on reserves | Central bank where reserves held | | Comment |
	Home	Host	
Market rate	A	B	No "tax" on intermediation
Positive, below market	C	D	
Zero	E	F	

Source: Based on Sub-Group Studying the Establishment of Reserve Requirements on Euro-currency Deposits (1980).

redeposited at the People's Bank of China (PBoC) through the clearing bank. This means that renminbi deposits in Hong Kong have been feeding a "narrow" banking system in which assets consist solely of government liabilities (PBoC reserves in this case). With the introduction of trade credit in July 2009, the reserve requirement has been effectively lowered, but for practical purposes will remain above 25 percent given that the HKMA imposes a 25 percent liquidity ratio requirement on such deposits.

In London, owing to the absence of reserve requirements, banks could and did pay a premium on time deposits over yields on large-denomination certificates of deposits in New York. (The same absence of reserve requirements allowed Libor-based loan pricing to be competitive versus prime-based loan pricing in the United States.) By contrast, renminbi deposit rates, constrained by the de facto high reserve requirement and the rate of remuneration thereon, have been lower in Hong Kong than on the mainland (box 10.2).

Box 10.2
Offshore and onshore interest rates and the renminbi deposits in Hong Kong

Owing to the absence of reserve requirements, deposit insurance fees, and the like, offshore banking can operate with narrower intermediation margins. Thus offshore wholesale deposits typically yield more than their onshore counterparts, while offshore loans can be priced below their onshore counterparts (if the markets are segmented; see graph A). In view of this regularity, the pricing of renminbi deposits in Hong Kong below comparable rates on the mainland is at variance with euromarket experience.

Box 10.2
(continued)

(a)

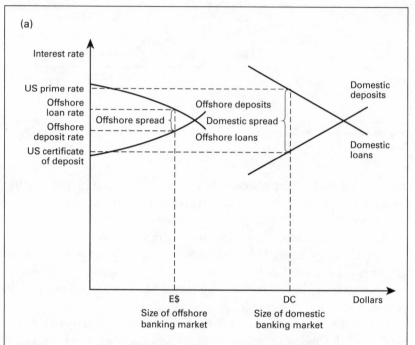

Building on Aliber (1980), Kreicher (1982) conceived of the linkage of domestic and euro market deposit rates in terms of an arbitrage tunnel. This tunnel was based on the arbitrage between the all-in cost of domestic certificates of deposit compared with Libor.

$$r_t^{eurodollar} = \frac{r_t^{domestic\ certificate\ of\ deposit} + FDIC_t}{1 - RR_t},$$

where
$r_t^{eurodollar}$ is Libid or Libor at time t;
$r_t^{domestic\ certificate\ of\ deposit}$ is the US domestic wholesale certificate of deposit rate at time t;
$FDIC_t$ is the premium for Federal Deposit Insurance at time t; and
RR_t is the reserve requirement on large, nonpersonal deposits at time t.

The arbitrage takes place in a tunnel as a result of bid-ask spreads (e.g., Libor vs. Libid, placing costs for the US certificate of deposit). It follows that the eurodollar market is more competitive at higher rates of (unremunerated) required reserves, at higher premia for deposit insurance and at higher interest rates overall.

Such pricing, of course, induces borrowers and placers of funds to move to the offshore market. Historically sovereign borrowers and large firms found it easy to shift to US dollar loans syndicated largely or exclusively with offshore banks and priced off the offshore reference rate,

Box 10.2
(continued)

Libor. Both classes of borrower were quick to insist on their large bank loans being priced off Libor in addition to (or instead of) the domestic benchmarks of prime or US certificates of deposit shortly after Libor gained ground against the latter (McCauley 2001). By the end of the 1980s, Libor was the pricing reference for most corporate loans and prime had been relegated to the status of benchmark for consumer loans.

US depositors showed greater stickiness in their holding of domestic wholesale deposits. One can call it a home bias, or a perceived country risk or inertia, but institutional investors took their time in the 1980s to switch to more remunerative deposits in the Caribbean or London. Money market funds, which compete fiercely on the basis of yield, were among the first to give a substantial weight to offshore deposits among their bank paper. By mid-2008 about half of prime money market funds were invested in foreign bank paper, including eurodollar deposits (Baba et al 2009).

Yields on offer on renminbi deposits in Hong Kong, by contrast, have not been very tempting when seen from the mainland. The savings rate on renminbi deposits in Hong Kong lies well below wholesale rates as represented by the seven-day repo rate in China in the graph below. Admittedly, the renminbi accounts in Hong Kong have not been structured for large-denomination time deposits that would be more comparable to money market yields on the mainland. But the Hong Kong renminbi savings yield has even, until late 2008, laid below the regulated renminbi savings rate in China (graph B). Nevertheless, the yields of renminbi bonds issued in Hong Kong, which were priced by the market, were closer to those on the mainland (table A).

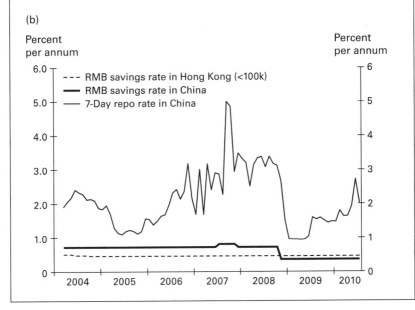

(b)

Box 10.2
(continued)

Box 10.2 Table A
Renminbi-denominated bond issues in Hong Kong through August 2010

Issuers	Issuance date	Issuance size	Maturity	Interest rate
China Development Bank	July 2007	CNY 5bn	2 years	3.00%
Export and Import Bank of China	July 2007	CNY 2bn	2 and 3 years	3.05% and 3.2%
Bank of China	September 2007	CNY 3bn	2 and 3 years	3.15% and 3.35%
Bank of Communication	July 2008	CNY 3bn	2 years	3.25%
Export and Import Bank of China	September 2008	CNY 3bn	3 years	3.4%
China Construction Bank	September 2008	CNY 3bn	2 years	3.24%
Bank of China	September 2008	CNY 3bn	2 and 3 years	3.25% and 3.4%
Bank of East Asia (China)	July 2009	CNY 4bn	2 years	2.8%
HSBC (China)	July 2009	CNY 1bn	2 years	38 bp over 3-m Shibor
China Development Bank	August 2009	CNY 1bn	2 years	38 bp over 3-m Shibor
China Development Bank	August 2009	CNY 2bn	2 years	2.45%
HSBC (China)	September 2009	CNY 2bn	2 years	2.6%
Ministry of Finance	October 2009	CNY 6bn	2, 3 and 5 years	2.25%, 2.7% and 3.3%
Hopewell Infrastructure	July 2010	CNY 1.38bn	3 years	2.98%
McDonalds	August 2010	CNY 200mn	3 years	3%

Source: Hong Kong Monetary Authority.

10.3.3   Reserve Requirements on Net Funding from Offshore Markets

Even if the home authorities cannot control the growth of offshore deposits with reserve requirements, they may still be able to use this tool to control domestic bank credit, if not all credit extended from offshore. US precedents show that the absence of reserve requirements on eurodollars led to the adaptation of the monetary management tool to cover net funding from the eurodollar market. This way domestic credit extension that depended on net funding from the eurodollar market was not able to circumvent this tool of monetary control.

Under Federal Reserve Regulation D, which governs reserve requirements, banks had to hold a non–interest-bearing account when they sold a large certificate of deposit in the United States. In addition, once a bank's US offices had collectively run up a net obligation to its branches outside the United States, the bank had to hold a non–interest-bearing account against additional eurodollar liabilities funding US assets. US-chartered banks' eurodollar reserve requirements were assessed against not only their borrowing from their foreign branches but also their lending to US nonbank customers booked at their foreign branches. Obviously this required the collection of detailed data on the branches outside the United States. But as a result, US-chartered banks could not get around the eurodollar reserve requirement by booking loans to domestic customers off shore.

However, foreign banks operating in the United States did not provide such information on their offshore operations and were assessed the eurodollar reserve requirement on a less inclusive base. As a result, foreign banks operating in the United States could, and did (McCauley and Seth 1992), engage in regulatory arbitrage by booking loans to US firms offshore in financial centers that did not impose reserve requirements. In the hotly contested US corporate loan market in the 1980s, foreign banks claimed a market share of half or more.

Thus a measure of monetary control was achieved by the US authorities at the cost of the competitive position of US-chartered banks in their home corporate loan market. And the distortion did not stop there. US multinationals could borrow dollars from US or other banks offshore and funnel the funds into their US operations. So both US banks and strictly US-based firms without banking relationships with non–US offshore banks could be placed at a competitive disadvantage by the working of the eurodollar reserve requirement. However, the distortion of competition should not be overstated. At an interest rate of 4 percent and a reserve requirement of 3 percent, the cost is only about 12 basis points. The distortion can also be reduced by remunerating required reserves.

The conclusion to be drawn from the US experience is that the monetary control that could not be unilaterally extended to offshore deposits could be imposed on credit to domestic borrowers funded offshore. Such a policy left a loophole, namely non–US banks' lending to US firms from offshore. The policy thus entailed distortions in competition in the banking market owing to the uneven application of rules on foreign and domestic banks. But these distortions can be mitigated by a nonzero rate of remuneration on reserves.

10.3.4   Offshore Markets and the Yield Curve

For central banks that implement monetary policy by targeting some short-term interest rate, the influence of offshore markets on onshore interest rates needs to be factored in. If such influence is significant and undesired, they can choose to intervene in the offshore markets, through private or public sector agents in such markets. Below we discuss the effect of the development of an offshore market on domestic interest rates under two headings: with and without capital controls. Experience to date with the offshore market in nondeliverable renminbi or rupees suggests little feedback to domestic money or fixed income markets. Under more liberalized conditions, however, the effect is likely to depend negatively on the size of the economy and positively on the level of domestic interest rates relative to global levels.

Offshore Markets with Capital Controls   For a number of emerging market currencies, offshore nondeliverable money and fixed income markets already trade quite actively. The nondeliverable forward exchange market serves as a money market, and the nondeliverable interest rate swap markets serve as the fixed income market. For the Brazilian real, Chinese renminbi, and Indian rupee, these "virtual" markets had, by April 2007, become quite sizable in relation to their onshore counterparts (table 10.7).

In other words, more or less well developed yield curves for these currencies offshore are already traded offshore. In such cases, adding an offshore deliverable money and bond market may not represent a large change.

But because of capital controls, these offshore yield curves are quite distinct from their domestic, onshore counterparts. No doubt there are

Table 10.7
Onshore and offshore money and fixed income markets for Brazil, China, and India: daily turnover (billions of USD)

| | Foreign exchange Forwards and Forex swaps | | | | | | Currency swap | | | | | | Interest rate swaps, forward rate agreements, interest rate options | | | | | |
| | Total | | Domestic | | Offshore | | Total | | Domestic | | Offshore | | Total | | Domestic | | Offshore | |
	2007	2010	2007	2010	2007	2010	2007	2010	2007	2010	2007	2010	2007	2010	2007	2010	2007	2010
BRL	5.5	14.1	0.3	2.5	5.3	11.6	0.31	0.39	0.27	0.36	0.04	0.03	1.749	3.3	0.071	1.2	1.678	2.02
CNY	5.6	22.1	0.9	8.0	4.7	14.0	0.13	0.07	...	0.00	...	0.07	0.185	2.0	...	1.5	...	0.51
INR	12.1	20.8	8.5	10.0	3.6	10.8	0.41	0.05	0.40	0.02	0.01	0.03	3.494	2.3	3.080	1.5	0.414	0.78

Source: BIS, Triennial Central Bank Survey, 2007, 2010.
Notes: In addition to the BRL forwards and swaps, BRL/USD futures traded $16.1 billion per day in 2007 and $24.6 billion per day in 2010. Offshore amounts in 2010 are to some extent higher than those in 2007 because these currencies graduated from voluntary to required reporting in the 2010 survey. "..." = not available.

opportunities for arbitrage between them, but such transactions do not carry sufficient weight to force these yield curves into line. Making the currency deliverable offshore would not necessarily alter this state of affairs appreciably. After all, Chinese equities can be delivered offshore, namely H shares in Hong Kong, but the price gap between otherwise identical onshore (A shares in Shanghai) and offshore shares (H shares in Hong Kong) can be very substantial indeed (Peng, Miao and Chow 2007; McCauley and Ma 2009; McCauley 2011).

In particular, when these currencies are under upward pressure, the offshore yield curves tend to be below their onshore counterparts. Perhaps of greater possible concern to the domestic authorities would be the opposite configuration: if the offshore yield curve trades above the domestic yield curve, it provides incentives for domestic residents to shift bank deposits offshore. Such a situation could emerge owing to downward pressure on the currency, and could become destabilizing.

Under these circumstances the home central bank may have concerns. There are precedents for the home central bank to do liquidity operations in the offshore markets. Toniolo (2005: 461) reports:

[C]entral banks and the BIS were already intervening, if quietly, in the market to try to keep the differential between interests paid on Eurocurrency and on domestic currency deposits within desirable limits. From 1965 onward the BIS itself, together with the Swiss National Bank, intervened in the market in order to moderate interest rate differentials caused by seasonal movements in and out of the Eurocurrency market. In December 1966, for instance, the Federal Reserve Bank of New York and the Swiss National Bank made available to the BIS, through swaps, close to $500 million, which the BIS then channelled in to the Eurodollar market. Such operations . . . became more frequent and more important in size as the market grew larger.

During the global financial crisis of 2007 to 2009, under conditions of widespread disruption to markets, the Federal Reserve partnered with central banks all over the world to try to manage Libor, the benchmark (and offshore) US dollar rate. In the case of emerging market currencies such as the renminbi, one could easily imagine the home central bank carrying out such operations through public or private sector agents in the offshore market were circumstances to warrant interventions. Such policy options should help alleviate concerns for instability that may arise because of interest rate differentials between the onshore and offshore markets.

Offshore Markets without Capital Controls   With liberalized capital flows between onshore and offshore markets, it is possible for offshore markets to dominate onshore markets in the determination of interest rates, especially when the onshore market is small as compared with the offshore markets. The recent case of New Zealand sounds a warning regarding the interaction between monetary policy and a thoroughly internationalized currency. At the outset it should be recognized that this is an extreme case in that the New Zealand bond market is among the most internationalized in the world. Most of it is offshore: only about a quarter of New Zealand dollar bonds are domestic issues in the domestic market, versus 50 percent for euro-denominated bonds or 75 percent for US dollar bonds (McCauley 2010; Munro and Wooldridge 2011; Spencer 2011).

As the Reserve Bank of New Zealand tightened in 2005 to 2007, heavy Japanese purchases of offshore kiwi bonds kept important private sector term yields from rising in step. In particular, heavy purchases in Japan of two- to three-year kiwi notes meant that only about half of the 300 basis point tightening of the overnight rate was communicated to the three-year interest rate swap yields. Since historically the New Zealand mortgage market financed houses with floating rate loans, this inverted yield curve might have tempted only a few more firms to sell bonds to replace bank debt. However, mortgage borrowing shifted out of floating based on 90-day rates to fixed off three-year rates. The combination of the weight of Japanese money on term yields and the responsiveness of the mortgage market in taking advantage of these low-term yields illustrates strikingly how an internationalized bond market can pose a challenge to monetary policy.

For larger economies, the offshore markets are less likely to play a crucial role if there are no impediments to investment in the domestic bond market. For New Zealand and Australia, given their relatively small government debt, there was a shortage of high-quality bonds issued by domestic obligors. The offshore markets in effect recruit opportunistic high-quality global issuers (e.g., European agencies or supranational organizations) to supplement the scarce supply of quality domestic issuers. For a big country there is less likely to be such a constraint, and the marginal contribution of the offshore market to the investment menu in the domestic bond market is likely to be smaller.

For the United States in recent years, the argument is made that foreign investment in domestically issued bonds of the Treasury and agencies has lowered bond yields (e.g., see Warnock and Warnock's 2006 accounting for the so-called conundrum) and stimulated such interest-sensitive sectors as residential housing. Whatever the truth of this claim,[10] for present purposes it is worth noting that the argument makes no reference to the offshore US dollar bond market. For big economies the onshore bond markets have offered better secondary market liquidity, and dominated offshore markets in determining the yield curve.

10.3.5 Offshore Markets and the Exchange Rate

Again, it is useful to discuss the effect of the development of an offshore market on the exchange rate under two headings: with and without capital controls. Under capital controls, the offshore use of a currency has in general an ambiguous effect on the exchange rate. While experience to date with the offshore market in renminbi suggests that it has tended to put upward pressure on the renminbi's exchange rate, this should be seen as a result of the prevailing foreign exchange, macroeconomic and political circumstances, such as increasing movements of other currencies, current account surpluses, and international pressures for a faster pace of appreciation. Under more liberalized conditions, however, the overall effect of offshore use of a currency is likely to depend on whether it is used as both an investment and a borrowing currency or mostly one or the other. And this in turn is likely to depend on the level of domestic interest rates relative to global levels.

Offshore Markets with Capital Controls Offshore trading in nondeliverable contracts can already affect the exchange rate. Existing nondeliverable forward markets might at first seem to have no effect on the spot exchange rate, since nondeliverable contracts can be considered nothing but side bets by offshore players with no net effect. But market participants with operations both outside and inside the country can take one side of the offshore market and the other in the domestic market and thereby transmit selling or buying pressure from the offshore nondeliverable market to the onshore cash market. For instance, if foreign investors want to take long positions in the currency, multinational firms can accommodate them by retaining local currency earnings within the country that would otherwise have been paid out in foreign currency as dividends. Such long cash positions in the domestic currency can be profitably hedged through the short sale of the currency in the nondeliverable market. As a result demand for dollars on the part of the multinational firm would be lower than it would have been otherwise, and the onshore spot market would feel the effect.[11]

When offshore markets develop under capital controls, the sequencing of permissible activities can determine the direction of effect on the exchange rate. In the case of Hong Kong, until the recent introduction of trade credit, renminbi banking had favored the creation of deposits over the creation of loans, or the accumulation of long over short positions. To the extent that Hong Kong residents end up holding more long positions in renminbi than they would otherwise have held, the mainland ends up with a larger domestic currency liability, and larger foreign currency claims on the rest of the world, than it would otherwise have had. In flow terms, the sale of Hong Kong or US dollars by a Hong Kong resident to purchase the renminbi account could put upward pressure on the renminbi's exchange rate and lead, ceteris paribus, to a larger purchase of foreign exchange by the PBoC (which forms the counterpart to the reserve liability), although in practice the scale of such flows was insignificant as compared with the overall inflows that the mainland experienced. It is also interesting that the demand for the renminbi balances has not been a one-way bet and has had a speculative element, increasing when the nondeliverable forward pointed to appreciation but decreasing in the absence of such a signal (figure 10.2). We can expect that developments to allow nonresidents to issue liabilities in renminbi would help balance out the pressures on the exchange rate from long-only positions.

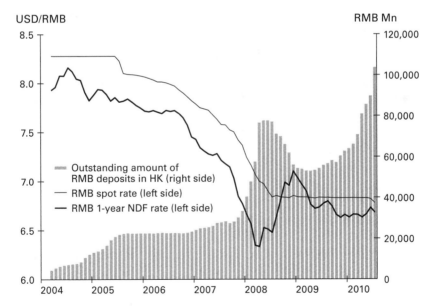

Figure 10.2
Demand and supply for domestic and offshore loans and deposits. Source: Author's adaption of Dufey and Giddy (1994: 97).

Offshore Markets without Capital Controls   It is useful to distinguish symmetrical use of a currency offshore from asymmetrical use. In the first case, nonresidents both invest in a currency and borrow in it. The net of the two may vary over time, but, as a broad observation, both take place. In the asymmetrical case, nonresidents mostly borrow or mostly invest in a currency. This distinction was introduced by Sakakibara and Kondoh (1984), who feared that the yen would attract foreign investment but not foreign borrowing. Of course, it has turned out the opposite: the yen has served international investors more as a funding currency than as a vehicle in which to invest.

The yen is not the only case of what Sakakibara and Kondoh called "lopsided" internationalization. The Australian and New Zealand dollars do not seem to attract any consistent borrowers from outside their economies. If one considers these cases, and contrasts them with the euro and the dollar as instances of balanced internationalization, interest rate levels seem to be key. Investors have been drawn to the Antipodean currencies by their high coupons; borrowers (and shorts) have been drawn to the yen by its low interest rate; and the euro and the dollar have tended to be in the middle.

So that poses the question of whether an emerging market contemplating the offshore use of its currency sees itself as a high or low interest rate economy. The authorities in Brazil or India probably would not pause before answering "high," though noting that interest rates have come down with inflation and that further progress can be anticipated. The authorities in China, by contrast, with its high savings, large current account surpluses and low inflation, might look forward to theirs being a low interest rate economy. That would make the renminbi a borrower's currency and its offshore use a net source of downward pressure on its exchange rate. The case of Japan suggests that this outcome does not exclude a tilt toward appreciation against major currencies like the dollar.

10.4   Financial Stability

The internationalization of a currency raises not only monetary policy issues but also financial stability issues. In what follows, we highlight those that bear on a bank-dominated financial system, such as that in China and India. We organize the discussion in three parts. First, we outline the risks arising from the international operation of domestic banks in foreign currency. These precede, logically and in practice, the risks created by the internationalization of the domestic currency, and serve as a baseline. Then we consider the risks that arise when domestic banks are able to swap domestic currency for foreign currency, thereby lowering the credit standing required of domestic banks to engage in foreign currency lending. Finally, we highlight the risks that arise from the lending of both domestic and foreign banks in domestic currency.

10.4.1 International Operation of Domestic Banks in Foreign Currency

It is important to recognize that the domestic banking system runs risks in participating in international banking operations even on the basis of established international currencies. These risks arise before the domestic authorities permit the domestic currency to be internationalized to any substantial extent and need to be appreciated in order to focus on the risks that are proper to the internationalization of the domestic currency. When domestic banks operate branches abroad, and these borrow and lend in foreign currency, the banks' domestic capital buffers must absorb any losses on foreign currency assets. The position is much the same if domestic banks open subsidiaries abroad. Unless these are substantially overcapitalized, unanticipated losses on foreign currency assets require the injection of capital in foreign currency.

Examples of such risks can readily be provided. In 2007 to 2008 European banks reported substantial losses on holdings of asset-backed securities based on US assets. These securities were generally denominated in US dollars. As write-offs were taken on these dollar assets, the European banks found themselves with more liabilities than assets denominated in the dollar, and had to buy dollars to square their position. In this manner, European banks' losses on dollar assets reduced not only their share prices but also the value of the euro against the US dollar (McCauley and McGuire 2009).

European banks were not alone in realizing such risks. Chinese commercial banks reported significant exposures to troubled US-based asset-backed securities. These sums, however, were not large relative to the banks' capital or relative to China's net assets in foreign exchange. Nevertheless, this case highlights that the internationalization of a country's banks poses financial stability risks, quite apart from the internationalization of the same country's currency.

Next we consider the intermediate case in which domestic banks continue to lend in foreign currency. But now, instead of having to borrow outright in foreign currency, domestic banks can swap domestic currency for foreign currency and thereby fund foreign currency assets. From the standpoint of the counterparty, the exposure to the domestic bank is much reduced. Instead of risking the entire amount, as in an uncollateralized deposit, the foreign counterparty is now exposed to the domestic bank only insofar as the domestic currency received in the swap depreciates against the foreign currency. The implication can be the decline in credit exposure by an order of magnitude and a corresponding increase in the access of domestic banks to foreign currency funding.

The implication of this from the standpoint of the domestic authorities is not entirely benign, however. The internationalization of the domestic currency permits previously strictly domestic banks to enter into foreign currency operations on the basis of domestic liquidity. As a result smaller, less internationally known and less creditworthy domestic banks can now more readily participate in the risks of lending in major currencies. In principle, this should allow them to diversify away from domestic risks and thereby to build a more robust portfolio of credits. In practice, inexperienced domestic banks can sail into deep water in foreign currency lending and take new risks.

10.4.2   Cross-border Lending in Domestic Currency

The discussion on the risks of lending in domestic currency can be divided into those posed by domestic banks' international lending in domestic currency and those posed by foreign banks' international lending in domestic currency.

If a wide range of domestic banks can more readily participate in foreign currency lending funded by swaps against domestic currency, an even wider range can participate in international lending that is denominated in domestic currency. An example is the distribution of loans to developing countries in Latin America across US banks by size in June 1982.[12] These were overwhelmingly dollar-denominated, so any US bank could readily join a syndicated loan on the basis of nothing other than domestic deposits. The top nine banks had $47.7 billion in exposure—for many of them a life-threatening multiple of capital that led to extraordinary official efforts to keep these loans from becoming nonperforming. For the present purpose, however, of more significance is the $16.0 billion in exposure to the same borrowers held by the next 15 banks and the $16.6 billion held by the rest of the surveyed banks. Most of the last group did not have foreign branches or much involvement with foreign exchange, so if the loans had not been denominated in the US dollar, they presumably would not have taken on the risk.

The financial stability implication of this broader participation in home currency lending is two-edged. For a given exposure on the part of US banks to developing countries, the wider syndication of dollar-denominated loans reduced the concentration of holdings in the largest banks and thereby systemic risk. However, the exposure was not given, and arguably the buildup of the stock of risky claims went further because the big banks were able to sell down their exposures to their correspondent banks around the country. On this view, spreading the foreign loans around the banking system only allowed the emerging markets to borrow more in relation to their underlying cash flows, increasing systemic risk.

Foreign banks' international lending in domestic currency can also raise financial stability issues. In this case the host central bank that issues the currency may look to the home authorities to deal with any credit losses that threaten the survival of the foreign bank. But the interaction of credit and liquidity difficulties of foreign banks using the home currency may not be so neatly handled by foreign banks' home authorities. In particular, events during the global financial crisis of 2007 to 2009 showed that the Federal Reserve, as issuer of the US dollar and the host central bank, was called upon to provide dollar liquidity to foreign banks, both directly through operations with foreign bank affiliates in the Unites States and indirectly through partner central banks.

The backdrop of these operations to provide dollar funding to non–US banks was a large buildup of dollar assets by foreign banks, especially European banks. While some European banks built up retail deposit bases in the United States, most depended on more wholesale sources of dollar funding, including money market funds in the United States (Baba, McCauley, and Ramaswamy 2009). Through these aggregators of funds, companies and individuals provided funds through both uncollateralized funding, such as certificates of deposit and commercial paper purchases, and collateralized funding in the form of reverse repurchase agreements. Added to these nonbank sources of funds were outright interbank placements as well as collateralized placements in the form of foreign exchange swaps.

Overall, European banks had built up net claims on nonbanks of very large proportions (McGuire and von Peter 2009a, b). Net dollar claims on nonbanks that needed to be funded, much at short maturities, reached an estimated $1 to $1.2 trillion in mid-2007. If one adds the wholesale funding from money market funds, the amount reached $2 to $2.2 trillion. When the banks suffered large losses on their dollar claims after the crisis broke out, they faced great difficulty in rolling over their dollar funding and had to resort to central bank liquidity support facilities.

As noted, the Federal Reserve used both direct operations with foreign banks and indirect operations involving partner central banks. The New York Second District auction of term funding reached a maximum of $240 billion in mid-April 2009, much of which was said to have been extended to foreign bank affiliates in New York. In addition, swaps with central banks reached a maximum of $580 billion in mid-December 2008.

To be sure, these are extreme events in the history of the euro market, but they were not without precedents. A generation ago, European central bankers considered that any liquidity needs of their banks' operations in US dollars represented a call on their own official reserves. And this was the way various crises played out. For instance, in the Nordic banking crises, the Norwegian and Swedish central banks in effect advanced dollars to their respective banks when these had a hard time rolling over their dollar deposits. And the Japanese authorities were said to have advanced dollars to the Japanese banks in the late 1990s, thereby limiting the "Japan premium" paid by Japanese banks in the international interbank market. Also, when such support for Korean banks overwhelmed the Korean authorities' capacity in 1997, the Korean authorities resorted to IMF and associated credit. In 2007 to 2008, the need was so large and pervasive that the Federal Reserve, as the dollar's bank of issue, provided funding liquidity to foreign banks as it never had previously.

10.4.3 Policy Lessons

What are the financial stability lessons for a central bank standing at the very beginning of the process of internationalization of its currency? Following the discussion above, three can be identified.

First, to the extent that its domestic banks are already actively engaged in intermediation in dollars (and euros, etc), the domestic banking system is already exposed to important credit and cross-currency liquidity risks. It would be a mistake to overstate the additional risks entailed in the internationalization of the home currency.

Second, the opening of a deep and liquid foreign exchange swap in the domestic currency will alone widen these risks to domestic banks that do not possess a deposit base in foreign currency or the credit standing or name recognition to attract wholesale foreign currency deposits. Domestic banking supervision needs to be alive to the potential risks. At a minimum, supervision needs to consolidate risks. Country risk exposures need to be defined and monitored to prevent undue concentrations in relation to domestic banks' capital.

Third, when borrowing in the domestic currency by the rest of the world becomes possible, it will become even easier for domestic banks to expose themselves to the risks of foreign borrowers. Again, consolidation and, in particular, the measuring and monitoring of country exposures, become critical.

Fourth, in the event that the domestic currency becomes very widely used, it might be necessary to have contingency arrangements to provide funding to foreign banks. These arrangements can take the form of operations directly with them, or facilities to provide the funding to partner central banks. But until such time as the domestic currency is widely used by third parties, such arrangements are probably not a high priority.

Box 10.3
Macroprudential policy and the rapid growth of euro market lending in the 1970s

Macroprudential regulation is a term that has been in use at the BIS since the late 1970s. It was used in connection with possible policies to respond to concerns over the excessively rapid growth of international lending in the mid- to late 1970s. The Governors of the G10 central banks gave the Eurocurrency Standing Committee (ECSC, now known as the Committee on the Global Financial System (CGFS)) the task of monitoring the broad risks originating in the offshore markets. At their September 1978 meeting, the Governors considered a report from this Committee and agreed that a "joint group of representatives from the Euro-currency Standing Committee and the Cooke Committee [as the Basel Committee on Banking Supervision (BCBS) was then known] . . . should consider whether there were ways in which the use of prudential measures might be extended into the macroeconomic field for the purpose of controlling the expansion of international bank credit."

The background note for this milestone meeting in November 1978 (BIS 1978) considered the following measures, any one of which could have served to slow the growth of international lending:

• Limiting the international element in banks' balance sheets, either to a maximum percentage of the balance sheet or to a maximum growth rate in relation to the total balance sheet.

• Limiting exposure by country—for instance, to some percentage of bank capital (e.g., 10 percent).
• Limiting maturity transformation in foreign currency.

There was little support at the meeting for such limits. Instead, there was a consensus for accelerating a supervisory development already in train in the Cooke Committee: consolidation of banks' accounts on a global basis. At their November 1978 meeting, the Governors had already endorsed this effort as an instrument of banking supervision, but it was seen as important from the macroeconomic viewpoint as well.

The consensus of the meeting did suggest that more data be collected and published, as a means of informing market participants of the risks that they were collectively running (Larre 1978). Thus Governors were also urged to support the gathering and publishing of statistics on country risk and maturity transformation. More controversial was the suggestion that Governors make a joint statement drawing attention to the risks of the narrowing of spreads of syndicated eurocurrency loans.

Unfortunately, we know that this story did not turn out well. This international lending boom ended in tears for Latin America in August 1982. Consolidated supervision, mandated processes of country risk analysis, publication of data showing a buildup of short-term debt, even a certain amount of jawboning, proved unequal to the task. In the 1980s heavy infusions of public funds through the IMF and multilateral banks allowed major banks to grow out of their claims on developing countries.

Still, a global trend towards more and looser international lending had been identified four years before the onset of the crisis, and the central bankers charged with understanding such broad trends in credit and the risk therein (the ECSC) sought to enlist the aid of the bank supervisors in doing something about it. For present purposes, it is worth noting that a generation ago, supervisory tools were being sought at the international level in order to address a recognized excess of credit.

In addition to the prudential measures just outlined (consolidation, country risk definition, and monitoring in relation to bank capital), there are precedents for the consideration of macroprudential regulation to check the growth of international lending. Box 10.3 recalls discussions along these lines in 1978 in Basel that brought together banking supervisors and those charged with following the broad implications of international banking.

10.5 Conclusions

We have observed in this chapter that offshore markets have intermediated a large chunk of financial transactions in major reserve currencies such as the US dollar. This was not a historical accident but reflected the fact that offshore markets perform essential economic functions, including a separation of currency risk from country risk and diversification of operational risks associated with the financial infrastructure that provides vital clearing and settlement services for the currency. For emerging market economies that are interested in seeing a larger share of their international balance sheets denominated in their own currencies, offshore markets can help increase the recognition and acceptance of the currency among exporters, importers, investors, and borrowers outside the country. This process can begin (but not end) while substantial capital controls are still in place, allowing the authorities to retain a measure of control over the pace of capital account liberalization.

The development of offshore markets could pose risks to monetary and financial stability in the home economy, and these risks need to be prudently managed. In the first instance, capital controls can be applied to cross-border movements of the domestic currency, but eventually other tools are required. The experience of the Federal Reserve and of the authorities of the other major reserve currency economies in dealing with the euro markets shows that policy options are available for managing such risks. The lesson to be learned is that the home authorities need to be alert to such risks, and factor in the additional influence of offshore markets on domestic monetary conditions and financial risks when making monetary and financial policies.

Would the global financial system benefit from a wider array of internationalized currencies with offshore markets? The offshore dollar markets described in the first part of this chapter, dominated by non–US banks, issuers, and investors, have limited the rents flowing to the United States from the global use of the dollar, at least by comparison with the heyday of sterling (DeCecco 1975). So the issue may be less distributional and more whether greater pluralism in international finance is conducive to global financial stability. The long-standing arguments regarding the stability of leadership/hegemony, on the one hand, and pluralism, on the other, need to be revisited in the light of the experience with the dollar shortage during the financial crisis (Ban for International Settlements 2010: 55–58).

Notes

1. The authors thank Robert Aliber, Edward Frydl, and Alexandre Swoboda for discussions, and S. K. Tsang and Lukas Vogel for comments on earlier versions of the chapter, as well as participants of the CESifo Venice Summer Institute 2010 on "The Evolving Role of China in the Global Economy," July 23 to 24, 2010, and of the Hong Kong Monetary

Authority conference on "Financial Reforms, Macro Policies and Currency Internationalization: The Case of China," October 19 to 20, 2009, and a seminar at the BIS, without implicating them in the views expressed. The authors thank Piet Clement for help with the BIS archives and Christian Dembiermont, Magdalena Erdem, Serge Grouchko, Carlos Mallo, Denis Pêtre, and Swapan-Kumar Pradhan for help with the data. Views expressed are those of the authors and not necessarily those of the HKMA or the BIS.

2. The development of renminbi banking in Hong Kong is described in Hong Kong Monetary Authority (2005, 2006, 2009).

3. See also Gao and Yu (2011).

4. Kindleberger (1973, p. 225) refers to the interest equalization tax as a "prohibitive tax."

5. For a discussion of some issues, see Gao (2010).

6. So-called "sweep" accounts are borderline cases. With these accounts, amounts outstanding in a domestic transaction account as of a certain hour are swept into an offshore account.

7. Whether control of base money given reserve requirements sufficed to control monetary or credit aggregates in a textbook fashion is a question beyond the scope of this chapter. Borio (1997: 48) notes that during the period of nonborrowed reserve targeting (October 1979 to October 1982), the Federal Reserve used semi-lagged reserve requirements where required reserves were largely predetermined, working against causation going from reserves to money. Only after this period were reserve requirements made contemporaneous. See Ho (2008: 12–16) for contemporary use of reserve requirements in Asia.

8. A study group was formed at the Bank for International Settlements chaired by the head of the Board of Governors' Division of Monetary Affairs, Stephen Axilrod. Its report became part of the public domain in 2010.

9. Henderson and Waldo (1980) refer to this as the "redenomination incentive." US dollar deposits sold forward against Canadian dollars were already important in the Canadian dollar money market.

10. Rudebusch, Swanson, and Wu (2006) found that foreign official purchases of US Treasuries played little or no role in the "conundrum." See also Genberg et al. (2005). Ben Bernanke stated in a speech in March 2006 that "a reasonable conclusion is that the accumulation of dollar reserves abroad has influenced US yields, but reserve accumulation abroad is not the only, or even the dominant, explanation for their recent behavior."

11. To the extent that the central bank aims at stabilizing the exchange rate, it may need to accumulate larger international reserves.

12. Federal Financial Institutions Examination Council (1982), summing "non–oil developing countries of Latin America and Caribbean" and Venezuela.

References

Aliber, R. 1980. The integration of the offshore and domestic banking system. *Journal of Monetary Economics* 6 (4): 509–26.

Aliber, R. 2002. *The New International Money Game*, 6th ed. Chicago: University of Chicago Press.

Baba, N., R. McCauley, and S. Ramaswamy. 2009. US dollar money market funds and non-US banks. *BIS Quarterly Review* (March): 65–81.

Baba, N., and F. Packer. 2009. From turmoil to crisis: Dislocations in the FX swap market before and after the failure of Lehman Brothers. Working Paper 285. BIS, Basel.

Balbach, A and D Resler. 1980. Eurodollars and the US money supply. *Federal Reserve Bank of St Louis, Review* (June/July): 2–12.

Bank for International Settlements. 1965. *34th Annual Report*. Basel: BIS.

Bank for International Settlements. 1978. Possible uses of banking supervisory instruments for controlling the expansion of international banking credit. Background note for a meeting of a joint group of representatives of the Eurocurrency Standing Committee and the Cooke Committee, Basel, 15 November 1978, in BIS Archives, 7.18(15) – Papers Alexandre Lamfalussy, box LAM20, f56, Eurocurrency Standing Committee.

Bank for International Settlements. 2010. *80th Annual Report*. Basel: BIS.

Bank for International Settlements. 2007, 2010. Triennial Central Bank Survey of Foreign Exchange and Derivatives Market Activity in 2007, 2010. BIS, Basel. Available at: http://www.bis.org/publ/rpfxf07t.htm, and at: http://www.bis.org/publ/rpfxf10t.htm.

Borio, C. 1997. Implementation of monetary policy in industrial economies: A survey. Economic Paper 47. BIS, Basel.

Cheung, Y.-W., G. Ma, and R. McCauley. 2011. Renminbising China's foreign assets. *Pacific Economic Review* 16: 1–17.

DeCecco, M. 1975. *Money and Empire: The International Gold Standard, 1890–1914*. Totowa, NJ: Rowman and Littlefield.

Dufey, G., and I. Giddy. 1994. *The International Money Market*, 2nd *ed*. Englewood Cliffs, NJ: Prentice Hall.

Einzig, P. 1970. *The Eurodollar System*, 5th ed. New York: St Martin's Press.

Federal Financial Institutions Examination Council. 1982. Country Exposure Lending Survey, June 1982. FFIEC, Washington, DC.

Friedman, M. 1969. The eurodollar market: Some first principles. *The Morgan Guaranty Survey* (October): 4–15.

Frydl, E. 1982. The eurodollar conundrum. *Federal Reserve Bank of New York, Quarterly Review* 7 (1): 11–19.

Gao, H. 2010. Internationalization of the renminbi and its implications for monetary policy. In C. Shu and W. Peng, eds., *Currency Internationalization: International Experiences and Implications for the Renminbi*. Basingstoke: Palgrave Macmillan, 209–220.

Gao, H., and Y. Yu. 2011. Internationalisation of the renminbi. In *Currency Internationalisation: Lessons from the Global Financial Crisis and Prospects for the Future in Asia and the Pacific*. BIS Papers, 61. Basel: Bank for International Settlements, 105–24..

Genberg, H. 2011. Currency internationalisation: Analytical and policy issues. In *Currency Internationalization: Lessons from the Global Financial Crisis and Prospects for the Future in Asia and the Pacific*. BIS Papers, 61. Basel: Bank for International Settlements, 221–30.

Genberg, H., R. McCauley, Y.-C. Park, and A. Persaud. 2005. *Official Reserves and Currency Management in Asia: Myth, Reality and the Future.* Geneva Reports on the World Economy 7. Geneva/ London: International Center for Monetary and Banking Studies and Centre for Economic Policy Research.

Henderson, D., and D. Waldo. 1980. Reserve requirements on eurocurrency deposits: Implications for eurodeposit multipliers, control of a monetary aggregate, and avoidance of redenomination incentives. International Finance Discussion Paper 164. Board of Governors of the Federal Reserve System, Washington, DC.

Ho, C. 2008. Implementing monetary policy in the 2000s: Operating procedures in Asia and beyond. Working Paper 253. BIS, Basel.

Hong Kong Monetary Authority. 2005. Renminbi banking business in Hong Kong. *Hong Kong Monetary Authority, Quarterly Bulletin* 42 (March): 22–26.

Hong Kong Monetary Authority. 2006. Hong Kong's renminbi business two years on. *Hong Kong Monetary Authority, Quarterly Bulletin* 46 (March): 38–43.

Hong Kong Monetary Authority. 2009. Renminbi trade settlement pilot scheme. *Hong Kong Monetary Authority, Quarterly Bulletin* 60 (September): 1–6.

Hui, C.-H., H. Genberg, and T.-K. Chung. 2009. Funding liquidity risk and deviations from interest-rate parity during the financial crisis of 2007–2009. Working Paper 13/2009. Hong Kong Monetary Authority.

Kindleberger, C. 1973. *International Economics,* 5th ed. Homewood, IL: Irwin.

Kreicher, L. 1982. Eurodollar arbitrage. *Federal Reserve Bank of New York, Quarterly Review* 7 (2): 10–22.

Larre, R. 1978. Telex to A. Lamb, S. Ogata, H. Wallich and D. Willey, 24 November. In *BIS Archives, 7.18(15)—Papers Alexandre Lamfalussy, box LAM20, f56.* Eurocurrency Standing Committee.

Ma, G., and R. McCauley. 2008a. Do China's capital controls still bind? In B. Eichengreen, Y.-C. Park, and C. Wyplosz, eds., *China, Asia, and the New World Economy.* Oxford: Oxford University Press, 312–40.

Ma, G., and R. McCauley. 2008b. The efficacy of China's capital controls: Evidence from price and flow data. *Pacific Economic Review* 13 (1): 104–23.

McCauley, R. 2001. Benchmark tipping in the money and bond markets. *BIS Quarterly Review* (March): 39–45.

McCauley, R. 2005. Distinguishing global dollar reserves from official holdings in the United States. *BIS Quarterly Review* (September): 57–72.

McCauley, R. 2010. Internationalizing the Australian dollar. In C. Shu and W. Peng, eds., *Currency Internationalisation: International Experiences and Implications for the Renminbi.* Basingstoke: Palgrave Macmillan, 56–77.

McCauley, R. 2011. Renminbi internationalisation and China's financial development, *BIS Quarterly Review* (December): 41–56.

McCauley, R., and G. Ma. 2009. Resisting financial globalisation in Asia. In *Financial Globalization and Emerging Market Economies. Proceedings of an International Symposium,* November 7–8. Bangkok: Bank of Thailand, 177–222.

McCauley, R., and P. McGuire. 2009. Dollar appreciation in 2008: Safe haven, carry trades, dollar shortage and overhedging. *BIS Quarterly Review* (December): 85–93.

McCauley, R., and R. Seth. 1992. Foreign bank credit to US corporations: the implications of offshore loans. *Federal Reserve Bank of New York, Quarterly Review* 17 (1): 52–65.

McGuire, P., and G. von Peter. 2009a. The US dollar shortage in global banking. *BIS Quarterly Review* (March): 47–63.

McGuire, P., and G. von Peter. 2009b. The US dollar shortage in global banking and the international policy response. Working Paper 291. BIS, Basel.

Munro, A., and P. Wooldridge. 2011. Motivations for swap-covered foreign currency borrowing. In *Currency Internationalization: Lessons from the Global Financial Crisis and Prospects for the Future in Asia and the Pacific*. BIS Papers, 61. Basel: Bank for International Settlements, 19–56.

Peng, W., H. Miao, and N. Chow. 2007. Price convergence between dual-listed A and H shares. China Economic Issues 6/07. Hong Kong Monetary Authority. Available at: http://www.hkma.gov.hk/eng/publications-and-research/research/china-economic -issues/2007/.

Rudebusch, G., E. Swanson, and T. Wu. 2006. The bond yield "conundrum" from a macro-finance perspective. Working Paper 2006–16. Federal Reserve Bank of San Francisco.

Sakakibara, E., and A. Kondoh. 1984. Study on the internationalisation of Tokyo's money markets. Japan Center for International Finance Policy Study Series, no 1, June.

Spencer, G. 2011. Panel discussion. In *Currency Internationalization: Lessons from the Global Financial Crisis and Prospects for the Future in Asia and the Pacific*. BIS Papers, 61. Basel: Bank for International Settlements, 243–47.

Sub-group Studying the Establishment of Reserve Requirements on Euro-currency Deposits. 1980. Reserve requirements on euro-currency deposits, 20 February, in BIS Archives, 1.3a(3)j—Working Party on Constraining Growth of International Bank Lending, vol 2.

Swoboda, A. K. 1968. *The Eurodollar Market: An Interpretation*. Essays in International Finance, 64. Princeton: Princeton University.

Swoboda, A. K. 1980. Credit creation in the euromarket: Alternative theories and implications for control. Occasional Paper 2. Group of Thirty, New York.

Toniolo, G. 2005. *Central Bank Cooperation at the Bank for International Settlements, 1930–1973*. Cambridge: Cambridge University Press.

Warnock, F., and V. Warnock. 2006. International capital flows and US interest rates. Working Paper 125. NBER, Cambridge, MA.

11 Crisis, Capital Controls, and Covered Interest Parity: Evidence from China in Transformation

Jinzhao Chen

11.1 Introduction

Covered interest parity (CIP) condition states that there will be no advantage to borrowing or lending in one currency rather than in another. In the absence of impediments to capital movement, the market arbitragers will equalize the rate of return for assets of similar risk characteristics denominated in different currency to maintain the CIP. In this chapter I study the renminbi (RMB) covered interest differential that is closely related to capital controls in China.

During the East Asia financial crisis of 1997, China's relatively closed capital accounts were considered by some commentators to be an important element in its ability to maintain a stable exchange rate (IMF 2000) and in preventing it from suffering harmful effects. Twelve years later, while most European countries were experiencing the downturn triggered by the financial crisis of 2007, China and the developing countries of the East Asia–Pacific region were the first to recover from the global crisis, and it is likely that they will grow rapidly during the next decade.

To sustain the brisk economic recovery of Asian economies and benefit the global economic growth, the public debate and discussions underscore the fact that capital controls limiting capital inflows (or swings in hot monies searching for higher yielding assets) may be a means to avoid overheating and bubble formation in these emerging economies. That is an important issue since large and sudden capital movements can pose a risk to their economies and financial systems and stem the sustainability of economic recovery. Under this circumstance, it is interesting to note how China coped with this financial turmoil and the implied economic slowdown. To this end, it is especially important to not look at the de jure capital controls but at their impact through an assessment of their effectiveness.

In this chapter, I investigate the intensity and the effectiveness of the capital controls in China from 2003 to 2010, and give special attention to the period of financial turbulence that erupted in the summer of 2007. The evidence I use is based on the CIP, with the measuring of the RMB yield differential between the onshore interest rate and its nondeliverable forward (NDF) implied offshore interest rate. I employ a two-regime threshold autoregressive model to study the RMB yield differential, with the estimated thresholds determined by the intensity of controls on capital inflows and transaction costs. An increase of the threshold indicates the strengthening of the de facto capital control intensity; a lower speed of adjustment to the threshold implies a more effective capital control, whereas a higher speed means either less effectiveness or a more integrated market.

I divide the sample into three subperiods to examine the effects of the Chinese exchange rate reform in 2005 and the recent global financial turbulence, with more attention to the latter. The financial crisis highlighted the pivotal role of the US dollar and gave rise to an acute dollar shortage, more acute than that of the 1950s (Cheung et al. 2011). As is well known, China and other Asian countries subsequently experienced stronger deviations from CIP and accompanying volatility. But what is less known is that the financial crisis interrupted the experiment of managing a gradual strengthening of RMB against trading partners' currencies (Ma and McCauley 2011). The resulting re-linkage to the dollar would hinder the RMB's internationalization (Cheung et al. 2011), which itself could serve to break the dependence of the international financial system on a currency subject to national management. In this circumstance the investigation of the capital controls of China and its monetary policy during this subperiod is needed.

This chapter is organized as follows: In section 11.2, I present the capital controls adopted in China. In section 11.3, main studies and methods related to covered interest parity are briefly reviewed. In section 11.4, I discuss the empirical methodologies adopted: the measuring of RMB yield differential between onshore and offshore market, and the threshold autoregressive model with conditional variance. Section 11.5 involves the data. In section 11.6, the results of estimation and hypothesis testing are presented and discussed. Section 11.7 concludes.

11.2   Capital Controls in China

As for the implementation of capital controls in China, the "all-included" foreign exchange management system has been replaced and transformed into a government-administrated control regime over transactions and currency exchanges in capital accounts. Long-run capital inflows are generally welcomed, while China maintains controls on both short-term capital inflows and outflows, focusing more on the regulation of the volatility of capital flows rather than their volumes. Quantitative and regulatory controls are implemented on the exchange between the RMB and foreign currencies. The evolving restrictions on financial accounts have three aspects: the management of foreign direct investments (FDI), the controls over international portfolio investment, and controls over foreign debts. And their implementations involve two forms of management (Zhang 2003). As for the first form, most cross-border capital transactions need to be approved by the relevant government departments, for instance, the People's Bank of China, or regulatory authorities like the China Securities Regulatory Commission (CSRC). The Qualified Foreign Institutional Investor (QFII) program issued in 2002, the Qualified Domestic Institutional Investor (QDII) program started in 2006, and its further extensions issued in 2007 and 2008, greatly relaxed the restrictions in this form on access by foreign investors to domestic financial markets and by Chinese investors to overseas financial markets. The second form lies in the controls imposed by the State Administration of Foreign Exchange (SAFE) on foreign exchange transactions related to relevant capital transactions, such as the repatriation of foreign currency denominated funding raised overseas by domestic companies, cross-border remittance. The strengthened supervision in 2008 on the balance of payments by SAFE mainly takes this form, and it aims to prevent the entry of hot money via the channels of trade, FDI and RMB-denominated accounts of nonresidents. In summation, China's controls are a direct restriction on cross-border capital flows, based mainly on administrative approval and quantitative limitation.

11.3   Learn from the Covered Interest Parity: A Brief Review

The CIP condition is an unalloyed criterion used to judge for "capital mobility" in the sense of the extent of financial market integration across national boundaries.[1] Today the CIP is widely recognized as the most appropriate indicator of the degree of the financial integration across countries (Frankel 1992; Holmes 2001) and the indicator of capital controls; for example, these controls have been found to interfere with the achievement of CIP in Germany between 1970 and 1974 (Dooley and Isard 1980) and in Japan in the 1970s (Otani and Tiwari 1981; Ito 1987).

According to the CIP criterion, the interest differential between two assets, identical in every aspect except currency of denomination, should be zero once allowance is made for cover in the forward exchange. Deviations from the CIP condition would reflect transactions costs (Frankel 1992).[2] For noncomparable assets (i.e., assets issued in different political jurisdictions), as concluded by Aliber (1973) in his seminal paper, political risk accounts for much of the observed differential. For an economic agent who formulates his portfolio including assets of different political jurisdiction, political risk can be composed of different tax/tariff structure or capital controls. In the latest financial turbulence, Baba and Packer (2009) rationalize the deviation from CIP with the counterparty risk and the liquidity risk. This chapter focuses on the determinant of the deviation associated with capital controls to propose some evidence for their effectiveness.

There are few studies in the literature about the evidence of CIP in China. The principal reason lies in the fact that neither a liquid onshore forward exchange market nor the euro-currency market of RMB exists. In this circumstance the difference between RMB's onshore interest rate and its offshore counterpart cannot be measured directly, as Dooley and Isard (1980) did for German mark; neither could it be done indirectly for the difference of the arbitrage gains, as Ito (1987) devised for the Japanese yen. Nevertheless, with the implicit assumption that the covered interest parity condition holds for RMB in the offshore financial market, Ma and McCauley (2008) calculated the yield differentials between the onshore interest rate of RMB and its offshore counterpart implied by CIP. By comparing these rates between two markets, where different regimes of capital controls exist, interest rate yield differential is showed as a quantitative indicator of the effect of capital controls. They have also showed that though these differentials have been shrinking over time, especially after the peg to the USD was abandoned in July 2005, the capital controls in China are still binding, as these interest rate differentials remain large and allow the Chinese government to retain a short-term monetary autonomy to some extent. However, their data sample does not include the recent period of turbulence. The soar and the slump of the yield differential cannot be simply explained by the effectiveness or powerlessness of the capital controls. In this context, further quantitative modeling seems necessary, and via this mean, I aim to fill the gap and shed some light on the efficacy of China's capital controls.

11.4   Methodology

11.4.1   Quantifying the Interest Yield Differential from Covered Interest Parity

If the covered parity condition holds, the international capital movements are free from capital controls. The ratio of the forward exchange rate to the spot rate is then equal to the ratio of the domestic interest yield against that of its foreign counterpart:

$$\frac{F}{S} = \frac{1+R}{1+R^F},\tag{11.1}$$

where F is the forward rate for a given maturity, S is the spot rate (domestic price of foreign currency), R is the interest rate of the home currency, and R^F is the foreign interest rate. When the capital controls bind, nonresidents may not have full access to the onshore monetary market; also, when an onshore forward exchange market does not exist or the existing one is not well developed, nonresidents cannot make use of the forward exchange contracts to cover the exchange rate risk exposure of their onshore portfolios, giving rising to the nondeliverable forward (NDF) contract.[3] With this financial instrument, a gain equivalent to that of euro-currency deposit—which does not exist for most of the countries having offshore NDF markets—can be obtained. Assuming that the offshore NDF market, which is considered as a benchmark market, is very active and the CIP holds there, we have

$$\frac{NDF}{S} = \frac{1+i}{1+R^F},\tag{11.2}$$

where i is the NDF-implied yield rate of the home currency offshore. To the extend that the arbitrage between the onshore money market and the offshore NDF market is effectively constrained by capital controls, the NDF-implied offshore interest rate, i, can differ considerably from the interest rate prevailing in the onshore money market, R. This yield differential (or spread) can be written as

$$Y = R - i = R - \left[\frac{NDF(1+R^F)}{S} - 1 \right].$$ (11.3)

A large and persistent onshore/offshore spread Y indicates the presence of effective cross-border restrictions.[4] Moreover a positive sign of the yield gap imply appreciation pressures on the home currency in the presence of capital controls and vice versa (Ma and McCauley 2008).

If we assume that, on the offshore market, CIP does not hold for some reasons (discussed in section 11.6), and there exists a deviation from this parity, we write this deviation as π, and rewrite equation (11.3):

$$\pi = \frac{S}{NDF}(1+i) - (1+R^F),$$ (11.4)

$$Y = R - \left[\frac{NDF(1+R^F)}{S} - 1 \right] - \pi \frac{NDF}{S},$$ (11.5)

$$Y' = Y + \pi \frac{NDF}{S} = R - \left[\frac{NDF(1+R^F)}{S} - 1 \right].$$ (11.3′)

Y' consists of two parts: the yield differentials measured in Ma and McCauley (2008), which represent capital controls and transaction costs, and some other factor resulting in the deviation from CIP in the offshore market. This is the variable of interest that I will calculate and model. I continue to name it the yield differential as well.

As to the empirical approaches relevant to the deviation from CIP, I consider only the univariate analysis in studying the behavior and the dynamics of Y'.[5] The early approaches attempted first at a branch of univariate analysis computing actual deviations from the interest parity (e.g., Frenkel and Levich 1975), and then the stationary or unit-root analysis was applied to the deviation from CIP (e.g., Holmes 2001). It was found that the speed with which deviations from CIP are eliminated is an indicator of the effectiveness of the capital controls and the extent of financial integration between different countries.[6] A more recent approach consists of assuming and testing the behaviors of deviation from CIP based on the regime (or space) in which they lie by means of estimating a threshold autoregressive model, which I will present next (e.g., Peel and Taylor 2002; Taylor and Tchernykh-Branson 2004).[7]

11.4.2 Threshold Autoregressive (TAR) Model

The TAR model was first proposed by Tong (1978) and further developed by Tong and Lim (1980). It is motivated by several commonly observed nonlinear characteristics such as asymmetry in declining and rising patterns of a process, or by limit cycles of a cyclical time series.

A special (or restricted) case of TAR, called the band-TAR model, was applied by Obstfeld and Taylor (1997) for testing the theory of purchasing power parity and the nonlinear adjustment of price.[8] It was later employed to investigate the validity of CIP by taking into account arbitrage costs in the financial market (e.g., Peel and Taylor, 2002; Taylor and Tchernykh-Branson, 2004).[9] The presence of fixed costs does not allow the agents to adjust continually their positions. Within the band that implies the extent of the transaction costs, the agent will not arbitrage, as the covered interest differential (CID) would not bring the excessive profit. The CIDs follow a random walk and will never revert to zero. Outside the band, unexploited profit will trigger the covered interest arbitrage and quickly reduce the CID to a certain level (the edge of the band), with this process characterized by an autoregressive model (e.g., AR(1)). A simple version of such band-TAR model may be written as

$$\Delta y_t = \begin{cases} \rho^{out}\left(y_{t-1} - c^{up}\right) + \varepsilon_t^{out} & \text{if} \quad y_{t-1} > c^{up}, \\ \rho^{in} y_{t-1} + \varepsilon_t^{in} & \text{if} \quad c^{low} \leq y_{t-1} \leq c^{up}, \\ \rho^{out}\left(y_{t-1} - c^{low}\right) + \varepsilon_t^{out} & \text{if} \quad y_{t-1} < c^{low}, \end{cases} \tag{11.6}$$

where c^{up} (c^{low}) is the upper (lower) threshold, ε_t^{out} is $N(0, \sigma^{out^2})$, and ε_t^{in} is $N(0, \sigma^{in^2})$. Here ρ^{in} could be restricted to zero, and ρ^{out} is the convergence speed outside the thresholds of arbitrage (or inaction).

The TAR model outlined above has three regimes or two thresholds. However, when the theory is not specific about the complete structure of the model, the number of regimes (or thresholds) in the model cannot be assumed to be known a priori. As this specification is supported by the transaction cost theory, the assumption of such a band-TAR model proposes a simple interpretation of the results.[10] Hutchison et al. (2010) use this three-regime TAR model to investigate capital control liberalization in India. Nevertheless, I applied some formal tests to confirm this hypothesis of nonlinearity or even further the number of thresholds if the linearity rejected.[11]

As shown in figure 11.1, there are insufficient data points during the sample period that will pass through the lower threshold, which is

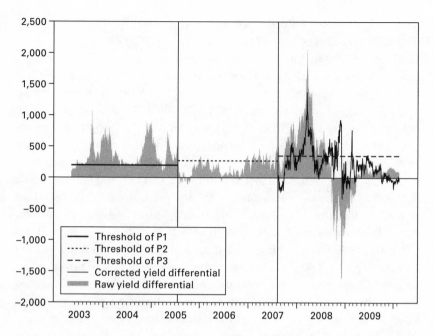

Figure 11.1
Interest yield differentials of RMB. Sources: Datastream, WM/Reuters, and author's calculations (daily data).

supposed to be negative. This is explained by the pressure exerted by capital inflows to China and by the corresponding bindingness of capital controls. Therefore the asymmetric band-TAR model outlined above cannot be identified, with the upper and lower bands representing the different degree of controls on capital inflows and outflows. Nevertheless, Taylor and Tchernykh-Branson (2004) point out that this is the case in most emerging markets, which lead consequently to the specification of a single upper threshold model (e.g., figure 11.2).[12] By this approach the model may be written in the form[13]

$$\Delta y_t = \begin{cases} \rho^{out}(y_{t-1} - c^{up}) + \varepsilon_t^{out} & \text{if} \quad y_{t-1} > c^{up}, \\ \varepsilon_t^{in} & \text{if} \quad y_{t-1} \le c^{up}. \end{cases} \tag{11.7}$$

When c^{up} is known, simple least-squares methods can be applied to each subset of the data partitioned by the single threshold. In the absence of prior knowledge about the threshold, this model can still be estimated via a grid search of all possible values of the threshold variable (here y_{t-1}), which either minimizes the sum of squared residuals

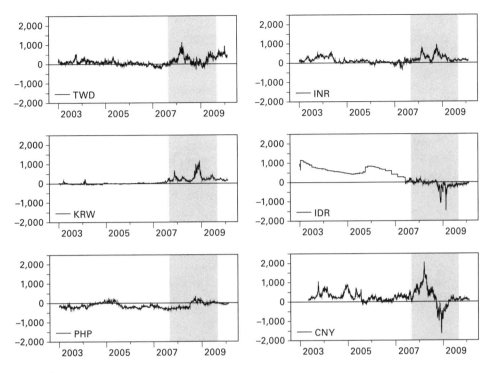

Figure 11.2
Covered differentials of Asian currencies/USD (basis points). Sources: Datastream, WM/Reuters, and author's calculations (daily data).

or maximizes the log-likelihood function of the model.[14] For correcting the autocorrelation and the heteroskedasticity prevalent in the residual, the model can be refined by adding the lag(s) of the dependent variable and the GARCH effect, as in Levy Yeyati et al. (2009), and rewritten as

$$\Delta y_t = 1_{out}\,\rho^{out}\left(y_{t-1}-c^{up}\right)+1_{in}\left(\rho^{in} y_{t-1}+C^{in}\right)+\sum_{j=1}^{k}\varphi_j \Delta y_{t-j}+\varepsilon_t,$$

$$\sigma_t^2 = \alpha_0 + \sum_{j=1}^{p}\alpha_j \varepsilon_{t-j}^2 + \sum_{j=1}^{q}\lambda_j \sigma_{t-j}^2,$$

(11.8)

where 1_{in} (1_{out}) is the indicator function and is equal to 1 when $y_{t-1} < c^{up}$ ($y_{t-1} \geq c^{up}$) and 0 otherwise, C^{in} is the constant term in the inner regime. In this specified TAR (2, k, d) model, 2 is the number of regimes, k is the augmented lag length, and d is the delay parameter. As I will show later, the sample can be divided into three subperiods, as the structural change and the outbreak of the financial crisis are represented in the data, and k can be set to 0 or 1 to correct the autocorrelation in the residuals. Due to the lack of a precise theoretical prior about the delay parameter d, I will set it to 1 for all subsamples, following the existing studies (e.g., Bec et al. 2004). ρ^{in} and ρ^{out} represent the convergence speed in the no-arbitrage and arbitrage regime, respectively.[15] Moreover the same error terms and conditional variance could be assumed for both of the two regimes.[16] The number of ARCH and GARCH terms (p and q) could be specified differently for each subsample. Generally, a GARCH (1, 1) is sufficient for each subsample to take into account the heteroskedasticity.[17]

I estimated the outlined model by following the procedure described in Obstfeld and Taylor (1997): by a grid search—for the potential threshold—on all values of the threshold variable, I estimated the TAR model with the threshold that maximizes the log likelihood ratio $LLR = 2(L_a - L_n)$, in which L_a (L_n) is the log likelihood of the alternative TAR model (null AR model).[18] The likelihood function of the above TAR can be written as

$$L_a\left(\rho^{out}, \rho^{in}, \sigma^2, c^{up}, C^{in}\right) = -\frac{1}{2}\sum_t\left[\ln(\sigma^2) + \frac{\varepsilon_t^2}{\sigma^2}\right].\qquad(11.9)$$

Once the TAR model is estimated, a threshold test can be run as a test of specification for checking the adequacy of the TAR alternative relative to the AR null. Because the threshold is not defined under the null, the LLR does not follow the standard distribution, and the standard inference is invalid. One way to resolve this problem is to use the Monte Carlo simulation to derive the critical value of the LLR test (e.g., Obstfeld and Taylor 1997; Hansen 1999): estimate and fit an AR(1) null model with GARCH effect on the actual data $(y_1, \ldots, y_T)$. With estimated parameters, the fitted linear model can be simulated.[19] Next the TAR model would be estimated for each simulated series and the corresponding LLR calculated. The empirical distribution of the LLR is then tabulated and used as an inference to judge the alternative TAR model against the AR null. However, this method suffers from the tail heaviness of the residuals, which violates the hypothesis of normally distributed residual assumed in the aforementioned Monte Carlo simulation; consequently the LLR test may have low power.[20]

11.5 Data

The sample I used for computing the yield differential spans from May 6, 2003 to February 12, 2010. The short span of the sample is dictated by the availability of the data. The onshore–offshore Chinese currency (RMB) yield differential is derived from the RMB spot rate, the 3-month RMB NDF rate, the 3-month US dollar Libor rate, and the 3-month PBOC (People's Bank of China: Central Bank of China) bill rate (proxy of the onshore interest rate), which is only available since May 6, 2003.[21] Datasets used for calculation, estimation, and hypothesis testing are of daily frequency and extracted from Datastream and Bloomberg.

Despite the relatively short sample span, it is possible to have some structural breaks or dramatic policy changes during the entire period, particularly the global crisis of 2007. In fact I divided the whole sample into three subsamples as follows: the first period (5/06/2003–7/20/2005), the second (7/21/2005–8/8/2007), and the third (8/9/2007–2/12/2010), based principally on the historical events that had an impact on the monetary or foreign exchange policy. Two eventual structural changes are documented in the literature. The first event was the reform of the Chinese exchange rate regime taken into effect in July 2005, which ended the peg of RMB to USD and created a management float based on a basket of currencies.[22] The second one was the recent financial turmoil triggered in August 2007, with August 8 considered as the timing of the break (e.g., Baba and Packer 2009, and the references therein). I implemented the hypothesis testing and the estimation on these subperiods, respectively. Furthermore, with the test of Lee and Strazicich (2003), which can identify the structural changes and at the same time test for stationarity, I could compare these dates with my ex ante choices.

11.6 Empirical Results

Figure 11.1 shows the yield differentials calculated with equation (11.3'). The substantial and persistent RMB yield differential may indicate large transactions costs and effective capital controls. As for the speed of reversion to "equilibrium," I relied on a TAR model with upper threshold as described above. Before presenting the estimation results, I will implement below some of my preliminary analyses.

11.6.1 Unit-Root (UR) Analysis

If the yield differentials have a unit root, this indicates that the deviations are persistent and not mean reverting, which implies that capital controls are effective enough to maintain a gap between the onshore and the offshore RMB interest rate. In contrast, the stationary characteristics represent a process of returning to the equilibrium level, via the activity of arbitrage in the market. Furthermore the speed of the convergence can be calculated by estimating the autoregressive parameter of the stationary process validated. A relatively low speed can still imply the binding control on capital flows. However, high-speed mean reversion may indicate the ineffectiveness of capital controls or a higher degree of financial market integration.

Following the traditional practice in the literature, a nonstationarity check should be executed before specifying the nonlinear characteristic of the series. However, standard UR tests are known to be biased toward the nonrejection of a unit root when they are applied to time series with nonlinear dynamics.[23] Numerous UR tests with various alternative hypothesis of nonlinearity can be used to increase the power of the UR test. Here, I only apply the generalized least-squares UR test (NP test hereafter) of Ng and Perron (2001) and the momentum-TAR test of Enders and Granger (1998), which assumes an M-TAR model in the alternative. My statistical inferences are mainly based on the latter, whereas I use the former for comparison.[24]

The two UR tests are applied to the whole sample and to each subsample, with the results reported in table 11.1. Not surprisingly, for the whole sample, both lead to the rejection of the UR null, as the tests become biased because of the structural changes. To adequately model and carefully investigate the series of the yield differentials, I also apply these two tests to each subsample. The results do not always provide the same evidence: the NP test cannot reject the UR null for any of the three subperiods (see table 11.1), implying the absence of the mean reversion of the yield differential, while the M-TAR test only accepts the UR for the third subperiod. Based on the results of M-TAR test during the first two subperiods, the yield differentials are stationary but nonlinear. As to the third one (the period the financial turbulence), even with the same conclusion of the two tests, the nonstationarity of the yield differential may be accepted with caution. The reason for this violation of the interest rate parity is still unclear: is it induced by the liquidity risk or the strengthening of the capital controls or even both (see figures 11.2 and 11.3)? I provide an answer at the end of this section.

Finally, I use the UR test proposed by Lee and Strazicich (2003) (LS test hereafter) to identify the structural changes. Their minimum Lagrange multiplier unit-root test endogenously determines the location of (up to) two structural breaks in level and/or in trend, and tests

Table 11.1
Stationarity tests

Period	N-P ADF model			M-TAR model	
	MZa	MZt	$\hat{k}$	φ^*	$\hat{k}$
Whole	−14.8024**	−2.7204**	12	4.3266*	12
1st	−5.0047	−1.4061	5	5.5520**	8
2nd	−1.0801	−0.7262	8	4.8262*	1
3rd	−3.7493	−1.3353	12	1.3486	12
3rd^c	−12.1675**	−2.4665**	3	6.7896**	2

Notes: $\hat{k}$ is the number of lags that is auto-selected by minimizing the AIC criteria. To ensure that the estimation is run over the same sample for each subperiod, we fix the number of first usable observation as the sum of k-max, the times of first difference of dependent variable and 1. For the second period, when we discard the first ten points of this period (because of their abnormal behavior due to the beginning period effect), the power of the M-TAR test has increased to 5 percent. *, **, and *** denote significance at the 10, 5, and 1 percent levels, respectively.

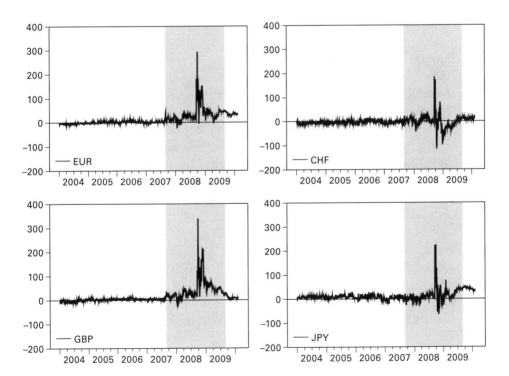

Figure 11.3
Covered differentials of major currencies/USD (basis point). Sources: Datastream, WM/ Reuters, and author's calculations (daily data).

Table 11.2
LS unit-root test with structural breaks

	$\hat{k}$	$\hat{T}_B$		Test statistic	Critical value break points		
Level	8	2005:08:15, 2006:07:26		−4.1634	$\lambda = (0.3, 0.5)$		
First difference	6	2006:07:26, 2008:09:15		−3.0095	$\lambda = (0.5, 0.8)$		
Break timing		(0.2, 0.4)	(0.2, 0.6)	(0.2, 0.8)	(0.4, 0.6)	(0.4, 0.8)	(0.6, 0.8)
	1%	−6.16	−6.41	−6.33	−6.45	−6.42	−6.32
CV	5%	−5.59	−5.74	−5.71	−5.67	−5.65	−5.73
	10%	−5.27	−5.32	−5.33	−5.31	−5.32	−5.32

Notes: $\hat{k}$ is the optimal number of lagged first-differenced terms included in the unit-root test to correct for serial correlation. T_B denotes the estimated break points. Critical values (CV) are shown below for the two-break minimum LM unit-root test with linear trend (model C) at the 1, 5, and 10 percent levels for a sample of size $T = 100$, respectively, depending on the location of the breaks $\lambda = (T_{B1}/T, T_{B2}/T)$. The critical values for LM test with breaks come from Lee and Strazicich (2003). *, **, and *** denote significance at the 10, 5, and 1 percent levels, respectively.

the null of a unit root, without diverging in the presence of breaks under the null.[25] The results are shown in table 11.2; for the timing of the structural breaks, the first one basically corresponds to the date of the exchange rate regime reform, whereas the second one failed to confirm the advent of the financial crisis. Because the timing of the breaks may be data dependent, I keep the dates of breaks exogenously determined under the guidance of historical facts. As for the result of the unit root of the LS test, the fact that the null cannot be rejected is possibly due to the aforementioned low power of the test when the nonlinearity is not specified in the alternative.[26]

11.6.2 AR versus TAR

Although the TAR model has theoretical support, it is nevertheless worth searching for its empirical support by testing the existence of threshold-type nonlinearity before its estimation. Can linearity be rejected? Even in that case, is the outlined TAR model well specified? The result of M-TAR does not give a clear-cut answer, as the rejection of the unit-root null does not imply that the real data definitely follow the process of M-TAR, notably because the nonlinear alternative could be misspecified. To answer these questions, I applied several widely used linearity tests: the F-test of Tsay (1989), the sup-LM test of Hansen

(1996), and a simulation-based log-likelihood ratio test (LLR test) as the tests of specification for the TAR model.

For the first two ready-to-wear tests, fitting an AR(k) model (k is the kth of lags) for each subsample is needed to ensure that the residuals contain no serial correlation. Then these two tests are applied to the residuals; the results are reported in table 11.4. Tsay's test rejects the linearity only for the corrected series of third period, and Hansen's test only for the first period. I provide two main possible explanations for this failure of nonrejecting the linear null: first, these two tests assume homoskedastic errors, which are evidently not the case for my samples. Second, failing to reject the linearity may be explained by the nonstationarity of volatility of the specified linear model, that is, the sum of and superior to 1 (see the coefficients of variance equation reported in table 11.3),[27] because the nonstationarity of volatility may affect the consistency, convergence rates and asymptotic distributions of the coefficients. Turning on the LLR test, the linearity is rejected at 5 percent but only for the first subperiod (see the LLR test in table 11.4).[28] In view of the absence of the unanimous rejection of linearity, the presence of nonstationarity volatility in the linear autoregressive model, and the low power of the simulation-based LLR test for discerning the competing models, I focus on the specified TAR model and compare with its linear counterpart for a balanced interpretation.

Following the method described in subsection 11.4.2, I estimate the threshold and the TAR model using the same specification of the AR-GARCH model. When some coefficients are nonsignificant, I impose some restrictions on the fitted models and re-estimate them. The results are reported in table 11.5.

11.6.3 Discussion

Here I discuss the results of the estimation for each subperiod. The estimated upper threshold indicates the de facto extent of capital controls, and the autoregressive parameter measures the speed of convergence to the zero-profit point under the force of arbitrage. Before the abandonment of the dollar peg of RMB in July 2005, the threshold estimated is about 200 base points, which approximates its unconditional mean (367 points), and it indicates the extent of capital controls and pure transaction costs. Below the threshold, the yield differential follows a random walk. When lying above, it reverts to the threshold under the force of the arbitrage but with a low speed (half-life of 36 days). The AR model reports a shorter half-life (HL) of 21 days. Both

Table 11.3
Autoregressive model with asymmetric GARCH effect

| Period | Augmented AR(1) with asymmetric GARCH(1, 1) | | | | | | | | Ljung–Box Q-statistic | |
	C_0	ρ	HL	k	α_0	α_1	λ_1	γ_1	SR	SSR
1st	9.211 (0.000)	-0.033 (0.002)	20.66	0	28.349 (0.006)	0.479 (0.000)	0.742 (0.000)	-0.329 (0.000)	0.34[10] 0.87[20]	0.17[10] 0.21[20]
2nd	8.054 (0.005)	-0.049 (0.001)	13.80	1	347.656 (0.006)	0.180 (0.006)	0.689 (0.000)	-0.149 (0.026)	0.21[10] 0.21[20]	0.19[10] 0.28[20]
3rd	0	-0.015 (0.015)	45.86	1	-0.865 (0.734)	0.137 (0.000)	0.915 (0.000)	-0.085 (0.002)	0.57[10] 0.89[20]	0.99[10] 0.997[20]
3rd[c]	15.265 (0.000)	-0.069 (0.015)	9.69	1	706.645 (0.003)	0.298 (0.000)	0.707 (0.000)	-0.160 (0.015)	0.74[10] 0.48[20]	0.80[10] 0.98[20]

Estimated equation

$$\Delta y_t = C_0 + \rho y_{t-1} + \sum_{j=1}^{k} \varphi_j \Delta y_{t-j} + \varepsilon_t$$

$$\sigma_t^2 = \alpha_0 + \alpha_1 \varepsilon_{t-1}^2 + \lambda_j \sigma_{t-1}^2 + \gamma_1 \varepsilon_{t-1}^2 I_{t-1} \qquad I_{t-1} = 1 \text{ if } \varepsilon_{t-1} < 0$$

$$I_{t-1} = 0 \text{ otherwise}$$

Notes: SR (SSR) denotes standardized residual (squared standardized residual). The half-life (HF) is calc,ated as $\ln(0.5)/\ln(1+\rho^{out})$. The figures in squared brackets denote the numbers of autocorrelations in SR(SSR). There is no augmented term in the mean equation when $k = 0$. γ_1 measures the asymmetric effect of residuals on the variance.

Table 11.4
Nonlinearity tests

Period	Lag(n)			Tsay's TAR-F		Hansen's sup-LM			LLR		
1st	1, 4, 6			1.544 (0.188)		26.874*** (0.004)			9.511** (0.047)		
2nd	1,2			0.366 (0.777)		11.966 (0.189)			4.190 (0.433)		
3rd[c]	1			3.559** (0.029)		9.779 (0.123)			4.169 (0.314)		
Fra.	Min.	1%	5%	10%	25%	50%	75%	90%	95%	99%	Max.
1st	0.41	0.69	1.22	1.52	2.45	3.87	5.99	8.06	9.37	13.68	19.82
2nd	0.79	0.98	1.50	1.81	2.69	3.79	5.65	7.75	9.25	13.00	36.39
3rd[c]	0.10	0.47	0.90	1.17	1.80	2.98	4.79	7.04	8.41	11.05	12.75

Notes: AR models are fitted with different lags for removing any serial correlation in the data, then TAR-F and sup-LM tests are applied to the residual series of the model. For sup-LM test, heteroscedasticity-consistent estimates are used for calculating the standard errors. Bootstrapped p-value (with 2,000 draws) are calculated and shown in parenthesis. Delay parameter d is set to 1. *, **, and *** denote significance at the 10, 5, and 1 percent levels, respectively. The fractiles (Fra.) of LLR test statistics are tabulated, based on 600 simulations.

of them show a long HL of mean reversion and the nonstationary volatility, allowing some conclusions to be drawn about the market's segmentation and the effectiveness of the capital controls. The nonstationary volatility is possibly due to the short period of the data. In other words, as the mean reversion is long, the conditional variance did not end the reverting cycle during the short time of the first subperiod.[29] Actually, since 2002, the expectation of the revaluation has been reinforced, along with the leap of current account surplus and the accumulation of the US dollar as the foreign exchange reserve, and the forward premium has increased gradually. However, the dollar peg was well maintained until the reform (see Ma and McCauley 2011). Meanwhile the evolution of RMB onshore interest rate did not follow, and it even ran in the opposite direction of the US Libor, indicating an independence of monetary policy (see figure 11.4). In this context the fixed exchange rate regime is maintained with the effective restrictions on cross-border capital flows, which are represented by the persistent and volatile yield differential.

After the introduction of the new managed float regime in July 2005, the threshold estimated by the TAR model has, contrary to what was expected, increased to about 270 base points, even exceeding its reduced

Table 11.5
Augmented threshold autoregressive model with GARCH effect

Period	TAR(2, k, d)						GARCH(1, 1) effect				Ljung–Box Q-statistic	
		c^{up}	c^{in}	ρ^{out}	ρ^{in}	HL	k	α_0	α_1	λ_1	γ_1	SR	SSR
1st	U	199.71	-4.578 (0.671)	-0.019 (0.055)	0.069 (0.276)	36.13	0	19.7 (0.025)	0.469 (0.000)	0.750 (0.000)	-0.310 (0.000)	0.45[10] 0.91[20]	0.23[10] 0.25[20]
	R		0	-0.019 (0.056)	0.042 (0.000)	36.13	0	20.1 (0.029)	0.468 (0.000)	0.751 (0.000)	-0.309 (0.000)	0.46[10] 0.91[20]	0.22[10] 0.26[20]
2nd	U	271.84	7.685 (0.007)	-0.204 (0.007)	-0.049 (0.021)	3.04	1	340.5 (0.010)	0.170 (0.007)	0.692 (0.000)	-0.134 (0.037)	0.27[10] 0.24[20]	0.14[10] 0.28[20]
	R		0	-0.212 (0.000)	0	2.91	1	314.3 (0.053)	0.116 (0.018)	0.701 (0.000)	0	0.17[10] 0.09[20]	0.22[10] 0.29[20]
3rd[c]	U	314.62	13.430 (0.003)	-0.170 (0.000)	-0.056 (0.023)	3.72	1	721.0 (0.002)	0.299 (0.000)	0.702 (0.000)	-0.161 (0.016)	0.75[10] 0.55[20]	0.86[10] 0.99[20]
	R		0	-0.162 (0.000)	0	3.92	1	761.63 (0.002)	0.240 (0.000)	0.680 (0.000)	0	0.75[10] 0.31[20]	0.84[10] 0.98[20]

Estimated equations

$$\Delta y_t = \rho^{out}(y_{t-1} - c^{up}) + \sum_{j=1}^{k} \Delta y_{t-j} + \varepsilon_t \qquad \text{if } y_{t-d} > c^{up}$$

$$\Delta y_t = \rho^{in} y_{t-1} + \sum_{j=1}^{k} \varphi_j \Delta y_{t-j} + \varepsilon_t \qquad \text{if } y_{t-d} \leq c^{up}$$

$$\sigma_t^2 = \alpha_0 + \alpha_1 \varepsilon_{t-1}^2 + \lambda_1 \sigma_{t-1}^2 + \gamma_1 \varepsilon_{t-1}^2 I_{t-1}$$

$y_{t-d} \leq c^{up}$ if $\varepsilon_{t-1} < 0$, $I_{t-1} = 0$ otherwise

Notes: Figures in parentheses denote marginal significance levels of the estimated parameters. Figures in squared brackets denote the numbers of autocorrelations in SR(SSR). SR, SSR, and HL are as defined above. U(R) denotes unrestricted (restricted) model. There is no augmented term in the mean equation when $k = 0$. The threshold delay (d) is set to 1.

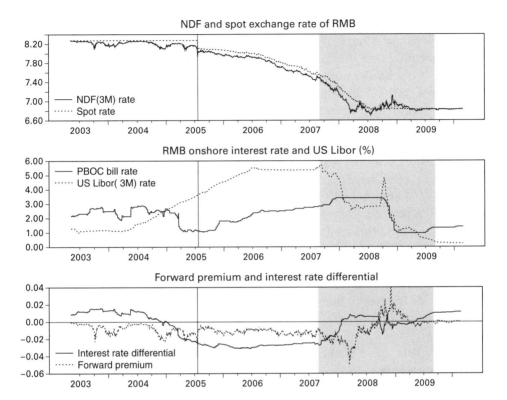

Figure 11.4
Components of CIP. Sources: Datastream, WM/Reuters, and author's calculations (daily data).

unconditional mean. Nevertheless, a HL of only 3 days indicates a more unified and active monetary and exchange market where the unexploited profits are quickly reduced by arbitrage to the level of the threshold once the yield differential exceeds it. In contrast to the TAR model, the linear AR reports a much longer HL (about 14 days), which is lower compared to the one of the first subperiod. The significant constant term in the differenced mean equation indicates a positive trend in the level of the yield differential. It means that the extent of the de facto capital control increases over time. Moreover, even if the conditional variance persists, the volatility becomes stationary according to both models, providing more evidence of the increased liquidity of this market.

Here I provide some possible explanations for the increased threshold and the far shorter HL. On one side, the higher threshold implies that during this subperiod the capital controls are still binding and that the extent of controls is even strengthened. This is mainly due to some policy measures introduced later in this subperiod to stem the short-term cross-border financial activities; one such measure is the guideline issued by SAFE in October 2006 on restricting mainland entities' participation in NDF market. This is in response to the participation of some mainland entities, mainly corporations for hedging purposes, in arbitrage between markets to exploit price differences. This result is consistent with the explanation that for the initial episode of the new regime, considered a transitional phase, the narrowing of the onshore and offshore RMB yield differential is a chosen policy outcome rather than as the waning effectiveness of the capital controls interpreted by market observers (see Ma and McCauley 2008), which is used to interpret the much lowered unconditional mean after the regime change. On the other side, the quick mean-reverting process (or a shorter HL) implies that once the unexploited profit appears and exceeds the transaction costs and risk associated with capital controls, the active arbitrage funds take the risks and assume the costs to obtain the excess portion of the profit, even despite the binding capital controls. This action reduces quickly the yield differential to the level of the threshold.

There is a considerable but well-managed appreciation of RMB against the dollar and a clear comovement between the NDF and the spot rate. However, what is less known is that it was managed against a basket of trading partner currencies, with a moderate (2 percent per annum) upward crawling and within narrow (±2 percent) bands (Ma and McCauley 2011).[30] Meanwhile a persistent and sizable gap between the RMB onshore rate and the US Libor rate has been maintained, despite the similar evolutionary tendency, suggesting that Chinese monetary authorities could still use independent domestic policy in an effort to prevent the economy from overheating and curb accelerating inflation. The PBOC has increased the lending rates five times during this period. All of these facts in 2007 corroborate the effectiveness of capital controls.

Capital Control since the Financial Crisis   Entering into a period of turbulence, the upward and downward spirals of the yield differential could not be fully explained by the eventual strengthening of capital controls implemented by the Chinese government. A look at both the countries with high financial integration (figure 11.3) and some Asian economies with NDF markets (figure 11.2) reveals some common factor(s) in the abnormal behavior of the yield differentials.

For those major currencies, the appearance and even the persistence of deviation from CIP during periods of uncertainty and turmoil are not a recent story (e.g., Taylor 1989). However, the liquidity risk caused by the US dollar funding shortage of non–US institutions and the significantly increased counterparty risk have been documented as the main reasons for the deviation of CIP in the recent turmoil. Furthermore the dollar Libor has been reported to have underestimated the funding costs that European financial institutions actually faced, as the measurement error of the true dollar funding costs over the period could have increased and therefore been misleading (e.g., Baba et al. 2008; Baba and Packer 2009). After the bankruptcy of Lehman Brothers, the dollar liquidity problem for European banks deepened and translated into a phenomenon of global dollar shortage.

In this context it is possible to assume that the impact of the financial turmoil on the evolution of yield differentials can be represented by a few latent common factors mentioned above, especially the liquidity risk (e.g., Baba and Packer 2009; Levy Yeyati et al. 2009; Fong et al. 2010). Here I use factor analysis based on a principal component approach to estimate this latent factor for six Asian economies owing the NDF market.[31] The results are reported in table 11.6 and table 11.7.[32] I then regress the raw data of yield differential of the third period over the first factor index, which measures the increased liquidity risk associated with the financial crisis. The residual net of this common factor is the "deflated series," with which the alternatives models are estimated and the hypothesis testing is implemented.

These corrected yield differentials are plotted in figure 11.1, accompanied by the raw series of the whole sample. Its volatility (the standard deviation) is largely reduced to half of the one computed with the original data but is still higher than the first two subperiods. During the period of turbulence, the yield differentials are mean reverting, as shown in the results of the UR tests (see the last row of table 11.1). An HL of about 10 days (shorter than the second subperiod) estimated by the linear AR model confirms this result; even this model reports a nonstationary volatility (see table 11.3). In contrast with the model estimated using the original data of the period of turmoil, the HL are much shorter once the volatility is deflated. In other words, when the dollar funding shortage triggers the lack of liquidity; the liquidity risk premium incurs extra volatility, makes the mean-reverting process

Table 11.6
Factor analysis with principal component approach (1)

Factor	Eigenvalue	Difference	Proportion	Cumulative
Factor1	**2.80195**	**1.72728**	**0.4670**	**0.4670**
Factor2	**1.07467**	**0.15833**	**0.1791**	**0.6461**
Factor3	0.91634	0.33062	0.1527	0.7988
Factor4	0.58572	0.13863	0.0976	0.8964
Factor5	0.44709	0.27286	0.0745	0.9710
Factor6	0.17423	—	0.0290	1.0000

Variable	Factor1	Factor2	Uniqueness
twd	0.5044	0.3483	0.6243
krw	−0.7440	0.3594	0.3174
php	−0.7525	−0.0886	0.4258
idr	−0.3556	0.8333	0.1792
inr	0.7347	0.0234	0.4596
cny	0.8726	0.3486	0.1170

Note: *hkd, twd, krw, php, idr, inr*, and *cny* denote the currency of Hong Kong, Taiwan, South Korea, Philippines, Indonesia, India, and China mainland, respectively.

Table 11.7
Factor analysis with principal component approach (2)

Factor	Eigenvalue	Difference	Proportion	Cumulative
Factor1	**1.86160**	**1.03497**	**0.6205**	**0.6205**
Factor2	0.82663	0.51485	0.2755	0.8961
Factor3	0.31178	—	0.1039	1.0000

Variable	Factor1	Uniqueness
twd	0.7035	0.5050
inr	0.7349	0.4599
cny	0.9091	0.1735

much slower, and consequently creates the illusion that the longer HL reflects tighter and more effective capital controls, which may not exist. Therefore the comparison between the HL estimated with raw series and that of corrected series shows that the longer HL induced by liquidity risk or some other factor during the period of turbulence makes the interpretation of HL by the effectiveness of the capital controls infeasible.

Our TAR model provides the different results: the threshold has increased to 315 basis points (see table 11.5) and the HL (about 4 days) is slightly extended, indicating that the extent of the de facto capital control has been strengthened. For instance, in August 2008 the issued regulation requires companies with FDI to submit the certified reports of their capital denominated in foreign currency, aiming to limit the inflows of "hot money" via the aforementioned FDI channels. As for the HL, estimated either by AR or TAR model, it changes only slightly relative to that of the second subperiod, implying that the markets are more and gradually integrated with the advent of new currency regime, even if they were partly affected by the financial turbulence.

In fact, with the eruption of financial turmoil and the continual dollar depreciation against most major currencies, there has been more Western short-term capital pursuing high earnings flow into emerging Asian markets, causing the appreciation of these Asian currencies, and the expectation of a further and more rapid appreciation of the RMB than what the spot rate actually had. This increases the forward discount, and there is even expectation of depreciation at the end of 2008 when the PBOC returns to the dollar peg as a special measure during the financial turmoil. The fluctuation of NDF makes the forward premium and consequently the RMB yield differential volatile. Even the bilateral spot exchange rate of RMB with the US dollar was stabilized, its nominal effective rate with trading partners is not well managed and more volatile—contrary to what the Chinese monetary authority committed to do with the regime of managing float—than the previous period during which the nominal effective rate crawled gradually within a narrow band, as the currencies composing the targeted currency basket of RMB went through appreciation and depreciation against the US dollar during the turmoil.[33] On the other side, in the monetary market, the interest gap was reduced (middle panel of figure 11.4) to approach the interest parity after the failure of Lehman Brothers. To attenuate the shock on the domestic economy and stimulate the domestic consumption, the Chinese monetary authority has adopted an expansionary monetary policy, decreasing the benchmark deposit and lending rate five times and the deposit reserve requirement ratio four times since September 2008 (until October 2010). This is in line with the purpose of the US Federal Reserve to provide the liquidity to the market. The introduction of the RMB currency swap market in August 2008 and that of the foreign exchange dealer system into the interbank foreign exchange market in October of the same year can be interpreted as a commitment of the Chinese government to further develop and deepen the foreign exchange market and to increase the liquidity of the associated derivatives market, which is an important condition to facilitate the outward foreign investment and to compensate the inflows of hot money. This could explain the rapid reversion to the threshold when excessive profit emerged in the market. Since the quick recovery of Chinese economic growth, the interest rate was moderately adjusted upward, resulting in a persistent gap with the US Libor. In sum, it was evident that during the financial turmoil the de facto intensification of capital controls translated into an increased threshold. Also evident was the effectiveness of the capital controls, as the speed of adjustment (the HL) was slightly reduced. However, despite this slower adjustment, it is still much quicker than during the period of the dollar peg, which implies that the development of a more liquid foreign exchange market is not fully hindered by the financial turbulences.

11.6.4   Robustness Check

Conditional on De jure Capital Controls   Government policies restricting capital flows can never be perfectly implemented because individuals and firms always find ways to circumvent regulations when higher returns are available. Thus, even if the legal restrictions remain unchanged, the measure of de jure capital controls may not capture the degree or the effectiveness of their enforcement, which can change over time (Kose et al. 2006). Because capital control policies may also change during the sample period, it is better to control this variable to check for their ineffectiveness. Specifically, the de jure capital control relaxation of some extent allows a more open capital account and may reduce the yield differential or the threshold, while it does not mean a noneffective capital control. Alternative (de jure) capital control indexes are constructed to represent the evolution of the policy and are widely used in empirical studies (Cheung et al. 2006; Cheung and Qian 2011).[34] One incompatibility of these indexes, let alone their intrinsic drawbacks when constructed, is that they are time-invariant during the sample period I use, whereas the degree of capital control appears not to be constant.[35] Accordingly, I assume in this chapter that China's overall de jure degree of capital control period is constant during the sample period and estimate the de facto capital control intensity represented by the estimated threshold for each subperiod under this hypothesis.

Conditional on Exchange Rate Expectation   The NDF rates are determined outside China in the deep, liquid offshore market. They are the results of the interplay between market forces and may be interpreted as a market proxy for the expected future Chinese RMB exchange rate (Cheung and Qian 2011).[36] In this context the NDF-implied interest yield differential also depends on the exchange rate expectations. If the expectation reverses, the implied offshore RMB interest rate and consequently the yield differential measuring the degree of capital control may change equally without any change in capital control policy. Following Cheung and Qian (2011), I calculate the deviation from CIP using the RMB deliverable forward rate of Chinese onshore market, which is developed recently and rapidly after the reform of exchange rate regime in 2005 but remains shallow and strictly regulated. The advantage of this onshore rate is that its pricing is mainly influenced by the CIP (see Peng et al. 2007). With this less expectation-driven rate, I re-estimated the outlined TAR model as a robustness check.[37]

The calculated covered interest deviation shows a similar pattern as the yield differential derived with NDF, especially for the period of turmoil, but both the level and the volatility are significantly reduced in this case. What is entirely different is that, during the subperiod after the 2005 reform and before financial turmoil, this deviation fluctuated around zero. A much lower estimated threshold (43 versus 272 estimated with NDF) distinguishes two stationary regimes for which the deviations from CIP are mean reversing. More surprisingly, the adjustment to the threshold is more rapid for the nonarbitrage regime, with a HL of only 1.2 days relative to 5.2 days of the arbitrage regime. However, this last result is counterintuitive and is not easy to interpret. In contrast, the linear specification produces a HL of 3.6 days, which is in the neighborhood of that estimated with NDF series.

For the period of turmoil, the estimated threshold is about 83 basis points, almost double relative to the previous subperiod. However, the quicker adjustment pattern in the nonarbitrage regime during the second subperiod has been sustained until the period of crisis. Moreover the adjustments to the threshold in both regimes have slowed correspondingly (with HL of 10.7 and 2.3, respectively). The linear estimation of HL shows a lower speed of adjustment to zero than its counterpart in the quiet subperiod (about 17 days). Estimated with NDF, the linear (TAR) HL is 10 days (4 days).

In summary, the use of the onshore forward rate of RMB (which is less influenced by the expectations of currency appreciation or depreciation) reduces both the level and the volatility of deviation (or yield differential) from CIP. It also decreases the thresholds that indicate the de facto degree of capital control. However, the threshold is found increasing during the period of financial turmoil and is similar to the result obtained using the NDF-based TAR model, which partly confirms the robustness of our conclusion. As for the threshold gap between the onshore forward-based and NDF-based estimations, it may be due to the understatement of the deviation from CIP and consequently the intensity of capital control by using onshore forward rate. Despite the pricing based on CIP; the onshore forward market is shallow relative to the NDF market because of the "real demand principle" and restrictive regulations on participants (Peng et al. 2007). Therefore the capital controls persist even if the deviation does not, as the onshore forward is less liquid and may be unrepresentative. For this reason the results from the TAR model with the NDF series are still informative and robust. After all, because the onshore forward market develops and deepens, there may be some information transmission from the CIP-based onshore forward rate to the NDF rate. It makes the NDF rate not so much expectation-driven and still acceptable for measuring the yield differential of currencies.

11.7   Concluding Remarks

This chapter proposes an assessment of the effectiveness of the capital controls in China. Using a two-regime TAR model, it studies the RMB interest yield differential between the onshore rate and the NDF-implied offshore rate for the period from mid-2003 to the beginning of 2010. With the threshold and half-life estimated for each subperiod, I find that the de facto intensity of capital controls increases over time, as reflected by the rising threshold of arbitrage, even during the period of financial crisis. When excessive profits appear, the time of adjustment toward the threshold measuring the intensity of capital controls and transaction costs is reduced after the abandonment of the RMB's dollar peg, as the force of arbitrage plays a more important role in a more liquid forward foreign exchange market. The eruption of the financial crisis did not fully interrupt this process; even it inflates the yield differential with both increased liquidity risk and dollar funding shortage. Moreover a slightly lower speed of adjustment to the threshold implies that the capital controls are effective in this context.

The PBOC announced on June 19, 2010, the abandonment of the dollar peg that it adopted as a "special measure" to deal with the period of financial turbulence and the re-switching to a managed floating regime with reference to a basket of currencies. This announcement confirms the end of the anticipation of a stable RMB-dollar rate by the market. If the Chinese monetary authority commits to implement this managed float regime, as it did from mid-2006 to mid-2008, more developed forward and derivatives markets as well as more open capital accounts seem needed and can thus facilitate the internationalization of the RMB. Because the option of lifting the capital controls to allow the full internationalization of the RMB is less possible (Cheung et al. 2011), the issue of how the implementation of the capital controls will be done is challenging and promising.

Notes

This work was supported by *Ile-de-France*. Part of the chapter was written when the author was PhD candidate at University of Paris Nanterre and was research assistant at CEPII research center where the suggestions and help of Director Agnès Bénassy-Quéré are gratefully acknowledged. I thank Michel Aglietta, Jung-Hyun Ahn, Raphaelle Bellando, Sophie Béreau, Mélika Ben Salem, Bertrand Blancheton, Régis Breton, Changsheng Chen, Chia-Shang J. Chu, Gilbert Colletaz, Anne-Laure Delatte, Jin-Chuan Duan, Eric Girardin, Jean-Yves Gnabo, Bertrand Gobillard, Bruce E. Hansen, Sébastien Laurent, David G. Mayes, Valérie Mignon, Nikolay Nenovsky, Yamina Tadjeddine, and Wing Thye Woo, especially Vincent Bignon, for their valuable and detailed comments. I thank specially the participants of the CESifo Venice Summer Institute workshop on "The Evolving Role of China in the Global Economy," my discussant Alessandro Rebucci, Bertrand Candelon, Yin-Wong Cheung, Menzie Chinn, Guonan Ma, Robert McCauley, Xingwang Qian, and Tara Sinclair for their constructive suggestions. Xingwang is acknowledged for providing some data. I also thank participants of the CERC-CCER Conference, 7th International Conference on the Chinese Economy, University of Orléans LEO seminar, 27th Symposium on Money, Banking and Finance, 21st CEA conference, and CEPII seminair. I thank referees for their valuable comments. The usual disclaimer applies.

1. Other methods defining capital mobility include Feldstein–Horioka definition, real interest parity, uncovered interest parity.

2. Transaction costs in broad sense. Studies in the literature attempted to rationalize this departure in terms of transactions costs (e.g., Branson 1969; Frenkel and Levich 1975, 1977); capital market imperfection (e.g., Frenkel 1973); capital controls (e.g., Otani and Tiwari 1981); data imperfection or mismatch (e.g., Taylor 1987, 1989).

3. Like standard forward contracts, NDF contracts fix exchange rates for a future date. However, there is no delivery of the underlying foreign currency. Instead, the net US dollar is settled with a compensating payment made or due based upon the difference between the NDF contract rate and the exchange rate prevailing at maturity. For recent development of Asian NDF markets and specifically that of RMB NDF market, see Ma et al. (2004) and Peng et al. (2007).

4. An Alternative way to investigate the effect of the capital controls is to calculate the price differential of RMB exchange rate from CIP, that is, assume that RMB has same interest rate in both the onshore and the offshore markets.

5. See, for example, Taylor and Tchernykh-Branson (2004) for the multivariate regression analysis.

6. Higher convergence speed implies a quicker convergence to CIP and hence tighter financial integration.

7. By estimating a band-TAR model, Peel and Taylor (2002) have supported the conjecture of Keynes and Einzig that deviations from CIP in the interwar period did not tend to be arbitraged at all until they were of the order of fifty basis points.

8. A standard model with transportation costs implies that real exchange rates should follow a band threshold model in which the process is a random walk within the band and a mean reversion outside it.

9. To test the law of one price and to shed some light on the international financial integration, Levy Yeyati et al. (2009) estimate an augmented band-TAR model with generalized autoregressive conditional heteroskedastic (GARCH) effect for the cross-market premium of the stock price.

10. A nonarbitrage band exists for small deviations from the CIP. The upper and the lower thresholds are determined by intensity of the capital controls and transaction costs.

11. Tsay (1989) proposed a graphical approach for locating the values of the thresholds and the number of the regimes. Alternatively, Hansen (1999) has generalized the sup-LR test and sequential least-squares estimations to the SETAR models with more than two regimes.

12. They estimate a single-threshold model for the deviation from the CIP of Thai baht, Indonesian rupiah, Philippine peso, Singapore dollar, Korean won, and Taiwan dollar, with the covered interest arbitrage involving the arbitrage along the term structure.

13. Once the data allow, with longer time span, the asymmetric band-TAR model could be estimated in the same way, by adding another dimension in the grid search of the thresholds that I discuss later in this subsection.

14. When the threshold variable for the grid search is the lagged value of the dependent variable with delay d (here $d = 1$), the TAR model is called self-exciting TAR or SETAR.

The band-TAR model estimated in this chapter is an extended SETAR model with some restrictions. I simply use TAR hereafter.

15. If the estimated coefficient of ρ^{in} is not significant (as can be expected based on the assumption that the yield differentials follow a random walk within the band), a restricted model can be estimated by imposing this coefficient to zero.

16. In other words, here the threshold effect is assumed to exist only in the mean equation. See, for example, Obstfeld and Taylor (1997) and Taylor and Tchernykh-Branson (2004), for the cases where the variance is assumed different for each regime, and Glosten et al. (1993), for a threshold (or asymmetric) volatility (GARCH) model. Another extension is to relax the assumption of same error terms and same conditional variance in the different regimes, and to specify a model with threshold effect in both the mean and the variance equations.

17. Generally, lower orders such as (1, 1), (1, 2), and (2, 1) are adopted in applications since higher orders models are difficult to estimate and to interpret.

18. Maximizing this ratio equals the maximization of the log-likelihood function of the TAR alternative mentioned earlier. To ensure an adequate number of observations on each side of the threshold (or in each threshold space), here I exclude the highest 15 percent and the lowest 15 percent values of the threshold variable from the grid search, as widely implemented in practice.

19. For example, 600 simulations are generated for the fitted model. I start each simulation with $y_{-b} = 0$, end at, and then discard the first b (set to 50) to avoid the initial value bias.

20. Hansen (1999) provides an alternative simulation approach based on bootstrapping, instead of other possible forms of distribution, such as the Student-t distribution, the generalized error distribution (GED), and the skewed-Student distribution. However, to simulate with bootstrapping an augmented AR(1) model with the GARCH effect complicates the traditional Monte Carlo procedure and is very time-consuming. Hence I leave it for the future research, and simply use, in this chapter, the test of specification based on the aforementioned simulation, and with caution when the TAR alternative is rejected.

21. For the reason why these proxies are chosen and for a detailed description of their characteristics, see, for example, Ma and McCauley (2008).

22. However, several authors have doubts about the real effect of this change (e.g., see Goldstein and Lardy 2006).

23. For the discussion on the low power of the traditional unit-root tests in the presence of asymmetric adjustment, see, for example, Enders and Granger (1998).

24. Using Monte Carlo experiment, Choi and Moh (2007) showed that the M-TAR test and the Inf–t test due to Park and Shintani (2005) outperform the others, and that they have reasonable power of discerning the unit root.

25. Alternatively, Hutchison et al. (2009) employ the method suggested by Bai and Perron (1998) to detect the structural changes. I do not adopt this approach because of the technical constraint on the sample size (less than 500 observations) of their GAUSS code.

26. The construction of an UR test with the nonlinear alternative capable of detecting the structural breaks is expected for the future study, which is out of scope of this chapter.

27. In my case, the ARCH and the GARCH effect are significant for all subsamples, while the volatility is stationary only in the second subsample.

28. As discussed in section 11.4.2, because of the low power of LLR test, the probability with which the TAR model is mistakenly rejected is high.

29. The author acknowledges Jin-Chuan Duan for this point. The short sample is due to the data availability of the PBOC bill rate. When I use China Interbank Offered Rate (Chibor) as the proxy of onshore interest rate, I observe the stationary volatility. Since the central bank bill rate is more liquid and a better proxy for the onshore interest rate than the Chibor, I keep using this rate to estimate my TAR model for all three subperiods.

30. The period of this stable managed float regime spans from June 2006 to May 2008.

31. In the offshore markets like Hong Kong and Singapore where the Asian NDF transactions are highly active, there are less conterparty risk since the NDF contracts do not entail currency delivery of the notional amounts at the maturity.

32. Two common factors are retained (boldface figures in upper panel of table 11.6) based on Kaiser criterion which drops all components with eigenvalues less than 1. Varimax rotation is then used to differentiate the original variables by extracted factor. Each factor will tend to have either large or small loadings of any particular variable, in our case the first factor (I assume it as the liquidity risk) has large positive loadings on *twd*, *inr*, and *cny* (see lower panel of table 11.6). I restart the factor analysis only on these three variables, and obtain the index of this first common factor (see table 11.7).

33. With standard regression, graphical analysis and error-correction model, Ma and McCauley (2011) find that from mid-2006 to mid-2008, RMB strengthened gradually against trading partners' currencies. This process was interrupted by the financial crisis, resulting in a re-peg to the US dollar.

34. Cheung and Qian (2011) include a dummy variable to take into account the change of capital control policy when studying the deviation from the covered interest parity between China and the United States. It captures the shift of China's policy bias from tightening to loosening and from primarily controlling outflow to controlling both inflows and outflows. It is assigned a value of +1 for the observations before September 2001, when China tightened capital outflow; a value 0 for the observations between September 2001 and October 2002, when it is deemed as a transition period; and a value −1 for the observations after October 2002, when Chinese authorities started to encourage or promote capital outflow.

35. In Cheung and Qian (2011), no extra dummy variable that captures the timing of China's capital control policy changes has been introduced after October 2002; China's financial openness index of Chinn and Ito (2008) is constant from 1993.

36. The pricing of the RMB NDF is proved not tied to its financial fundamentals (Peng et al. 2007).

37. Since the onshore market-based forward rate did not exist before the reform of 2005, I estimate only for the second and the third subperiods. Aforementioned statistical tests are applied to this deviation, with the results allowing us to estimate the TAR model. These results are not reported because of limit of space.

References

Aliber, R. Z. 1973. The interest rate parity theorem: A reinterpretation. *Journal of Political Economy* 81 (6): 1451–59.

Baba, N., F. Packer, and T. Nagano. 2008. The spillover of money market turbulence to FX and cross-currency swap markets. *BIS Quarterly Review* (March): 73–86.

Baba, N., and F. Packer. 2009. Interpreting deviations from covered interest parity during the financial market turmoil of 2007–08. *Journal of Banking and Finance* 33 (11): 1953–62.

Bai, J., and P. Perron. 1998. Estimating and testing linear models with multiple structural changes. *Econometrica: Journal of the Econometric Society* 66 (1): 47–78.

Bec, F., M. Ben Salem, and M. Carrasco. 2004. Tests for unit-root versus threshold specification with an application to the purchasing power parity relationship. *Journal of Business and Economic Statistics* 22: 382–95.

Branson, W. H. 1969. The minimum covered interest differential needed for international arbitrage activity. *Journal of Political Economy* 77 (6):1028–35.

Cheung, Y. W., M. D. Chinn, and E. Fujii. 2006. The Chinese economies in global context: The integration process and its determinants. *Journal of the Japanese and International Economies* 20 (1): 128–53.

Cheung, Y. W., G. Ma, and R. N. McCauley. 2011. Renminbising China's foreign assets. *Pacific Economic Review* 16 (1): 1–17.

Cheung, Y. W., and X. Qian. 2011. Deviations from covered interest parity: The case of China. In Y. W. Cheung, G. Ma, and V. Kakkar, eds., *The Evolving Role of Asia in Global Finance*. Bradford, UK: Emerald Group Publishing, 369–86.

Chinn, M. D., and H. Ito. 2008. A new measure of financial openness. *Journal of Comparative Policy Analysis: Research and Practice* 10 (3): 309–22.

Choi, C. Y., and Y. K. Moh. 2007. How useful are tests for unit-root in distinguishing unit-root processes from stationary but non-linear processes. *Econometrics Journal* 10: 82–112.

Dooley, M. P., and P. Isard. 1980. Capital controls, political risk, and deviations from interest-rate parity. *Journal of Political Economy* 88 (2): 370–84.

Enders, W., and C. W. J. Granger. 1998. Unit-root tests and asymmetric adjustment with an example using the term structure of interest rates. *Journal of Business and Economic Statistics* 16 (3): 304–11.

Fong, W. M., G. Valente, and J. K. Fung. 2010. Covered interest arbitrage profits: The role of liquidity and credit risk. *Journal of Banking and Finance* 34 (5): 1098–1107.

Frankel, J. A. 1992. Measuring international capital mobility: A review. *American Economic Review* 82 (2): 197–202.

Frenkel, J. A. 1973. Elasticities and the interest parity theory. *Journal of Political Economy* 81 (3): 741–47.

Frenkel, J. A., and R. M. Levich. 1975. Covered interest arbitrage: Unexploited profits? *Journal of Political Economy* 83 (2): 325–38.

Frenkel, J. A., and R. M. Levich. 1977. Transaction costs and interest arbitrage: Tranquil versus turbulent periods. *Journal of Political Economy* 85 (6): 1209–26.

Glosten, L. R., R. Jagannathan, and D. E. Runkle. 1993. On the relation between the expected value and the volatility of the nominal excess return on stocks. *Journal of Finance* 48 (5): 1779–1801.

Goldstein, M., and N. Lardy. 2006. China's exchange rate policy dilemma. *American Economic Review* 96 (2): 422–26.

Hansen, B. E. 1996. Inference when a nuisance parameter is not identified under the null hypothesis. *Econometrica: Journal of the Econometric Society* 64 (2): 413–30.

Hansen, B. E. 1999. Testing for linearity. *Journal of Economic Surveys* 13 (5): 551–76.

Holmes, M. J. 2001. New evidence on real exchange rate stationarity and purchasing power parity in less developed countries. *Journal of Macroeconomics* 23 (4): 601–14.

Hutchison, M., J. Kendall, G. K. Pasricha, and N. Singh. 2010. Indian capital control liberalization: Evidence from NDF markets. MPRA Working Paper 21771. University Library of Munich, Germany.

International Monetary Fund. 2000. Capital controls: Country experiences with their use and liberalization. Occasional Paper 190. IMF, Washington, DC.

Ito, T. 1987. Capital controls and covered interest parity. Working Paper 1187. NBER, Cambridge, MA.

Kose, M. A., E. Prasad, K. Rogoff, and S.-J. Wei. 2006. Financial globalization: A reappraisal. Working Paper 06/189. IMF, Washington, DC.

Lee, J., and M. C. Strazicich. 2003. Minimum Lagrange multiplier unit root test with two structural breaks. *Review of Economics and Statistics* 85 (4): 1082–89.

Levy Yeyati, E., S. L. Schmukler, and N. Van Horen. 2009. International financial integration through the law of one price: The role of liquidity and capital controls. *Journal of Financial Intermediation* 18 (3): 432–63.

Ma, G., C. Ho, and R. N. McCauley. 2004. The markets for non-deliverable forwards in Asian currencies. *BIS Quarterly Review* (June): 81–94.

Ma, G., and R. N. McCauley. 2008. Efficacy of China's capital controls: Evidence from price and flow data. *Pacific Economic Review* 13 (1): 104–23.

Ma, G., and R. N. McCauley. 2011. The evolving renminbi regime and implications for Asian currency stability. *Journal of the Japanese and International Economics* 25 (1): 23–38.

Ng, S., and P. Perron. 2001. Lag length selection and the construction of unit root tests with good size and power. *Econometrica: Journal of the Econometric Society* 69 (6): 1519–54.

Obstfeld, M., and A. M. Taylor. 1997. Nonlinear aspects of goods-market arbitrage and adjustment: Heckscher's commodity points revisited. *Journal of the Japanese and International Economies* 11 (4): 441–79.

Otani, I., and S. Tiwari. 1981. Capital controls and interest rate parity: The japanese experience, 1978-81. *IMF Staff Papers* 28: 793–815.

Park, J. Y., and M. Shintani. 2005. Testing for a unit root against transitional autoregressive models. Working Paper 05010. Department of Economics, Vanderbilt University.

Peel, D. A., and M. P. Taylor. 2002. Covered interest rate arbitrage in the interwar period and the Keynes–Einzig conjecture. *Journal of Money, Credit and Banking* 34 (1): 51–75.

Peng, W., C. Shu, and R. Yip. 2007. Renminbi derivatives: Recent development and issues. *China and World Economy* 15 (5): 1–17.

Taylor, M. P. 1987. Covered interest parity: A high-frequency, high-quality data study. *Economica* 54 (216): 429–38.

Taylor, M. P. 1989. Covered interest arbitrage and market turbulence. *Economic Journal* 99 (396): 376–91.

Taylor, M. P., and E. Tchernykh-Branson. 2004. Asymmetric arbitrage and default premiums between the U.S. and Russian financial markets. *IMF Staff Papers* 51 (2): 257–75.

Tong, H. 1978. On a threshold model. In C. Chen, ed., *Pattern Recognition and Signal Processing*. Alphen aan den Rijn, Netherlands: Sijthoff and Noordhoff, 575–86.

Tong, H., and K. S. Lim. 1980. Threshold autoregression, limit cycles and cyclical data. *Journal of the Royal Statistical Society, Series B. Methodological* 42 (3): 245–92.

Tsay, R. S. 1989. Testing and modeling threshold autoregressive processes. *Journal of the American Statistical Association* 84 (405): 231–40.

Zhang, X. 2003. Capital account management and its outlook in China. *China's Capital Account Liberalization: International Perspective*. BIS Working Papers, 15. Basel: Bank for International Settlements Basel, 19–24.

IV   China's FDI and Quest for Resources

12   China's Outward Direct Investment and Its Oil Quest

Xingwang Qian

12.1   Introduction

The People's Republic of China (henceforth, China) has experienced a miracle of economic development since it "opened its door" in 1978. Three decades of astonishing growth have propelled China to become the second largest economy in the world. However, behind such a miracle, there are numerous challenges and issues that China has to confront and resolve. Such issues include the shortage of domestic natural resources, a widening income inequality, the global payments imbalance, and the valuation of the Chinese currency, renminbi, among others. How China resolves those issues has profound implications for both China and the global economic outlook.

China's global quest for energy to ease the shortage of the domestic supply, particularly of oil and gas, is eliciting increased attention. Once a top oil producer in Asia, China became a net oil importer in 1993. Decades of rapid economic growth caused soaring demands for oil, resulting in China's inability to produce enough domestic oil to meet the desired consumption. The domestic oil demand–supply gap has continued to widen ever since; in 2008, 45 percent of total oil consumption in China relied on imported foreign oil (figure 12.1). Energy security therefore quickly became an imperative issue that imposed serious risks, potentially hampering China's long-term economic growth.

In response to this situation, the Chinese government has initiated and implemented a series of policy directives to secure a stable energy supply, notably the infamous "going global" policy that promotes Chinese enterprises for international operations to improve resource allocation and enhance global competitiveness (UNCTAD 2006). Under the "going global" policy, China's national oil companies[1](NOCs), perceived as "China Inc.," stepped up to invest globally and acquire

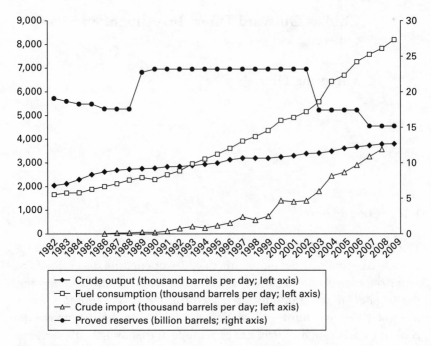

Figure 12.1
China's oil output, consumption, and imports. Source: Energy Information Administration (EIA).

oil and gas quite aggressively. As expected, billion-dollar energy deals emerged all over the world (*The Economist* 2008). For instance, Sinopec offered over $2 billion to secure the right to explore for oil in three parcels of Angola's territorial waters in 2006.[2]

China's global oil quest has consequently stirred growing uneasiness, controversy, and criticisms from the rest of the world. Some complained that China's huge and growing appetite for oil contributed to the oil price hike in 2005. Others found that China's economic arrangement with "rogue" oil states, such as Sudan, enabled China to gain an unfair advantage in the competition for both oil and regional influences. Still others believe that Chinese NOCs, shipping the equity oil[3] exclusively to China, rather than selling on the world oil market, significantly reduce the capacity of the world oil market to respond flexibly to oil demand shocks, hence jeopardizing global energy security (Downs 2000; Kreft 2006; *The Economist* 2008).

There has been a plethora of discussions and studies on China's global oil quest, its oil policies, and the implication of those oil policies (e.g., Downs 2000, 2007; Klare and Volman 2006; Lee and Shalmon 2007). Most of them, however, only provide anecdotal arguments about China's oil quest and lack formal econometric analysis on its determinants. In this study I investigate empirically the factors that determine China's outward direct investment (ODI) in the conventional oil-producing countries, including oil producers in Middle East, Africa, Russia and Central Asia, and Latin America.

In light of the hyped discussion about China's global energy quest, I specifically examine the role of energy[4] in determining China's investment in oil-producing countries. I also control for other relevant factors, including some canonical determinants (the market-seeking motives and political risks) and some China-specific determinants (the exports of oil countries to China, China's total imports of crude oil, and the infamous "going global" policy).

Further I separate the entire country sample into three subsamples—the Middle East, Africa, and other oil-producing countries—and study them individually. It is believed that the strategies that China uses to deploy its ODI are different in different regions (Lee and Shalmon 2007; Chen 2008). For example, on one hand, although the Middle East remains China's main source of oil supply and accounts for about 50 percent in 2008, China is diversifying away from it due to the prolonged instability in the area. Africa, on the other hand, has received increased oil involvement from China's ODI, especially after the implementation of the "going global" policy in 2002 (Cheung et al. 2010). In addition to the Middle East and Africa areas, China's ODI also aggressively engages in oil operations in other areas such as Central Asia and Latin America. According to China Industry Warning Net (2006), China had allocated 15 and 11 percent of its total oil-related ODI to Russia–Central Asia and Latin America by mid-2006,[5] respectively.

This chapter uses two sets of China's ODI data: the approved ODI data and the new ODI data in the OECD-IMF standard. The former contains official data on China's outward foreign direct investment initiated by Chinese enterprises, and approved by the Chinese authorities. The sample period is from 1991 to 2005. The latter is the ODI data (2003 to 2007) compiled by the Ministry of Commerce of China according to the OECD-IMF standard.[6]

Both ODI datasets contain the flow data of China's ODI and are censored at zero from below. Thus I first use the Tobit (1958) model to study their behavior. Then I consider the Heckman (1979) two-stage method that allows the investment decision to be separated into two stages. Essentiallyin the first stage decision can be assumed to be whether or not to invest in a host country. If China decides to invest, the decision in the second stage is then over the amount of committed investment.

China's ODI is found to go to oil-producing countries with high energy output, notably after the implementation of the "going global" policy. China's surging demand for oil and its increasing reliance on imported foreign oil have pushed China's ODI to quest for more foreign oil. There is evidence of the market-seeking motive and the political risk effect. Interestingly, the estimated results indicate that China tends to invest in corrupted oil-producing countries. In line with some anecdotal evidence, China's ODI behaves differently in different oil regions. While stepping up the quest for oil in Africa and other regions, such as Russia–Central Asia and Latin America under the directive of the "going global" policy, China has been reducing its overdependence on the Middle East. In addition, rather than concentrate in a few major Middle Eastern oil countries, China's ODI has diversified across countries in that region. Nevertheless, the Middle East is still the major oil supplier for China.

The remainder of the chapter is organized as follows. In section 12.2, I briefly discuss the evolution of China's oil and energy production and consumption. The empirical model specifications and results are presented in section 12.3. Section 12.4 concludes.

12.2   The Background of China's Energy Production and Consumption

Three decades of economic boom have resulted in a surge in China's demand for energy, which spans the whole spectrum of energy—coal, oil, gas, electricity, hydropower, nuclear power, and other renewable energy sources as well. Thanks to its vast reserves, coal supplies about 70 percent of China's total energy need (figure 12.2). Although China's demand for electricity has soared and keeps growing, it is conceivable that electricity will remain only a fraction of China's total energy supply. The use of natural gas accounted for about 3 percent of China's total energy consumption in 2006 (EIA 2009). It is likely to play a larger role in meeting the country's energy need, as the Chinese government promotes the use of more natural gas (primarily because of the concern over China's growing dependency on oil imports and widespread envi-

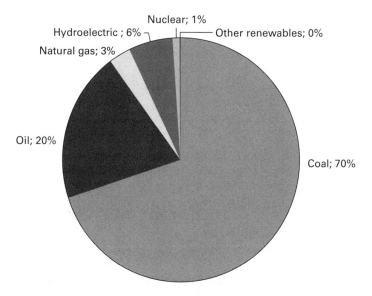

Figure 12.2
Total energy consumption in China, by type (2006). Sources: International Energy Annual (2006), Energy Information Administration (EIA).

ronmental degradation caused by coal). The rapid pace of economic growth has particularly led to dramatic growth in the demand for oil. In the past three decades China's consumption of oil increased fivefold from 1.7 in 1982 to 8.2 million barrels per day in 2009, making China the second-largest oil consumer in the world.

China had been a net oil importer in the 1950s and early 1960s, receiving the bulk of its imports from the former Soviet Union. However, the discovery of the Daqing oil field in 1959 transformed China into Asia's largest oil producer, enabling China not only to become self-sufficient in oil by the mid-1960s but also to begin to export small amounts of oil in 1970s.

Despite the expansion of oil production, the demand continued to outstrip the supply; as a result China started to import oil in 1993. Since then the volume of imports has continuously increased, and eventually China began to rely heavily on foreign oil and imported 45 percent of its total oil supply in 2008.

One main reason for this is the very limited nature of China's domestic oil output. Despite its vastness in geographic area, China has never discovered large oil reserves. Its traditional fields in and around Daqing and Shengli are turning old and their production is either flat or declining. New efforts in developing offshore oil fields in both the South China and East China Seas so far have been unimpressive. The newer discoveries in the Junggar and Tarim basins, in contrast to its initial optimistic estimation, turned out to be modest. Therefore substantial imports of oil to meet the widening gap between the demand and domestic supply are inevitable (EIA 2009).

Up until 2008, China's net oil imports were 3.6 million barrels per day, ranking China the third-largest oil importer in the world. International Energy Agency (IEA) forecasts that China will import almost 13.2 million barrels per day by 2025 (EIA 2006). That means China would have to import some 80 percent of its oil supplies. The Middle East remained the primary source of China's oil imports (about 50 percent of the total oil imports in 2008), and Africa contributed a significant and increasing amount of oil to China, accounting for about 30 percent in 2008. In terms of individual countries, Saudi Arabia and Angola were China's two largest sources of oil imports. Together they accounted for more than one-third of China's total crude oil imports (figure 12.3).

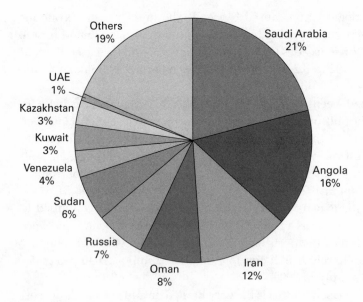

Figure 12.3
China's crude oil imports, by source (2008). Source: International Energy (2009), Energy Information Administration (EIA).

The increasing dependence on oil imports has stirred a strong sense of insecurity in the Chinese government and has promoted concerns that an interruption of oil supplies or unexpected price hikes could put the brakes on economic growth, which would eventually result in political and social instability (IEA 2000).

In response, China has launched an "all-out" program of domestic reform and a global energy import security strategy. On one hand, it aims to keep production going in traditional oil fields in northeastern China while expanding the production in the western part of China. In addition, developing offshore oil field exploration in both the South China and East China seas has been raised to a high-priority mission. On the other hand, China has implemented a "going global" strategy to encourage and financially support China's NOCs to secure more foreign oil and gas equities, diversify import sources, build pipelines, and sign long-term provision contracts with energy-producing countries.

The "going global" strategy focuses not only on purchasing oil in the international energy market but, more important, seeking to accelerate China's access to long-term foreign energy equity assets (Leverett and Bader 2005). Access to foreign oil assets could diversify China's oil supply sources and avoid international price fluctuations. Furthermore, in 2003, China's State Council issued a directive of "leapfrog strategy in the energy field" through 2020 to reinforce the "going global" policy and secure more oil supplies from overseas (Bremner et al. 2004). As a result Chinese equity oil investments are all over the world. For instance, CNPC held international assets in 29 oil countries at the end of 2008. The overseas equity production represented roughly 29 percent of China's total oil production in 2008 (EIA 2009).

China's aggressive policies in response to its foreign oil dependence are likely to pose implications not only to the world energy market but also to the global economy and security issues.

12.3   Data and Empirical Determinants

In this section I discuss two datasets of China's ODI, the approved ODI data (1991 to 2005) and China's ODI data in OECD-IMF standard (2003 to 2007). Then I use Tobit (1958) and Heckman (1979) methods to analyze the determinants of China's ODI in conventional oil-producing countries.

12.3.1   China's ODI Data

While China's ODI has been extensively discussed, there are only a few formal econometrics analyses in the literature, including Buckley et al. (2007), Cheng and Ma (2009), Cheung and Qian (2009), and Cheung et al. (2010).[7] The primary reason perhaps is because of the issues associated with the quality and availability of Chinese ODI data. China has published two ODI datasets. However, they have different definitions and different time period coverage, and each dataset has its limitations.

The first ODI dataset, China's approved ODI data, is comprised of data on China's ODI approved by Chinese authorities. Since the Chinese government published the host country-specific approved ODI data starting from 1992 and ending in 2006, the approved ODI data cover sample periods from 1991 to 2005. There are some limitations associated with the approved ODI data, such as that it may understate the actual volume of Chinese ODI (Cheung and Qian 2009). This dataset, nevertheless, provides us some advantages in studying China's ODI. First, it offers longer time period coverage, allowing us to study the evolution of China's ODI in oil-producing countries. Second, the ODI projects are managed by Chinese business enterprises but approved by the authorities. Thus the approved ODI data contain market information and reflect China's policy stance.

Naturally, it makes sense for the energy quest of China's ODI in oil-producing countries to be a mixture of government policy mission and business venture (Downs 2007; Lee and Shalmon 2007). Although many studies argue that the political dimension of China's ODI is gradually fading away (Besada et al. 2007: 15), the Chinese government still, arguably, directs China's ODI, as about 70 percent of total China's ODI is from state-owned enterprises.[8] Therefore the approved ODI dataset gives us the leverage to identify both the policy and market determinants of China's ODI simultaneously.

Besides the approved ODI data, China has also published its ODI data in a format in accordance with the OECD-IMF standard since 2003 in *The Statistical Bulletin of China's Outward Foreign Direct Investment* and later in the *2009 China Commerce Yearbook*. While it is in the OECD-IMF standard and provides country specific time series data, the dataset is relatively short in time periods, from 2003–2008. The data from 2003 to 2007 are comprised of nonfinancial ODI data. But the financial ODI data[9] were added to the year 2008 data, making the 2008 data incompatible with 2003 to 2007 data. Thus we use 2003 to 2007 OECD-IMF standard ODI data for China in the current exercise.

12.3.2 Results Based on the Approved ODI Data

In this subsection I use the Tobit (1958) and Heckman (1979) methods to study the determinants of China's ODI in oil-producing countries based on China's approved ODI data. Both methods consider a unique feature of China's approved ODI data; that is, the dataset comprises nonnegative observations, and many of the observations are zeros—61 percent of total observations are zeros. Recall that the approved ODI is approved by Chinese authorities. However, Chinese authorities might not approve any ODI to an oil producer every year. For instance, there is no ODI approved to be invested in Algeria from 1991 to 1999. For such a case the observations of ODI to Algeria from 1991 to 1999 are zeros.

Technically the Tobit method, censoring China's ODI data at zero from below, avoids the possible downward bias of OLS regression due to the nonnegative data structure of China's ODI. It is conceivable that China's ODI decision is made in two ordered steps: first, it decides in which countries to invest; if it decides to invest, the second step determines the amount to be invested in a selected country. Heckman's two-stage method provides a convenient framework to model such a decision making process. I study the factors determining the invest-or-not-to-invest decision in the first stage; in the second stage, I examine what determines the amount of investment.

In specifying the empirical models, I consider some commonly identified determinants of FDI (market-seeking motives, resource-seeking motives, and political risks, etc.) and some China specific factors, for example, China's reliance on foreign oil and the competition from other FDIs.

It is conceivable that oil-producing countries' abundant resource of oil and gas is one of the important factors that attract Chinese investments. I thus investigate how energy abundance of an oil-producing country affects China's ODI behavior. *Engy* is selected to proxy the energy abundance. It is measured as the return in dollar units from the energy output (crude oil, natural gas, and coal) scaled by a host country's gross national income (GNI).[10] I expect a positive effect of *Engy* to China's ODI in oil-producing countries. Data on *Engy* are from the *World Development Indicators* database provided by the World Bank. A detailed description of all variables used in the current study and their sources is listed in appendix A at the end of this chapter.

China's ODI is found to have market-seeking motives in other studies, such as Cheung and Qian (2009). Does China's ODI also seek markets in oil-producing countries? To answer this question, I study three market-seeking factors of China's ODI—the host-country's gross domestic product (*GDP*), the real *per capita* income (*RGDPpc*), and the real income growth rate (*RGDPG*). *GDP* represents the market size that the ODI accesses (Frankel and Wei 1996; Kravis and Lipsey 1982; Wheeler and Mody 1992). *RGDPpc* is another commonly used indicator of market opportunities and is a typical measure for the level of infrastructure as well (Eaton and Tamura 1994, 1996; Kinoshita and Campos 2004; Lane 2000; Lipsey 1999). Finally, *GDPG* is a measure of market growth potential (Billington 1999; Lipsey 1999). These three variables are expected to have positive coefficients under the market-seeking strategy.

FDIs are adversely affected by political risks, particularly in the developing countries. In the oil-producing countries, it is commonly believed that oil countries are associated with all kinds of political risks, such as state instability, corruption, and poor law and order (Atkinson and Hamilton 2003; Ross 1999). High levels of corruption and poor law and order are two prominent components of the political risks that affect FDIs in oil nations (Ross 1999). I consider *RISK*, a vector comprised of six dimensions of political risk indexes, in the regression to assess how political risks impact China's ODI in oil countries. These six political risk indexes are the economic condition risk index (*Econ*), the political system risk index (*Polt*), the confliction risk index (*Cnfl*), the social tension risk index (*Scnt*), the corruption risk index (*Crpt*), and the law and order risk index (*Law*). A higher value of each risk index indicates a lower risk level in that country. The six risk indexes are constructed from the twelve country risk indexes from the *International Country Risk Guide* (ICRG). For example, I create the *Econ* variable by adding the socioeconomic condition index and the investment profile index of ICRG. Appendix A provides the details of how the other five political risk indexes were created.

The two-way causality relation between FDI and trade is a traditional topic in the FDI literature (Aizenman and Noy 2006). Such a two-way interaction between trade and FDI is expected between China and oil-producing countries. It is conceivable that the primary purpose of China investing it ODI in an oil country is to produce oil and export the majority of it back to China (IEA 2000). Therefore the export from the ODI host country to China could be a good proxy in capturing the possible effect of trade on the ODI. Thus XP, measured by the exports from an oil-producing country to China over the total exports of that country, is used in my regression.

Some of China's specific factors are also expected to play important roles in determining China's ODI in oil-producing countries. China has been increasingly reliant on foreign oil due to its surging demand against the limited domestic supply for oil, pushing China to work out a "going out" strategy to encourage its NOCs to invest overseas and secure more foreign oil. I consider the reliance on foreign oil to be a push factor that presses China to be actively involved in investing in oil-producing countries. To evaluate the importance of such a push factor in determining China's ODI, I include a proxy variable for China's reliance on foreign oil, $OilM$, measured by China's import of crude oil (thousand barrels per day) divided by China's total oil consumption (thousand barrels per day). A greater reliance on foreign oil is expected to push China to seek more foreign oil supplies via ODI.

In the business of acquiring foreign oil, China is a late comer (Downs 2007). Most oil industries in conventional oil-producing countries are tied up by the US and European interests. To avoid direct competition with international oil companies (IOCs), such as Exxon and Shell, China circumvents those locations with a strong foothold of IOCs and looks for the areas that are outside of the IOCs' spheres of influence. I incorporate $SFDI$, a variable measured as the existing stock of FDIs from countries other than China, to capture the potential competition that China's ODI could encounter when investing in an oil country. A higher value of $SFDI$ indicates more competition from the existing interests of IOCs.

Tobit Specification   The Tobit regression equation I used to study China's ODI behavior in oil-producing countries takes the following form:

$$ODI_{it}^{*} = \alpha + \beta_1 Engy_{it-1} + \beta_2 MKT_{it-1} \\ + \beta_3 RISK_{it} + \beta_4 XP_{it-1} + \beta_5 OilM_{t-1} + \beta_6 SFDI_{it-1} + v_{it},$$

(12.1)

where $ODI_{it}^{*} = ODI_{it}$ if $ODI_{it} > 0$ and $ODI_{it}^{*} = 0$ if $ODI_{it} \leq 0$. The variable ODI_{it} is China's ODI flow to a host country i, at time t, normalized by the host country's population. All the relevant factors that are discussed in the previous subsection are included as the explanatory variables. Three market-seeking factors, *GDP*, *RGDGpc*, and *RGDPG* are contained in *MKT* vector; six political risk dimensions are in the vector of *RISK*.

To avoid possible endogeneity issues, I used lagged values of all explanatory variables in the regression except for the six political risk variables. I assumed that China's ODI does not affect an oil country's risk characteristics due to China's proclaimed foreign policy principle of "noninterference in internal affairs." Clearly, China's ODI is small compared with the total FDI in oil-producing countries. Hence the contemporaneous political risk variables could be considered exogenous.[11]

The panel data Tobit regression with random effects[12] is used and the estimate results pertaining to specification (12.1) are presented in table 12.1. I had a total of 29 conventional oil-producing countries[13] from 1991 to 2005 in my data sample. For brevity, I dropped very insignificant variables (e.g., *p*-value >20 percent) [14]and report the results in the column "Tobit-All-1" of table 12.1.

The estimated coefficients are largely consistent with the conventional wisdom, except for the corruption (*Crpt*) and energy output (*Engy*) variables. Out of three market-seeking factors, only the market size, *GDP*, is estimated to be both positive and significant. That is, an oil-producing country with a larger market attracts China's ODI. The other two market factors, the income level (*RGDPpc*) and the growth potential (*GDPG*), are not the significant reasons for China's ODI in oil countries.

A big factor that limits the FDI's flow to many oil-producing countries is political risk. A US government report acknowledges that increased oil investment is being hampered by widespread corruption, outmoded investment laws, internal disorder and conflict, and a systemic lack of governmental transparency in oil nations (Klare and Volman 2006).

Unlike the common view, the estimate of the corruption variable *Crpt* reveals interesting information: an oil-producing country with worse levels of corruption received a higher amount of China's ODI. The plausible reason may relate to the strategy that China's ODI carried out to compete against IOCs. Being a relatively small competitor and the latecomer in the foreign oil game, China strategically avoids direct confrontation with other FDIs in some oil countries where IOCs have a strong foothold (Downs 2007). Chinese ODI instead goes to "rogue" states, such as Sudan and Iran, which are traditionally shunned by

Table 12.1
Empirical determinants of China's outward direct investment in the oil-producing countries

	Tobit-All-1	Tobit-All-2	Tobit-All-3
$GDP(-1)$	1.516***	1.542***	1.660***
	(0.43)	(0.41)	(0.44)
$XP(-1)$	6.056***	5.983***	5.043***
	(1.79)	(1.78)	(1.80)
$OilM(-1)$	0.931*		
	(0.55)		
$Engy(-1)$	0.039	0.042	0.026
	(0.04)	(0.04)	(0.04)
$Crpt$	−1.108***	−1.125***	−1.050***
	(0.33)	(0.31)	(0.31)
GG		1.203**	−1.204
		(0.59)	(1.08)
$GG*Engy(-1)$			0.121***
			(0.05)
Constant	−30.571***	−33.336***	−36.048***
	(11.07)	(10.32)	(10.93)
Adjusted pseudo R^2	0.11	0.12	0.12
Observed	345	345	345

Sources: Tobit (1958) with the approved ODI data (1991–2005).
Notes: Reported are the results of random effect Tobit panel regression in equation (12.1). All insignificant (>20 percent in p-value) variables are dropped, except for variables associated with interaction terms. The column "Tobit-All-1" reports the results of regression in equation (12.1); the column "Tobit-All-2" gives the results of regression with "GG" dummy; the "Tobit-All-3" column presents the results with both "GG" and the interaction variable $GG*Engy(-1)$. Robust standard errors are in parentheses. ***, **, and * denote significance at the 1, 5, and 10 percent levels, respectively. The adjusted pseudo R^2 is the adjusted McFadden's.

IOCs due to a high level of political risk. In addition some Western countries (e.g., the United States) do not permit their corporations to engage in bribery activities in foreign markets, which creates an investment vacuum in these corruption loaded countries. China thus finds less competition when investing in these countries (Cheung et al. 2010). Apparently other aspects of political risks seem not to significantly affect China's ODI to invest in oil-producing countries.

In theory, the FDI promotes the trade, and the trade in turn positively feeds back to the FDI (Aizenman and Noy 2006). My result is in accordance with such a feedback theory: an oil country exporting more to China draws more ODI from China. Indeed, in contrast to China's supercharged exporting prowess to other countries, China is consistently in trade deficits against most oil-producing countries. The trade deficits to the group of 29 oil countries in our sample reached as high as \$39 billion in 2008. To conduct the booming business of exporting oil to China, including both purchased oil and the equity oil, more Chinese investments in oil-producing countries are needed. Building secure and convenient ways to ship the acquired oil is also crucial to China's global oil quest, which may require China's ODI to build transportation tools such as pipelines that allow China to ship oil safely and smoothly. [15]

China's reliance on foreign oil ($OilM_{t-1}$) yields a positively significant estimate. It is in line with the notion that increased dependence on foreign oil pushes China's ODI to acquire more oil in a more stable way than simply purchasing oil from international markets (Downs 2000). Although purchasing oil from the international energy markets is still the main channel through which China satisfies its energy thirst, Chinese energy planners appear to have a strong distrust of energy markets (Lieberthal and Herberg 2006). Many believe that the United States, a major political competitor that controls critical energy transport sea-lanes and has enormous power in the global oil industry and institutions, exerts a powerful influence on global oil prices and flows. Such threats from the United States over China's energy weakness and insecurity via international energy markets have concerned many Chinese leaders. Hence there appears a strong perception among Chinese energy planners and analysts that long-term equity holdings on overseas oil fields will increase China's control over the imported oil (Downs 2000; Kreft 2006). Accordingly, ODI, a long-term investment, has become a primary way for the Chinese government to utilize its quest for stable foreign oil supplies.

While I identify a few determinants of China's ODI in oil-producing countries, I do not find a significant effect of energy output on China's ODI—the *Engy* variable is not estimated to be significant. Recall from section 12.2 that China's "going global" policy has been driving China's ODI quest for oil globally since 2002. To capture the "going global" policy effect, I augment specification (12.1) by adding a policy dummy variable, *GG* ($I(t >= 2002) = 1$; otherwise 0) and an interaction variable ($GG*Engy(-1)$) to capture the "going global" policy effect and its implication for the energy output of oil-producing countries. The regression results of the augmented specification (12.1) are presented in the "Tobit-All-2" and "Tobit-All-3" columns of table 12.1, respectively. The *"GG"* variable in "Tobit-All-2" yields a positive and significant result, confirming that the "going global" policy promotes more ODI to oil nations to secure China's oil supply. Further, as shown in "Tobit-All-3," the estimate of the "GG*Engy(−1)" variable indicates that the "going global" policy not only pushes China's ODI to oil-producing countries but also concentrates China's ODI in oil nations more abundant in energy output. Adding the policy dummy variable and the interaction variable does not affect the results of other standard variables, except that the push factor $OilM(-1)$ becomes insignificant.

Heckman Method   In this subsection, I utilize the Heckman (1979) method to examine the determinants of China's ODI in oil-producing countries. Conceivably the decision-making of China's ODI perhaps is comprised of two discrete steps. In the first step, China assesses the host oil country and decides whether to invest. After a positive decision is made to invest in a host country, in the second step, China decides the amount of ODI to be invested in that country. The Heckman two-stage method offers an empirical framework to sequentially analyze such a decision-making process.

In the first stage of the Heckman method, China selects which country to invest its ODI and the selection specification is constructed as

$$D_{it} = \alpha + \beta_1 Engy_{it-1} + \beta_2 MKT_{it-1}$$
$$+ \beta_3 RISK_{it} + \beta_4 XP_{it-1} + \beta_5 OilM_{t-1} + \beta_6 SFDI_{it-1} + v_{it}, \qquad (12.2)$$

$D_{it} = 1$ if $ODI_{it} > 0$ and zero otherwise. In essence, I assume that the likelihood of China to invest in an oil-exporting country is determined by the factors used in the censored regression (12.1). Given the panel data of my sample, I adopt the Wooldridge (1995) method that modified the Heckman (1979) procedure for panel data analysis. A panel data Probit regression with random effects[16] is performed on the entire sample.

The second column of table 12.2 gives the results. Again, very insignificant variables (p-value > 20 percent) are dropped from the regression. Except for $cnfl$ and $RGDPpc$, the results are similar to those of the Tobit regression above. China's ODI is found to be more likely to go to an oil-producing country with larger market size, more exports to China, and more corruption. The level of energy output does not significantly affect the probability that China invests in an oil-producing country.

Table 12.2
Empirical determinants of China's outward direct investment in the oil-producing countries

	Heckman-All-1		Heckman-All-2		Heckman-All-3	
	First stage	Second stage	First stage	Second stage	First stage	Second stage
GDP(−1)	0.822***		0.792***		0.822***	
	(0.16)		(0.16)		(0.17)	
RGDPpc(−1)	−0.345**		−0.389**		−0.396**	
	(0.16)		(0.16)		(0.17)	
XP(−1)	5.434***		5.168***		4.964***	
	(1.69)		(1.70)		(1.71)	
Erngy(−1)	0.012	0.037*	0.010	0.024	0.007	0.028
	(0.01)	(0.02)	(0.01)	(0.02)	(0.01)	(0.02)
Cnfl	0.150		0.141		0.121	
	(0.09)		(0.09)		(0.10)	
Polt		0.488***		0.453***		0.463***
		(0.13)		(0.12)		(0.11)
Sctn		0.545***		0.614***		0.566***
		(0.14)		(0.20)		(0.16)
Crpt	−0.455***	−0.766***	−0.392***	−0.693***	−0.372***	−0.636**
	(0.11)	(0.25)	(0.12)	(0.25)	(0.13)	(0.23)
Law		−1.086***		−1.012**		−0.998**
		(0.33)		(0.39)		(0.36)
GG			0.324	1.378**	−0.189	0.085
			(0.25)	(0.52)	(0.49)	(0.50)

Table 12.2
(continued)

	Heckman-All-1		Heckman-All-2		Heckman-All-3	
	First stage	Second stage	First stage	Second stage	First stage	Second stage
$GG*Engy(-1)$					0.030	0.074***
					(0.04)	(0.03)
Mills		0.675		1.791**		1.853**
		(0.68)		(0.86)		(0.84)
Constant	−17.243***	0.875	−16.397***	−0.668	−16.961***	−0.925
	(3.75)	(1.83)	(3.80)	(1.87)	(3.97)	(1.87)
Adjusted $R^{2\dagger}$	0.37	0.26	0.37	0.31	0.37	0.32
BJL test	0.94		1.19		1.28	
Observed	334	150	334	150	334	150

Sources: Heckman (1979) with the approved ODI data (1991–2005).

Notes: Reported are the results of estimation in equation (12.1) and equation (12.2) using the Heckman (1979) two-stage method. All insignificant (>20 percent in p-value) variables are dropped, except for variables associated with interaction terms. The columns of "Heckman-All-1" report the results of regressions in equations (12.1) and (12.2). The columns of "Heckman-All-2" give the results of regression controlling "going global" policy with GG dummy; "Heckman-All-3" presents the results with both GG dummy and the interaction variable $GG*Engy(-1)$. Robust standard errors are in parentheses. ***, **, and * denote significance at the 1, 5, and 10 percent levels, respectively. The coefficient of interaction variable $GG*Engy(-1)$ in the columns of "Heckman-All-3" is reported as the marginal effect of $GG*Engy(-1)$ (Ai and Norton 2003).

† Numbers in the column "First stage" report the adjusted MacFadden's pseudo R^2; the numbers in the column "Second stage" report the adjusted R^2. The Bera, Jarque, and Lee (1984) normality test is done after the Heckman first-stage regression. All results are insignificant and do not reject the null hypothesis of normal distribution.

The confliction risk variable *Cnfl* is only marginally insignificant at the 10 percent level with a positive sign. It thus provides weak evidence that China's ODI inclines to invest in oil countries with less conflict, including both internal and external conflict.

The estimated coefficient on real GDP per capita (*RGDPpc*) suggests that an oil nation with a lower level of real income is more likely to receive China's ODI. It may seem counterintuitive at quick glance; however, if one considers *RGDPpc* as a proxy for the level of infrastructure, the result appears reasonable. That is, China's ODI tends to go to an oil nation with poor infrastructure. Indeed, China usually offers "oil-for-infrastructure" deals in order to bid oil deals over IOCs. American and European IOCs, with a century of operating in oil-rich nations, often focus on taking out crude oil and reselling oil products back to those countries and the rest of the world, while failing to build up the infrastructure and therefore raising people's living standard in those oil countries. China, however, is more willing than Western IOCs to establish an entire chain of an oil industry, including local refinery facilities, petrochemical industries, as well as other infrastructure that is not directly related to oil exploration, such as roads, bridges, and dams. Oil nations are consequently willing to offer oil deals to China in exchange for such infrastructure buildup (Jakobson and Zha 2006).

The first stage of the Heckman enables us to identify what determines the likelihood of China's ODI; it also allows us to generate an inverse Mills ratio that contains information on the unobserved factors associated with the selection process on zero-censored data. The inverse Mills ratio is then added to the second-stage regression of the Heckman method as an explanatory variable to control for the possible effect of unobserved factors that affects China's decision on the amount of ODI to be invested.

The regression equation for the second stage of the Heckman method is specified as

$$ODI_{it} = \alpha + \beta_1 Engy_{it-1} + \beta_2 MKT_{it-1}$$
$$+ \beta_3 RISK_{it} + \beta_4 XP_{it-1} + \beta_5 OilM_{t-1} + \beta_6 SFDI_{it-1} + \beta_7 Mills_{it} + v_{it} ,$$

$$(12.3)$$

where ODI_{it} is comprised of only positive ODI observations. Except for the inverse Mills ratio, $Mills_{it}$, all other explanatory variables are the same as in specification (12.2). A panel data regression with fixed effects is performed to estimate equation (12.3). The column "second stage" in "Heckman-All-1" of table 12.2 contains the estimation results.

Even though I considered the same set of explanatory variables, the significant determinants in the second stage are not identical to those in the first stage. This suggests that the factors driving the amount of investment are not necessarily the same as those determine the invest-or-not-to-invest decision. The two-stage procedure offers a convenient framework to scrutinize China's investment behavior in oil-producing countries.

The inverse Mills ratio, $Mills_{it}$, is estimated to be insignificant, and hence we have no statistical evidence that there are unobserved factors in the first stage selecting process that affect China's ODI decision in the second stage. Albeit insignificant, the inverse Mills ratio, $Mills_{it}$, ensures that the coefficient estimates in the second stage are purged of bias resulting from the possible selection bias problem.

The energy variable ($Engy$) has a positive and significant coefficient. This confirms that a higher energy output draws more China's ODI to an oil-producing country. However, my results suggest a sophisticated view of China's ODI strategy in seeking for oil in oil-producing nations. If the estimate results in both stages of the Heckman method are combined, we find that an oil country with a large energy production alone does not increase the likelihood that China's ODI invests. However, once selected by China, an oil country with more energy output draws a higher volume of China's ODI.

In addition to the corruption effect, the Heckman method reveals other aspects of political risks that China's ODI may consider. A selected oil-producing country with a stable political system and less social tensions attracts China's ODI, which is in line with the finding of Arezki and Brückner (2009) and Asiedu (2006). Both the negative and significant estimates for $Crpt$ and Law suggest that, among the selected oil countries, China invests more ODI to countries loaded with corruption and poor in law and order. Such a result perhaps is not surprising as poor law and order is usually associated with a high level of corruption (Cheung et al. 2010).

To evaluate China's "going global" policy effect, I added the policy dummy variable (GG) and both "GG" and its interaction term "$GG*Engy(-1)$" to equations (12.2) and (12.3). These regression results are reported in "Heckman-All-2" and "Heckman-All-3" in table 12.2, respectively. As indicated in the "first stage" of "Heckman-All-2," the "going global" policy does not increase the likelihood of China to invest its ODI in an oil-producing country. However, once a positive investment decision is made to invest in an oil country, the "going global" policy directs Chinese enterprises to place a higher amount of its ODI in that country ("second stage" of "Heckman-All-2"). I obtained similar results when both the policy dummy and its interaction variable are included in the regressions ("Heckman-All-3").

The significance of the inverse Mills ratio in both regressions suggests the existence of unobserved factors that affect China's ODI behavior in oil nations. It allows us to control the selection bias associated with the approved ODI data.

Augmenting the model by including "GG" and its interaction term "GG*Engy(–1)" does not change the results of other variables, except for $Engy(-1)$, whose significance is reduced to be marginally insignificant at the 10 percent level.

A comparison of the results of the Tobit and Heckman regressions reveals a few differences in the composition of the significant explanatory variables. For instance, on one hand, the push factor of China's ODI—China's reliance on foreign oil, $OilM$, is a significant factor in the Tobit regression but not in the Heckman procedure. On the other hand, the real income level, $RGDPpc$, is significant in the Heckman but not in the Tobit regression. The different results of $OilM$ may attribute to the different estimating procedures. The procedure of the Heckman method is to assess the probability that an individual country receives China's ODI in the first stage and then evaluate how much ODI to be invested in the second stage. With respect to each individual host country of China's ODI, the aggregated foreign oil reliance of China might be an unobserved factor that is essentially contained in the inverse Mills ratio. I thus was not able to isolate the detailed pushing effect of $OilM$ in the Heckman method.

Arguably, the two-stage Heckman procedure is the finer method than the Tobit method in analyzing China's ODI in oil-producing countries. Under the scenario that both China and oil nations prefer "oil-for-infrastructure" deals, it is plausible that $RGDPpc$, a proxy for the infrastructure level, may only increase the probability of China's ODI to get an oil deal; it is still less likely to affect how much of China's ODI is to be placed in that country after the first-stage decision. The Tobit method, as a one-stop treatment, may be too coarse to capture such a detailed decision-making process.

Three components of political risks—$Polt$, $Sctn$, and Law—are significant in the second stage of the Heckman regression in table 12.2, whereas they are insignificant in the Tobit regression in table 12.1. Such differences perhaps, again, attribute to the finer specification of the Heckman than the Tobit method.

Empirical Results from Individual Country Groups   China has carried out a strategy of diversifying energy sources and markets that is similar to the energy policy pursued by the United States and Japan decades ago (Downs 2000). Diversity is deemed to be the foundation of stability in natural resource supply in China (Gu 1998). As such, an important goal of Chinese investment in oil-producing counties is to diversify China's oil import channels[17].

Among numerous oil sources, it is not surprising that the Middle East remains the main source for China's oil import. The Middle East possesses more than 61 percent of world proved oil reserves and has the lowest production costs. It currently produces 24 million barrels a day and keeps growing, projected to reach 35 million barrels a day by 2020.[18] Much of this growth will be targeted toward Asian markets, from which China will take a lion's share. Further most of China's refinery facilities are better suited to handle crude oil from the Middle East. In fact 50 percent of China's total imported oil in 2008 was from the Middle East.

Despite relying heavily on the Middle Eastern oil, China has been strategically diversifying and reducing its dependence on that region primarily due to (1) the volatile political situation, especially, the prolonged civil wars; (2) that the oil transportation sea-lanes stretching from the Persian Gulf to the South China Sea are controlled by the US Navy, which theoretically jeopardizes the security of the oil supply (Khan 2008).

Meanwhile African oil has gained weight on the equation of China's diversification strategy. Up until 2008, about 30 percent of China's imported oil was from Africa. This seems to be an interesting move in China's diversification game, since Africa accounts for only about 9 percent of the world proved oil reserve. However, as noted by the US Department of Energy (DoE), Africa is believed to hold significant undiscovered oil reserves and possesses great upward potential of oil output. Not only China, but also other major oil consumers, such as the United States and Europe have paid extraordinary interest to African oil. Moreover, in contrast to other oil nations, African countries are open to foreign investments in oil exploration and production, which is particularly attractive to China's ODI that is on mission to secure long-term oil supply.

In addition China has comparative advantages over others in gaining oil deals in Africa. For example, China takes a "win-win" tactic when interacting with African oil nations. In order to get deals with African oil nations, China usually offers comprehensive packages as an exchange, such as debt cancellations (Cheung et al. 2010) and the "oil-for-infrastructure" package. Such an exchange essentially establishes a China–Africa strategic partnership that matches the comparative advantages of both parties. On one hand, China discovers a new market for its supercharged export industry and expertise in infrastructure building. It also receives the much needed natural resources supply from Africa. On the other hand, Africa also finds a new market for its natural resources and takes advantage of Chinese goods and China's expertise on infrastructure buildup in raising African peoples' living standard, which Western nations have failed to do for more than a century. Besides, China's embraced investment policy of "no strings attached" or "noninterference in internal affairs" is especially welcomed by many African oil nations, authoritarian African nations, in particular.

Some political risks, for instance, the possible interruption of China's oil transporting sea-lanes by the US Navy, have pushed China to seek oil resources other than those from the Middle East and Africa. An obvious solution is the neighboring oil countries, such as Russia and Kazakhstan, where transportation interruption from the United States is largely absent (Guo 2006; He 2008). In fact Kazakhstan is China's biggest equity oil producer. It accounted for 33 percent of China's total oversea equity oil production in 2006 (Downs 2008). Another solution that China pursues is to go to oil nations that have weak ties or are hostile toward the United States or Europe; such countries include Venezuela (Tu 2008).

To investigate whether China's ODI takes different approaches in different regions in the quest for oil, I fit regression models, both the Tobit and Heckman models, to the sample of the Middle East, the sample comprised of African oil-producing countries, and the sample of the rest of the conventional oil producers, to study the different behaviors of China's ODI in each individual region. The results are presented in tables 12.3 through 12.8.

The coefficient estimates are supportive of the conjecture that factors determining China's ODI in the Middle East, Africa, and the rest of oil nations are not the same. In the Middle Eastern countries (tables 12.3 and 12.4), China's ODI expresses a strong market-seeking motive—

Table 12.3
Empirical determinants of China's outward direct investment in Middle East oil-producing countries

	Tobit-Mdest-1	Tobit-Mdest-2	Tobit-Mdest-3
$GDP(-1)$	3.056***	3.064***	3.027***
	(0.86)	(0.88)	(0.86)
$RGDPpc(-1)$	1.587**	1.586**	1.642**
	(0.77)	(0.77)	(0.77)
$XP(-1)$	13.358*	13.414*	13.605*
	(8.01)	(8.09)	(8.14)
$OilM(-1)$	2.126	2.172	2.178
	(1.38)	(1.67)	(1.67)
$Engy(-1)$	−0.140	−0.139	−0.113
	(0.15)	(0.15)	(0.16)
$Polt$	−1.038*	−1.039*	−1.062*
	(0.60)	(0.60)	(0.60)
Law	−4.280***	−4.280***	−4.325***
	(1.33)	(1.33)	(1.34)
GG		−0.089	2.101
		(1.83)	(6.05)
$GG*Engy(-1)$			−0.098
			(0.26)
Constant	−53.910**	−53.944**	−53.937**
	(21.54)	(21.63)	(21.04)
Adjusted pseudo R^2	0.09	0.09	0.09
Observed	106	106	106

Sources: Tobit (1958) with the approved ODI data (1991–2005).
Notes: Reported are the results of random effect Tobit panel regression in equation (12.1). All insignificant (>20 percent in p-value) variables are dropped, except for variables associated with interaction terms. The column "Tobit-Mdest-1" reports the results of regression in equation (12.1); the column "Tobit-Mdest-2" gives the results of regression with GG dummy; the "Tobit- Mdest -3" column presents the results with both GG dummy and the interaction variable $GG*Engy(-1)$. Robust standard errors are in parentheses. ***, **, and * denote significance at the 1, 5, and 10 percent levels, respectively. The adjusted pseudo R^2 is the adjusted McFadden's.

Table 12.4
Empirical determinants of China's outward direct investment in the Middle East oil-producing countries

	Heckman-Mdest-1		Heckman-Mdest-2		Heckman-Mdest-3	
	First stage	Second stage	First stage	Second stage	First stage	Second stage
GDP(−1)	1.112***	4.765**	0.969***		0.917***	1.217
	(0.33)	(1.44)	(0.31)		(0.30)	(0.88)
XP(−1)	4.644*	8.809	3.878		3.927	
	(2.45)	(4.89)	(2.42)		(2.53)	
OilM(−1)				0.731***	0.355	0.836*
				(0.15)	(0.43)	(0.42)
Engy(−1)	0.004	−0.007	−0.015	−0.017	−0.018	−0.037*
	(0.03)	(0.03)	(0.04)	(0.02)	(0.04)	(0.02)
Crpt		0.890***		0.846***		0.934**
		(0.14)		(0.22)		(0.27)
Law	−0.625**	−2.934**	−0.542**	−1.740***	−0.669**	−1.773***
	(0.28)	(0.81)	(0.26)	(0.18)	(0.28)	(0.24)
GG			0.289	1.633**	1.558	2.224
			(0.43)	(0.64)	(1.74)	(1.34)
GG*Engy(−1)					−0.016	−0.034
Mills		5.326*		2.715***		2.917***
		(2.18)		(0.62)		(0.68)

Table 12.4
(continued)

	Heckman-Mdest-1		Heckman-Mdest-2		Heckman-Mdest-3	
	First stage	Second stage	First stage	Second stage	First stage	Second stage
Constant	−25.131***	−109.454**	−21.002***	6.818***	−20.023***	−22.901
	(7.86)	(34.59)	(7.27)	(1.78)	(7.49)	(22.19)
Adjusted R²	0.11	0.21	0.14	0.21	0.19	0.22
BJL test	1.51		1.32		1.15	
Observed	117	35	117	35	106	34

Sources: Heckman (1979) with the approved ODI data (1991–2005).

Notes: Reported are the results of estimation in equation (12.1) and equation (12.2) using the Heckman (1979) two-stage method. All insignificant (>20 percent in p-value) variables are dropped, except for variables associated with interaction terms. The columns of "Heckman-Mdest-1" report the results of regressions in equations (12.1) and (12.2); the columns of "Heckman-Mdest-2" give the results of regression controlling "going global" policy with GG dummy; "Heckman-Mdest-3" presents the results with both GG and the interaction variable $GG^*Engy(-1)$. Robust standard errors are in parentheses. ***, **, and * denote significance at the 1, 5, and 10 percent levels, respectively. The coefficient of interaction variable $GG^*Engy(-1)$ in the columns of "Heckman-Mdest-3" is reported as the marginal effect of $GG^*Engy(-1)$ (Ai and Norton 2003).

[†] Numbers in the column "First stage" report the adjusted MacFadden's pseudo R^2; the numbers in the column "Second stage" report the adjusted R^2. The Bera, Jarque, and Lee (1984) normality test is done after the Heckman first-stage regression. All results are insignificant and do not reject the null hypothesis of normal distribution.

both *GDP* and *RGDPpc* are significantly positive. Indeed China's approach to the Middle East is not to simply treat it as an oil resource destination but as an important part of a greater interdependent trade relationship (Lee and Shalmon 2007). The bilateral trade volume between China and the Middle East increased from $2.4 billion in 1991 to $142 billion in 2008.

In supplying about 50 percent of China's foreign oil need, the Middle Eastern oil exporters serve as the major oil suppliers to satisfy China's fast-growing foreign oil appetite. China's ODI is one of the primary tools that China can utilize to sustain the oil supply from the Middle East. The estimated positive effect of *XP* and *OilM* on China's ODI in Middle Eastern countries lends support to such a conjecture. China's ODI flows to the Middle East to facilitate the increasing exports volume from the Middle Eastern countries (*XP*) and the growing foreign oil need (*OilM*) pushes China's ODI to invest more in the Middle Eastern countries. Further, as suggested from the result in the "second stage" column of "Heckman-Mdest-2" in table 12.4, China's "going global" policy directs more of China's ODI to the selected Middle Eastern countries to maintain the important position of the Middle East as China's major oil suppliers.

While the Middle East remains China's major oil suppliers, China has strategically reduced its overreliance on that region to trim down the risk of possible oil supply interruption due to the traditional political instability in the Middle East. Indeed China's oil import share from the Middle East has reduced from 61 percent in 1998 to 50 percent in 2008. [19]

Furthermore China's ODI might diversify across the Middle Eastern oil countries. All the estimated coefficients of the *Engy* variable in the Tobit regression (table 12.3) and five out of six from the Heckman regression (table 12.4) are negative, though most are insignificant. This suggests, albeit the evidence is rather weak, that China's ODI does not concentrate in a few Middle Eastern oil producers with high energy output. Further China's "going global" policy does not seem to promote the ODI to concentrate in the Middle Eastern oil producers with higher energy output either. As shown in columns of "Tobit-Mdest-2" and "Tobit-Mdest-3" in table 12.3, both *GG* and "*GG*Engy*(−1)" are negative, although insignificant. A similar result is obtained in the "Heckman-Mdest-3" in table 12.4.

All these results point out that China's ODI has been diversifying across the Middle Eastern oil countries and reducing its overreliance on a few major oil exporters. More interesting, the diversification move is not a recent event. In the "second stage" of "Heckman-Mdest-3" in table 12.4, statistically significant evidence is found that China's ODI had been reducing its involvement in the Middle Eastern oil producers with high energy output before the launch of "going global" policy in 2002.

The estimated results of *Polt* and *Law* in table 12.3 indicate that in questing for oil in the Middle East, China place more of its ODI in the Gulf states where the political system is unstable and poor in law and order.

As shown in tables 12.5 and 12.6, the regression results for the African country samples are quite different from those of the Middle Eastern samples. The significant estimate for *RGDPpc* (table 12.6) suggests that the "oil-for-infrastructure" has drawn China's ODI to Africa, where the infrastructure level is rather poor. *SFDI*(−1), the proxy for the degree of competition that China's ODI could face, garners a negative and significant coefficient, indicating that an African oil country that had many other FDIs deters China's ODI. This again attests to China's investment strategy—avoiding direct competition against Western FDIs and investing in countries that lack influence of other FDIs. Indeed the estimate of *Crpt* echoes such a strategy—China's ODI goes to more corruption-heavy African oil countries where fewer Western FDIs are present.

Although China's ODI invests in corrupted African oil countries, it does seem to prefer a country with better economic conditions for business. Both estimates for *OilM* and *Engy* are in accordance with the anecdotal evidence that China has moved up the priority to rely more on the African oil. The "going global" policy strengthens such a strategic move (table 12.6).

With regard to the sample of conventional oil producers other than the Middle East and Africa (I label these oil countries as "others"), I would like to point out three prominent results that are different from those of either the Middle East or Africa. First, rather than avoid competition, China's ODI actively competes against other FDIs for oil in "others," such as Russia, Kazakhstan, Ecuador, and so on.

Second, the "going global" policy seems to change the course of China's ODI in questing for oil in "others." As shown in the "Tobit-Others-3" in table 12.7, the variable "*Engy*(−1)" gets a coefficient of −0.15 and the interaction term "*GG*Engy*(−1)" has a coefficient with a value of 0.21; both are significant. That is, prior to the implementation

Table 12.5
Empirical determinants of China's outward direct investment in African oil-producing countries

	Tobit-Africa-1	Tobit-Africa-2	Tobit-Africa-3
SFDI(−1)		−0.740*	−0.727*
		(0.44)	(0.44)
OilM(−1)	3.691***	2.258**	2.336**
	(1.04)	(1.13)	(1.14)
Engy(−1)	0.078	0.096**	0.103**
	(0.05)	(0.05)	(0.05)
Econ	1.282***	1.272***	1.191***
	(0.40)	(0.38)	(0.39)
Crpt	−1.140	−1.143*	−1.063
	(0.73)	(0.71)	(0.71)
GG		2.325**	1.325
		(1.00)	(1.47)
GG*Engy(−1)			0.045
			(0.05)
Constant	5.347	2.706	2.556
	(3.67)	(3.72)	(3.78)
Adjusted pseudo R^2	0.11	0.12	0.12
Observed	95	95	95

Sources: Tobit (1958) with the approved ODI data (1991–2005).
Notes: Reported are the results of random effect Tobit panel regression in equation (12.1). All insignificant (>20 percent in p-value) variables are dropped, except for variables associated with interaction terms. The column "Tobit-Africa-1" reports the results of regression in equation (12.1); the column "Tobit-Africa-2" gives the results of regression with "going global" dummy; the "Tobit-Africa-3" column presents the results with both GG and the interaction variable GG*Engy(−1). Robust standard errors are in parentheses. ***, **, and * denote significance at the 1, 5, and 10 percent levels, respectively. The adjusted pseudo R^2 is the adjusted McFadden's.

of "going global" policy, China's ODI goes away from "others" with high oil output; however, the "going global" policy has changed such a pattern and significantly pushed China's ODI to quest for oil in high-oil-output "others." In other words, the "going global" policy directs $0.21 more ODI per capita if an oil nation in "others" increases its energy output by 1 percent. This result is confirmed by the Heckman method ("Heckman-others-3" in table 12.8).

Third, interestingly, the values of the coefficients on XP are more than ten times as large as the ones estimated with the Middle Eastern samples. The possible interpretation is that because of the transportation security issue associated with the imported oil from the Middle

Table 12.6
Empirical determinants of China's outward direct investment in African oil-producing countries

	Heckmam-Africa-1		Heckman-Africa-2		Heckman-All-3	
	First stage	Second stage	First stage	Second stage	First stage	Second stage
$RGDPpc(-1)$	−0.722*** (0.24)		−0.867 ** (0.41)		−0.819* (0.48)	
$Engy(-1)$	−0.003 (0.01)	0.078*** (0.02)	0.002 (0.02)	0.124*** (0.02)	0.003 (0.02)	0.138*** (0.03)
$Econ$	0.539*** (0.19)		0.594** (0.26)	1.801*** (0.33)	0.606** (0.25)	2.000*** (0.31)
$Cnfl$	0.219* (0.12)					
$Sctn$		0.455** (0.16)				
$Crpt$	−0.811*** (0.18)	−1.281*** (0.28)	−0.568** (0.26)	−2.707*** (0.44)	−0.626** (0.28)	−3.076*** (0.47)
Law		−1.301** (0.52)				
$SFDI(-1)$				−0.527*** (0.12)		−0.460** (0.14)
GG			1.341* (0.75)	3.735*** (0.57)	2.237 (1.40)	3.323*** (0.37)
$GG^*Engy(-1)$					−0.007 (0.01)	0.053** (0.02)
Mills		−1.018* (0.43)		4.283*** (0.74)		5.406*** (0.84)
Constant	3.455*** (1.24)	8.313*** (1.28)	4.242* (2.23)	−0.576 (0.79)	3.996* (2.11)	−1.943** (0.77)
Adjusted R^2	0.33	0.38	0.37	0.40	0.39	0.51
BJL test	0.07		1.58		1.58	
Observed	101	55	95	51	95	51

Sources: Heckman (1979) with the approved ODI data (1991–2005).
Notes: Reported are the results of estimation in equation (12.1) and equation (12.2) using Heckman (1979) two-stage method. All insignificant (>20 percent in p-value) variables are dropped, except for variables associated with interaction terms. The columns of "Heckman-Africa-1" report the results of regressions in equations (12.1) and (12.2); the columns of "Heckman-Africa-2" give the results of regression controlling "going global" policy with GG dummy; "Heckman-Africa-3" presents the results with both GG and the interaction variable $GG^*Engy(-1)$. Robust standard errors are in parentheses. ***, **, and * denote significance at the 1, 5, and 10 percent levels, respectively. The coefficient of interaction variable $GG^*Engy(-1)$ in column "Heckman-Africa-3" is reported as the marginal effect of $GG^*Engy(-1)$ (Ai and Norton 2003).
†Numbers in the column "First stage" report the adjusted MacFadden's pseudo R^2; the numbers in the column "Second stage" report the adjusted R^2. The Bera, Jarque, and Lee (1984) normality test is done after Heckman first-stage regression. All results are insignificant and do not reject the null hypothesis of normal distribution.

Table 12.7
Empirical determinants of China's outward direct investment in other oil-producing countries

	Tobit-Others-1	Tobit-Others-2	Tobit-Others-3
$GDP(-1)$	0.984***	1.024***	1.075**
	(0.36)	(0.36)	(0.46)
$SFDI(-1)$	0.594*	0.721*	0.607
	(0.33)	(0.39)	(0.43)
$XP(-1)$	64.439***	66.490***	56.023***
	(12.03)	(12.58)	(15.99)
$Engy(-1)$	−0.072	−0.071	−0.150*
	(0.07)	(0.07)	(0.09)
$Sctn$	0.733***	0.687***	
	(0.26)	(0.26)	
$Crpt$	−1.566***	−1.618***	−1.473***
	(0.33)	(0.34)	(0.37)
GG		−0.641	−4.294**
		(1.07)	(1.76)
$GG*Engy(-1)$			0.212**
			(0.09)
Constant	−28.421***	−29.426***	−23.201*
	(10.39)	(10.46)	(12.58)
Adjusted pseudo R^2	0.24	0.24	0.23
Observed	114	114	114

Sources: Tobit (1958) with the approved ODI data (1991–2005).
Notes: Reported are the results of random effect Tobit panel regression in equation (12.1). All insignificant (>20 percent in p-value) variables are dropped, except for variables associated with interaction terms. The column "Tobit-Others-1" reports the results of regression in equation (12.1). The column "Tobit-Others-2" gives the results of regression with GG dummy; the "Tobit-Others-3" column presents the results with both the GG dummy and the interaction variable $GG*Engy(-1)$. Robust standard errors are in parentheses. ***, **, and * denote significance at the 1, 5, and 10 percent levels, respectively. The adjusted pseudo R^2 is the adjusted McFadden's.

East, China has made extraordinary efforts[20] to secure oil imports from the "others," in order to diversify the risk of possible oil supply interruption and the consequent energy insecurity.

In sum, splitting the country samples allows some similar patterns of China's ODI to be identified across different regions, namely a market-seeking motive in all three regions. More important, it uncovers the unique ways in which China's ODI serve to diversify the risk of oil supply interruption and hence provide a better energy security for China's sustainable economic growth.

Table 12.8
Empirical determinants of China's outward direct investment in other oil-producing countries

	Heckman-Others-1		Heckman-Others-2		Heckman-Others-3	
	First stage	Second stage	First stage	Second stage	First stage	Second stage
$GDP(-1)$	1.010*** (0.29)		0.981*** (0.28)		1.139*** (0.33)	-0.104 (0.07)
$XP(-1)$	41.348*** (15.08)	37.407** (11.41)	41.118*** (15.11)	13.110*** (2.96)	39.798*** (14.06)	
$SFDI(-1)$		0.675** (0.29)				
$Engy(-1)$	0.045 (0.04)	-0.053 (0.07)	0.042 (0.04)	-0.041 (0.06)	0.034 (0.04)	
$Polt$		0.768** (0.30)		0.987** (0.39)		0.708* (0.32)
$Sctn$		0.871** (0.34)		0.932** (0.34)		0.165 (0.16)
$Crpt$	-0.394*** (0.15)	-0.777*** (0.19)	-0.432*** (0.15)	-0.957*** (0.19)	-0.398** (0.16)	-0.998*** (0.17)
Law		-1.417* (0.60)		-1.378 (0.84)		
GG			-0.392 (0.51)	1.504*** (0.32)	-1.052 (0.74)	-1.864** (0.61)

Table 12.8
(continued)

	Heckman-Others-1		Heckman-Others-2		Heckman-Others-3	
	First stage	Second stage	First stage	Second stage	First stage	Second stage
$GG*Engy(-1)$					0.009	0.206***
Mills		0.625 (1.55)		0.511 (2.54)		0.715 (1.76)
Constant	-22.339*** (6.86)	-10.372* (5.25)	-21.940*** (6.63)	-8.497* (4.48)	-25.272*** (7.83)	-1.392 (4.29)
Adjusted R^2	0.17	0.49	0.20	0.50	0.24	0.47
JBL test	1.94		2.77		1.42	
Observed	114	48	114	48	114	48

Sources: Heckman (1979) with the approved ODI data (1991–2005).

Notes: Reported are the results of estimation in equation (12.1) and equation (12.2) using the Heckman (1979) two-stage method. All insignificant (>20 percent in *p*-value) variables are dropped, except for variables associated with interaction terms. The columns of "Heckman-Others-1" report the results of regressions in equations (12.1) and (12.2). The columns of "Heckman-Others-2" give the results of regression controlling "going global" policy with GG; "Heckman-Others-3" presents the results with both GG and the interaction variable $GG*Engy(-1)$. Robust standard errors are in parentheses. ***, **, and * denote significance at the 1, 5, and 10 percent levels, respectively. The coefficient of interaction variable $GG*Engy(-1)$ in the columns of "Heckman- Others -3" is reported as the marginal effect of $GG*Engy(-1)$ (Ai and Norton 2003).

¹Numbers in the column "First stage" report the adjusted MacFadden's pseudo R^2; the numbers in the column "Second stage" report the adjusted R^2. The Bera, Jarque, and Lee (1984) normality test is done after the Heckman first-stage regression. All results are insignificant and do not reject the null hypothesis of normal distribution.

12.3.3 Results Based on the ODI Data in IMF-OECD Standard

In this subsection, I report the empirical results based on China's ODI data in IMF-OECD format. The dataset covers 29 oil-producing countries from 2003 to 2007. Despite the relatively short time dimension, the dataset covers the period in which China experienced a strong growth in its overseas investment activity (Cheung and Qian 2009) and a drastic increase in its appetite for oil (figure 12.1). These data could therefore offer more information as to the link between China's overseas investment and its quest for foreign oil during this growth period.

As in the approved data, there are zero-value observations (about 15 percent of total observations) in this new ODI dataset. To be consistent, I should perform both Tobit and Heckman two-stage regressions in this section. However, due to the limited number of observations in this new dataset, the Heckman method, especially the second-stage regression, would suffer from insufficient degrees of freedom. For instance, there are only 26 observations in the Middle Eastern sample (table 12.9). I therefore drop the Heckman (1979) method and only report results from the Tobit regression. The results of the random effects panel data Tobit regression for the sample of all countries, the Middle East, Africa, and "others" are reported in the "Tobit-All," "Tobit-Mdest," "Tobit-Afr," and "Tobit-Others" columns of table 12.9, respectively.

Overall, the results are consistent with the findings based on the approved ODI data. For instance, strong presence is found of a market-seeking motive of China's ODI in oil-producing countries. A higher level of exports from oil nations to China requires a higher level of China's ODI. In addition a greater reliance on imported foreign oil pushes more of China's ODI to oil countries. Finally, China's ODI goes to those countries with relatively abundant in energy output and to more corrupted oil countries.

The results for different country samples are largely in line with those in the previous section, with a few exceptions. For example, in "Tobit-Mdest," the estimate of $SFDI(-1)$ indicates that China flexed its ODI muscle in the Middle Eastern countries to compete with other FDIs during 2003 to 2007 time period; I did not find such a competitive spirit of China's ODI in the previous section. There are a couple of plausible interpretations. (1) The Middle Eastern region is in a dominant position in the world energy supply market. Walking away from the Middle East would only worsen China oil security position. It is therefore realistic to compete against other FDIs in order to get a share of the Middle Eastern oil pie. (2) Although perceived as a small competitor

Table 12.9
Empirical determinants of China's outward direct investment in oil-producing countries

	Tobit-All	Tobit-Mdest	Tobit-Afr	Tobit-Others
GDP(−1)	1.263***	1.409***	1.476***	1.415***
	(0.31)	(0.45)	(0.57)	(0.46)
RGDPG(−1)		0.600***		
		(0.21)		
SFDI(−1)		1.679***		−0.968**
		(0.49)		(0.45)
XP(−1)	2.951**	10.330	1.942**	36.739***
	(1.40)	(6.51)	(0.92)	(12.89)
OilM(−1)	8.018**	10.231*		
	(3.31)	(5.53)		
Engy(−1)	0.049*	0.204*	0.061**	0.115*
	(0.03)	(0.12)	(0.03)	(0.06)
Econ	0.355	−1.370**		
	(0.26)	(0.55)		
Cnfl	0.520	2.491**		
	(0.40)	(1.06)		
Sctn				0.718**
				(0.29)
Crpt	−1.073***		−1.801**	
	(0.38)		(0.84)	
Law		−1.893**		
		(0.76)		
Constant	−19.593*	−44.873***	−28.596**	−34.539***
	(10.61)	(14.31)	(13.76)	(12.43)
Pseudo adjusted R^2	0.12	0.29	0.07	0.15
Observed	94	26	31	37

Sources: Tobit (1958) with the OECD-IMF format ODI data (2003–2007).
Notes: Reported are the results of random effect Tobit panel regression in equation (12.1). All insignificant (>20 percent in p-value) variables are dropped. The column "Tobit-All" reports the results of regression with all country samples; the column "Tobit-Afr" gives the results of regression with African countries sample; the "Tobit-Mdest" column presents the results with the Middle East oil-producing countries sample; and the column "Tobit-Others" reports the results of regression with all other oil-producing countries sample. Robust standard errors are in parentheses. ***, **, and * denote significance at the 1, 5, and 10 percent levels, respectively. The adjusted pseudo R^2 is the adjusted McFadden's.

and a latecomer, China has two advantages over others in getting the Middle Eastern oil: it offers a paucity of political packages to the negotiation table that the Middle Eastern countries are unable to get from Western countries, and it has an enormous market for Middle Eastern goods and services (Lee and Shalmon 2007).

The significant estimates for three political risk components, *Econ*, *Cnfl*, and *Law*, reveal the complicated behavior of China's ODI in the Middle East. While evidence that China's ODI prefers a country with less conflict is in line with conventional wisdom, the fact that better economic conditions deter China's ODI is intriguing. It might be related to China's routine strategy—going to "rogue" oil states where there is less competition and it is relatively easy to set foot. These "rogue" states usually have relatively bad economic conditions for FDI business. The negatively significant estimate for *Law* lends credit to such an interpretation.

Interestingly, the *SFDI*(−1) in the "others" sample has an opposite sign from its counterpart estimations in tables 12.7 and 12.8. Did China shift the strategy of investment in "others" during 2003 to 2007? We may need data over a longer time period to answer this question. At this moment one plausible explanation may again point to China's involvement with "rogue" state, such as Venezuela, where other FDIs, particularly those from the United States, largely retreated after Mr. Hugo Chavez took power in 1998.[21]

A comparison of the results from the three individual samples shows a few common determinants of China's ODI. For example, China's ODI seeks markets, more of China's ODI goes to facilitate the higher exports to China from oil countries, and of course, an abundance of energy output in an oil-producing country draws China's ODI to quest for energy there.

In sum, China's ODI keeps to routine behavior toward oil producers after 2003: namely market seeking, favoring energy abundance, and choosing more corruption. It has, however, developed a few new features in investing in different regions. For instance, facing rough reality, China's ODI leverages its own advantages to compete actively in the Middle East against other FDIs; in contrast, it still plays as a weak competitor to avoid brutal competition in other regions.

12.4   Concluding Remarks

In this chapter, I examine the empirical determinants of China's ODI in conventional oil-producing countries. These determinants include the canonical economic factors and some China specific factors, such as the push factor and Chinese government policies that affect China's ODI in oil countries. Both China's officially approved ODI data and the ODI data, which reportedly follow the OECD-IMF standard, are used in my empirical exercise.

Some common economic factors are found to be significant determinants of China's ODI in oil-producing countries. For example, China's ODI tends to go to oil countries with a large market size and more exports to China. In line with the natural resource-seeking strategy, China's ODI responses positively to the energy output of a host oil country. Heavily relying on foreign oil has pushed China's ODI to secure the oil supply that underpins China's long-term economic growth. Apparently China does not make the "invest or not-to-invest" decision based on a country's energy output. Once a positive investment decision is made, however, China tends to invest more in oil countries with a higher energy output.

China's ODI is generally averse to political risks—a result that is in accordance with theory and intuition. In terms of the level of corruption in a host country, my findings indicate that corruption in oil-producing countries tends to draw in China's ODI.

Although the Chinese economy has been transitioning gradually from a centrally planned economy to one that is market driven since the adoption of the open door policy in 1978, government policies still play a significant role in affecting China's economic activities. Apparently there is no exception in the ODI arena. The "going global" policy is a typical example. Under the directive of deploying investments overseas to support the economic development at home, China's "going global" policy induces a higher volume of ODI to oil countries and a higher concentration in countries with higher oil production.

Subject to the different investment strategies that China implemented, the behavior of China's ODI in the Middle East, Africa, and other oil-producing countries is different. While diversifying globally to reduce the risk of oil supply interruption, China's ODI has put more weight in Africa and other oil nations, and has been diversifying away from and across the Middle Eastern region; nevertheless, the Middle East remains China's main source of imported oil.

I note that there are a few issues related to the ODI data. For instance, the two datasets used in my empirical exercises are compiled according to different methodologies. The results generated by these two different datasets using two different econometric methods are encouraging in that they are quite comparable and compatible; my empirical results are robust.

China has been diversifying its ODI activities globally. The options for China's ODI are rather limited, however, due to the highly competitive nature of the global energy market. As a latecomer, China's ODI has to confront much stronger FDIs in traditional oil-producing countries, such as in the Middle East. This obviously puts China in a disadvantaged position.

Consequently China has to consider other options for its ODI. One option is connecting to the "rogue" states that Western FDIs deliberately avoid due to the political risk. Other options include going to some nontraditional oil-producing countries that produce limited energy that, for IOCs, is not commercially viable. Such nontraditional oil producers include Equatorial Guinea and Cameroon, for example.

To better understand China's ODI in questing for oil, we need access to better information about the "rogue" states and include more data samples of nontraditional oil producers. Therefore, while my analyses offer some insights into the factors affecting China's investment decisions, further research is warranted to broaden our understanding of the related economic and political interactions between China and the oil-producing nations.

Appendix A: Data—Definition and Sources

Variable Definition

ODI	China's approved outward direct investment scaled by the host country's population. [Source: Editorial Broad of the Almanac of China's Foreign Economic Relations and Trade (1992–2006)]; China's outward direct investment in IMF-OECD standard scaled by the host country's population. [Source: *Statistical Bulletin of China's Outward Foreign Direct Investment* and *China Commerce Yearbook*, the Ministry of Commerce, China (2005–2008)]
GDP	Host country's nominal GDP in current US dollar (log value). [Source: World Bank, World Development Indicators]
RGDPpc	Host country's real per capita GDP in constant 2000 US dollar (log value). [Source: World Bank, World Development Indicators]
GDPG	Host country's real GDP growth rate. [Source: World Bank, World Development Indicators]
OilM	China's imports of crude oil (thousand barrels per day) divided by China's total consumption (thousand barrels per day). [Source: Energy Information Administration (EIA)]

XP	Share of exports of an oil-producing country to China to the total exports of that country. [Source: IMF, DOT]
SFDI	Total FDI stock in a host country except China's ODI (log value). [Source: UNCTAD FDI Statistics]
Engy	Energy depletion (percent of GNI) is equal to the product of unit resource rents and the physical quantities of energy extracted. It covers crude oil, natural gas, and coal. [Source: World Bank, World Development Indicators]
Econ	Economic condition risk index of a host country, calculated as the sum of socioeconomic condition index and investment profile index of ICRG. [Source: International Country Risk Guide (ICRG)]
Polt	Political system risk of a host country, calculated as the sum of government stability, military in politics, and democratic accountability index of ICRG. [Source: International Country Risk Guide (ICRG)]
Cnfl	Confliction risk index of a host country, calculated as the sum of internal conflict and external conflict index of ICRG. [Source: International Country Risk Guide (ICRG)]
Sctn	Social tension index of a host country, calculated as the sum of religious tensions and ethnic tensions index of ICRG. [Source: International Country Risk Guide (ICRG)]
Crpt	Corruption risk index of a host country, calculated as the sum of corruption and bureaucracy quality index of ICRG. [Source: International Country Risk Guide (ICRG)]
Law	Law and order risk index of a host country. [Source: International Country Risk Guide (ICRG)]
GG	Time dummy variable for China's "going global" policy. $I(t >= 2002) = 1$; otherwise 0.

Appendix B: List of Conventional Oil-Producing Countries

African Oil Producers
Algeria, Angola, Congo Republic, Egypt, Gabon, Libya, Nigeria, Sudan.

Middle Eastern Oil Producers
Bahrain, Iran, Iraq, Kuwait, Oman, Qatar, Saudi Arabia, Syria, United Arab Emirates, Yemen.

Other Oil Producers
Azerbaijan, Brunei, Colombia, Ecuador, Indonesia, Kazakhstan, Mexico, Norway, Russia, Trinidad and Tobago, Venezuela.

Notes

Qian acknowledges the financial support from the Dean of School of Natural and Social Science at Buffalo State. He thanks Lauren Malone, Shu Yu, and participants of the 2010 CESifo Venice Summer Institution Workshop for their helpful comments and suggestions.

1. They are China National Petroleum Corporation (CNPC), China Petroleum and Chemical Group (Sinopec), and China National Offshore Oil Corporation (CNOOC).

2. There are also some failed attempts and aborted deals, such as CNOOC's failed acquisition of Unocal in the United States in 2005.

3. The equity oil is the proportion of oil production that a concession owner has the legal and contractual right to retain. The "concession" means the operating right to explore and develop petroleum fields in consideration for a share of production in-kind (equity oil).

4. In the current study, "energy" includes oil, gas, and coal. The major part of "energy" produced in a conventional oil country, however, is comprised of oil and gas.

5. There is no updated information available for more recent years, such as 2008.

6. I do not consider the 2008 OECD-IMF format data because these data were reported based on the definition different from those of the 2003 to 2007 data.

7. Most studies on China's ODI are policy oriented or descriptive in nature, including two early studies on China's ODI, Sung (1996) and Wall (1997), as well as Asia Pacific Foundation of Canada (2005, 2006), UNCTAD (2003, 2007), Wang and Bio-Tchané (2008), Wong and Chan (2003), and Wu and Chen (2001).

8. According to *the 2008 Statistical Bulletin of China's Outward Foreign Direct Investment*, state-owned enterprises account for 69.6 percent of total China's ODI stock in 2008.

9. The financial ODI include China's direct investment in banking, insurance, securities, and other financial institution sectors.

10. There are other proxies for the energy abundance. For instance, the data on the ratio of total fuel exports to total merchandise exports from the *World Development Indicators* database. However, these data are not available for many of our sample countries.

11. As a robustness check, we have also considered lagged political risk variables. The results are qualitatively similar to those reported in the text, and hence are not reported for brevity.

12. The fixed effects Tobit panel data regression generates biased estimates; see, for example, the discussions in Greene (2004a, b).

13. The selection of 29 conventional oil-producing countries (appendix B) follows IMF papers and reports, for example, Arezki and Brückner (2009), Policy Development and Review Department of IMF Policy Development and Review Department (2005), and World Economic Outlook (2008).

14. To reveal the energy-seeking information about China's ODI, the *Engy* variables are included even if they are insignificant more than 20 percent. Nevertheless, dropping the insignificant *Engy* variables does not affect the results of other variables.

15. For instance, China started to invest in a 620-mile pipeline from northern Kazakhstan to Xinjiang, China, in 2006, and it is scheduled to complete in 2011. The pipeline eventually leads to the oil field in Iran. And in 2009 China signed an agreement with Myanmar to build a pipeline crossing Myanmar as an alternative transport route for crude oil from the Middle East and Africa that would bypass the potential sea-lane choke point of the Strait of Malacca (EIA 2009).

16. Similar to the fixed effects Tobit regression, the fixed effect Probit regression generates biased estimates, see, for example, the discussions in Greene (2004a, b).

17. "Kao duoyuanhua baozhang Zhongguo youqi gongying" ("Rely on diversification to guarantee China's oil and gas supply"), *Zhongguo shiyou bao (China Oil News)*, January 12, 2000, p. 1; "Di san zhi yan kan Zhongguo shiyou" ("The third eye looks at China's oil"), *Zhongguo shiyou bao (China Oil News)*, January 18, 2000, p. 2.

18. OPEC database, 2006.

19. See Lewis (2002) and EIA (2009).

20. Most efforts that have been seen are multi-billion dollar investments in pipeline enabling China to directly ship oil and gas across the Chinese border, for example, the pipeline from Kazakhstan to Xinjiang in western China.

21. According to UNCTAD FDI statistics, the FDI inflow to Venezuela continuously declined from about 5 billion in 1998 to about –0.6 billion dollars in 2006.

References

Ai, C., and E. Norton. 2003. Interaction terms in logit and probit models. *Economics Letters* 80: 123–29.

Aizenman, J., and I. Noy. 2006. FDI and trade—Two-way linkages? *Quarterly Review of Economics and Finance* 46 (3): 317–37.

Arezki, R., and M. Brückner. 2009. Oil rents, corruption, and state stability: Evidence from panel data regressions. Working Paper 09/267. IMF, Washington, DC.

Asia Pacific Foundation of Canada. 2005. *China Goes Global: A Survey of Chinese Companies' Outward Direct Investment Intentions.* Vancouver: Asia Pacific Foundation of Canada.

Asia Pacific Foundation of Canada. 2006. Survey of Chinese companies' outward direct investment intentions. In *China Goes Global*, vol. 2. Vancouver: Asia Pacific Foundation of Canada.

Asiedu, E. 2006. Foreign direct investment in Africa: The role of natural resources, market size, government policy, institutions and political instability. *World Economy* 29 (1): 63–77.

Atkinson, G., and K. Hamilton. 2003. Savings, growth and the resource curse hypothesis. *World Development* 31 (11): 1793–1807.

Bera, A., C. Jarque, and L.-F. Lee. 1984. Testing the normality assumption in limited dependent variable models. *International Economic Review* 25 (3): 563–78.

Billington, N. 1999. The location of foreign direct investment: An empirical analysis. *Applied Economics* 31: 65–76.

Bremner, B., D. Roberts, A. Aston, S. Reed, and J. Bush. 2004. Asia's great oil hunt. *Business Week.* Available at: http://www.businessweek.com/magazine/content/04_46/b3908044.htm.

Buckley, P., J. Clegg, A. Cross, X. Liu, H. Voss, and P. Zheng. 2007. The determinants of Chinese outward foreign direct investment. *Journal of International Business Studies* 38: 499–518.

Chen, S. 2008. China's outward FDI and energy security. Working paper 143. East Asia Institution, Singapore National University.

Cheng, L., and Z. Ma. 2009. China's outward FDI: Past and future. Manuscript. Hong Kong University of Science and Technology.

Cheung, Y.-W., and X. Qian. 2009. Empirics of China's outward direct investment. *Pacific Economic Review* 14 (3): 312–41.

Cheung, Y.-W., J. de Haan, X. Qian, and S. Yu. 2010. China's outward direct investment in Africa. Working Paper. SUNY Buffalo State.

China, Industry Warning Net. 2006. Zhongguo Shiyou Quye Haiwai Touzi fenbu (The distribution of overseas investment by Chinese oil companies). http://www.calert.com.cn/ReadNews.asp?NewsId= 362.

Downs, E. 2000. *China's Quest for Energy Security.* Santa Monica: RAND.

Downs, E. 2007. The fact and fiction of Sino-African energy relations. *China Security* 3 (3): 42–68.

Downs, E. 2008. China's NOCs: Lessons learned from adventures abroad. *Fundamentals of the Global Oil and Gas Industry.* London: Petroleum Economist, 27–31.

Eaton, J., and A. Tamura. 1994. Bilateralism and regionalism in Japanese and U.S. trade and FDI patterns. *Journal of the Japanese and International Economies* 8: 478–510.

Eaton, J., and A. Tamura. 1996. Japanese and US exports and investment as conduits of growth. Working Paper 5457. NBER, Cambridge, MA.

Energy Information Administration (EIA). 2006. *World Oil Consumption by Region, Reference Case, 1990–2030 (Table A4).* Washington, DC: US Department of Energy.

Energy Information Administration (EIA). 2009. *Country Analysis Briefs—China.* Washington, DC: US Department of Energy.

Frankel, J., and S.-J. Wei. 1996. ASEAN in a regional perspective. Working paper C96–074. University of California, Berkeley.

Greene, W. 2004a. Fixed effects and bias due to the incidental parameters problem in the Tobit model. *Econometric Reviews* 23 (2): 125–47.

Greene, W. 2004b. The behavior of the fixed effects estimator in nonlinear models. *Econometrics Journal* 7: 98–119.

Gu, S. 1998. PRC resources security assessed. *Zhongguo kexue bao* (China Science News), p. 3. *WNC* (Document ID: 0f55msm01fsior).

Guo, X. 2006. Energy security in central Eurasia. *China and Eurasia Forum Quarterly* 4: 130.

He, Z. 2008. China's energy strategy in Central Asia. *Shanghai Economic Research* 1: 37–46.

Heckman, J. 1979. Sample selection bias as a specification error. *Econometrica: Journal of the Econometric Society* 47 (1): 153–61.

IMF Policy Development and Review Department. 2005. Oil market developments and issues. Policy Paper. IMF, Washington, DC.

International Energy Agency (IEA). 2000. *China's World Wide Quest of Energy Security*. Paris: OECD.

Jakobson, L., and D. Zha. 2006. China and the worldwide search for oil security. *Asia–Pacific Review* 13 (2): 60–73.

Khan, H. 2008. China's energy drive and diplomacy. *International Review* (Shanghai Institute for International Studies, SIIS): 93–94.

Kinoshita, Y., and N. Campos. 2004. Estimating the determinants of foreign direct investment inflows: How important are sampling and omitted variable biases? BOFIT Discussion Paper 10/2004. Bank of Finland, Helsinki.

Klare, M., and D. Volman. 2006. The African "oil rush" and American national security. *Third World Quarterly* 27: 4.

Kravis, I., and R. Lipsey. 1982. Location of overseas production and production for export by U.S. multinational firms. *Journal of International Economics* 12: 201–23.

Kreft, H. 2006. China's quest for energy. Policy review. Hoover Institution, Stanford University.

Lane, P. 2000. International investment positions: A cross-sectional analysis. *Journal of International Money and Finance* 19: 513–34.

Lee, H., and D. Shalmon. 2007. Searching for oil: China's oil initiatives in the Middle East. Faculty Research Working Paper. John F. Kennedy School of Government, Harvard University.

Leverett, F., and J. Bader. 2005. Managing China–U.S. energy competition in the Middle East. *Washington Quarterly* 29: 187–201.

Lewis, S. 2002. China's oil diplomacy and relations with the Middle East: Post September 11–updated report. James A. Baker III Institute for Public Policy, Rice University.

Lieberthal, K., and M. Herberg. 2006. China's search for energy security: Implications for US policy. Analysis Paper 40. NBR (National Bureau of Asian Research), Seattle.

Lipsey, R. 1999. The location and characteristics of US affiliates in Asia. Working Paper 6876. NBER, Cambridge, MA.

Ministry of Commerce of China. 2005–2008. *Statistical Bulletin of China's Outward Foreign Direct Investment and China Commerce Yearbook*. Beijing.

Ross, Michael. 1999. The political economy of the resource curse. *World Politics* 51: 297–322.

Sung, Y.-W. 1996. Chinese outward investment in Hong Kong: Trends, prospects and policy implications. Technical paper 113. OECD Development Centre, Paris.

The Economist. 2008. Intrepid explorers: China's mining and oil firms pop up everywhere. *The Economist Journal.* http://www.economist.com/node/10795755.

Tobin, J. 1958. Estimation of relationships for limited dependent variables. *Econometrica* 26 (1): 24–36.

Tu, T. 2008. China's strategic petroleum reserves in Sino–Venezuela Relations. *China Brief* (Jamestown Foundation, Washington, DC) 8: 19.

UNCTAD (UN Conference on Trade and Development). 2003. *China: An Emerging FDI Outward Investor. E-Brief.* New York: United Nations.

UNCTAD. 2006. *World Investment Report.* New York: United Nations.

UNCTAD. 2007. *Asian Foreign Direct Investment in Africa: Towards a New Era of Cooperation among Developing Countries.* New York: United Nations.

Wall, D. 1997. Outflow of capital from China. Technical paper 123. OECD Development Centre, Paris.

Wang, J.-Y., and A. Bio-Tchané. 2008. Africa's burgeoning ties with China. *Finance and Development* 45 (1): 44–47.

Wheeler, D., and A. Mody. 1992. International investment location decisions: The case of U.S. firms. *Journal of International Economics* 33: 57–76.

Wong, J., and S. Chan. 2003. China's outward direct investment: Expanding worldwide. *China. International Journal* (Toronto) (1/2): 273–301.

Wooldridge, J. 1995. Selection corrections for panel data models under conditional mean independence assumptions. *Journal of Econometrics* 68: 115–32.

World Economic Outlook. 2008. Financial stress, downturns, and recoveries. In *Divergence of Current Account Balances across Emerging Economies.* Washington, DC: IMF, 129–58.

Wu, H.-L., and C.-H. Chen. 2001. An assessment of outward foreign direct investment from China's transitional economy. *Europe–Asia Studies* 53: 1235–54.

13 China's Investments in Africa

Yin-Wong Cheung, Jakob de Haan, Xingwang Qian, and Shu Yu

13.1 Introduction

China's fast-growing economic ties with Africa have attracted considerable attention. China's trade (exports plus imports) with Africa increased steadily, albeit at a slow pace, in the 1990s, but surged from $9.5 billion in 2000, to $36.3 billion in 2005, and to $79.8 billion in 2009. Likewise China has become one of the major capital providers for countries in Africa (UNCTAD 2007). According to the 2009 *China Commerce Yearbook*, China's outward direct investment (ODI) in Africa relative to its total ODI increased from 2.6 percent in 2003 to 9.8 percent in 2008. Africa has in fact become the third largest recipient of China's ODI in recent years (Besada et al. 2008). In addition to trade and ODI, contracted projects are another important channel through which China interacts with Africa. These contracted projects include building of highways and roads, bridges, schools, shopping centers, housing and office buildings, water conservancy, dams, and power plants. The dollar value of China's contracted projects dwarfs its ODI in Africa.

According to Morrison (2009), several factors drive China's ODI. First, the increase in foreign exchange reserves has led China to seek more profitable ways of investing these reserves (which traditionally have mainly been put into relatively safe, low yield assets, e.g., US Treasury securities). Second, China purchases existing companies and their brand names. Third, acquisition of energy and raw materials has been an important priority of China's ODI strategy.

Indeed a very common view is that China's interest in Africa is mainly driven by its concern to achieve more security of supply for natural resources, rather than relying on global markets.[1] Likewise worries have been raised that Chinese investments could crowd out African manufacturing industry, causing unemployment. The number of high-quality jobs created by Chinese investments is perceived to be quite limited, since Chinese firms tend to bring along their own workers. Some other concerns include the possible negative impacts of China's ODI on the environment, governance, and political reforms in Africa. Some observers criticize China's policy as it tolerates, and passively exacerbates, authoritarian regimes and human right violations. For instance, Brookes (2007, p. 5) argues that "Chinese policies are . . . troubling, especially when they support authoritarian African regimes, . . . and exacerbate conflicts and human rights abuses in countries such as Sudan and Zimbabwe."[2]

Yet the benefits of China's ODI may be enormous (UNCTAD 2010a). Chinese capital offers a valuable source of financing for African countries. Arguably China has played a positive role in improving infrastructures, increasing productivity, boosting exports, and raising the living standards of millions of Africans. Sometimes China's ODI is credited for diversifying economic activity and creating jobs in manufacturing, mining, processing trade, and construction.

Although China's economic relations with Africa have attracted some attention in the academic literature (e.g., see Besada et al. 2008; Morck et al. 2008; Broadman 2007; Wang 2007), formal econometric evidence of the driving factors of China's ODI in Africa is scarce.[3] In previous work (Cheung et al. 2012) we have examined to what extent China's ODI is driven by standard economic determinants of foreign direct investment. We concluded that there is evidence in support of the market-seeking motive, the risk-avoiding motive, and the resources-seeking motive. The economic links with China that are captured by trade relations and contracted projects affect China's investment decision. Once an investment decision is made, China tends to invest more in oil-producing African countries. The effects of natural resources on China's investment decision are especially visible after the adoption of the "going global" policy in 2002.

This chapter extends our previous work by examining to what extent also political considerations and host-country characteristics affect China's ODI in Africa. For instance, does China invest more in countries that are political allies? Do autocratic and corrupt regimes receive more Chinese ODI? Most important, what happens with the economic drivers of China's ODI in Africa once political factors are included in the analysis?

We use two sets of China's ODI data. The first one contains data on China's ODI approved by Chinese authorities. The sample period is from 1991 to 2005. The end of the sample period is dictated by the availability of the officially approved ODI data. The sample starts in 1991 because host-country specific ODI data are available only after 1991. The second dataset comprises ODI data (2003 to 2007) compiled by the Ministry of Commerce of China using the OECD-IMF standard. The second dataset only contains observations after 2002, when the "going global" policy was announced, allowing us to test whether this policy change had any implications for the importance of economic vs. political determinants of Chinese ODI in Africa.

Since the ODI data are "censored" at zero and below, we estimate Tobit models. In addition we use the Heckman (1979) method that allows us to separate the investment decision process into two stages. First, a decision is taken whether to invest in a host country. If this is the case, the second decision is how much to invest in the country concerned.

Our main findings are that in the Tobit models for the first dataset political variables seem to dominate economic determinants of China's ODI in Africa. The likelihood that a country receives ODI from China increases if the country concerned is a political ally of China, has diplomatic relations with China, is corrupt, democratic, and politically stable. In contrast, for the second dataset most political variables turn out to be insignificant. According to our estimates for the more recent period, China's ODI in Africa is mainly driven by economic ties (trade and projects) and the drive for natural resources. The Heckman models suggest that the decision to invest in a country is driven by different factors than the decision how much to invest in a country.

The remainder of the chapter is structured as follows. Section 13.2 describes the data used in this chapter, while section 13.3 presents the hypotheses tested. Sections 13.4 and 13.5 contain the estimation results, and the final section concludes.

13.2   China's ODI in Africa

The ties between China and Africa can be traced back to the Bandung Conference in Indonesia—the first large-scale Asian—African Conference held in 1955. On May 30, 1956, China established its first formal diplomatic relationship in Africa, with Egypt. Ever since, China has been cultivating and maintaining ties by spreading revolutionary ideology and offering economic and military support to its "third world" African friends. However, China changed course in the 1980s. As pointed out by Cheung and Qian (2009), its policy has been transformed from a purely political devise to a more market-oriented strategy. Before 1985, only state-owned and local-government-owned enterprises were allowed to invest overseas, but after 1985 private enterprises were permitted to apply for ODI projects. However, the state is still heavily involved in the FDI activity.

One Chinese policy action that has attracted some attention is the establishment of special economic zones in Africa. For China, special economic zones play a crucial role in its recent astonishing economic performance. Conceived to be an effective policy to promote the manufacturing sector and employment in Africa, China has assisted some African countries in developing their own special economic zones and encouraged Chinese companies to invest in them. The first special economic zone established under this initiative is in the Chambishi copper belt region in Zambia. Despite its potential benefits to the African economies, China's involvement in these African special economic zones is not without critics.[4] At the beginning of the 1990s, Chinese ODI surged, especially in Hong Kong. After the 1997 Asian financial crisis, China adjusted its ODI strategy. In 1999, a directive was issued to encourage direct investment abroad that promotes China's exports via "processing trade" investment, while in 2002, the Chinese authorities pushed the "going global" strategy to sustain the economic reform process and to promote global industry champions in the wake of the WTO accession. This policy represents China's concerted efforts to encourage investments in overseas markets to support economic development and sustain economic reform in China.

Despite all these changes, the absolute amount of China's ODI is quite small and it accounted for only 1.2 percent of the world's total FDI in 2009. Still China's ODI as a share of FDI from developing countries has increased steadily since the 1990s and reached the 9 percent level in 2003 and 17 percent in 2009. Indeed the 2010 United Nations survey reported that China is ranked as the second most promising global investor (UNCTAD 2010b).

We use data on approved ODI as annually published by the Ministry of Commerce and the former Ministry of Foreign Trade and Economic Cooperation in the *Almanac of China's Foreign Economic Relations and Trade*. Country-specific approved ODI data are available since 1991, offering a reasonably long time series to investigate the linkages between Chinese ODI in Africa and the characteristics of its host countries. Chinese ODI is still to a great extent determined by the government, and using ODI projects approved by the authorities thus allows examining China's policies.[5] This dataset is available for the period 1991 to 2005. The top three receivers in Africa of ODI from China are South Africa, Sudan, and Algeria.

We have a second dataset on China's ODI from the China Commerce Year Book that runs from 2003 to 2007 in which ODI is measured differently, so that both datasets cannot be merged. This dataset reports the data according to the IMF-OECD standard, thereby mitigating one of the drawbacks of the other dataset that we use. The top three receivers in Africa of ODI from China are now Nigeria, South Africa, and Sudan.

In the remainder of this chapter we will investigate the driving forces of Chinese ODI in Africa by testing various hypotheses, building on our previous work (Cheung et al. 2012).

13.3 Hypotheses and Data

Table 13.1 shows the hypotheses to be tested. We distinguish between three groups of hypotheses. The first set of hypotheses refers to "standard" economic determinants of ODI on which we focused in our previous work. The second group of hypotheses focuses on political ties between the host country and China, while the third subset of hypotheses refers to political and institutional host-country characteristics. Data availability primarily determined the list of hypotheses tested. The appendix offers summary statistics of the data used and provides detailed information on their sources.

The first hypothesis is that Chinese ODI in Africa is determined by the drive for new markets. Numerous studies (surveyed by Chakrabarti 2001) show that FDI and market size are associated positively. In our previous work we employed various proxies to test the importance of the market-seeking motive, and it turned out that the host country's gross domestic product, measured in current US dollars in logs (GDP) outperforms other indicators. GDP represents the market size and has been used in previous research (Frankel and Wei 1996; Kravis and Lipsey 1982; Wheeler and Mody 1992). Data were drawn from the *World Development Indicators* database of the World Bank. According to our first hypothesis, GDP is expected to have a positive impact on Chinese ODI in Africa.

The second hypothesis is that China will invest in African countries with which it has close economic ties. We use two proxies to test this

Table 13.1
Hypotheses

Hypothesis	Proxies	Expected sign
Standard economic determinants		
1. China invests in African countries with large market potential	GDP	+
2. China invests in African countries with which it has strong economic ties	EX, Proj	+
3. China invests in African countries with low risk	RISK	+
4. China invests in African countries with large amounts of natural resources	Engy, Min	+
Political ties with China		
5. China invests in African countries that are close political allies	UN Voting	−
6. China invests in African countries with which it has long-standing diplomatic relations	Diplomatic	+
Host country characteristics		
7. China invests in African countries that are nonauthoritarian	Autocracy	−
8. China invests in African countries with low levels of corruption and a good bureaucracy	Corruption, Law and Order	+/− +
9. China invests in African countries that are politically stable	ExecChn	−

hypothesis, namely *EX* and *Proj*. The first variable, *EX,* is the ratio of the host country's total exports to China and total exports of the host country.[6] Although it is more common to use total trade, a case can be made that exports to China may be more relevant. China's recent investment in Africa is generally perceived to follow the state-driven strategy of giving infrastructure and taking natural resources (see Foster et al. 2008). If true, exports of African countries to China should increase ODI.

The second element, *Proj,* is the amount of China's contracted projects in a host country normalized by the host country's population. Contracted projects are an important channel through which China interacts with Africa. Conceivably, contracted projects require endorsements by local authorities. Thus the amount of contracted projects is indicative of the existing economic ties between China and the host country. To facilitate comparison across countries of different size, we normalize the data by the host country's population. We expect *Proj* to have a positive impact on China's ODI.

The incentive to invest could be adversely affected by the presence of risk factors (hypothesis 3). Traditionally many African countries are considered to be very risky (Asiedu 2002). This explains why Africa receives little capital from Western investors. We include *RISK* to assess the effect of a host country's risk characteristics on China's ODI. This variable is the sum of the socioeconomic conditions index and the investment profile index as provided by the *International Country Risk Guide* (ICRG) divided by two. The socioeconomic conditions index is an assessment of the socioeconomic pressures at work in society that could constrain government action or fuel social dissatisfaction. The rating assigned is the sum of three subcomponents, each with a maximum score of 4 points (very low risk) and a minimum score of 0 points (very high risk). The subcomponents are unemployment, consumer confidence, and poverty. The investment profile index is an assessment of factors affecting the risk to investment that are not covered by other political, economic, and financial risk components. The rating assigned is the sum of three subcomponents, each with a maximum score of 4 points (very low risk) and a minimum score of 0 points (very high risk). The subcomponents are contract viability/ expropriation, profits repatriation, and payment delays. Our *RISK* index runs from 0 (high risk) to 12 (low risk). According to our third hypothesis, *RISK* is expected to have a positive impact on Chinese ODI in Africa.

China seriously lacks natural resources to support its high rates of economic growth. Growing at double digits requires access to natural resources. However, the evidence in support of natural resources as a pull factor (hypothesis 4) is mixed. Whereas Ramasamy et al. (2010) report that China's ODI is attracted to countries with abundant natural resources, Cheung and Qian (2009) found otherwise. The different focus between these two studies could explain these diverging results. The study of Ramasamy et al. (2012) refers to the number of international location decisions made by private and nonprivate Chinese firms during the period 2006 to 2008, while Cheung and Qian (2009) use similar data as the present study but focus on Chinese ODI in all countries.

Two endowment-related variables, *Engy* and *Min*, are used to examine whether China's drive for natural resources impacts its ODI in Africa. *Engy* is a host country's energy output that includes crude oil, natural gas, and coal output. *Min* is the mineral output that includes bauxite, copper, iron, and gold. Both *Engy* and *Min* are normalized by the host country's gross national income. The data on *Engy* and *Min* were also retrieved from the World Bank.

The next set of hypotheses refers to China's political ties with the host country. According to Besada et al. (2008, p. 15), "A key element in understanding what is behind the growth in China's involvement in Africa is the central Chinese precept that business should not be mixed with politics. China's growing presence in Africa thus largely reflects commercial rather than other political considerations." These authors claim in fact that the Chinese position is not to interfere in other countries' internal affairs, and thus respecting their right to choose the road of development that best suits them. In contrast, it can be hypothesized that China has a preference for countries that are political allies (hypothesis 5). We test this hypothesis using data on voting behavior in the UN General Assembly. Unfortunately, data on voting in line with China are not available, and therefore we follow Barro and Lee (2005) and use a variable reflecting the extent to which a country voted in line with the United States, discarding those votes where more than 80 percent of the countries agreed (*UN Voting*). The data were provided by Axel Dreher (see Dreher and Sturm 2012). The expected sign of this proxy is negative.

Under hypothesis 6, China is expected to invest in those countries with which it has diplomatic relations. In the course of time China has established diplomatic ties with many African countries. In 2010 China has a formal diplomatic relationship with 49 of the 54 countries on the African continent. Our variable *Diplomatic* is a dummy indicating whether country *i* and China have a diplomatic relationship in year *t*. If so, the dummy is one and it is zero otherwise. The data come from the Ministry of Foreign Affairs of the People's Republic of China (http://www.fmprc.gov.cn/eng/). The expected coefficient is positive.

The final set of hypotheses refers to host-country characteristics. The view outlined concerning China's noninterference policy above also implies that China should not have a preference for democratic versus autocratic states. At the same time China supports African leaders, like Mugabe in Zimbabwe and Bashir in Sudan (Brookes 2007). A possible reason is that making a deal with an autocrat is easier than with a democratic country. Still most previous evidence reports that democracy enhances FDI (see Adam and Filippaios 2007; Busse and Hefeker 2007 and references cited therein). Under hypothesis 7, China is therefore assumed to invest in non-autocratic states. We use the sum of the Political Rights and Civil Liberties indicators of the Freedom House to proxy *Autocracy*. The Freedom House indicators have a value between 1 and 7 (where 7 = autocracy and 1 = democracy), so our indicator ranges between 2 and 14. According to hypothesis 7, *Autocracy* is expected to have a negative impact on Chinese ODI in Africa.

Next we test whether China invests in countries with low corruption and good governance (hypothesis 8). On the one hand, a poor institutional environment is often argued to deter foreign investment (Globerman and Shapiro 2002). On the other hand, corruption may be seen as facilitating transactions and speeding up procedures that would otherwise occur with more difficulty, if at all (Cuervo-Cazurra 2006). Therefore the expected sign of corruption is ambiguous. To capture corruption, we include a variable *Corruption* provided by the International Country Risk Guide (ICRG). The ICRG data are based on perceived corruption by a panel of experts. The level of corruption is expressed on a scale between zero and six, where a higher score means less corruption. Although there are many proxies available for measuring corruption, this index is the only one that is available for a long period of time for many countries and that has been constructed in a consistent way (see Seldadyo and de Haan 2011). To capture governance, we include the *Law and Order* index of ICRG. This indicator assesses (on a 6-point scale) the strength and impartiality of the legal system (the law component) as well as popular observance of the law (the order component). The expected sign of *Law and Order* is positive.

Finally, hypothesis 9 states that China prefers to invest in countries that are politically stable (Schneider and Frey 1985). Not all evidence supports this hypothesis. For instance, Ramasamy et al. (2012) conclude that Chinese investments are attracted to countries that are politically unstable. For testing hypothesis 9, we use the variable *ExecChn*, which is defined as the number of times in a year that effective control of the executive power changes hands (source: Databanks International). The expected sign is negative.

13.4 Censored Regression Results

The Chinese ODI data we are dealing with are left-censored, since either positive or zero ODI flows from China are observed. Using OLS would lead to biased estimates for coefficients and that is why we estimate Tobit models. We estimate various panel models that are specified as follows:

$$ODI^*_{i,t} = \alpha + \beta_1 GDP_{i,t-1} + \beta_2 ECI_{i,t-1}$$
$$+ \beta_3 RISK_{i,t-1} + \beta_4 NTR_{i,t-1} + \beta_5 POL_{i,t-1} + \beta_6 ICC_{i,t-1} + \varepsilon_{i,t},$$

(13.1)

where $ODI_{i,t} = ODI^*_{i,t}$ if $ODI^*_{i,t} > 0$ and $ODI_{i,t} = 0$ if $ODI^*_{i,t} \leq 0$. While $ODI^*_{i,t}$ being the latent variable, the observed dependent variable, $ODI_{i,t}$, is the host country i's amount of ODI from China in year t normalized by the host country's population to facilitate comparison across countries of different size. The variable is expressed in logarithmic form. GDP is our proxy for market seeking. ECI is a vector comprising two variables EX and Proj that measure China's economic interactions with the host countries. RISK is the economic condition risk index, while the vector NTR includes the variables Engy and Min. The vectors POL and ICC contain our proxies for the political relationship between the host country and China (UN Voting and Diplomatic) and individual country characteristics (Autocracy, Corruption, Law and Order, ExecChn), respectively. To facilitate interpretation and avoid endogeneity issues, lagged variables are used in the regression, except for Diplomatic.

The maximum likelihood estimates obtained from the panel data censored regression with the random effect specification are presented in table 13.2.[7] As explained before, the data refer to officially approved ODI for the period 1991 to 2005. Because data on some explanatory variables is not available, the regressions are based on data for 31 African countries.

Column 1 shows the results if we use GDP as proxy for market size. In addition we include the variables EX, Proj, RISK, Engy, and Min. We take this model, which is very similar to the model used in our previous work, as our base model. In line with our previous findings, we find that GDP is only significant at the 20 percent level of significance, while the variables Engy and Min are not significant. Of the two variables that measure China's economic interactions with the host countries (exports and contracted projects), the contracted projects Proj is statistically significant at the 1 percent level, while EX is significant at 5 percent. Finally, RISK comes out significantly at the 10 percent level with the expected sign.

Column 2 shows the results when we add all the variables in the vectors POL and ICC simultaneously to the base model and follow the general to specific procedure. The main conclusion that follows from

Table 13.2
Chinese ODI in Africa, 1991 to 2005 (Tobit with random effects)

	(1)	(2)	(3)	(4)	(5)
GDP_{it-1}	0.140		0.139	0.126	0.126
	1.346		1.380	1.291	1.223
EX_{it-1}	2.588**	2.333**	1.947*	2.271**	2.691**
	2.251	2.084	1.681	1.982	2.344
$Proj_{it-1}$	0.018***	0.014**	0.016***	0.017***	0.017***
	3.155	2.555	2.760	2.973	3.047
$RISK_{it-1}$	0.131*		0.120	0.150**	0.114
	1.742		1.629	2.024	1.523
$Engy_{it-1}$	0.003		0.002	0.002	0.002
	0.320		0.203	0.170	0.197
Min_{it-1}	−0.140		−0.132	−0.085	−0.141
	−1.323		−1.262	−0.788	−1.339
UN Voting$_{it-1}$		−3.802***	−3.764***		
		−2.765	−2.723		
Diplomatic$_{it}$		0.703**			
		2.040			
Autocracy$_{it-1}$		−0.060*			
		−1.685			
Corruption$_{it-1}$				−0.204**	
				−2.081	
ExecChn$_{it-1}$		−0.624**			−0.590**
		−2.338			−2.169
Constant	−4.516*	−0.211	−3.967*	−3.762*	−4.045*
	−1.949	−0.425	−1.777	−1.734	−1.760
Observations	434	433	433	434	434
Number of id	31	31	31	31	31
LR-test	24.09	16.45	24.29	18.48	24.72
Pseudo R^2	0.03	0.02	0.03	0.02	0.03

Notes: t-Statistics are reported below coefficient *, **, and *** denote significant levels at the 10, 5, and 1 percent levels, respectively. The pseudo R^2 gives the McFadden's R^2.

this regression is that inclusion of the political variables causes most of the economic determinants to become insignificant. Most coefficients of the variables in the vectors POL and ICC are in line with the hypotheses spelled out in table 13.1. In line with hypothesis 7, the coefficient of *Autocracy* is significant, albeit only at the 10 percent level, with a negative sign. So our findings suggest that autocratic regimes do not receive more Chinese ODI (recall that a higher number for the variable *Autocracy* implies a more authoritarian regime). Our results also suggest that political allies of the United States, politically unstable regimes, and countries without diplomatic ties with China receive less ODI from China.

As an alternative approach, we add the variables in the vectors *POL* and *ICC* to the base model one by one; only those variables that turn out to be significant at the 10 percent level are shown. The results are presented in columns 3 to 5 of table 13.2. It turns out that now also corruption is significant: more corrupt countries in Africa receive more ODI from China in the period under consideration (recall that a higher number of *Corruption* implies less corruption). Although corruption is often perceived to deter FDI because it represents an extra tax and increases investment costs (Bardhan 1997; Abed and Davoodi 2000; Wei 2000), empirical evidence on the deterrent effect of corruption is very mixed. For instance, some studies found no significant corruption effect (Wheeler and Mody 1992) and some found that corruption could in fact positively affect investment and economic growth (Swaleheen and Stansel 2007). Cuervo-Cazurra (2006) argues that investors who have been exposed to bribery at home will not be deterred by corruption abroad but instead seek countries where corruption is prevalent. The similarities in the conditions of the institutional environment induce these investors to focus their FDI there. Our result that for the period under consideration China has a preference for investing in countries that are corrupt are in line with the findings of Swaleheen and Stansel (2007) and Cuervo-Cazurra (2006).

Overall, our results suggest that in the period under consideration, political factors played a key role in China's ODI decisions. Inclusion of political factors makes some previously significant economic determinants of ODI become insignificant, although exports and contracted projects remain significant in all specifications.

Table 13.3 presents the estimation results for ODI data in IMF-OECD format, following the same setup as table 13.2. As said, the sample period is 2003 to 2007. We start with the baseline model in column 1, including *GDP*, *EX*, *Proj*, *RISK*, *Engy*, and *Min*. Column 2 shows the results when we add all the variables in the vectors *POL* and *ICC* simultaneously and follow the general to specific procedure. In stark contrast to the results as reported in table 13.2, it turns out that none of the variables in the vectors *POL* and *ICC* are significant, while various traditional economic determinants of ODI turn out to be significant. The coefficients of *GDP* and *Proj* are significant, while there is also strong evidence for the resource-seeking motive as *Min* turns out to be significant. Our findings for the resource-seeking motive are

Table 13.3
Chinese ODI in Africa, 2003 to 2007 (Tobit with random effects)

	(1)	(2)	(3)
GDP_{it-1}	0.298**	0.356***	0.287**
	2.135	2.875	2.195
EX_{it-1}	2.483	3.007**	2.378
	1.456	2.147	1.477
$Proj_{it-1}$	0.008*	0.009**	0.007
	1.669	2.159	1.544
$RISK_{it-1}$	−0.022		0.085
	−0.164		0.613
$Engy_{it-1}$	0.017		0.014
	1.173		1.024
Min_{it-1}	0.518***	0.519***	0.544***
	5.869	6.078	6.276
Law and Order$_{it-1}$		−0.292*	−0.313*
		−1.871	−1.885
Constant	−6.794**	−7.251**	−6.121**
	−2.202	−2.523	−2.109
Observations	123	123	123
Number of id	31	31	31
LR-test	2.53	1.87	1.15
Pseudo R^2	0.01	0.00	0.00

Notes: t-Statistics are reported below coefficient *, **, and *** denote significant levels at the 10, 5, and 1 percent level, respectively. The pseudo R^2 gives the McFadden's R^2.

broadly in line with the results of Buckley et al. (2007) who also find that their proxy for this motive is only significant in the latter part of their sample period.

Likewise, when we add the variables in the vectors POL and ICC one by one to the base model, only Law and Order turns out to be significant at the 10 percent level as shown in column 3. However, the coefficient has the wrong sign, so our results do not confirm hypothesis 8.[8]

13.5   Results for Heckman Models

So far we have found support for many of our hypotheses, although our results also suggest that during the first period political factors played a more important role than during the second. However, there is a potential problem with our estimates. In a Tobit regression the occurrence of Chinese FDI and the amount of Chinese FDI are assumed to be determined by the same mechanism and the same set of explanatory variables. However, it might not be true that the occurrence of Chinese ODI and the amount of Chinese ODI are driven by the same variables. That is why we have applied a Heckman two-step estimator, which assumes two mechanisms: one for the occurrence of Chinese ODI and one for the amount of Chinese ODI. Compared with the censored model used in the previous subsection, the two-step procedure offers a framework to sequentially analyze the decision-making process. The first decision is to make an investment or not. If the first decision is positive, then the amount of the investments has to be determined. The decision to invest or not is studied using the regression specification:

$$D_{i,t} = \alpha + \beta_1 GDP_{i,t-1} + \beta_2 ECI_{i,t-1}$$
$$+ \beta_3 RISK_{i,t-1} + \beta_4 NTR_{i,t-1} + \beta_5 POL_{i,t-1} + \beta_6 ICC_{i,t-1} + \mu_{i,t}, \quad (13.2)$$

where $D_{i,t} = 1$ if $ODI_{i,t} > 0$ and is zero otherwise.

In essence, we postulate that the likelihood of China to invest in an African country is determined by the variables used in the censored regression. The technical issue of zero-censored data—selection bias problem—is controlled for using the inverse Mills ratio (also known as the hazard rate). The ratio that contains information about the unobserved factors that determine China's ODI in an African country is retrieved from equation (13.2) and will be included in the second stage of the Heckman regression. The significance of the inverse Mills ratio reflects the importance of selection bias.

We adopted the Wooldridge (1995) procedure that extends the Heckman procedure to panel data. Specifically, the panel data Probit regression with random effects is used to estimate (13.2) with both zero and positive ODI observations. In the second stage of the Heckman procedure, we assess the determinants of the amount of China's ODI. The assessment using only positive ODI data is based on the following regression:

$$ODI_{i,t} = \alpha + \beta_1 MKT_{i,t-1} + \beta_2 ECI_{i,t-1}$$
$$+ \beta_3 RISK_{i,t-1} + \beta_4 NTR_{i,t-1} + \beta_5 POL_{i,t-1} + \beta_6 ICC_{i,t-1} + \rho Mills + \upsilon_{i,t}.$$
$$(13.3)$$

Table 13.4 presents the results for the officially approved ODI data for the period 1991 to 2005. We start with a general-to-specific approach in the first stage and report all remaining significant variables in column 1. In the second stage, we again employ the general-to-specific approach

Table 13.4
Chinese ODI in Africa, 1991 to 2005 (Heckman two-stage estimates)

	(1)	(2)
	First stage	Second stage
GDP_{it-1}	0.346***	
	3.708	
EX_{it-1}	3.692**	5.204***
	2.473	2.618
$Proj_{it-1}$		0.024**
		2.486
$UN\ Voting_{it-1}$	−2.877**	−5.447*
	−2.112	−1.885
$Autocracy_{it-1}$	−0.112***	−0.269***
	−3.101	−3.402
$Corruption_{it-1}$	−0.266***	−0.353*
	−2.861	−1.915
$Law\ and\ Order_{it-1}$	0.140*	
	1.749	
$ExecChn_{it-1}$	−0.501**	−1.213**
	−2.129	−2.033
Mills		1.942**
		2.191
Constant	−6.308***	−0.477
	−3.020	−0.304
Year-fixed effects	No	Yes
Observations	433	205
Number of id	31	29
Pseudo R^2	0.05	
Hausman test		chi^2(20) = 3.65
LM test		chi^2(1) = 17.57
R^2		0.29

Notes: Reported are the estimation results from the random effect Probit panel regressions for the first-stage regression. For the second stage we use the random effect estimator and include year-fixed effects, which are jointly significant at least 10 percent. The Breusch and Pagan Lagrange multiplier test for random effects (short for LM test) is performed here, and the result suggests random effects estimator is more appropriate than pooled OLS. The t-statistics (robust in second stage) are reported in second rows. The pseudo R^2 gives the McFadden's R^2. *, **, and *** denote significant levels at the 1, 5, and 10 percent levels, respectively.

including the estimated reverse Mills ratio based on the results of column 1. As to the estimator used: the Hausman test did not reject the null hypothesis, suggesting that the use of a random-effects estimator is not inappropriate, while the Lagrange-multiplier test (LM test, which compares the OLS estimator with the random effects estimator) shows the existence of random effects, which makes pooled OLS estimates less efficient and thus inappropriate. We use a random effects estima-tor[9] with year-fixed effects. The F-statistic indicates that the year-fixed effects are jointly significant.

The results for the first-stage regression are broadly in line with the findings as reported in table 13.2, suggesting that the decision to invest is primarily driven by political factors and host-country characteristics, although also *GDP* and *EX* come out highly significant. Table 13.4 also suggests that the factors determining the decision to invest are not the same as the factors determining the amount to be invested. For instance, *GDP* and *Law and Order* are significant in the first stage regression but not in the second. Likewise *Proj* is significant in the second stage but not in the first. Now the coefficient of *Law and Order* has the expected sign, while the results for *Corruption* are in line with our previous findings.

Table 13.5 presents the estimation results for ODI data in IMF-OECD format, following the same setup as table 13.4. It is quite remarkable that in the first-stage regression, only *GDP* and *Law and Order* turn out to be significant, the latter again with the wrong sign. In the second-stage regression, only economic determinants of ODI (*EX, Proj, Min*) turn out to be significant, in line with the results reported in table 13.3. None of the political variables that turned out to be significant in the regressions for the period 1991 to 2005 have a significant coefficient.

13.6 Conclusions

Extending Cheung et al. (2012), we have examined to what extent political considerations and host-country characteristics affect China's ODI in Africa. We come up with nine hypotheses on factors that may drive China's ODI that are tested using two sets of China's ODI data. The first one contains data on China's ODI approved by Chinese authorities. The sample period is from 1991 to 2005. The end of the sample period is dictated by the availability of the officially approved ODI data. The sample starts in 1991 because host-country-specific ODI data are available only after 1991. The second dataset comprises ODI

Table 13.5
Chinese ODI in Africa, 2003 to 2007 (Heckman two-stage estimates)

	(1)	(2)
	First stage	Second stage
GDP_{it-1}	0.767** 2.280	
EX_{it-1}		4.259** 2.524
$Proj_{it-1}$		0.011*** 3.265
Min_{it-1}		0.167*** 3.207
Law and Order$_{it-1}$	−0.823* −1.917	
Mills		−0.567 −0.513
Constant	−12.880* −1.920	−1.373*** −3.009
Year-fixed effects	No	Yes
Observations	123	104
Number of id	31	30
Pseudo R^2	0.07	
Hausman test		chi2(7) = 13.61
LM test		chi2(1) = 27.23
R^2		0.31

Notes: Reported are the estimation results from the random effect Probit panel regressions for the first-stage regression. For the second stage we use the random effect estimator and include year-fixed effects, which are jointly significant at least 10 percent. The Breusch and Pagan Lagrange multiplier test for random effects (short for LM test) is performed here, and the result suggests random effects estimator is more appropriate than pooled OLS. The t-statistics (robust in second stage) are reported in second rows. The pseudo R^2 gives the McFadden's R^2. *, **, and *** denote significant levels at the 1, 5, and 10 percent levels, respectively.

data (2003 to 2007) compiled by the Ministry of Commerce of China using the OECD-IMF standard. The second dataset only contains observations after 2002, when the "going global" policy was announced, allowing us to test whether this policy change had any implications for the importance of economic vs. political determinants of Chinese ODI in Africa.

Since the ODI data are "censored" at zero and below, we estimate Tobit models. In addition we use the Heckman (1979) method that allows us to separate the investment decision process into two stages. First, a decision is taken whether to invest in a host country. If this is the case, the second decision is how much to invest in the country concerned.

Table 13.6 summarizes our results. Our main findings are that in the models for the first dataset political variables seem to dominate economic determinants of China's ODI in Africa. The likelihood that a country receives ODI from China increases if the country concerned is a political ally of China, has diplomatic relations with China, and is corrupt, democratic, and politically stable. In contrast, for the second dataset most political variables turn out to be insignificant. According to our estimates for the more recent period, China's ODI in Africa is mainly driven by economic ties (trade and projects) and the drive for natural resources. The Heckman models suggest that the decision to invest in a country is to some extent driven by different factors than the decision how much to invest in a country.

Table 13.6
Summary of findings

Hypothesis	Expected sign	First data set (1991–2005)			Second data set (2003–2007)		
			Heckman			Heckman	
		Tobit	First stage	Second stage	Tobit	First stage	Second stage
1. China invests in African countries with large market potential	+		+		+	+	
2. China invests in African countries with which it has strong economic ties	+	+	+	+	+		+
3. China invests in African countries with low risk	+	+					
4. China invests in African countries with large amounts of natural resources	+				+		+
5. China invests in African countries that are close political allies	−	−	−	−			
6. China invests in African countries with which it has long standing diplomatic relations	+	+					
7. China invests in African countries that are nonauthoritarian	−	−	−	−			
8. China invests in African countries with low levels of corruption (first line) and a good bureaucracy (second line)	+/−	−	−	−			
	+		+		−	−	
9. China invests in African countries that are politically stable	−	−	−	−			

Appendix: Sources and Summary Statistics

Chinese ODI in Africa, 1991 to 2005

Variable	Description	Observed	Mean	SD	Min	Max
ODI_{it}	China's approved outward direct investment scaled by the host country's population (in logs). Source: Editorial Broad of the Almanac of China's Foreign Economic Relations and Trade (1992–2006).	434	0.25	0.91	0	11.09
GDP_{it-1}	Lagged value of the host-country's gross domestic product, measured in current USD in logs and represents the market size. Source: WDI.	434	22.57	1.41	18.70	26.10
EX_{it-1}	Lagged ratio of the host country's total exports to China and total exports of the host country. Source: IMF DOTS and WTO.	434	0.03	0.07	0	0.59
$Proj_{it-1}$	Amount of contracted projects China has in a host African country in the previous year in USD per capita. Source: Editorial Broad of the Almanac of China's Foreign Economic Relations and Trade (1992–2008).	434	5.52	14.96	0	157.86
$RISK_{it-1}$	Lagged value of the sum of the socioeconomic condition index and the investment profile index divided by two as provided by the International Country Risk Guide (ICRG).	434	5.36	1.52	0.50	8.73
$Engy_{it-1}$	Lagged value of a host country's energy output (includes crude oil, natural gas, and coal output) normalized by the host country's gross national income. Source: WDI.	434	6.15	13.78	0	81.31

Variable	Description	Observed	Mean	SD	Min	Max
Min_{it-1}	Lagged value of a host country's mineral output (includes bauxite, copper, iron, and gold) normalized by the host country's gross national income. Source: WDI.	434	0.34	1.04	0	8.99
$UN\ Voting_{it-1}$	Lagged value of Inlineblhetusa (voting in line with USA, votes where more than 80 percent of the countries agreed discarded, definition according to Barro and Lee), as provided by Dreher and Sturm (2012).	433	0.12	0.06	0	0.27
$Diplomatic_{it}$	Dummy indicating whether country i and China have a diplomatic relationship in year t. Information is obtained from the Ministry of Foreign Affairs of the People's Republic of China (www.fmprc.gov.cn/eng/).	434	0.88	0.32	0	1
$Autocracy_{it-1}$	Lagged value of the sum of the Political Rights and Civil Liberties indicators provided by the Freedom House	434	9.36	2.95	3	14
$Corruption_{it-1}$	Lagged value of the corruption index provided by the International Country Risk Guide (ICRG).	434	2.56	1.00	0	5
$Law\ and\ Order_{it-1}$	Lagged value of the law and order index provided by the International Country Risk Guide (ICRG).	434	3.18	1.22	0.08	6
$ExecChn_{it-1}$	Number of times in the previous year that effective control of the executive power changes hands, as provided by Databanks	434	0.11	0.34	0	2

Chinese ODI in Africa, 2003 to 2007

Variable	Description	Observed	Mean	SD	Min	Max
ODI_{it}	China's outward direct investment in the IMF-OECD standard scaled by the host country's population (in logs). Source: Statistical Bulletin of China's Outward Foreign Direct Investment and China Commerce Yearbook, the Ministry of Commerce, China (2005–2009).	123	0.89	1.82	−2.03	9.69
GDP_{it-1}	Lagged value of the host country's gross domestic product, measured in current USD in logs and represents the market size. Source: WDI.	123	23.01	1.47	19.72	26.28
EX_{it-1}	Lagged ratio of the host country's total exports to China and total exports of the host country. Source: IMF DOTS and WTO.	123	0.073	0.12	0	0.57
$Proj_{it-1}$	Amount of contracted projects China has in a host African country in the previous year in USD per capita. Source: Editorial Broad of the Almanac of China's Foreign Economic Relations and Trade (1992–2008).	123	18.13	37.52	0	241.33
$RISK_{it-1}$	Lagged value of the sum of the socioeconomic condition index and the investment profile index divided by two, as provided by the International Country Risk Guide (ICRG).	123	5.66	1.45	1.08	8.75
$Engy_{it-1}$	Lagged value of a host country's energy output (includes crude oil, natural gas, and coal output) normalized by the host country's gross national income. Source: WDI.	123	8.52	16.11	0	77.67

Variable	Description	Observed	Mean	SD	Min	Max
Min_{it-1}	Lagged value of a host country's mineral output (includes bauxite, copper, iron, and gold) normalized by the host country's gross national income. Source: WDI.	123	0.60	1.81	0	15.06
$UN\ Voting_{it-1}$	Lagged value of Inlineblhetusa (voting in line with USA, votes where more than 80 percent of the countries agreed discarded, definition according to Barro and Lee), as provided by Dreher and Sturm (2012).	123	0.05	0.04	0	0.14
$Diplomatic_{it}$	Dummy indicating whether country i and China have a diplomatic relationship in year t. Information is obtained from the Ministry of Foreign Affairs of the People's Republic of China (www.fmprc.gov.cn/eng/).	123	0.94	0.25	0	1
$Autocracy_{it-1}$	Lagged value of the sum of the Political Rights and Civil Liberties indicators provided by the Freedom House	123	8.50	3.02	3	14
$Corruption_{it-1}$	Lagged value of the corruption index provided by the International Country Risk Guide (ICRG).	123	1.99	0.76	0	4
$Law\ and\ Order_{it-1}$	Lagged value of the law and order index provided by the International Country Risk Guide (ICRG).	123	3.19	1.12	0.5	6
$ExecChu_{it-1}$	Number of times in the previous year that effective control of the executive power changes hands, as provided by Databanks	123	0.06	0.30	0	2

Notes

1. Indeed oil and gas accounted for over 60 percent of Africa's exports to China in 2006, followed by nonpetroleum minerals and metals that take up 13 percent, while Africa's imports from China comprised mainly manufactured products and machinery and transport equipment, which together accounted for about three-fourths of total imports (Wang and Bio-Tchané 2008).

2. For an alternative view, we refer to Bräutigam (2009) who takes issue with the image of China propping up dictatorial regimes.

3. Some previous studies (e.g., Buckley et al. 2007; Cheung and Qian 2009; Ramasamy et al. 2012) have analyzed China's ODI strategy.

4. See, for example, UNCTAD (2010b) for a detailed discussion on China's role in Africa's development and related issues.

5. These data do not cover ODI that does not go through the formal approval process, thereby underestimating China's total ODI. However, as we are interested in the Chinese authorities' policies, this is not a serious drawback. In addition we use a second dataset that covers all Chinese ODI. Unfortunately, this dataset is available for a short period only.

6. Here we slightly deviate from our previous work in which we used total trade of the host country with China.

7. The fixed effect specification would generate biased estimates (Greene 2004a, b).

8. So our results are not in line with the findings of previous studies like Busse and Hefeker (2007).

9. To be more precise: our random effects estimator is sometimes referred to as GLS random effects estimator (e.g., see Cameron and Trivedi 2005).

References

Abed, G. T., and H. R. Davoodi. 2000. Corruption, structural reforms and economic performance in the transition economies. Working Paper 00/132. IMF, Washington, DC.

Adam, A., and F. Filippaios. 2007. Foreign direct investment and civil liberties: A new perspective. *European Journal of Political Economy* 23 (4): 1038–52.

Asiedu, E. 2002. On the determinants of foreign direct investment to developing countries: Is Africa different? *World Development* 30 (1): 107–19.

Bardhan, P. K. 1997. Corruption and development: A review of issues. *Journal of Economic Literature* 25: 1320–46.

Barro, R., and J.-W. Lee. 2005. IMF programs: Who is chosen and what are the effects? *Journal of Monetary Economics* 52: 1245–69.

Besada, H., Y. Wang, and J. Whalley. 2008. China's growing economic activity in Africa. Working Paper 14024. NBER, Cambridge, MA.

Brautigam, D. 2009. *The Dragon's Gift: The Real Story of China in Africa*. Oxford: Oxford University Press.

Broadman, H. G. 2007. *Africa's Silk Road: China and India's New Economic Frontier*. Washington, DC: World Bank.

Brookes, P. 2007. Into Africa: China's grab for influence and oil. Heritage Lecture 1006. Available at: http://www.heritage.org/research/africa/HL1006.CFM (assessed at March, 9, 2009).

Buckley, P. J., L. J. Clegg, A. R. Cross, X. Liu, H. Voss, and P. Zheng. 2007. The determinants of Chinese outward foreign direct investment. *Journal of International Business Studies* 38: 499–518.

Busse, M., and C. Hefeker. 2007. Political risk, Institutions and foreign direct investment. *European Journal of Political Economy* 23 (2): 397–415.

Cameron, A. C., and P. K. Trivedi. 2005. *Microeconometrics: Methods and Applications*. New York: Cambridge University Press.

Chakrabarti, A. 2001. The determinants of foreign direct investment: Sensitivity analyses of cross-country regressions. *Kyklos* 54 (1): 89–113.

Cheung, Y.-W. and X. W. Qian. 2009. Empirics of China's outward direct investment. *Pacific Economic Review* 14: 312–41.

Cheung, Y.-W., J. de Haan, X.W. Qian, and S.Yu. 2012. China's outward direct investment in Africa. *Review of International Economics* 20 (2): 201–20.

Cuervo-Cazurra, A. 2006. Who cares about corruption? *Journal of International Business Studies* 37 (6): 807–22.

Dreher, A., and J.-E. Sturm. 2012. Do IMF and World Bank influence voting in the UN General Assembly? *Public Choice* 151 (1): 363–97.

Foster, V., W. Butterfield, C. Chen, and N. Pushak. 2008. *Building Bridges: China's Growing Role as Infrastructure Financier for Sub-Saharan Africa*. Washington, DC: World Bank.

Frankel, J. A., and S.-J. Wei. 1996. ASEAN in a regional perspective. Working Paper C96-074. UC Berkeley.

Globerman, S., and D. Shapiro. 2002. Global foreign direct investment flows: The role of governance infrastructure. *World Development* 30 (11): 1899–1919.

Greene, W. H. 2004a. Fixed effects and bias due to the incidental parameters problem in the Tobit model. *Econometric Reviews* 23: 125–47.

Greene, W. H. 2004b. The behavior of the fixed effects estimator in nonlinear models. *Econometrics Journal* 7: 98–119.

Heckman, J. J. 1979. Sample selection bias as a specification error. *Econometrica* 47 (1): 153–61.

Kravis, I. B., and R. E. Lipsey. 1982. Location of overseas production and production for export by U.S. multinational firms. *Journal of International Economics* 12: 201–23.

Morck, R., B.Yeung, and M. Zhao. 2008. Perspectives on China's outward foreign direct investment. *Journal of International Business Studies* 39 (3): 337–50.

Morrison, W. M. 2009. China's economic conditions. Congressional Research Service 7-5700.Washington, DC.

Ramasamy, B., M. Yeung, and S. Laforet. 2012. China's outward foreign direct investment: Location choice and firm ownership. *Journal of World Business,* 37 (1): 17–25.

Schneider, F., and B. Frey. 1985. Economic and political determinants of foreign direct investment. *World Development* 13 (2): 161–75.

Seldadyo, H. G., and J. de Haan. 2011. Is corruption really persistent? *Pacific Economic Review* 16: 192–206.

Swaleheen, Mishfiq, and Dean Stansel. 2007. Economic Freedom, Corruption, and Economic Growth. *Cato Journal* 27: 343–58.

UNCTAD. 2007. *Asian Foreign Direct Investment in Africa: Towards a New Era of Cooperation among Developing Countries, United Nations.* Geneva: United Nations.

UNCTAD. 2010a. *Economic Development for Africa Report 2010: South—South Cooperation: Africa and the New Partnership for Development.* Geneva: United Nations.

UNCTAD. 2010b. *World Investment Prospects Survey 2010–2012.* Geneva: United Nations.

Wang, J.-Y. 2007. What drives China's growing role in Africa? Working Paper 07/211. IMF, Washington, DC.

Wang, J.-Y., and A. Bio-Tchané. 2008. Africa's burgeoning ties with China. *Finance and Development* 45 (1): 44–47.

Wei, S.-J. 2000. How taxing is corruption on international investors. *Review of Economics and Statistics* 82: 1–11.

Wheeler, D., and A. Mody. 1992. International investment location decisions: The case of U.S. firms. *Journal of International Economics* 33: 57–76.

Wooldridge, J. M. 1995. Selection corrections for panel data models under conditional mean independence assumptions. *Journal of Econometrics* 68: 115–32.

Index